Agriculture, Environment, and Health

The University of Minnesota Press
gratefully acknowledges assistance provided
for the publication of this volume
by the John K. and Elsie Lampert Fesler Fund.

Agriculture, Environment, and Health:
Sustainable Development in the 21st Century

Vernon W. Ruttan, editor

University of Minnesota Press
Minneapolis
London

Published by the University of Minnesota Press
2037 University Avenue Southeast, Minneapolis, MN 55455-3092
♻ Printed on recycled paper (50% recycled/10% postconsumer)

Library of Congress Cataloging-in-Publication Data

Agriculture, environment, and health : sustainable development in the
　21st century / Vernon W. Ruttan, editor.
　　　p.　cm.
　　Based on papers presented at a conference held in Bellagio, Italy, in
　October 1991.
　　Includes index.
　　ISBN 0-8166-2291-4 (acid-free)
　　ISBN 0-8166-2292-2 (pbk. : acid-free)
　　1. Agriculture—Environmental aspects—Congresses.
　　2. Agriculture—Economic aspects—Congresses.　3. Rural health—
　Congresses.　I. Ruttan, Vernon W.
　　3589.75.A39　1993
　　338.1′4—dc20　　　　　　　　　　　　　　　　　　　93-8527
　　　　　　　　　　　　　　　　　　　　　　　　　　　　　　CIP

Contents

Preface

The objective of this book is to examine the implications of a series of changes under way at the global level for institutional design and policy reform to achieve sustainable agricultural development. These changes include population growth and the resource and environmental impacts of the intensification of agricultural and industrial production. Particular attention is given to the institutions that conduct research and implement changes in technology and practice in the fields of agriculture, environment, and health; and that monitor the changes in resource endowments, the quality of the environment, and the health and productivity of the human resources employed in agricultural production.

The chapters in this book are concerned with issues identified during a series of consultations held during 1989 and 1990 with leading agricultural, environmental, and health scholars and practitioners around the following topics: (1) biological and technical constraints on crop and animal production; (2) resource and environmental constraints on sustainable agricultural production; and (3) health constraints on agricultural production. The implications of these three consultations for agricultural, environmental, and health research are summarized in chapter 13.

Initial drafts of most of the papers on which the chapters in this book are based were presented and discussed at the Conference on

Agriculture, Environment, and Health, held at the Rockefeller Foundation Conference and Study Center, Villa Serbelloni, in Bellagio, Italy, October 14 to 18, 1991. Following critique and discussion at the Bellagio conference, authors were asked to revise their papers to take into account the comments by discussants. Chapters 6 and 14, while drawing on discussion at the Bellagio conference, were written following the conference.

A unique feature of the book is its interdisciplinary breadth. The agricultural, environmental, and health communities have often acted as separate "island empires." Sustainable development will require that effective bridges be built between these several research communities. An important object of this book is to contribute to the construction of such bridges.

Financial support for the consultations and for the Bellagio conference was provided by the Rockefeller Foundation, the University of Minnesota Agricultural Experiment Station, and the Center for Food and Agricultural Policy. I am indebted to Suzanne Denevan for editorial assistance in translating the draft papers presented at the Bellagio conference into a manuscript that could be transmitted to the University of Minnesota Press.

Vernon W. Ruttan

Part I
Introduction

CHAPTER 1

SUSTAINABLE AGRICULTURAL GROWTH

Vernon W. Ruttan

We are in the closing years of the 20th century, completing one of the most remarkable transitions in the history of agriculture. Prior to this century almost all the increase in food production was obtained by bringing new land into production. There were only a few exceptions to this generalization—in limited areas of East Asia, the Middle East, and western Europe.

In most of the world the transition from a resource-based to a science-based system of agriculture is occurring within a single century. Most of the countries of the developing world have been caught up in the transition only since midcentury. Among developing countries, the countries of East, Southeast, and South Asia have proceeded further in this transition than most countries in Latin America or Africa.

Recent historical trends in production and consumption of the major food grains could easily be taken as evidence that one should not be excessively concerned about the capacity of the world's farmers to meet future food demands. World wheat prices, corrected for inflation, have declined since the middle of the last century. Rice prices have declined since the middle of this century (Edwards, 1988; Pingali, 1988). These trends suggest that productivity growth has been able to more than compensate for the rapid growth in demand, particularly during the decades since World War II.

As we look toward the future, however, the sources of productivity growth are not as apparent as they were a quarter century ago. The developing economies will place exceedingly high demands on their agricultural producers from population growth and growth in per capita consumption arising out of higher income. Population growth rates are expected to decline substantially in most countries during the first quarter of the next century. But the absolute increases in population size will be large, and increases in per capita incomes will add substantially to food demand. The effect of growth in per capita income will be more rapid growth in demand for animal proteins and for maize and other feed crops. During the next several decades growth in food and feed demand arising from growth in population and income will run upwards of 4 percent per year in many countries. Many will experience more than a doubling of food demand. Questions are increasingly being raised as to whether it will be possible to sustain the demands that will be placed on agricultural production systems, on environmental resources, and on rural communities and families.

It is clear that the effort to achieve sustainable growth of agricultural production must be carried out along a broad multidisciplinary front. Closer linkages must be established between the "island empires" of agricultural, environmental, and health sciences. In this book an effort is made to outline a vision of the structures of global agricultural, health, and environmental research institutions that must be put in place to assure sustainable agricultural and rural development into the 21st century.

The Sustainability Agenda

During the 1980s the concept of sustainability achieved wide currency in the agroecological and international development communities. The term *sustainability* was first advanced in 1980 by the International Union for the Conservation of Nature and National Resources (IUCN; Lele, 1991). Prior to the mid-1980s the term had achieved its widest currency among critics of what was viewed as "industrial" approaches to the process of agricultural development (Harwood, 1990:3-19). Proponents have utilized a number of rhetorical vehicles, such as biodynamic agriculture, organic agriculture, farming systems, appropriate technology, and, more recently, regenerative and low-input agriculture, in advancing the sustainability agenda (Dahlberg, 1991). Many reform movements with widely disparate views have been able to march under the sustainability umbrella while avoiding confrontation over their often mutually inconsistent agendas.

Definitions of Sustainability

Writing in the early 1980s, Gordon K. Douglass identified three alternative conceptual approaches to the definition of agricultural sustainability (Douglass, 1984:3-29). One group defined sustainability primarily in technical and economic terms — in terms of the capacity to supply the expanding demand for agricultural commodities on increasingly favorable terms. For this group, primarily mainstream agricultural and resource economists, the long-term decline in the real prices of agricultural commodities has represented evidence that the growth of agricultural production has been following a sustainable path. In contrast, a sustained rise in the real prices of agricultural commodities would be interpreted as raising serious concern about sustainability.

Douglass identified a second group that regards agricultural sustainability primarily as an ecological question — "for its advocates an agricultural system which needlessly depletes, pollutes, or disrupts the ecological balance of natural systems is unsustainable and should be replaced by one which honors the longer-term biophysical constraints of nature" (Douglass, 1984:2). Among those advancing the ecological sustainability agenda there is a pervasive view that present population levels are already too large to be sustained at present levels of per capita consumption (Goodland, 1991).

A third group traveling under the banner of "alternative agriculture," places its primary emphasis on sustaining not just the physical resource base but a broad set of community values (Committee on the Role of Alternative Farming Methods in Modern Production Agriculture, 1989). This third group draws substantial inspiration from the agroecological perspective. But it often views conventional science-based agriculture as an assault not only on the environment, but also on rural people and rural communities. Its adherents take as a major objective the strengthening or revitalization of rural culture and rural communities guided by the values of stewardship and self-reliance and an integrated or holistic approach to the physical and cultural dimensions of production and consumption.

By the mid-1980s the sustainability concept was diffusing rapidly from the confines of its agroecological origins to the broader development community. The definition that has achieved the widest currency was that adopted by the Bruntland Commission: "Sustainable development is development that meets the needs of the present without compromising the ability of future generations to meet their own needs" (World Commission on Environment and Development, 1987:43).

The Bruntland Commission definition raises the possibility that it may be necessary for those of us who are alive today, particularly those of us living in the more affluent societies, to curb our level of material consumption in order to avoid an even more drastic decline in the consumption levels of future generations. This is not a welcome message to societies that have found it difficult to discover principled reasons for the contemporary transfer of resources across political boundaries in support of efforts to narrow the level of living between rich and poor nations or rich and poor people. Historical experience, at least in the West, has often led to lack of concern about our obligations to future generations. It was only a generation ago that Robert Solow, a leading growth theorist, noted in his Richard T. Ely address to the American Economic Association, "We have actually done quite well at the hands of our ancestors. Given how poor they were and how rich we are, they might properly have saved less and consumed more" (Solow, 1974:9). In most of the world the ancestors have not been so kind! This suggests that the future may be too important to be left to either market forces or historical accident—even for the more affluent societies.

In spite of its challenge to current levels of consumption in the developed countries, it is hard to avoid a conclusion that the popularity of the Bruntland Commission definition is due, at least in part, to the fact that the definition is so broad that it is almost devoid of operational significance. Over the last decade the sustainability concept has been undergoing "establishment appropriation" (Buttel, 1988).

Sustainable Agricultural Systems in History

We are able to draw on several historical examples of systems that proved capable of meeting the challenge of achieving sustainable increases in agricultural production. One example is the forest and bush fallow (or shifting cultivation) systems practiced in most areas of the world in premodern times and today in many tropical areas (Pingali, Bigot, and Binswanger, 1987). At low levels of population density, these systems were sustainable over long periods of time. As population density increased, short fallow systems emerged. Where the shift to short fallow systems occurred slowly, as in western Europe and East Asia, systems of farming that permitted sustained growth in agricultural production emerged. Where the transition to short fallow has been forced by rapid population growth, the consequence has often been soil degradation and declining productivity.

A second example can be drawn from the agricultural history of East Asian wet rice cultivation (Hayami and Ruttan, 1985). Traditional wet rice cultivation resembled farming in an aquarium. The rice grew tall and rank; it had a low grain-to-straw ratio. Most of what was produced, straw and grain, was recycled in the form of human and animal manures. Mineral nutrients and organic matter were carried into and deposited in the fields with the irrigation water. Rice yields rose continuously, although slowly, even under a monoculture system.

A third example of sustainable agriculture was the system of integrated crop-animal husbandry that emerged in western Europe in the late Middle Ages to replace the medieval two- and three-field systems (van Bath, 1963; Boserup, 1965). The "new husbandry" system emerged with the introduction and intensive use of new forage and green manure crops. These in turn increased the availability and use of animal manures, permitting the emergence of intensive crop-live-stock systems of production through the recycling of plant nutrients in the form of animal manures to maintain and improve soil fertility (Pretty, 1990).

The three systems that I have described, along with other similar systems based on indigenous technology, have provided an inspiration for the emerging field of agroecology. Many traditional systems were sustainable under conditions of slow growth in food demand. But none has demonstrated a capacity to respond to modern rates of growth in demand generated by some combination of rapid increase in population and in growth of income. Some traditional systems were able to sustain rates of growth in the range of .5 to 1 percent per year. But modern rates of growth in demand are in the range of 1 to 2 percent per year in the developed countries. They often rise to the range of 3 to 5 percent per year in the less developed and newly industrializing countries. Rates of growth in demand in this range lie outside of the historical experience of the presently developed countries!

In developed countries the capacity to sustain the necessary increases in agricultural production will depend largely on our capacity for institutional innovation. If our capacity to sustain growth in agricultural production is weakened, it will be a result of political and economic failure. It is quite clear, however, that the scientific and technical knowledge is not yet available that will enable farmers in most poor countries to meet the current demand their societies are placing upon them or to sustain the increases that are currently being achieved. Further, the research capacity has not yet been established that will be necessary to provide the knowledge and the technology. In these countries, achievement of sustainable agricultural surpluses is dependent on advances in scientific knowledge and on technical and institutional innovation (Technical Advisory Committee/Consultative Group on International Agricultural Research, 1989).

The agricultural research community will have to broaden its agenda. It has, in many parts of the world, been exceedingly successful in contributing to the capacity of the agricultural system to meet the demands for food and fiber that have been placed on it. And these demands have been met, in most cases, at lower and lower cost. The result has been that consumers in both developed and developing countries have had access to agricultural commodities on increasingly favorable terms.

But the costs of the production-enhancing agricultural technology have not been fully captured in market measures (Conway and Pretty, 1991). The spillover of the residuals from agricultural intensification have in many areas eroded the capacity of the resource base itself, as in the case of rising water tables, salinization, and erosion; agriculture has also *become* in some locations a source of atmospheric pollution, contributing methane, nitrous oxides, and carbon dioxide to global climate change. And the fertilizers that it employs to enhance production and the pesticides it employs to protect crops and animals have in some situations become costly in terms of human health. When environmental health concerns are added to the health concerns arising from malaria and tuberculosis resurgence, failure to make progress on parasitic disease, the high cost of dealing with infectious diseases, and the AIDS epidemic, it becomes strikingly apparent that any approach to sustainable development must confront directly the health problems of rural people.

Concerns about Resources and the Environment

We are now in the midst of the third wave since World War II of social concern about the implications of natural resource availability and environmental change for the sustainability of improvements in human well-being.

The first wave of concern, in the late 1940s and early 1950s, focused primarily on the quantitative relations between resource availability and economic growth—the adequacy of land, water, energy, and other natural resources to sustain growth. In the United States, reports of the President's Water Resources Policy Commission (1950) and the President's Materials Policy Commission (1952) were the landmarks of the early postwar resource assessment studies generated by this wave of concern. The primary response to this first wave of concern was technical change. In retrospect it appears that a stretch of high prices has not yet failed to induce the new knowledge and new technologies needed to locate new deposits, promote substitution, and enhance productivity (Barnett and Morse, 1963; Ausubel and Sladovich, 1989).

The second wave of concern about resources and the environment occurred in the late 1960s and early 1970s, and focused on the capacity of the environment to assimilate the multiple forms of pollution generated by growth (Meadows et al., 1979; Nordhaus, 1973). An intense conflict emerged between the two major sources of demand for environmental services. One was the rising demand for environmental assimilations of residuals derived from growth in commodity production and consumption—asbestos in our insulation, pesticides in our food, smog in the air, and radioactive wastes in the biosphere. The second was the rapid growth in consumer demand for environmental amenities—for direct consumption of environmental services—arising out of rapid growth in per capita income and high income elasticity of demand for such environmental services as access to natural environments and freedom from pollution and congestion (Ruttan, 1971). The response to these concerns, still incomplete, was the design of local institutions to induce individual firms and other organizations to bear the costs arising from the externalities generated by commodity production.

Since the mid-1980s these two earlier concerns have been supplemented by a third. These newer concerns center around a series of environmental changes that are occurring on a transnational scale—issues such as global warming, ozone depletion, acid rain, and others (Committee on Global Change, 1990; Committee on Science, Engineering and Public Policy, 1991). The institutional innovations needed to respond to these will be more difficult to design. They will, like the sources of change, need to be transnational or international. Experience with attempts to design incentive-compatible transnational regimes, such as the Law of the Sea Convention, or even the somewhat more successful Montreal Protocol on reduction of chloro-flourocarbon emissions, suggests that the difficulty of resolving free-rider and distributional equity issues imposes a severe constraint on how rapidly effective transnational regimes to resolve these new environmental concerns can be put in place.

With each new wave the issues that dominated the earlier waves were recycled. The result has been an ever-widening agenda of concerns about the relationships between resource and environmental change and sustainable growth in agricultural production. During the 1980s, for example, there was heightened concern about the effects of more intensive agricultural production on (1) resource degradation through erosion, salinization, and depletion of groundwater; and (2) the quality of surface and groundwater through runoff and leaching of plant nutrients and enhanced use of pesticides. Concepts that had initially been advanced by the populist critics of agricultural research—such as alternative, low-input, regenerative, and sustainable agriculture—began to enter the vocabulary of those responsible for agricultural research resource allocation. It is this broader agenda—embracing the technical, environmental, and health constraints—that we, in this book, attempt to interpret within the rubric of sustainable rural development.

Biological and Technical Constraints

The first of a series of consultations on agriculture, environment, and health, held in 1989 and 1990, focused on the new "postgreen" revolution: biological and technical constraints in growth in crop and animal production. Advances in crop yields in areas that have already achieved the highest levels of crop productivity—in Western Europe, North America, and parts of East Asia—have come about primarily by increasing the production of grain relative to straw in individual plants and by increasing plant populations per unit area. Advances in animal productivity have come about largely by decreasing the proportion of food consumed that is devoted to animal maintenance and increasing the proportion used to produce usable animal products. There are severe physiological constraints to continued improvement along these conventional paths. As a result, in the future almost all increases in agricultural production must come from further intensification of agricultural production on land that is presently devoted to crop and livestock production.

A major inference is that the gains in agricultural production required over the next quarter century will be achieved with much greater difficulty than in the immediate past. Difficulty is currently being experienced in raising yield ceilings for the cereal crops that have experienced rapid yield gains in the recent past. The incremental response to increases in fertilizer use has declined. Expansion of irrigated area has become more costly. Maintenance research, the research required to prevent yields from declining, is rising as a share of research effort (Plucknett and Smith, 1986). The institutional capacity to respond to these concerns is limited, even in the countries with the strongest national research and extension systems. Indeed, there has been considerable difficulty in many countries during the 1980s in maintaining the agricultural research capacity that had been established during the 1960s and 1970s (Cummings, 1989).

It seems apparent that until well into the next century the necessary gains in crop and animal productivity will continue to be generated by improvements resulting from conventional plant and animal breeding and from more intensive and efficient use of technical inputs including chemical fertilizers, pest-control chemicals, and higher-quality animal feeds. But the productivity gains from these conventional sources are likely to come in smaller increments than in the past.

It is possible that advances in basic knowledge will create new opportunities for improvements in agricultural technology that will relax the urgency of some of the above concerns. Institutionalization of private-sector agricultural research capacity in some developing countries is beginning to complement public-sector capacity (Pray, 1983; Pray and Echeverria, 1990). Advances in molecular biology and genetic engineering are occurring rapidly. But the date when these promising advances will be translated into productive technology remains unclear. If these advances are to be translated into gains in agricultural production in the poor countries of the tropics, substantial research and training capacity will have to be established and strengthened to advance basic knowledge and to transfer the tools of genetic engineering to practicing scientists.

Resource and Environmental Constraints

The second consultation, focusing on issues of resource and environmental constraints on agricultural production, included scientists involved in climate change studies, agricultural scientists, and economists (Ruttan, 1992). One set of concerns explored during the consultation focused on the impact of intensification of agricultural production practices. These include loss of soil resources due to erosion, waterlogging and salinization, groundwater contamination from plant nutrients and pesticides, and growing resistance of insects, weeds, and pathogens to present methods of control. If agriculture is forced to continue to expand into more fragile environments, such problems as soil erosion and desertification can be expected to become more severe. Additional deforestation will intensify problems of soil loss and degradation of water quality and will contribute to the forcing of climate change.

A second set of concerns stems from the impact of industrialization on global climate and other environmental changes (Reilly and Bucklin, 1989; Parry, 1990). There can no longer be much doubt that the accumulation of carbon dioxide (CO_2) and other greenhouse gases—principally methane (CH_4), nitrous oxide (N_2O), and chlorofluorocarbons (CFCs)—has set in motion a process that will result in a rise in global average surface temperatures over the next 30 to 60 years. And there continues to be great uncertainty about the climate changes that can be expected to occur at any particular date or location in the future. It is almost certain, however, that the climate changes will be accompanied by rises in the sea level and that these rises will impinge particularly heavily on island Southeast Asia and the great river deltas of the region. Dryer and more erratic climate regimes can be expected in interior South Asia and North America. As a partial offset some analysts have suggested that higher CO_2 levels may have a positive effect on yield (Rosenberg, 1986).

The participants in the second consultation also found themselves particularly concerned with the limited capacity available to monitor the effects of resource and environmental change on growth in agricultural production. It was a matter of serious concern, for example, that only in the last decade and a half has it become possible to make firm estimates of the magnitude and productivity effects of soil loss even in the United States.

Health Constraints

The third consultation focused on health constraints on agricultural development (Ruttan, 1990). One might very well ask why this topic was included in a conference on agricultural research. Since the mid-1960s a number of commonly used health indicators, such as life expectancy and infant mortality, experienced substantial improvement for almost all developing countries. Concerns about nutritional deficiency as a source of poor health has receded in a large number of developing countries in the last several decades (Commission on Health Research for Development, 1990). Yet there are a number of other indicators that suggest that health constraints could become increasingly important by the early decades of the next century. Daily calorie intake per capita has been declining for as much as two decades in a number of African countries. While dramatic progress has been made in the control and reduction of losses due to infectious disease and in the control of diarrheal disease, little progress has been made in the control of several important parasitic diseases. The sustainability of advances in malaria and tuberculosis control are causing serious concern. The emergence of AIDS, combined with the other health threats, could emerge as a major threat to economic viability in both developed and developing countries.

One reason that the concern about health research in developing countries has emerged, or should emerge, as a priority on the development assistance agenda is the unfavorable location of most developing countries on the path of epidemiological transition. "The health problems associated with poverty and underdevelopment have been replaced by chronic and degenerative diseases of adult life, such as cancer, stroke, lung and heart disease, arthritis and impairment of the nervous system. . . . For many among the developing countries the transition has hardly begun. An unfinished agenda of pre-transitional health problems—infectious and parasitic disease, nutritional deficiencies, and reproductive health problems—still cause a substantial share of deaths in the Third World" (Commission on Health Research in Development, 1990:4).

There is also a second set of health concerns arising out of the environmental consequences of the intensification of agricultural and industrial production that were discussed in the second consultation. As the environmental impacts of agricultural and industrial intensification become clearer, it appears that they are already imposing significant health burdens in some countries, particularly in parts of the former Soviet Union and Eastern Europe, and may become more burdensome in the future.

If one visualizes a number of these health threats emerging simultaneously in a number of countries it is not too difficult to construct a scenario in which there are large numbers of sick people in many villages around the world. The numbers could become large enough to be a serious constraint on food production capacity.

It cannot be emphasized too strongly that the constraints on sustainable growth are both technical and institutional. The great institutional innovation of the 19th century was "the invention of the method of invention." The modern industrial research laboratory, the agricultural experiment station, and the research university were a product of institutional innovation. But it was not until well after mid-century that national and international agricultural research institutions became firmly established in most developing countries. The challenge to institutional innovation in the next century will be to design the institutions that can ameliorate the negative spillover into the soil, the water, and the atmosphere of the residuals from agricultural and industrial intensification while sustaining growth in agricultural production.

The capacity to achieve sustainable growth in agricultural production and income will also depend on the changes that occur in the economic environment in which developing country farmers find themselves. The most favorable economic environment for releasing the constraints on crop and animal productivity and for achieving sustainable adaptation to the resource and environmental constraints that will impinge on agriculture in developing countries is one characterized by slow growth of population and by rapid growth of income and employment in the nonagricultural sector. Failure to achieve sustainable growth in the nonfarm sector could place developing-country farmers in a situation in which they could make adequate food and fiber available to the nonfarm sector only at higher and higher prices—reversing the long-term trend—and in which the resources available to generate the needed investments in resource and technology development were inadequate.

This book consists of six parts, with Part 1 serving as an introduction. Part 2 sets the stage for later sections by assessing the constraints that will condition the design of new technologies and new institutions to sustain agricultural development. In chapter 2 Kirit S. Parikh assesses the state of current knowledge on the growth of demand for food arising out of growth of population and income over the first half of the 21st century. He then examines how these demands might be met in view of the constraints imposed by land and water resources and the opportunities for yield-enhancing technical change. Parikh has been forced, in both his projections and his analyses, to go beyond earlier official and unofficial estimates in an attempt to develop projections that stay robust over the large changes in population and income anticipated over the first half of the 21st century. His results suggest that if recent rates of growth in output per hectare, in the range of 1 percent per year, can be maintained, the projected demands can be met at the global level even in the presence of substantial slowing in the growth of area cultivated and in the rate of irrigation development. The outlook is, however, considerably less optimistic for a number of poor countries that are experiencing explosive growth in food demand as a result of rapid population growth and rising income. There is, of course, a substantial trade-off between productivity-enhancing technical change and land and water resource development. If productivity growth can be maintained at the relatively high rate of the recent "green revolution" period (1970-90), there will be much less pressure for investment in land and water development.

In chapter 3 Douglass C. North outlines a conceptual framework for analyzing the process of institutional and organizational change. He makes a careful distinction between institutions—the structures, including rules and norms, that condition human interaction—and organizations—consisting of groups of individuals engaged in purposeful group activity. The problem of how to design incentive-compatible institutions, capable of achieving compatibility between individual, organizational, and social objectives, has not been resolved at the theoretical level. Nevertheless, North draws on historical experience to provide important insights into the analytical and design issues that must be considered in making organizational and institutional reforms and innovations needed to achieve sustainable agricultural development.

Part 3 consists of three chapters on agricultural research, resource management, and technology dissemination. In chapter 4 Carl K. Eicher reviews the development of the international agricultural research system and efforts to strengthen national agricultural research systems, focusing especially on sub-Saharan Africa, where achieving scientific, economic, and political viability continues to be problematic. The international system is attempting to expand its emphasis to include the agricultural resource base and the environmental impacts of agricultural intensification during a period of limited resources.

Eicher raises serious questions about the wisdom of the 1990 decision by the Consultative Group on International Agricultural Research (CGIAR) to increase the number of international agricultural research centers (IARCs) from 13 to 17. Eicher questions this decision in light of the fact that the core resources of the system have stopped growing in real (inflation-adjusted) terms. Eicher also calls for a debate on a new CGIAR management structure to make the hard decisions facing the CGIAR system more quickly.

In chapter 5 B. L. Turner II and Patricia A. Benjamin address the problem of sustainable agricultural development in fragile resource areas. They draw on a wide variety of case materials, including their own research, ranging from Amazonia (Brazil), the Himalayas (Nepal), the Ordos Plateau (Inner Mongolia), and the Aral Basin (Uzbekistan and Kazakhstan). One of their more dramatic conclusions is that long-term sustainable cultivation has taken place on lands that, when classified on the basis of environmental criteria, have been regarded as too fragile to sustain agricultural production. One of the firm inferences from the Turner-Benjamin study is that the sustainability of agricultural production on fragile land areas is at least as much a function of the institutional as of the physical environment within which agriculture is practiced.

In chapter 6 Judith Tendler addresses the issue of linking agricultural research and extension to local initiative. Very few extension systems have been able to resolve the conflict between the transfer of technical knowledge through hierarchically organized systems and the mobilization of energies at the household and community levels to make effective use of new knowledge and new materials. Tendler presents case studies of successful dissemination in the area of plant protection and new crop varieties. She found that demand-side factors, particularly the efforts of potential users of the new technologies, played a greater part than anticipated.

The three chapters in Part 4 deal with health research and health systems. In chapter 7 Adetokunbo O. Lucas addresses the issue of strengthening the infrastructure for health research in developing countries. The health sciences have lagged relative to the agricultural sciences in establishing national and international infrastructures for health research, but the complementary structure of international agricultural research institutes and national agricultural research institutes that have been developed to serve the agricultural sector are probably inappropriate for the health sector. The time seems to have passed when the donor community would be prepared to support the development of an international system of health research institutes. Lucas argues, drawing on the work of the Commission on Health Research for Development (1990), on which he served, that the capacity of each country to carry out location-specific research in areas such as epidemiology and social and behavior analysis related to health policy and the design of health delivery is a national responsibility. Capacity should also be developed in a number of the stronger national health research systems to conduct research that has potential regional and international significance. These would include basic and generic biomedical research and research for the development of new and improved drugs, vaccines, and other health technologies of particular significance to developing countries. These centers should receive international support.

Chapters 8 and 9 focus on the development of health systems for rural areas. In most developed countries medical services are designed for health care — for recovery from illness rather than the promotion of health. A successful approach to advancing human health in the poor developing countries will depend on the development of health systems that enable families and communities to take greater responsibility for health maintenance and improvement. In chapter 8 Godfrey Gunatilleke traces the evolution of the food, nutrition, and health policies that have enabled Sri Lanka to achieve health indicators — birthrates, life expectancy, and others — comparable to the more developed countries even though per capita income remains at a relatively modest level. In chapter 9 Dan C. O. Kaseje describes the development of a community-based health care (CBHC) system, which he participated in designing, in which the family, particularly the wife and mother, is recognized as the key health provider. Kaseje also outlines the activities conducted at the community, district, and national level by governmental and nongovernmental organizations to sustain the effectiveness of the family effort.

Part 5 is devoted to a discussion of our capacity to monitor the environmental-resource and health changes that are significant for agricultural production. In chapter 10 Stephen L. Rawlins addresses the status of our capacity to monitor the effects of microenvironmental changes such as soil loss, salinization, and desertification. In chapter 11 J. A. Lee, David Norse, and Martin Parry address our ability to monitor the effects of acid deposition and global climate change on agricultural production. In chapter 12 David Bradley examines our capacity to monitor the impact of changes that impinge on the health status of rural people. A conclusion that emerges from the three chapters is the exceeding deficiency in our capacity, either at the national or international level, to monitor the environmental changes that impinge on the health of rural people and the productivity of the resources that are managed by rural people.

Chapters 13 and 14 present the recommendations for research priorities that emerged from the Rockefeller Foundation–sponsored conference on Agriculture, Environment, and Health held in Bellagio, Italy, in 1991 and from three preconference consultations. The research priorities reflect (1) the international scope of the problems; (2) the need for broadened options for action; (3) the importance of monitoring changes in agricultural productivity, the environment, and health status; and (4) the need for an institutional infrastructure that can sustain growth in agricultural production.

In chapter 14 David E. Bell, William C. Clark, and Vernon W. Ruttan describe the structure of global agricultural, health, and environmental research systems that will be required to meet the needs of the 21st century.

References

Ausubel, Jesse, and Hedy E. Sladovich, eds. 1989. *Technology and the Environment*. Washington, D.C.: National Academy Press.

Barnett, Harold J., and Chandler Morse. 1963. *Scarcity and Growth: The Economics of Natural Resource Availability*. Baltimore, Md.: Johns Hopkins University Press.

Boserup, E. 1965. *Conditions of Agricultural Growth*. Chicago: Aldine.

Buttel, Frederick H. 1988. *Agricultural Research and Development and the Appropriation of Progressive Symbols: Some Observations on the Politics of Ecological Agriculture*. Ithaca, N.Y.: Cornell University Rural Sociology Bulletin no. 151.

Commission on Health Research for Development. 1990. *Health Research: Essential Link to Equity in Development*. London: Oxford University Press.

Committee on Global Change of the Commission on Geoscience, Environment, and Resources. 1990. *Research Strategies for the U.S. Global Change Research Program*. Washington, D.C.: National Academy Press.

Committee on Science, Engineering, and Public Policy. 1991. *Policy Implications of Greenhouse Warming*. Washington, D.C.: National Academy Press.

Committee on the Role of Alternative Farming Methods in Modern Production Agriculture, Board on Agriculture, National Research Council. 1989. *Alternative Agriculture*. Washington, D.C.: Alternative Agriculture.

Conway, Gordon R., and Jules N. Pretty. 1991. *Unwelcome Harvest: Agriculture and Pollution*. London: Earthscan.

Cummings, Ralph W. 1989. *Modernizing Asia and the Near East: Agricultural Research in the 1990s*. Washington, D.C.: U.S. Agency for International Development, Bureau for Science and Technology. Mimeo.

Dahlberg, Kenneth A. 1991. Sustainable agriculture: Fad or harbinger? *BioScience* 41:337-40.

Douglass, Gordon K., ed. 1984. *Agricultural Sustainability in a Changed World Order*. Boulder, Colo.: Westview Press.

Edwards, Clark. 1988. Real prices received by farmers keep falling. *Choices* 3 (47): 22-23.

Goodland, Robert. 1991. The case that the world has reached limits. In *Environmentally Sustainable Economic Development: Building on Bruntland*, edited by Robert Goodland,

Herman Daly, and Salah El Serafy. World Bank Environmental Working Paper no. 46 (July), 5-17. Washington, D.C.: World Bank.

Harwood, Richard R. 1990. A history of sustainable agriculture. In *Sustainable Agricultural Systems*, edited by C. A. Edwards, R. Lal, P. Madden, R. H. Miller, and G. House. Ankeny, Iowa: Soil and Water Conservation Authority.

Hayami, Yujiro, and Vernon W. Ruttan. 1985. *Agricultural Development: An International Perspective*. 2d ed. Baltimore, Md.: Johns Hopkins University Press.

International Union for Conservation of Water and Natural Resources (IUCN). 1990. *World Conservation Strategy: Living Resource Conservation for Sustainable Development*. Glord, Switzerland: IUCN, United Nations Environmental Program and World Wildlife Foundation.

Lele, Sharachandra M. 1991. Sustainable development: A critical review. *World Development* 19(6): 607-21.

Meadows, Donella H., and Dennis L. Meadows, with Jorgen Randers and William W. Behrens III. 1972. *The Limits to Growth*. New York: University Books.

Nordhaus, William D. 1973. World dynamics: Measurement without data. *Economic Journal* 83:1156-83.

Parry, Martin. 1990. *Climate Change and World Agriculture*. London: Earthscan.

Pingali, Prabhu. 1988. *Intensification and Diversification of Asian Rice Farming Systems*. International Rice Research Institute (IRRI), AE 88-41. Los Baños, the Philippines: IRRI.

Pingali, P., Y. Bigot, and H. P. Binswanger. 1987. *Agricultural Mechanization and the Evolution of Farming Systems in Sub-Saharan Africa*. Baltimore, Md.: Johns Hopkins University Press.

Plucknett, Donald H., and Nigel J. H. Smith. 1986. Sustaining agricultural yields. *BioScience* 36(1): 40-45.

Pray, Carl E. 1987. Private agricultural research in Asia. In *Policy for Agricultural Research*, edited by Vernon W. Ruttan and Carl E. Pray. Boulder, Colo.: Westview Press.

Pray, Carl E., and Ruben Echeverria. 1990. *Determinants and Scope of Private Sector Research in Developing Countries*. International Service for National Agricultural Research (ISNAR), staff notes 90-82. The Hague ISNAR.

President's Materials Policy Commission. 1952. *Resources for Freedom*. Washington, D.C.: Government Printing Office.

President's Water Resources Policy Commission. 1950. *A Water Policy for the American People, Volume 1*. Washington, D.C.: Government Printing Office.

Pretty, Jules N. 1990. Sustainable agriculture in the Middle Ages: The English Manor. *Agricultural History Review* 3:1-19.

Reilly, John, and Rhonda Bucklin. 1989. Climate change and agriculture. In *World Agriculture Situation and Outlook Report*, Agricultural Research Service, WAS-55, pp. 43-46. Washington, D.C.: USDA/ARS.

Rosenberg, Norman J. 1986. Climate, technology, climate change, and policy: The long run. In *The Future of the North American Grainery: Politics, Economics, and Resource Constraints in North American Agriculture*, edited by C. Ford Runge. Ames: Iowa State University Press.

Ruttan, Vernon W. 1971. Technology and the environment. *American Journal of Agricultural Economics* 53:707-17.

———, 1989a. Why foreign economic assistance? *Economic Development and Cultural Change* 37:411-24.

_____, ed. 1989b. *Biological and Technical Constraints on Crops and Animal Productivity: Report on a Dialogue*. St. Paul: University of Minnesota, Department of Agricultural and Applied Economics.

_____, ed. 1990. *Health Constraints on Agricultural Development*. St. Paul: University of Minnesota Department of Agricultural and Applied Economics.

_____, ed. 1992. *Sustainable Development and the Environment: Perspectives on Growth and Constraints*. Boulder, Colo.: Westview Press.

Solow, Robert M. 1974. The economics of resources or the resources of economics. *American Economic Review* 64:1-14.

Technical Advisory Committee/Consultative Group on International Agricultural Research (TAC/CGIAR). 1989. *Sustainable Agricultural Production: Implications for International Research*. Rome: Food and Agriculture Organization.

van Bath, S. H. Slicker. 1963. *The Agrarian History of Western Europe, A.D. 500-1850*. London: Edward Arnold.

World Commission on Environment and Development. 1987. *Our Common Future* [The Bruntland Report]. New York: Oxford University Press.

Part II
Setting the Stage

The challenges to the achievement of sustainable development are both technical and institutional. We are concerned in this book with how to provide families and communities with the knowledge and the technology needed to enhance agricultural production, sustain environmental resources, respond to environmental change, and gain access to the knowledge and materials that will enable them to lead healthy lives.

In chapter 2 Kirit S. Parikh has responded to the challenge to explore demands that will be placed on the agricultural sector, arising out of population and income growth, to meet the food needs of their societies into the middle of the 21st century. He then attempts to identify the adequacy of resource endowments, the possible impacts of investments in land and water resource endowments, and prospects for generating the new knowledge and new technology that will be needed if the demands are to be met.

Parikh presents two scenarios. One is based on moderately rapid population growth and relatively slow growth of national income. A second is based on relatively high population and high national income growth. The two projections represent an attempt to capture the range of likely alternatives.

The task that the Bellagio conference organizers set out for Parikh represented an imposing challenge. The official projections of demand and potential supply of agricultural products have rarely looked beyond the early years of the 21st century. The projections that Parikh has produced should be viewed as plausible future production and consumption scenarios rather than predictions.

The scenarios that emerge are cautiously optimistic. They suggest that in spite of a more than doubling of population levels and fairly rapid growth in demand rising out of income growth, it should be possible to meet the demands that will be placed on the agricultural producers. But the demands will not be met easily. Substantial investments in land and water resource development and in the development of yield-enhancing technologies will be necessary. Whether these investments will be made will depend on the behavior of the institutions and organizations that provide the materials, the technology, and the incentives necessary for agricultural producers to respond effectively to the needs of their societies. The constraints that will limit the development of capacity to meet the future demands placed on rural communities are at least as much institutional as technological.

In chapter 3 Douglass C. North addresses the issues of institutional innovation and design. North employs an analytical framework that distinguishes between institutions and organizations. Institutions are the structures that humans impose on human interactions. Organizations are made up of individuals engaged in purposeful activity. "Institutions are the rules of the game; organizations are the players." But the incentives that act to mobilize and channel the activity of individuals and organizations are constrained and directed by the institutions of the society in which they live. North views institutional change as evolutionary and path dependent. The interests and skills invested in a particular path of institutional development impose high transaction costs on efforts to achieve institutional reform or to move institutional evaluation onto a new path. It is the continuous interaction between institutions and organizations in an economic setting of scarcity that generates institutional innovation.

In applying his framework North gives particular attention to the institutional constraints that have arisen out of the historical experience of particular societies, the mental models derived from cultural experience that condition or bias the ability of individuals to utilize new knowledge, and the conflicting interests of the organizations and individuals that influence the implementation of social policy.

In spite of the constraints on our capacity to design incentive-compatible institutions, North ends his chapter on a cautiously optimistic note. The public university system of the United States, nourished by a democratic polity with its roots in English constitutional development, has been a powerful instrument of economic growth. The establishment of national and international agricultural research systems has generated a path of technical change consistent with the resource endowments and economic conditions of countries characterized by intense pressure of population against resource endowments, particularly in Asia.

In the final section of his chapter North outlines a series of challenges for social-science research on issues related to institutional design and reform. He insists that we know too little about how to consciously design the changes in institutions needed to induce organizations to perform more efficiently. These changes involve both organizational leaning and changes in the ideologies or mental models held by individuals. We also know too little about how to achieve effective bureaucratic performance in large public and private organizations.

The issues outlined by Parikh and North highlight the challenge to provide the technology and the resources that rural people will need to meet the demands their societies will place on them, as well as the challenge to reform old institutions and design the new institutions that will enable rural people and their organizations to respond to these demands. These issues will emerge again in almost every chapter in this book.

CHAPTER 2

AGRICULTURAL AND FOOD SYSTEM SCENARIOS FOR THE 21ST CENTURY

Kirit S. Parikh

The Malthusian concern about the demand for food outstripping the limits of natural resources has time and again proved to be misplaced. Expansion of areas under cultivation in the "new" continents, as well as expansion of irrigation, progress of technology both in the manufacture of agrochemicals and in the breeding of high-yielding varieties, and innovations in institutional arrangements to encourage farmers to produce more, have enabled the supply of food and agricultural products to keep pace with the growth of demand. Even under conditions of unprecedented growth in populations and incomes, all of which have grown faster in this century than during any other period in human history, effective demands have been met.

Given this information, the question becomes, What is the problem? Why can't we continue to meet such demands in the future? There are two reasons why Malthusian concern may be of some relevance today. First, the plausible growth rates of population and incomes in the coming decades require demands to grow at very rapid rates. Annual additions to productions in absolute as well as in percentage terms will be large. It is questionable whether or not the rate of induced innovations will be sufficient to meet these demands. Second, the carrying capacity of the environment has become a scarce natural resource. It is likely to impose significant constraints on the techniques of production that may be adopted. Moreover, the stress on the environmental carrying capacity is not just the outcome of agricultural production but is synergistically aggravated by other economic activities. Thus, the constraints on adoptable new techniques are likely to become increasingly stringent in the future.

This discussion raises a number of questions. What will be the growth of demand for agricultural commodities arising out of population and income growth over the first half of the 21st century? Given the resource endowments, can these demands be met? What are the implications for required contributions of technical change and material input to enhance land productivity to meet projected demands for agricultural commodities? What institutional issues do these raise?

The Importance of Long-Term Demand Projections

In addressing these questions, projections of long-term demand play a critical role. Depending on the projections, the focus of discussion changes. If the projected demands are high, they will create a climate of doom and, perhaps, generate resolves and actions to fight it. Low demands might foster complacency. The response strategy will depend on the projected demands.

In spite of the importance of future demands, very long term projections for agricultural demands are seldom made. While energy analysts and now environmentalists frequently make very long term projections (of 50 to 100 years), such projections are not available for agricultural products. Perhaps this is because agriculture is characterized by millions of small competitive farmers. Very long term considerations do not affect their production decisions. However, many infrastructure projects have long gestation lags, and one would have expected that at least governments could use long-term projections in deciding on these projects.

A survey of global modeling and simulations by Robinson (1985) shows that apart from the global models of the 1970s, World 3 (Meadows et al., 1972), the Latin American World Model (Herrera et al., 1976), the Systems Analysis Research Unit Model (SARUM) (Roberts, 1977), the Model of International Relations in Agriculture (MOIRA) (Linnemann et al., 1979), and the World Integrated Model (Mesarovic and Pestel, 1974), none of the studies look beyond 25 years or beyond the year 2000.[1]

Moreover, the global models that look beyond 2000 have, in general, aggregated agriculture to one or two commodities. Thus MOIRA, with the most sophisticated treatment among these models of agriculture demand and supply, aggregates agriculture into just one commodity called consumable protein. The more recent model of the International Institute of Applied Systems Analysis (IIASA), which is called the basic linked system (Parikh et al., 1988; Fischer et al., 1988), has a detailed agricultural commodity classification but has been used to simulate only until the year 2000.

Fox and Ruttan (1983) have surveyed developing-country food balance projections. In addition to some of the global and sectoral models referred to above, they also survey trend projections.[2] Once again these projections do not go beyond the year 2000. A recent Organization for Economic Cooperation and Development (OECD) study by Brown and Goldin (1992) also does not go beyond 2000. The World 3 model of Meadows and colleagues has been widely criticized for using exponential growths without substitutions and adjustments in making long-term projections on the limits to growth. Fox and Ruttan observe that the Mesarovic and Pestel model is also done in the same spirit. Jonathan M. Harris (1990) has used trend projections to project cereal demand in 2050. Using trends for making long-term projections is quite unsatisfactory. It may as easily pro-vide a message of gloom and doom as it may create a false sense of security.

Future demand projections are useful for a number of reasons. First, they help target the problem and provide a feel for the magnitude of the problem. Second, they help to bound the problem. Bounds are important since there are many uncertainties in any future projection. Third, a surprise scenario that speaks gloom and doom also stimulates imagination. Clarity of mind increases when death seems imminent. Such scenarios also tell us where to go, what actions to take, what vicious circles to disrupt, and so on. However, misguided actions, initiated by unwarranted gloom and doom, can be very expensive, too, not just in money terms but also in their welfare impact. It is, therefore, necessary to have scenarios that bound the problem in a reasonable way.

To do this, I have taken two population-growth scenarios and two gross domestic product (GDP) growth scenarios. Food demands are projected for each of the four combinations of these. However, due to space limitations, results of only two scenarios, which bound the demand projections, are presented. It should be noted that the projections of demand presented are based on purchasing power rather than food requirements.

In the next section, the population and income-growth scenarios are described. This is followed by projection of demand using alternative methodologies. The subsequent step is comparing the required production estimate with estimates of production potentials and examining the resource needs. The chapter also explores some institutional issues in realizing the production potential. Finally, some conclusions are presented.

A Population and Income-Growth Scenario

Projections of population and income are critical determinants of demand. Long-term projections (of 60 years) by necessity involve a large number of assumptions. My approach to this is to make very simple assumptions. Considering the use to which these projections are put, I deem it a reasonable approach.

Population Projections

Typical models of population projections start from a given population with its age and sex composition, and age-specific fertility and mortality rates, and use these to project consistent future population. Since the vital rates are stable and change only gradually over time, for short-term or medium-term (less than 30 years) projections, a method that accounts for some demographic inertia yields fairly good projections and is preferred over crude trend projections.

However, for longer-term projections one would need to assume age-specific fertility and mortality rates. Such assumptions will be quite arbitrary, and a whole range of values for these are possible. This is because fertility and mortality rates are affected by income and public policy. An aggressive policy can attain a rapid demographic transition. Such large uncertainties in long-term population projections are unavoidable. The effect of such uncertainties is to generate very wide ranges in long-term population projections. For example, projections made by Frejka (1973) give a range of 5.7 billion to 15 billion for global population in the year 2100. I have, therefore, followed a simple approach to extend United Nations medium and high projections, which are available till the period 2020-25. (United Nations, 1991). Using the U.N. projections, we have extrapolated the *average annual growth rates* over five-year periods into the future to obtain future populations.

Future population projections for the world and major regions are shown in Table 2.1. These projections were constructed by extending

Table 2.1. Projected population
(in millions)

Year	World	Africa	Latin America	North America	Asia	Europe	Oceania	Former USSR
1990	5,292	642	448	276	3,113	498	26	289
Medium projections								
2020	8,092	1,452	716	326	4,700	516	37	344
2050	10,300	2,340	960	355	5,700	520	45	380
High projections								
2020	8,802	1,595	773	347	5,128	543	40	361
2050	12,810	3,175	1,140	435	6,940	565	55	420

Source: Calculations by the author.

the time trends of the U.N. 1990-2025 medium and high regional projections to 2050 (United Nations, 1991).[3]

Gross Domestic Product Projections

Long-term projections of economic growth involve even more uncertainties than projections of population growth. Once again, it is best to make plausible assumptions. In order to make our projections comparable to at least one long-term carbon dioxide and greenhouse gas model, I have made the same assumption as Alan Manne and R. G. Richels (1991) in what I call the "low-growth" scenario. Another set of assumptions has been made for a higher-growth scenario. In these assumptions, the growth rates of developing countries other than China are stepped up. The growth rates for China were already rather high in the Manne scenario and so they were not increased. These growth rate assumptions are shown in Table 2.2.

The Scenarios

Thus we have two GDP and two population scenarios. Demand projections were made for each of these four scenarios. However, we report the results of only the two extreme scenarios since they bound the projections. These scenarios are as follows: MP-LG, medium population growth and low GDP growth, and HP-HG, high population growth and high GDP growth.

Projections for Demand for Agricultural Commodities

The methodology for long-term projections of demands as opposed to requirements are not well developed. The approaches used generally

Table 2.2. Assumed growth rates of gross domestic product

Low-growth scenario

Period	China	India	USA, USSR,* OECD	Rest of the World
1989-2000	6.50	4.00	2.625	4.00
2000-2010	5.50	4.00	2.375	4.00
2010-20	4.50	3.75	2.125	3.75
2020-30	3.50	3.25	1.875	3.25
2030-40	2.75	2.75	1.625	2.75
2040-50	2.25	2.25	1.325	2.25

High-growth scenario

Period	China	India	USA, USSR,* OECD	Rest of the World
1989-2000	6.50	6.50	2.625	6.00
2000-2010	5.50	7.50	2.375	6.00
2010-20	4.50	6.75	2.125	5.375
2020-30	3.50	5.25	1.875	5.25
2030-40	2.75	4.75	1.625	4.75
2040-50	2.25	4.25	1.375	4.25

Source: Calculations by the author.
*Projections are for the countries formerly included in the Soviet Union.

are particularly inadequate for agricultural commodities. The composition of the food consumption basket changes significantly in relation to income. Additionally, the food intake by an individual is limited physiologically. Use of trend growth rates, as done by Jonathan Harris (1990), are inappropriate. Demand projections have to be made simultaneously for the whole basket of commodities. Such projections can be made on the basis of a complete expenditure system. However, empirically estimated systems are mostly linear expenditure systems, which are not appropriate for long-term projections involving large changes in incomes and expenditures. To illustrate these difficulties, projections will be made using different methods. Following this, I suggest a procedure that I think is more appropriate for this purpose. Projections derived from it will then be presented.

Alternative Methods of Demand Projections

Expenditure elasticities for individual commodities are often used for projecting commodity demands. I have used the elasticities obtained from the reference-run simulations of the basic linked system (BLS) of national models (Fischer et al., 1988) developed at IIASA. Using these, along with the projected per capita expenditure derived from the GDP and populations of the preceding section, we obtain the first set of projections. Assuming that the aggregate savings rate would remain constant at the level projected for the year 2000 in the BLS scenario, we obtain per capita expenditure given the GDP and the population. The demand, expenditure, and elasticities are related as follows:[4]

$$d_1 = d_0 \left[\frac{e_1}{e_0}\right]^\eta$$

where

d_1 = projected per capita demand;

d_0 = base year per capita demand;

e_1 = projected per capita expenditure;

e_0 = base year per capita expenditure;

and η = elasticity.

The results of this exercise generate very high levels of demand and imply unrealistically high calorie intake. For long-term projections involving substantial growth in incomes and expenditures, commodity-by-commodity demand projections using elasticities are therefore not satisfactory. One of the problems of such projections is that the implied expenditure for all the commodities does not add up to the total expenditure.

To test this conclusion we also employed a complete expenditure system to make demand projections for India. We had previously estimated a three-level hierarchical demand system (Suryanarayana, 1992) for India. The system has many desirable properties. It attempts to capture household preferences for both food and nonfood commodity items. It is a complete demand system based on a nested AIDS-Translog–LES cost function and is estimated separately for both rural and urban India. The projections gave absurdly high demand projections for the rural sector and unrealistically high demand projections for the urban sector. The results indicate that it is not enough to have a complete expenditure system. It should also be robust over large changes in income and expenditure. The projections made with this methodology did not meet this test.

Demand Projections for Regions of the World

The problem with these projections is that the implied calorie intake is too high to be physiologically credible. They imply whole nations of obese gluttons. What is needed is a demand projection method that respects some calorie constraint. Fortunately, the demand system used in some of the national models of IIASA's basic linked system (BLS) have such a feature. In these models a linear expenditure system is synthesized at each expenditure level given a set of prices.[5]

The details of this approach are given in Fischer and colleagues (1988). Such a system can be looked upon as an approximation to an underlying nonlinear demand system. Such a system is available for the following countries: Argentina, Brazil, Mexico, Canada, Austria, the European Community, Egypt, Turkey, Pakistan, Indonesia, and Japan. We use the demand systems of these countries to represent demands for their regions and estimate the demands for 2020 and 2050.

With the projected per capita consumption expenditure for the years 2020 and 2050, a consumption vector was estimated for each of these countries for each of the two scenarios. By multiplying those per capita consumption figures by the corresponding populations of the regions of which these countries are considered as representative we can project total demands for final human consumption.[6] Demands for feeds have to be added to these.

Projected Feed Needs

For projecting the feed needs, we simply take the feed norms for producing the major livestock products, namely milk, poultry, pork, and bovine and ovine meats. While substitution among different feeds is possible and does indeed take place in response to changes in relative prices, much scope also exists for technical progress. In projecting feed needs we neglect these and use the feed intakes of the European Community in the year 2000 as projected in the reference scenario of the IIASA model as the norm.[7]

The required productions, when feed needs are added to the demand for human consumption, are summarized in Table 2.3. It should be emphasized that the production of cereals and protein feeds includes the feeds needed to produce the various animal products. Thus, if we can produce the food grains and provide the needed pastures for bovine and ovine meat, then all the animal products can be produced. Similarly, the oils and protein feeds are joint products of oil seed production.

Table 2.3. Production needs and production ratios for 2020 and 2050 vis-à-vis 2000

Year	Cereals	Bovine & ovine meat	Dairy	Other animal products	Protein feeds	Oils and fats	Sugar
2000[a]	2082	86	642	27	106	96	286[b]
Medium population – low growth (MP-LG)							
2020	2305.8	124.8	640.6	97.4	88.3	99.1	219.4
2050	3262.4	175.5	855.9	130.5	128.3	158.6	324.7
High population – low growth (HP-LG)							
2020	2762.9	144.6	780.5	111.0	108.3	131.6	219.1
2050	4916.4	270.5	1347.3	184.5	205.3	288.6	523.8
MP-LG Ratio							
2020/2000	1.11	1.45	1.00	3.61	0.83	1.03	0.77
2050/2000	1.57	2.04	1.33	4.83	1.21	1.65	1.14
HP-LG Ratio							
2020/2000	1.33	1.68	1.22	4.11	1.02	1.37	0.98
2050/2000	2.36	3.15	2.10	6.83	1.94	3.01	1.83

Source: Calculations by the author.
Note: Units are as follows:
Cereals: million tons
Bovine and ovine meat: million tons carcass weight
Dairy: million tons whole milk equivalent
Other animal products: million ton protein equivalent
Protein feeds: million ton protein equivalent
Oils: 10^6 tons oil
Sugar: 10^6 tons refined sugar equivalent
[a]Production figures for 2000 are taken from the basic linked system reference scenario.
[b]1986-87

It may be noted that the projections refer to effective demand and not to any biological requirement. The fact that average per capita demands are large does not by itself imply that everyone's biological demand is met. However, if the scenarios of GDP growth are realized, then the scenarios imply virtually no hunger by the year 2020, if we assume that income distribution would not be worsened in the different countries of the world. The average per capita calorie intake exceeds 3,000 kilocalorie per person each day in most of our countries. With such intake, the incidence of hunger is likely to be very small.

Can these demands be met? We look at this in two steps. First, we examine the technical feasibility. Then we look at the institutional requirements to realize the production potential in a sustainable way. It is possible to take a sanguine view and say that the technical feasibility should pose no great problem. Can the needed institutions be developed in time to do this in a sustainable way? That is not so clear.

Production Possibilities and
Resource Needs — Technical Feasibility

The production potential for realizing the demands does exist. The projected demands for Europe, the United States and Canada, and Oceania have increased relatively modestly over their current values. Thus one would be justified in thinking that those countries that are net exporters of food grains and animal products at present will be able to meet their own demands comfortably. The Food and Agriculture Organization (FAO) estimates of population-supporting capacities for developing countries, excluding China, are given in Table 2.4.

We see from the table that the developing countries, excluding China, have a potential year 2000 population-supporting capacity, with high levels of inputs, of 5.11 persons per hectare. Thus the total land area of 6.495 billion hectares can support a population of 33.2 billion. Our projected demands imply roughly 50 percent more calorie intake than assumed in the FAO study. Adjusting for that, we still get a population-supporting capacity of the developing countries alone of 22.1 billion persons (33.2/1.5). These estimates (Higgins et al., 1982) do not adequately account for irrigated output. Input intensities do not seem to change in the FAO study on irrigated land across the low, intermediate, or high scenarios. Thus the actual population-supporting capacities must be higher still. The fact that production potential exists does not mean that it will be realized. We need to identify in some detail what is needed to realize these potentials.

Land Resources

Figures 2.1 and 2.2 depict land-use reserves and irrigation potential.[8] The "other land" category includes unused but potentially productive land, built-on areas, wasteland, parks, ornamental gardens, roads, lanes, barren land, and any other land not specifically listed under other items. Some of this land can be brought under cultivation to expand the area under arable and permanent crops. Area can also be expanded through multiple cropping. Figure 2.1 shows the scope for expanding cultivated area in 93 developing countries.

If at the global level arable land can be brought to the same proportion as in Asia, not to mention Europe, the net area under cultivation

Table 2.4. Developing country population-supporting capacities

Location	Total land area (million hectares)	Year 1975 population (million people)	Year 1975 population density (persons per hectare)	Year 1975 potential population-supporting capacity (persons per hectare)			Year 2000 population (million people)	Year 2000 population density (persons per hectare)	Year 2000 potential population-supporting capacity (persons per hectare)		
				Low inputs	Medium inputs	High inputs			Low inputs	Medium inputs	High inputs
Total	6,494.9	1,956.6	0.30	0.61	2.11	5.05	3,589.7	0.55	0.86	2.30	5.11
Africa	2,878.1	380.2	0.13	0.39	1.53	4.47	780.1	0.27	0.44	1.56	4.47
South-west Asia	677.4	136.3	0.20	0.16	0.25	0.40	264.7	0.39	0.27	0.35	0.48
South America	1,770.2	215.8	0.12	0.72	2.92	6.97	392.6	0.22	0.78	2.96	6.99
Central America	271.6	106.6	0.39	0.64	1.65	4.51	215.2	0.79	1.07	2.04	4.76
South-east Asia	897.6	1,117.7	1.25	1.29	3.76	6.34	1,937.1	2.16	2.74	4.86	7.06

Source: Higgins et al., 1982.

Notes: Land areas are derived from FAO-UNESCO Soil Map, and exclude areas mapped as water bodies.
U.N. data for 1975: *U.N. 1979: World Population Trends and Prospects by Country (1950–2000),* summary report of the 1978 assessment,
ST/ESA/Ser. R/33 (New York: United Nations).
Projected U.N. data for 2000: medium projection, 1979.

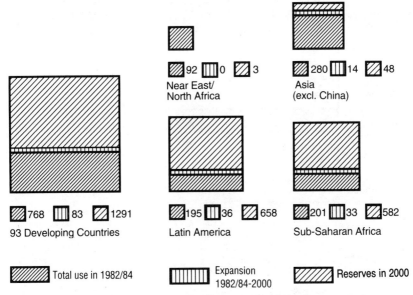

Figure 2.1. Land use and reserves (million hectares, arable land).

will increase by more than 50 percent. In addition the potential for the development of irrigation should also be considered. The potential shown in Figure 2.2 is really an underestimate. For example, for India it shows irrigation potential of about 90 million hectares. The estimate of India's irrigation potential has been periodically revised upward. A recent estimate places the area at 113 million hectares. Some argue however, that the potential is substantially higher than that. In any case, even in the relatively well developed irrigation system of India, only a little more than half the irrigation potential is realized.

The scope for further development of irrigation in many developing countries remains substantial. Even more important is the scope for improving the efficiency of water use through conservation practices and programs and spot applications. These, however, require capital investments and skills. Given the pressure of demand, one can expect that these investments will become profitable and irrigated area will expand substantially. This should result in higher cropping intensities as well as in higher yields. If irrigation expansion were to lead to a 15 percent expansion of harvested area, then area expansion alone can give 60 to 65 percent higher production. This agricultural production should be more than adequate by itself to meet the projected demand in 2020.

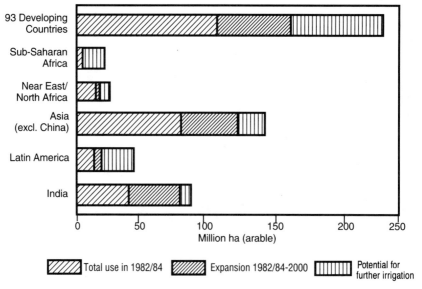

Figure 2.2. Irrigated land use and potential. (Agriculture toward 2000–FAO conference, 24th session, Rome, 1987.)

Of course, one would expect that along with expansion of area, yield improvements will also continue to take place. This would reduce the pace of expansion of area. What are the prospects for yield increases?

Yield Increases

Yields vary considerably across regions depending on agroclimatic resources, input use, and the genetic variety used. It shows that the yields for all cereals are quite high for Europe and North America. This is partly due to higher fertilizer-use intensity.[9] While Europe uses 142 kilograms per hectare, the world average of fertilizer use is only 30 kilograms per hectare. There is a significant scope for increasing the fertilizer intensity in all continents, except Europe, to raise yields, particularly in Africa and South America, which use less than 10 kilograms per hectare of fertilizer. The present production of cereals in these two continents is rather small, so yield increases will result in small increases in global production. However, in both Asia and North America, which are major cereal producers, scope exists for increasing yield through increased intensity of fertilizer.

To meet global demands for 2050, yields will have to increase by some 50 to 60 percent, an annual improvement of less than 1 percent. While this does not seem to present an impossible task, we need to realize that this implies agriculture in almost all continents performing at the European productivity level.

Technical Progress

Raising yield levels will require considerable technical progress. Even where it may be possible to raise yields using presently available technology through input intensification, it may not be desirable to do so to ensure environmental sustainability. In many other areas, new varieties will have to be developed that are appropriate to the agroclimatic conditions where potential for growth exists. Techniques will have to be evolved for more effective applications of inputs such as fertilizers and water and for integrated pest management.

Biotechnology offers great hope in realizing the necessary technical change. The recombinant DNA technologies, the developing of gene transfer systems, and the realization that genes have two major components, a product coding region and a control region, constitute three key elements of genetic engineering (Peacock, 1991). The promise is one of new varieties that give higher yields at the same level of inputs. The presently available high-yield varieties also do that (Parikh, 1978), and yet this is not enough to prevent wasteful applications of chemicals and water. However, the new information technology can be used to give more precise applications of inputs (Ruttan, 1992). The buildup of undesirable chemical residues in soils can thus be minimized. There are, therefore, few constraints, from the viewpoint of scientific knowledge, to attaining the yield levels needed to meet the demand for agricultural products.

Soil Degradation

Hard data on the impact of soil degradation on yields are not available. The waterlogging and salinization resulting from irrigation have become a major point of contention in the controversy surrounding large irrigation projects. While the environmentalists seem to exaggerate the loss, the economists tend to undervalue it. Thus in India, for the Narmada project, it has been argued that nearly 40 percent of the Narmada command area will become waterlogged (Alvares and Billorey, 1988). The same authors also assert, without citing any source, that 10 million hectares of land is lost due to waterlogging in the country. An estimate based on satellite data of 1982-83 (Singh,

1989) puts the total amount of land turned to wasteland due to waterlogging at 0.88 million hectares. Similarly, according to Alvares and Billorey (1988), 25 million hectares in the country are facing salinization, whereas Singh (1989) estimates wasteland due to salinization to be 3.9 million hectares. The estimates for the extent of land degradation also differ, ranging from 90 to 140 million hectares, reported by some activists, to 50 million hectares, much of it recoverable, based on satellite imagery. Part of the difference in these estimates may be due to differences in definitions. A partially waterlogged or salinized land may still be productive and used for cultivation. Some may include this in degraded land and others may not. What is necessary is a measure of the soil-quality degradation that accounts for the intensity of waterlogging and salinization.

Crosson reports losses of 3 to 10 percent in yields over a 100-year period due to soil erosion in the United States (Ruttan, 1992). An estimate for India indicates that a shift of fully 10 percent of the total cropped area from greater than 3 feet soil depth to less than 1 foot soil depth category will lead to a yield loss of around 2 percent. There is no estimate of the period of time over which such a shift will take place (Parikh and Ghosh, 1990). In any case, these losses are small when compared with the expected impact of technical change.

Institutional Obstacles and Needs

It is clear that it will be potentially feasible to increase the growth of agricultural supply to meet the demands that will be placed on agricultural production. To do so will require expansion of area under cultivation, development of irrigation potential, and research and extension efforts to bring modern technology to virtually all farmers in the world. The question becomes, Can this be done given the present institutional setup? Changes in organization behavior and institutional arrangements may be more difficult to achieve (see chapter 3). What are the problems and what kind of new institutional arrangements are required?

Expansion of Cultivable Area

First, we consider the problems associated with expansion of area under cultivation. To expand to the extent required may not be too difficult. In fact, if the population increases as projected, cultivated area will expand. That much is almost certain. However, what is uncertain is whether this will or can be done in an ecologically sustainable way. When cultivable area is expanded by using land around existing settlements, it is usually at the cost of village commons or surrounding forests or woods. Their destruction deprives the poor of fodder and fuel wood. The efforts to find new sources for these creates further deforestation. Each of these causes much ecological disturbance. This can be restrained, however, if the poor are not so impoverished that they have to depend on freely gathered fuels and if alternative fuels and fodder supplies are arranged. This requires that the impoverished countries develop rapidly in the coming one or two decades and eliminate poverty.

When cultivated area is expanded through new settlements, it can also lead to ecological stress (see chapter 5). Forests may be removed, and if the resulting agricultural use is not consistent with the ecological characteristics of the area, it may soon turn into wasteland. This happened in Brazil in the mideighties, when forests were cleared to promote agricultural operations under the influence of incentives provided by government policy but the fragile ecosystems of the Amazon could not sustain agricultural operations. The policies have subsequently been partially corrected. Yet it does point to the likelihood of ecological damage during and consequent to area expansion. Policies must be based on sound ecological knowledge. The provision of such knowledge to developing country governments is currently not ensured or coordinated. Institutions with the function of generating and disseminating such knowledge are needed.

Expansion of Irrigation

The needed expansion of irrigation and more efficient allocation and use of water must also be examined. A difficult problem for efficient use of water resources in many developing countries is the very small average farm size. In India the average farm size was 1.71 hectares in 1982, and that is often further subdivided into numerous smaller fragments. Small farmers do not have the resources to invest in irrigation. Even when finances are provided, with such small plots investment in tube-wells becomes economically unwise unless groundwater markets are developed.

Small holdings also make it much more difficult to construct drainage systems needed for sustainable irrigation. Cooperative water management can assist in solving these problems. However, such programs have not been very successful, except in isolated instances where a charismatic leader has organized, nurtured, and supervised such cooperatives. Nor is the experience with collective farming encouraging, to say the least, as far as efficient use of resources is concerned. When it comes to sustainable use of resources where externalities and free-riding opportunities abound, collectives and cooperatives are even less likely to succeed. The solution to the small-size farms is indeed rapid economic growth, migration out of agriculture, and consolidation of these small holdings into larger holdings under single ownership.

Research and Extension for Widespread Intensification

If production is to increase to meet the projected demands, widespread yield improvements will be needed. This will call for dispersal of new varieties and modern inputs throughout all parts of the world. The research and extension (R&E) institutions needed to create and widely circulate the needed technology have to be in place. The Indian experience with green revolution clearly brings out the importance of such institutions.

In India the tremendous potential of green revolution has been well recognized for 25 years. It has not yet been extended to cover all regions and all the major crops in India. The use of high-yield varieties is not universal even for rice. Rice varieties suitable for all the different agroclimatic conditions of the country are not available, because development of such varieties requires adaptive research. The agricultural research system in India is large and well developed, and yet it is not able to fully meet the needs of Indian agriculture.

The task of bringing about a global green revolution is not going to be trivial, nor will such a revolution take place without concerted effort. Adaptive research by local institutions is important (see chapter 6), yet international research institutions will have to play a major role in this task (see chapter 4).

An international network of institutions promotes exchange of genetic material, helps train critical work-force members, and, through exchange of information and knowledge, significantly increases the chances of success in breeding. This is obvious when one looks at the experience of breeding rice varieties. David and Evenson (1992) have documented this. Between 1966 and 1991, some 1,846 rice varieties have been released around the world. Of the 1,816 varieties for which data are available, only 640 had germ plasm independent of the International Rice Research Institute. The flow of germ plasm has been enormous. Indian material was in 1,249 varieties, including 579 varieties released in other countries. Similarly, of the 1,236 varieties released in China, 532 had germ plasm from India. Such flows would not have been easy without a network of research institutions, including international institutions. This highlights the extremely important role played by international cooperation and international research institutions. It also exposes the dangers of the growing tendency to patent biological resources and of the monopolization of emerging new biotechnology.

Concluding Observations

The expected demand in 2050 for agricultural products by a global population of some 12.8 billion (a pessimistically high projection, in my opinion) with a much larger per capita income can be met through expansion of area and technical progress in increasing yield and reducing excessive application of chemicals. In order for this possibility to be realized, developments in a number of areas will be needed. Induced technical change in response to demand pressures can be expected to lead to some advancements. Substantial institutional change will also be required to mobilize the efforts of rural people to make effective use of the technical changes that will become available (see chapter 6).

To expand area under cultivation, infrastructure facilities of roads, electricity, irrigation, drainage, and markets must be improved. In many developing countries where scope for area expansion exists, substantial investment is required. To increase yields, high-yield varieties appropriate for local agroclimatic conditions will have to be formed. International institutions, cooperation among national institutions, and free exchange of agricultural technology have been crucial in the past for breeding new plant varieties. Each of these will have to be boosted for a new widespread green revolution to occur. Extension efforts will also be needed to diffuse the new plant varieties to farmers. Research and development and extension institutions must be created in the near future.

To achieve environmental sustainability, conservation practices, some based on information technology, will need to be adopted widely. An educated farm community is a precondition for using such measures. Policies have to be devised to internalize some of the environmental externalities in farm management. Other policies will be needed to make it worthwhile for the farmers to pursue environment-friendly practices. Achievement of sustainable farming practices is possible, but widespread and rapid economic growth is imperative: Such growth would not only give the poor the means to buy the food they need but would also reduce the pressure to use land in an unsustainable way. Without economic growth, deforestation is unlikely to be contained. Only rapid economic growth in the developing countries can stem the flow of international migration. Thus, international assistance, both financial and technical, must be escalated to promote growth and thereby to eliminate hunger, to reduce population growth, to contain international migration, and to promote sustainable use of this planet's resources of land and forests.

Notes

The author has greatly benefited from the comments of the participants at the conference and particularly those of the chapter's discussants, Robert Kates and Randolph Barker. He also thanks Abbeek Barua for computational assistance.

1. The other studies surveyed include International Futures Simulation (Hughes, 1980); Grain Buffer Stock (Eaton et al., 1976); the U.N. World Model (Leontief, Carter, and Petri, 1977); the Interactive Agricultural Model (Enzer, Drobnick, and Alter, 1978); the Optimal Grain Reserve (Johnson and Sumner, 1976); Future of Global Interdependence (Kaya, Onishi, et al., 1977); the USDA Grains, Oils, and Livestock Model (Rojko and Schwartz, 1976); the Input-Output Model (Bottomley et al., n.d.); the FAO Price Equilibrium Model (FAO, 1971); and the World Food Economy Model (Takayami, Hashimoto, and Schmidt, 1976).

2. The trend projections surveyed include Iowa State University (Blakeslee, Heady, and Framingham, 1973), the International Food Policy Research Institute (1977), and the FAO (1981).

3. The historical (to 1990) and medium average annual projected growth rates (1990-2025) of the U.N. are presented in Appendix Tables A2.1 and A2.2. Because of space limitations it was not possible to include these and other appendix tables (A2.3-A2.9) in this volume. Copies may be obtained from the author.

4. The expenditure elasticities, base-year consumption levels, and projections for selected countries are given in Appendix Tables A2.3 and A2.4, available from the author.

5. This involves the following steps:

   a. A modified Engel Curve that expresses per capita demand as a function of per capita expenditure as well as own price of the commodity is estimated for each commodity from the historical data of the country. Thus,

$$d_i = f_i (e, p_i)$$

where:

d_i is per capita demand for ith commodity,

p_i is price of i, and

e is total per capita expenditure.

   b. An Engel Curve for aggregate calorie intake is also estimated from cross-country data. This curve is asymptotic to a level of 4,500 kcal/capita/per day.

   c. From these Engel Curves we estimate the demands d_i for all commodities and aggregate calories for an estimated expenditure level ê and assumed prices $\hat{p}_i$. In general, the demands do not add up to the projected expenditure, that is:

$$\sum_i p_i \hat{d}_i \neq \hat{e}.$$

Also in general, the implied calorie intake would not add up to the projected calorie intake $\hat{C}$, that is, with c_i the calorific value of ith commodity:

$$\sum_i c_i d_i \neq \hat{C}.$$

   d. Find a vector $\{d\}$ such that the weighted distance between $\{d\}$ and $\{\hat{d}\}$ is minimized subject to the conditions that the total expenditure on $\{q\}$ equals the given total expenditure ê and the calorie content of $\{d\}$ adds up to $\hat{C}$.

   e. Vector $\{d\}$ is the per capita projected demand. Multiply with projected population to obtain projected total demand.

  6. The detailed results for the year 2050 are given in Appendix Tables A2.61 and A2.62 (available from the author) for the MP-LG scenario.

  7. The feed input coefficients for the EC in the year 2000 are given in Appendix Table A2.63. The global feed needs for the projected demands are given in Appendix Table A2.64. Both tables are available from the author.

  8. The land-use pattern in 1985 is given in Appendix Table A2.7, available from the author.

  9. Appendix Table A2.8 shows the production and yield for different crops in different regions for 1986–87. Appendix Table A2.9 gives data on fertilizer use in different regions. Both tables are available from the author.

References

Alvares, C., and Billorey, R. 1988. *Damming the Narmada: India's Greatest Planned Environmental Disaster*. Pennang, Malaysia: Third World Network.

Blakeslee, L. L., E. O. Heady, and C. F. Framingham. 1973. *World Food Production, Demand and Trade*. Ames: Iowa State University Press.

Bottomley, A., M. Ergatoudes, L. C. Carpenter, and M. Lloyd. N.d. A six sector input-output world model. Undated manuscript. This and other data and material are available through Dr. A. Bottomley, University of Bradford, Bradford, W. Yorkshire BD 71P, U.K.

Brown, Martin, and Ian Goldin. 1992. *The Future of Agriculture: Developing Country Implications*. Development Centre Studies. Paris: Organization for Economic Cooperation and Development.

Crosson, P. 1992. Temperate region soil erosion. In *Sustainable Agriculture and the Environment: Perspectives on Growth and Constraints*, edited by Vernon W. Ruttan. Boulder, Colo.: Westview Press.

David, C., and R. E. Evenson. 1992. *Structural Adjustment and Technical Change in Rice Production*. A paper presented at the Expert Meeting on Structural Adjustment and Technological Change in Developing Country Agriculture, Organization for Economic Cooperation and Development Centre, Paris, January 20-21, 1992.

Eaton, D., W. S. Steele, J. L. Cohon, and C. S. ReVelle. 1976. A method to size world grain reserves: Initial results. In *Analysis of Grain Reserves: A Proceeding*, edited by D. J. Eaton and W. S. Steele. U.S. Department of Agriculture (USDA) Economic Research Service Report no. 634. Washington, D.C.: USDA.

Enzer S., R. Drobnick, and S. Alter. 1978. *Neither Feast nor Famine*. Lexington, Mass.: Lexington Books.

Food and Agriculture Organization (FAO). 1971. *A World Price Equilibrium Model*. Rome: General Commodity Analysis Group, Commodities and Trade Division and Research Division, UN Conference on Trade and Development (UNCTAD).

————. 1981. *Agriculture toward 2000*. Rome: FAO.

Fischer, G., Klaus Frohberg, Michel A. Keyzer, and Kirit S. Parikh. 1988. *Linked National Models — A Tool for International Food Policy Analysis*. Dordrecht: Kluwer.

Fox, G., and V. W. Ruttan. 1983. A guide to LDC food balance projections. *European Review of Agricultural Economics* 10:325-56.

Frejka, T. 1973. *The Future of Population Growth: Alternative Paths to Equilibrium*. New York: Wiley.

Harris, J. M. 1990. *World Agriculture and the Environment*. New York: Garland.

Herrera, A. O., H. D. Scholnik, Graciela Chichilnisky, Gilberto C. Gallopin, Jorge E. Hardoy, Diana Mosovich, Enrique Oteiza, Gilda L. de Romero Brest, Carlos E. Suarez, and Luis Talavera. 1976. *Catastrophe or New Society? A Latin American World Model*. Ottawa: International Development Research Center.

Higgins, G. M., A. H. Kassam, L. Naiken, G. Fischer, and M. M. Shah. 1982. *Potential Population Supporting Capacities of Lands in the Developing World*. Technical Report INT/75/P13. Rome: Food and Agriculture Organization.

Hughes, B. B. 1980. *World Modeling: The Mesarovic-Pestel World Model in the Context of Its Contemporaries*. Lexington, Mass.: Lexington Books.

International Food Policy Research Institute. 1977. *Food Needs of Developing Countries: Projections of Production and Consumption to 1990*. Research Report 3. Washington, D.C.: International Food Policy Research Institute.

Johnson, D. G., and D. Sumner. 1976. An optimization approach to grain reserves for developing countries. In *Analysis of Grain Reserves: A Proceedings*, edited by D. J. Eaton and W. S. Steele. USDA Economic Research Service Report no. 634. Washington, D.C.: USDA.

Kaya, Y., A. Onishi, and Y. Suzuki, et al. 1977. Report on project FUGI — future of global interdependence. Paper presented at Fifth Global Modeling Conference, International Institute for Applied Systems Analysis (IIASA), Laxenburg, Austria.

Leontief, W., A. Carter, and P. Petri. 1977. *Future of the World Economy: A United Nations Study*. New York: Oxford University Press.

Linnemann, H., J. De Hoogh, M. A. Keyzer, and H. D. J. Van Heemst. 1979. *MOIRA: Model of International Relations in Agriculture*. Amsterdam: North-Holland.

Manne, A. S., and R. G. Richels. 1991. Global CO_2 emission reductions — the impacts of rising energy costs. *Energy Journal* 12(1): 87-107.

Meadows, Donella H., and Dennis L. Meadows, with Jorgen Randers and William H. Behrens III. 1972. *The Limits to Growth*. New York: Universe Books.

Mesarovic, M., and E. Pestel. 1974. *Mankind at the Turning Point*. New York: Dutton.

Onishi, A. 1987. Alternative futures of the world economy, 1986-2000: Policy simulations by the FUGI global macroeconomic model. In *Dynamic Modeling and Control of National Economies 1986: Proceedings of the Fifth International Federation of Automatic Control/International Federation of Operations Research Societies Conference*, edited by B. Martos, L. F. Pau, and M. Ziemann, Budapest, June 17-20, 1986. Oxford: Pergamon.

Parikh, K. S. 1978. HYV and fertilizers — synergy or substitution: Implications for policy and prospects for agricultural development. *Economic and Political Weekly* 13(2): A2-A8.

Parikh, K. S., and U. Ghosh. 1990. *Natural Resource Accounting for Soils: Towards an Empirical Estimate of Costs of Soil Degradation for India*. Discussion Paper no. 48. Bombay: Indira Gandhi Institute of Development Research.

Parikh, K. S., G. Fischer, K. Frohberg, and O. Gulbrandsen. 1988. *Toward Free Trade in Agriculture*. Dordrecht: Nijhoff.

Peacock, J. W. 1991. Key elements of modern biotechnology of relevance to agriculture. *Papers of the Plenary and Invited Paper Sessions*. Twenty-first International Agricultural Economists' Association Conference, August 22-29. Tokyo: International Agricultural Economists' Association.

Roberts, P. C. 1977. *SARUM 76—Global Modeling Project*. Research Report no. 19. London: U.K. Department of Environment and Transport.

Robinson, J. 1985. Global modeling and simulations. In *Climate Impact Assessment*, edited by R. W. Kates, J. H. Ausubel, and M. Berberian. New York: Wiley.

Rojko, A. S., and M. W. Schwartz. 1976. Modeling the world grains, oilseeds and livestock economy to assess the world food prospects. *Agricultural Economics Research* 28:89-98.

Ruttan, V. 1992. *Sustainable Agriculture and the Environment: Perspectives on Growth and Constraints*. Boulder, Colo.: Westview Press.

Singh, P. 1989. *Problem of Wasteland and Forest Ecology in India*. New Delhi: Ashish.

Suryanarayana, M. H. 1992. *A Hierarchic Demand System Based on Nested AIDS-Translog-LES cost function*. Discussion paper. Bombay: Indira Gandhi Institute of Development Research.

Takayama, T., H. Hashimoto, and S. Schmidt. 1976. *Projection and Evaluation of Trends and Policies in Agricultural Commodity, Supply, Demand, International Trade, and Food Reserves*. Agricultural Extension Service, 4405 (Part I). Urbana-Champaign: University of Illinois.

United Nations. 1991. *World Population Prospects 1990*. Population Studies no. 120. New York: United Nations.

CHAPTER 3

CONSTRAINTS ON INSTITUTIONAL INNOVATION:

TRANSACTION COSTS, INCENTIVE COMPATIBILITY, AND HISTORICAL CONSIDERATIONS

Douglass C. North

Devising an institutional framework that will make possible sustainable agricultural development in the 21st century requires a clear understanding of the way institutions evolve as a prerequisite to effective policymaking. One cannot effectively design institutions without an insight into what institutions are, how they relate to organizations, and how they change. A theory of institutional change is essential because the tools of neoclassical theory (and other theories in the social scientist's toolbag) cannot satisfactorily account for the very diverse performance of societies and economies both at a moment of time and over time. The models derived from neoclassical theory may account for most of the differences in performance between economies on the basis of differential investment in education, savings rates, and so on, but they do not explain why economies would fail to undertake the appropriate activities if they have a high payoff (Mankiw, Romer, and Weil, 1991). Institutions determine the payoffs. They are the structure that humans impose on human interaction, and therefore they define the incentives that (together with the other constraints—budget, technology, and so forth) determine the choices individuals make that shape the performance of societies and economies over time.

In the first part of this chapter I sketch out a framework for analyzing institutions. This framework builds on the basic assumption of economic theory of scarcity and therefore competition and hence choices subject to constraints. However, it incorporates new assumptions both about the constraints that individuals face and about the process by which they make choices within those constraints. Traditional neoclassical assumptions that are relaxed are those of costless exchange, perfect information, and unlimited cognitive capabilities. Too many gaps still remain in our understanding of this new approach to call it a theory. What I do provide is a set of definitions, principles, and a structure that make up much of the scaffolding necessary to build a theory of institutional change.

With that scaffolding in place I can then explore the issues relevant to the subject of this book: the prospects for such an institutional framework coming to grips with problems posed by the scientists in three "dialogues" leading to the conference that inspired this volume. The second part applies the analytical framework to the issues, the third explores what we have learned, and the final section develops the policy implications and also points up the lacunae in our understanding of these issues.

The Analytical Framework

I begin by making a distinction essential to any understanding of institutional change—that between institutions and organizations.

Institutions consist of formal rules, informal constraints (norms of behavior, conventions, and self-imposed codes of conduct) and the enforcement characteristics of both. In short they consist of the structure that humans impose on their dealings with each other. The degree to which there is an identity between the objectives of the institutional constraints and the choices individuals make in that institutional setting depends on the effectiveness of enforcement. Enforcement is carried out by the first party (self-imposed codes of conduct), by the second party (retaliation), and/or by a third party (societal sanctions or coercive enforcement by the state). Institutions affect economic performance by determining (together with the technology employed) transaction and transformation (production) costs.

If institutions are the rules of the game, organizations are the players. They are made up of groups of individuals engaged in purposive activity. The constraints imposed by the institutional framework (together with the other standard constraints of economics) define the opportunity set and therefore the kind of organizations that will come into existence. Given the objective function of the organization—

maximizing profit, winning elections, regulating businesses, educating students—organizations such as firms, political parties, regulatory agencies, schools, or colleges will engage in acquiring skills and knowledge that will enhance their survival possibilities in the context of ubiquitous competition. The kinds of skills and knowledge that will pay off will be a function of the incentive structure inherent in the institutional matrix. If the highest rates of return in a society are from piracy, then organizations will invest in knowledge and skills that will make them better pirates; if the payoffs are highest from increasing productivity, then firms and other organizations will invest in skills and knowledge that achieve that objective. Organizations will not only directly invest in acquiring skills and knowledge but will indirectly (via the political process) induce public investment in those kinds of knowledge that they believe will enhance their survival prospects.

It would be a mistake to conceive of the role of organizations as some mechanical response to the institutional incentive structure. The ideal incentive framework will not only reward productive activities but will provide a hospitable environment for the creative designing by entrepreneurs of new institutions to solve new problems.

Institutional Change: Agents, Sources, Process, Direction

The agent of change is the (political or economic) entrepreneur, the decision maker(s) in organizations. The subjective perceptions (mental models) of entrepreneurs determine the choices they make.

The sources of change are the opportunities perceived by entrepreneurs. They will stem from either external changes in the environment or from the acquisition of learning and skills that, given the mental constructs of the actors, will suggest new opportunities. Changes in relative prices have been the most commonly observed external sources of institutional change in history, but changes in taste have also been important. The acquisition of learning and skills will lead to the construction of new mental models by entrepreneurs to decipher the environment, which in turn will alter perceived relative prices of potential choices. In fact it has usually been some mixture of external change and internal learning that determines the choices that lead to institutional change.

Deliberate institutional change will come about therefore as a result of the demands of entrepreneurs in the context of the perceived costs of altering the institutional framework at various margins. The entrepreneur will weigh the gains to be derived from recontracting within the existing institutional framework against the gains from devoting resources to altering that framework. Bargaining strength and the incidence of transaction costs are not the same in the polity as in the economy, otherwise it would not be worthwhile for groups to shift the issues to the political arena. Thus entrepreneurs who perceive themselves and their organizations as relative (or absolute) losers in economic exchange as a consequence of the existing structure of relative prices can turn to the political process to right their perceived wrongs by altering that relative price structure. In any case the perceptions of the entrepreneur—correct or incorrect—are the underlying sources of action.

Changes in the formal rules include legislative changes such as the passage of a new statute, judicial changes as a result of court decisions altering the common law, regulatory rule changes enacted by regulatory agencies, and constitutional rule changes, which alter the rules by which other rules are made.

Institutional change resulting from changes in informal constraints—norms, conventions, or personal standards of honesty, for example—will have the same originating sources of change, such as learning or relative price changes, but will occur far more gradually and sometimes quite subconsciously as individuals evolve alternative patterns of behavior consistent with their newly perceived evaluation of costs and benefits.

The process of change is overwhelmingly incremental (although I shall deal with revolutionary change below). The reason is that the economies of scope, complementarities, and network externalities that arise from a given institutional matrix of formal rules, informal constraints, and enforcement characteristics will typically bias costs and benefits in favor of choices consistent with the existing framework. The larger the number of rule changes, ceteris paribus, the greater the number of losers and hence opposition. Therefore, except in the case of gridlock (described below), institutional change will occur at those margins considered most pliable in the context of the bargaining power of interested parties. The incremental change will come from a change in the rules via statute or legal change. Alternatively, changes in informal constraints will be a very gradual withering away of an accepted norm or social convention or the gradual adoption of a new one as the nature of the political, social, or economic exchange gradually changes.

The direction of change is determined by path dependence. The political and economic organizations that have come into existence in consequence of the institutional matrix typically have a stake in perpetuating the existing framework. The complementarities, economies of scope, and network externalities mentioned above bias change in favor of the interests of the existing organizations. The interests of the existing organizations that produce path dependence and the mental models of the actors—the entrepreneurs—that produce ideologies "rationalize" the existing institutional matrix and therefore bias the perception of the actors in favor of policies conceived to be in the interests of existing organizations.

Alteration in or reversal of paths is a result of external sources of change, which weaken the power of existing organizations and strengthen or give rise to organizations with different interests, or a result of the unanticipated consequences of the policies of the existing organizations. That is, the entrepreneurs' mental models determining the choices they make produce consequences at variance with their desired outcomes; the weakening of the power of existing organizations and the rise of organizations with different interests follow. The critical actor(s) in such situations will be political entrepreneurs whose degrees of freedom will increase in such situations and, given their perception of the issues, will give them the ability to induce the growth of (or strengthen existing) organizations and groups with different interests.

Revolutionary change will occur as a result of gridlock arising from a lack of mediating institutions and organizations, which enable conflicting parties to reach compromises and bargains that capture some of the gains from potential trades. The key to the existence of such mediating political (and economic) institutions is not only formal rules and organizations but the existence of informal constraints that can foster dialogue between conflicting parties. The inability to achieve compromise solutions may also reflect limited degrees of freedom of the entrepreneurs to bargain and still maintain the loyalty of their constituent groups. Thus the real choice set of the conflicting parties may have no intersection, so that even though there are potentially large gains from resolving disagreements, the combination of the limited bargaining freedom of the entrepreneurs and a lack of facilitating institutions makes it impossible to do so.

However, revolutionary change is never as revolutionary as its rhetoric would have us believe. It is not just that the power of ideological rhetoric fades as the mental models of the constituents confront their utopian ideals with the harsh realities of postrevolutionary existence. It is rather that the formal rules may change overnight but the informal constraints cannot. Inconsistency between the formal rules and the informal constraints (which may be the result of a deep-seated cultural inheritance because they have traditionally resolved basic exchange problems) results in tensions that typically get resolved by some restructuring of the overall constraints—in both directions—to produce a new equilibrium that is far less revolutionary than the rhetoric.

The Implications of an Institutional Framework

Information processing by the actors as a result of the costliness of transacting underlies the formation of institutions. At issue are both the meaning of rationality and the characteristics of transacting that prevent the actors from achieving the joint maximization result of the zero-transaction-cost model.

The instrumental rationality postulate of neoclassical theory assumes that the actors possess information necessary to correctly evaluate alternatives and in consequence to make choices that will achieve the desired ends. In fact such a postulate implicitly assumes the existence of a particular set of institutions and costless information. If institutions play a purely passive role so that they do not constrain the choices of the players and the players are in possession of the information necessary to make correct choices, then the instrumental rationality postulate is the correct building block. If, on the other hand, the players are incompletely informed, devise subjective models as guides to choices, and can only imperfectly correct their models with information feedback, then a procedural rationality postulate is the essential building block to theorizing. Such a postulate not only accounts for the incomplete and imperfect markets that characterize much of the present and the past world, but also leads the researcher to the key issues of just what it is that makes markets imperfect—the cost of transacting.

The cost of transacting arises because information is costly and asymmetrically held by the parties to exchange. In consequence, any way that the players develop institutions to structure human interaction results in some degree of imperfection of the markets. In effect the incentive consequences of institutions provide mixed signals to the participants, so that even in those cases where the institutional framework is more conducive to capturing the gains from trade than an earlier institutional framework, there will be incentives to cheat, free ride, and so forth, that will contribute to market imperfections.

The success stories of economic history describe institutional innovations that have lowered the costs of transacting and permitted capturing more of the gains from trade and hence have permitted the expansion of markets. But such innovations, for the most part, have not created the conditions necessary for the efficient markets of the neoclassical model. The polity specifies and enforces the property rights of the economic marketplace, and the characteristics of the political market are the essential key to understanding the imperfections of markets.

Just as the efficiency of an economic market can be measured by the degree to which the competitive structure, via arbitrage and efficient information feedback, mimics or approximates the conditions of a zero-transaction-cost framework, so an efficient political market would be one in which constituents accurately evaluated the policies pursued by competing candidates in terms of the net effect on their well-being, in which only legislation (or regulation) that maximized the aggregate income of the affected parties to the exchange would be enacted, and in which compensation to those adversely affected would insure that no party was injured by the action.

To achieve such results, constituents and legislators would need to possess true models that allowed them to accurately evaluate the gains and losses of alternative policies; legislators would vote their constituents' interests—that is, the vote of each legislator would be weighted by the net gains or losses of the constituents; and losers would be compensated to make the exchange worthwhile to them—all at a transaction cost that still resulted in the highest net aggregate gain.

I do not wish to imply that the political process in democracies does not sometimes approach such a nirvana outcome, nor that economic markets do not sometimes approximate the zero-transaction-cost model implicit in much economic theory. But such instances are rare and exceptional. Voter ignorance, incomplete information, and, in consequence, the prevalence of ideological stereotypes, underpinning the subjective models individuals develop to explain their environment and make choices, result in political markets that can and do perpetuate unproductive institutions and consequent organizations (North, 1990a).

Let me conclude this discussion by summing up the key features of this analytical framework of institutional change:

> 1. The continuous interaction between institutions and organizations in the economic setting of scarcity and hence competition is the key to institutional change.

2. Competition forces organizations to continually invest in skills and knowledge to survive.

3. The institutional framework dictates the kind of skills and knowledge perceived to have the maximum payoff.

4. The mental constructs of the players, given the complexity of the environment, the limited information feedback on the consequences of actions, and the inherited cultural conditioning of the players, determine perceptions.

5. The economies of scope, complementarities, and network externalities of an institutional matrix make institutional change overwhelmingly incremental and path dependent.

The Framework Applied

The institutions in this essay are the set of rules and informal constraints of the political units that shape agricultural, environmental, and health policies of the world. The immense diversity in the rules of the game among the high-income polities and economies, third-world countries, and the currently in flux "centrally planned" economies results in enormous diversity of the consequent organizations among these economies. A necessary first step in this analysis is to sketch out, however incompletely, the incentive structure—the opportunity set—of these polities and economies in order to understand the kinds of organizations that each gives rise to, since it is the organizations and their entrepreneurs who are the action players in this essay.

But we need still another input in order to meaningfully structure the game to get some useful results. We also must know something about the mental models (theories, ideologies, dogmas, insights) that the players employ to interpret and analyze the issues. The combination of institutional constraints and mental models of the entrepreneurs dictates the direction they will take in acquiring knowledge to deal with the issues.

Finally we must explore the incentive characteristics of the resultant organizations and particularly the principal-agent problems that will arise.

Let me make clear the direction of the rest of this essay by creating a make-believe model of a (largely) zero-transaction-cost world (one that is implicitly assumed by many neoclassical economists in their models). In this world the actors possess "true" models about the sources of the constraints on technology, environment, and health that threaten sustained agricultural development. They can calculate the benefit-cost ratios of alternative policies to overcome these constraints and enact those policies that have the highest payoff (including compensating any losers); where the policies are privately profitable they will be enacted by voluntary organizations, and where they are socially but not privately profitable (because of free-rider or public-goods problems—here the zero-transaction-cost assumption has been lifted) they will be undertaken by public agencies.

Our task as I see it is to so structure the game that we can approximate this ideal model (within the context of the framework developed above). All of this is a tall order, and I see my task as sketching out broad outlines.

The Institutional Constraints

Polities define the formal rules and property rights of economies. A necessary condition for effective solutions to the problems of sustainable agricultural growth is the existence of institutional frameworks that provide positive incentives for the creation of alternative approaches. This means that institutions that broaden the opportunity set and therefore provide inducements for creative entrepreneurship are essential. The contrast between the performance of the Western economies and the centrally planned economies since World War II provides a sobering reminder of the critical importance of institutional frameworks that induce competition and decentralized decision making and that reward the acquisition of productive skills and knowledge. Whatever the defects of the institutional framework of Western societies for solving the problems we confront, it cannot be emphasized too strongly at the outset that a necessary condition for the creation of organizations in the third world and former centrally planned economies that can deal with the issues of agricultural growth is the evolution of institutional frameworks that provide the necessary incentives to create appropriate organizations and learning.

The ideal institutional framework is one that is adaptively efficient. Economists concentrate on allocative efficiency—a static concept concerned with "getting the prices right" at a moment of time—but our concern is with creating a flexible framework of rules and norms over time that maximizes the choices available and eliminates failures. In a world of uncertainty no one knows the correct solution to the problems we confront. Broadly speaking, democratic polities and decentralized market economies with well-specified and enforced property rights are the closest approximation we know to an adaptively efficient institutional framework. But such a broad generalization conceals wide variations even among Western economies in the extent to which polities and economies deal effectively with issues of sustainable agriculture. The variations stem from the different mental models of the actors and variations in the institutional frameworks that result in variations in organizational structures.

Information Processing

A necessary first step to resolving the issue of the absence of information needed to properly analyze and deal with constraints is the creation or expansion of research organizations to gather the necessary data (see chapter 4). But there is more to information processing than data. There is what I have termed earlier the mental models of the actors; that is, the way the relevant actors see the problems—not only immediate policymakers in democratic (and even in nondemocratic) polities but also the "public." Running through the three "dialogues" in the conference that preceded this book were persistent references to the perceptions of the actors (politicians, environmentalists, the public, and the scientists and the social scientists themselves). For example, in the "dialogue" on the environment, not only were different perceptions about the magnitude and consequences of global warming evident among the participants, but those differences were seen to be simplified, magnified, exaggerated, or minimized by the stereotyped ideologies embodied in the varying perceptions of the "public," which in turn are reflected in political policies. It is certainly correct that improved information (the first issue) is an essential step to improving the quality of public perceptions and hence policies, but it would be the height of folly to think that reduced scientific disagreement is all that is necessary to produce "sound" political policies. The ideological stereotypes that dominate political thinking in all the complex issues that concern us do get altered with changes in scientific knowledge, but the process reflects all the vagaries of political markets discussed earlier. Political markets simply do not approximate the efficient markets I've described, and, because so much of the "new political economy" is predicated on rational choice models, little of the literature confronts directly the issue of public policy formation under conditions of incomplete information and preconceived, stereotyped, and frequently conflicting "theories."

The mental models individuals possess are in part culturally derived, partly acquired through experience, and partly (nonculturally and nonlocally) learned. Culture consists of the intergenerational transfer of knowledge, values, and other factors that influence behavior, and it varies radically among different ethnic groups and societies. Experience is "local" to the particular environment and therefore varies widely with different environments. These first two sources of the mental models individuals possess are termed "folk psychology" in the cognitive science literature.[1] The term refers to the mundane everyday understanding of ourselves and others. It is "nonscientific" in origin and results in immense variation in mental models and, as a consequence, in different perceptions of the world and the way it "works." The decline in information costs of the past century has, on the other hand, provided a "homogenizing" influence to noncultural learning. While this third source of mental models can result in a reduction of divergent views (such as on the issue of global warming, on the assumption that the scientists themselves achieve some consensus), culture and "local" learning continue to produce immense differences. At the extreme these differences are between, for example, Shiite fundamentalists in Iran, a Western businessperson, and a Papuan tribesman. More prosaic but no less important for our purposes are the different mental models mirrored in different and conflicting ideological stereotypes that underlie not only conflicting public policies but also widely varying attitudes toward such values as honesty, integrity, hard work—values that are critical determinants of the costs of transacting in complex political and economic exchange. I have gone on at length about this aspect of information processing because, in my view, this is the most difficult and intractable source of the constraints confronting us.

Organizations

In the first part of this chapter organizations were conceived as creations of the opportunity set established by the institutional framework, and the direction of their evolution was seen as a function of the incentive structure embodied in that institutional framework. Such a characterization is fine as far as it goes, but there are two implicit assumptions in it that are critical to the issues of concern to us. The first is that the institutional framework provides clear, unambiguous, and unidirectional signals and incentives to the relevant entrepreneurs. The second is that the relevant entrepreneurs—agents—faithfully carry out the intentions of the principal(s). Incentive compatibility and principal-agent issues are inextricably interwoven, but before delving into the theoretical issues let me first outline their relevance to the subject matter of this conference.

Organizations and specifically their entrepreneurs are the actors in institutional innovation. If the resource, environmental, and health constraints discussed in this book are to be overcome it will be because the "proper" organizations are put in place and their entrepreneurs carry out the necessary policies.

The initial actors are politicians with constituencies made up of widely varying and frequently conflicting interests to which they are held accountable even within a particular country. Because the issues that concern us are worldwide, the relevant constituencies are those of politicians worldwide, with frequently conflicting actual or at least perceived interests. How will the politicians protect their interests when they are called on to create the necessary organizations?

The resultant organizations will be staffed by entrepreneurs with their own interests. A consequence of delegating authority to bureaucrats is that they will become more knowledgeable about their policy responsibilities than are the elected officials who created the bureau and as a result will pursue their own agendas (which can range from selling out to an interest group, to shirking, to pursuing their own objectives). How will the politicians and relevant interest groups assure themselves that the entrepreneurs of these bureaucracies will carry out their intentions, given the costs involved in monitoring performance?

The answer to the first question is that the politicians will develop an elaborate structure and procedures for the organization that will safeguard compromise solutions between conflicting interests. The answer to the second question is that the structure and procedures will require agencies to follow intricate and cumbersome decision-making processes that will facilitate monitoring by the politicians.[2] The consequences are public agencies that typically do not have the efficiency characteristics that would exist in a zero-transaction-cost framework. They are hamstrung not only by the constraints imposed to prevent divergent interest groups from being "gored" but also by severe restrictions on their freedom to pursue effective policies that might raise the costs of monitoring.

What Have We Learned?

The foregoing analysis has been essentially a depressing litany of the problems confronting an attempt to achieve sustained agricultural expansion in the 21st century. But clearly there is another story as well. The "Rise of the Western World" is a largely successful story (however admixed with failures) of institutional innovation that has overcome hunger, famine, disease, and poverty to produce the modern Western world. The path-dependent patterns that produced relative success in the Western world and persistent failure in much of the rest of the world give us important clues about not only what works but also what doesn't work in terms of fundamental institutional frameworks. At a more micro level of analysis there have been important success stories in the recent histories of third-world countries, and finally we have begun to realize that simple catchwords like "privatizing" cover up quite diverse ways by which successful organizations (public as well as private) have evolved to deal with collective action problems. Let me briefly explore some lessons from history.

Path Dependence

The contrast between the histories of England and of Spain and their colonies over the past five centuries is a sobering tale of the persistence of a path-dependent pattern of evolution. In the case of England, the Magna Carta, the evolution of secure property rights, and the eventual triumph of Parliament in 1689 were institutional stepping-stones that produced political democracy and long-run economic growth—a pattern reproduced and expanded in English North America. In the case of Spain, a large centralized bureaucracy administered an ever-growing body of decrees and juridical directives that defined the course of action. Every detail of the economy and polity was structured with the objective of furthering the interests of the crown in the creation of the most powerful empire since Rome. The ultimate consequences were repeated bankruptcies, decline, and centuries of stagnation. In the Spanish New World the pattern of centralized bureaucracies with detailed control of the polity and economy has produced three centuries of sporadic and uneven development and political instability (North, 1990b).

But there is more to this lesson of path dependence. The political and economic institutional framework that evolved in the North American colonies and then the United States led to the evolution of a thriving and productive agriculture. At the time of the Revolutionary War there were approximately 4 million colonists; more than 90 percent farmed and produced enough agricultural output to feed themselves and the other 10 percent and to produce thriving exports. Today farmers make up approximately 3 percent of the population of 253,000,000, yet feed themselves and the other 97 percent, and the United States is a leading world exporter of agricultural commodities. The institutional steps along the way in this success story include both a series of Land Ordinances (1784, 1785, and 1787), which efficiently paved the way for redistributing land from public to private hands and secured property rights providing incentives for rapid settlement and production for markets, and a series of governmental policies that effectively supplemented private incentives to increase agricultural productivity (the Department of Agriculture in 1862; the Morrill Act of 1862, to establish land grant colleges to promote the development and dissemination of agricultural knowledge; and the Hatch Act of 1887, to establish agricultural experiment stations in every state in the Union). It is not that there have not been many unproductive or even antiproductive agricultural policies enacted in the United States over the past several centuries, but the basic underlying institutional framework has rewarded productive activity and mitigated the consequences of poor public policies.

It is too much to claim that the successful institutional framework that evolved in England and was carried over to North America was a deliberate self-conscious creation—Whig history. However, contrasting the North American with the Spanish and Latin American case makes clear what works and what doesn't—notions that have been powerfully reinforced by recent events in Central and Eastern Europe. No one knows how to create adaptively efficient institutional frameworks, but we are learning, and ideas matter particularly in the context of low-cost information about the striking performance differences between the developed world and the rest of the world.

The Green Revolution

Let me turn to more recent history. The green revolution usually refers to the dramatic expansion of yields in certain grains during the 1960s and 1970s due to the development of what are referred to as modern varieties (MVs) and high-yield varieties (HYVs). For example, in the Indian Punjab, average yields of wheat rose from 1.24 tons per hectare in 1965-66 to 2.73 tons per hectare in 1980-81, an increase of 120 percent; yields of rice rose from 1 ton per hectare to 2.74 tons per hectare, a 174 percent increase (Lipton and Longhurst, 1989). However, the success of the green revolution has not been universal. The rate of adoption has varied widely both countrywide (80 percent of the rice area in the Philippines was planted with MVs as compared with 13 percent for Thailand in the early 1980s) and locally (in 1978 100 percent of the farmers in one Javanese village planted MVs, while only 14 percent did in another, 20 kilometers away) (Hayami and Kikuchi, 1982). Government policies have biased technological change in favor of mechanization and away from the adoption of MVs in Argentina and Brazil (Sanders and Ruttan, 1978; de Janvry, 1978); and while the view that HYVs tend to increase income inequality has been discredited (Lipton and Longhurst, 1989:7; Hayami and Ruttan, 1985:337-40), Hayami and Ruttan suggest that where inequality is already extreme the introduction of HYVs may exacerbate this tendency.

The green revolution is ongoing, but there appear to be some lessons from experience so far. The adoption of HYVs requires the adoption of a package of innovations involving not just seed but fertilizer and water management as well. For instance, several areas in Bangladesh failed to adopt HYVs because of uncertainty over water supplies (Lipton and Longhurst, 1989:63). The importance of the ability of agricultural groups to express their interests to scientists and administrators, as well as their ability to see that these interests are acted upon, has been repeatedly stressed in the literature. In particular Hayami and Ruttan suggest that a decentralized system with many small groups of farmers is the most effective.

Governing Common-Pool Resources

Hayami and Ruttan's findings are congruent with Elinor Ostrom's empirical study of successes and failures in the governing of common-pool resources (CPR)—"a natural or man made system that is sufficiently large as to make it costly (but not impossible) to exclude potential beneficiaries from obtaining benefits from its use" (Ostrom, 1990:30). As with public goods it is difficult to exclude people, but here one individual's consumption diminishes that of others. Ostrom found that there are certain similarities among situations where self-governing common-pool-resource institutions have developed and been successful. Although they exhibit a wide variety of specific rules, they all have complex and uncertain environments, stable populations, extensive norms governing informal relationships, and relatively homogeneous populations (Ostrom, 1990:88). In addition the institutions and organizations that have been successful also have similarities that she refers to as designed principles:

1) Clearly defined boundaries.

2) Congruence between appropriation and provision rules and local conditions.

3) Collective choice arrangements. . . . [M]ost individuals affected by the operational rules can participate in changing the operational rules.

4) Monitoring. . . . [M]onitors who actively audit common property resource conditions and appropriator behavior are accountable to the appropriators or are the appropriators.

5) Graduated sanctions. . . . Appropriators who violate operational rules are likely to be assessed graduated sanctions (depending on the seriousness and context of the offense).

6) Conflict resolution mechanisms.

7) Minimal recognition of rights to organize (by external government authorities).

8) Nested enterprises. . . . Appropriation, provision, monitoring, enforcement, conflict resolution, and governance activities are organized in multiple layers of nested enterprises. (Ostrom, 1990:90)

Sri Lanka provides interesting examples of how these principles apply. Ostrom examines two systems, Kirindi Oya and Gal Oya, both of which had large-scale irrigation systems but neither of which spontaneously developed institutions to govern the use of the CPR. Both were characterized by relatively unstable, heterogeneous populations. In the case of Kirindi Oya, a project completed under British colonial rule in 1920, a succession of management strategies imposed from above (although with sporadic attempts at greater democratic participation after independence in 1958) and an inept bureaucracy have resulted in the noncooperative dominant strategy of farmers cheating by taking more water than they are entitled to. Enforcement was the responsibility of state officials who had little incentive to carry out the task. In fact politicians used the irrigation system to provide "spoils" for supporters, and large farmers used political contacts to prevent enforcement (Ostrom, 1990:164). The overall result (which has been characteristic of Sri Lankan irrigation projects) has not only been ceaseless conflict but poor performance, high cost, and a wide discrepancy between project plans and project performance in Sri Lankan farmers' actual application of water to their paddy lands (which is a major determinant of rice yields).

The situation was similar on the left bank of the Gal Oya until a project was undertaken to improve the use of the irrigation system. The Agrarian Research and Training Institute (ARTI), assisted by the Rural Development Committee at Cornell University, developed a program in which "institutional organizers" met with farmers and attempted to discern what the farmers perceived to be problems. They then promoted the formation of small groups, of 10 to 15 farmers, to solve particular problems, "such as repairing a broken control gate or desilting a field channel." The members of these field channel organizations were also members of larger distributory channel organizations with 100 to 300 members. In areas where these organizations were developed, farmers almost unanimously agreed that water rotation schemes were being followed and were equitable. Perhaps most notable is the fact that cooperation took place despite traditional conflicts between Tamils and Sinhalese. As of 1986 the project had resulted in an increase of 1,000 acres under cultivation (Ostrom, 1990:167-71). Ostrom is careful to point out that the relative success of Gal Oya is "fragile" (180) because the population is unstable and heterogeneous. The perverse incentives that had prevailed had produced deep distrust and made it unlikely that the farmers or officials themselves would have overcome the situation. Rather it was the way the ARTI/Cornell team went about involving the participants, along the lines of Ostrom's design principles, that appeared to hold out promise of effective institutional innovation.

Institutional Innovation: Promise and Problems

The foregoing very brief lessons from history were aimed at showing the different levels at which institutional innovation must occur in order to achieve sustainable agricultural development in the 21st century. Before going on let me repeat the essence of my earlier argument. An economy's political and economic organizations and their entrepreneurs make the decisions that determine economic performance, and they are constrained by the existing institutional framework and the mental constructs that guide the way they process the information they receive.

Reversing Institutional Paths

We know all too little about altering the direction of economies toward adaptive efficiency, although it is easy enough to state the issues. Both the institutions and the ideological perceptions of the participants must change. Changing institutions entails the alteration of existing organizations or the creation of new organizations whose entrepreneurs will find it worthwhile to undertake productive activities and therefore directly or indirectly alter the institutional framework to create rules and informal constraints that are productive.

There are two ways this process can occur. Learning by the entrepreneurs of existing organizations can lead them to shift from unproductive to productive pursuits as their perception of the most profitable alternatives changes with changing relative prices. Alternatively, poor economic performance in the context of low information costs about contrasting performance elsewhere will undermine the influence and political clout of existing organizations and sometimes give political entrepreneurs sufficient degrees of freedom of policymaking to initiate productive rule changes (more on this subject later).

Changes in the ideologies or mental models of the participants stem from outcomes inconsistent with expectations. However, such changes in no way guarantee that new ideological constructs will be productivity enhancing. The widespread conviction after World War II that the future lay with planning and socialism stemmed from the traumatic consequences of the Great Depression and the perceived failure of market economies. And just as that set of perceptions turned out to be illusory, so too can today's faith in the efficacy of markets and private enterprise turn out to be illusory if the "transition" costs involved in the reversal of institutional paths produce a political reaction that negates or thwarts the transition.

Ideology and Political Markets

Ultimately the formal rules that would embody efficient property rights and enforce them are made by the polity, and, as noted earlier, political markets are inherently imperfect and swayed by ideologies and pressures that reflect the organizational interests of existing entrenched groups. The instability of Latin American polities, Robert Bates's (1981) studies of agrarian political policies in sub-Saharan Africa, and the rigid orthodoxy and inefficient bureaucracies that have characterized socialist planning in Central and Eastern Europe suggest some of the problems besetting political markets. Not only the formal rules but also the informal constraints embodied in deeply held convictions (which have evolved very slowly) have made Western polities persist in spite of tensions resulting from the costs of the second economic revolution.[3]

But if political markets are inherently imperfect, that very imperfection has at times made it possible for political entrepreneurs to alter the direction of economies. That is, the imperfection has sometimes given entrepreneurs degrees of freedom to pursue policies and encourage the growth of productive organizations that would not have been possible had they been held responsible to the existing interest groups and ideological perceptions of their constituents. In such contexts ideas matter a great deal, since it is their power that leads political entrepreneurs to gamble on new paths.

A Dilemma of Institutional Change

There exists no theory of the dynamics of polity evolution that can guide the policymaker in the many current restructuring efforts that are ongoing in the third-world and former socialist economies. But the dilemma is straightforward enough. Slow incremental change will be sabotaged by the creation of "corruption rights" by the existing bureaucracy. The policy implication is that radical alterations in policy should be accompanied by radical restructuring of the bureaucracy. But this will only be possible where the existing underlying ideology and resultant informal constraints are (at least partially) complementary to the creation of more efficient property rights. Economies without a heritage of informal institutions and ideological perceptions to enable them to adjust to the stresses and strains of impersonal markets, competition, and other institutional consequences that flow from the technological imperatives of the second economic revolution simply cannot adjust overnight. The institutional infrastructure that must be created entails shifting away from family-and-kin-centered social, political, and economic organizations to institutions and organizations that can cushion the insecurities associated with the extreme interdependence of an economy of specialization and impersonal markets. Rapid change will result in social and political turmoil, since the informal constraints and underlying ideological perceptions simply will not adjust overnight. But therein is the dilemma. Slow change will be sabotaged by existing bureaucracies and interest groups so that the reforms will be distorted, dissipated, and dissolved.

Organizations

"American public bureaucracy is not designed to be effective. The bureaucracy arises out of politics, and its design reflects the interests, strategies, and compromises of those who exercise political power" (Moe, 1989:267). What holds for American public bureaucracy is (with variations reflecting different political structures) applicable elsewhere. Moreover, designing organizations that are completely incentive compatible is probably impossible. "The difficulty is not due to our lack of inventiveness, but to a fundamental conflict among such mechanisms' attributes as the optimality of equilibria, incentive compatibility of the rules, and the requirements of informational decentralization. Concessions must be made in at least one of these directions" (Hurwicz, 1973:1-30). Curiously enough, these two quotations that summarize basic dilemmas of public bureacracy and incentive compatibility in hierarchies are, I believe, grounds for cautious optimism. Just as with institutions, one cannot design effective organizations without an understanding of the nature of the problems involved. And for far too long the literature on organizations has confused pious, normative hopes about what organizations should do with positive models of what organizations in fact do.

Let me take the issue of bureaucratic effectiveness and quote the same author:

> A politically powerful group, acting under uncertainty and concerned with solving a complex policy problem, is normally best off if it resists using its power to tell bureaucrats exactly what to do. It can use its power more productively by selecting the right types of bureaucrats and designing a structure that, although strategically constraining their behavior, still affords them substantial discretion and autonomy. Reputation and predictability make this an especially attractive strategy of group control compared to a strategy of detailed formal command. Through the judicious allocation of bureaucratic roles and responsibilities, incentive systems, and structural checks on bureaucratic choice, a select set of bureaucrats can be unleashed to follow their expert judgement, free from detailed formal instructions. (Moe, 1990:117)

What Terry Moe has attempted to do in this prescription of organizational design of public bureaucracies is to harness the self-interested concerns of politicians and interest groups together with the concern of experts to maintain their reputation in order to achieve the objectives of providing a safeguard against bureaucratic malfeasance and the creation of a more effective public organization.

Take the issue of incentive incompatibility. If we recognize the inability to achieve perfect incentive compatibility in organizations, then we must recognize that (wealth-maximizing) incentive structures in organizations must be complemented with appeals to other values in the utility functions of agents. Effective organizations have always supplemented material incentives with appeals designed to convince the agent that the interests of the principal and the agent were identical.[4] The success of Japanese firms in instilling standards of loyalty and hard work in their employees reflects a blend of material incentives and widely shared norms of behavior that have shaped the structure of the Japanese firm.

Some General Policy Implications

Let me conclude this essay by returning to the make-believe model of a (largely) zero-transaction-cost world described earlier. Transaction costs arise because of the costs of measuring the multiple valuable dimensions involved in exchange (broadly, information costs) and because of the costs of enforcing agreements. Information is not only costly but incomplete, and enforcement is not only costly but imperfect. Effective institutions and organizations can reduce the transaction costs per exchange so as to realize more of the potential gains of human interaction. Some specific conclusions follow:

1. We will never have "true" models about the sources of constraints on technology, environment, and health that threaten sustained agricultural development, but the closer we get to a scientific consensus on the major issues the greater the possibility of successful policies. Fundamental disagreement in the scientific community is going to be magnified and distorted in the ideological stereotypes that characterize political markets. Therefore a first requirement is the creation and financing of organizations that will not only undertake the research but also effectively disseminate the findings. It is only then that we can get an accurate assessment of the costs and benefits of alternative policies.

2. Enacting the necessary consequent policies is going to entail both restructuring institutions in much of the world and compensating losers. In a zero-transaction-cost world the gainers would compensate the losers in order to make it jointly worthwhile. In the real world compensation is unusual, and as a result opposition of the potential losers prevents the enactment of the necessary policies. Reducing the transaction costs in this case means getting better information on the

benefit/cost ratios of policies so as to measure the gains and losses and gainers and losers; devising institutional structures that can serve to reduce bargaining costs between gainers and losers; and, in the case of large losses to third-world economies, subsidizing by first-world economies. With respect to the last point it is probably politically unrealistic to expect third-world and (perhaps) former socialist economies to invest the necessary resources in pollution-abatement policies in the face of the short-run costs and foregone opportunities involved.

3. Voluntary, private organizations will evolve automatically to take advantage of profitable opportunities where the underlying institutional structure provides the proper incentives, and as the foregoing discussion of common-pool-resource problems makes clear, voluntary organizations can deal with a wide range of "common" problems. But for a range of problems where free-riding and public-goods aspects militate against the spontaneous development of private organizations, it is important that the social benefits (and costs) are clearly known to the polity so that they will be undertaken by governmental organizations.

Because of the inherent imperfection of political markets, this last point needs emphasis. Let me illustrate with respect to public education. If third-world governments do invest in education, they frequently misdirect that investment into higher education rather than primary education, which has a much higher social rate of return. Why the misdirection? Prestige, status, and imitation of the high-income countries all conspire to promote higher education. An "educated" polity would correct such misallocation of resources.

Notes

1. See Clark (1990) for the problems such mental constructs pose for cognitive science.

2. There is extensive literature dealing with the politics of bureaucracy (most of it drawn from U.S. experience) using the theoretical building blocks of the new political economy (Moe, 1990; *Journal of Law, Economics and Organization*, 1990).

3. The second economic revolution came about in the last half of the nineteenth century as a consequence of changes in the stock of knowledge arising from the development and implementation of modern scientific disciplines. It resulted in the systematic wedding of science and technology. For economies that could take advantage of this technology the result was increasing returns and high rates of economic growth. But taking advantage of this technology entailed fundamental reorganization of economies (and societies) to realize this potential. Specialization, division of labor, and impersonal exchange on an unprecedented scale have produced stresses and strains that have

threatened (and still do threaten) the continued adaptive efficiency of those Western economies that have, at least partially, realized the potential of this technology. It is an extraordinary irony that Karl Marx, who first pointed out the necessity of restructuring societies in order to realize the potential of a new technology, should have been responsible for the creation of economies that have foundered on that precise issue. For an elaboration of the nature and consequences of the second economic revolution, see chapter 12 in North (1981).

4. For a sophisticated analysis of the problems and solutions to incentive compatibility in organizations, see Miller (1991).

References

Bates, Robert. 1981. *Markets and States in Tropical Africa*. Berkeley: University of California Press.

Clark, A. 1990. Folk psychology thought and content. In *Microcognition*. Cambridge: MIT Press.

de Janvry, Alain. 1978. Social structure and biased technical change in Argentine agriculture. In *Induced Innovation*, edited by Hans Binswanger and Vernon Ruttan. Baltimore, Md.: Johns Hopkins University Press.

Hayami, Yujiro, and Masao Kikuchi. 1982. Cited in Y. Hayami and V. Ruttan, *Agricultural Development*. Baltimore, Md.: Johns Hopkins University Press, 1985.

Hayami, Yujiro, and Vernon W. Ruttan. 1985. *Agricultural Development*. Baltimore, Md.: Johns Hopkins University Press.

Hurwicz, Leonid. 1973. The design of mechanisms for resource allocation. *American Economic Review* 63:1-30.

Journal of Law, Economics, and Organization. 1990. Vol. 6, The organization of political institutions.

Lipton, M., and R. Longhurst. 1989. *New Seeds and Poor People*. Baltimore, Md.: Johns Hopkins University Press.

Mankiw, G., D. Romer, and D. Weil. 1991. *A Contribution to the Empirics of Economic Growth*. National Bureau of Economic Research Working Paper no. 3541.

Miller, Gary. 1991. *Managerial Dilemmas: The Political Economy of Hierarchies*. Cambridge: Cambridge University Press.

Moe, Terry. 1989. The politics of bureaucratic structure. In *Can the Government Govern?*, edited by J. E. Chubb and P. E. Peterson. Washington, D.C.: Brookings Institution.

_____. 1990. The politics of structural choice: Towards a theory of public bureaucracy. In *Organization Theory: From Chester Barnard to the Present and Beyond*, edited by O. Williamson. Oxford: Oxford University Press.

North, Douglass. 1981. *Structure and Change in Economic History*. New York: Norton.

_____. 1990a. A transaction cost theory of politics. *Journal of Theoretical Politics* 2:355-68.

_____. 1990b. *Institutions, Institutional Change and Economic Performance*. Cambridge: Cambridge University Press.

Ostrom, Elinor. 1990. *Governing the Commons: The Evolution of Institutions for Collective Action*. Cambridge: Cambridge University Press.

Sanders, John, and Vernon Ruttan. 1978. Biased choice of technology in Brazilian agriculture. In *Induced Innovation*, edited by Hans Binswanger and Vernon Ruttan. Baltimore, Md.: Johns Hopkins University Press.

Part III
Agricultural Research, Resource Management, and Technology Dissemination

The two major sources of growth in agricultural production have been expansion of area cultivated into land that was not previously cultivated and more intensive production on lands already cultivated. Prior to the beginning of this century most increases in agricultural production came from expanding the area cultivated. During the last century an increasing share of the growth in agricultural production has come from more frequent cropping and higher yields on land already in cultivation.

The development of agricultural research capacity has been the central institutional innovation leading to higher yields. In most presently developed countries substantial agricultural research capacity was not established until well into this century. In most developing countries it was not established until well after midcentury, and in those countries essential national agricultural research capacity is still lacking. An important institutional innovation of the 1960s was the establishment of a network of international agricultural research centers designed both to generate new yield-enhancing technology and to serve as collaboration research networks enhancing both the emerging national systems and the new international agricultural research system.

In chapter 4 Carl K. Eicher examines the development of the international agricultural research system and efforts to strengthen national agricultural research organizations, with special emphasis on sub-Saharan Africa, where the problem of achieving scientific, economic, and political viability remains unresolved. Even the most successful national systems have experienced growth and erosion of capacity. The international system, in response to emerging concerns about the negative resource and environmental impacts of agricultural intensification, is attempting to expand its original commodity focus to include a stronger emphasis on the agricultural resource base and on the environmental effects of agricultural intensification during a time when the resources available to the system are more severely constrained than in the past. Eicher is concerned about the decision in 1990 to expand the number of centers organized under the Consultative Group for International Agricultural Research (CGIAR) at a time when the core resources available to the system have stopped growing.

Eicher is also concerned about the cycles of capacity growth and erosion that have characterized many national research systems, particularly in Latin America. It has been difficult to generate and sustain domestic political and financial support. This issue is particularly acute in Africa. Africa has lost market share of major export crops, particularly oil-palm, to Malaysia, which invested heavily in oil-palm research. Per capita food crop production in Africa is now lower than two decades ago. At the conference in Bellagio, Eliseu Alves of Brazil raised the question of whether it is possible to sustain the development of a productive agricultural research system in an environment in which other elements of a nation's institutional infrastructure, including its political institutions, are eroding or failing to develop effectively. Eicher does not attempt to provide an answer to Alves's question. He does identify four areas that need further discussion and debate. These include (1) how to establish basic research capacity in the third world to provide the scientific foundation for advances in the knowledge that will be needed to advance agricultural and health technology; (2) how to achieve more effective articulation and synergy between university, ministry, and international research organizations; (3) how to achieve sustainable improvements in the capacity of national agricultural research organizations; and (4) how to supply the knowledge and the technology needed by producers in those countries that are too small, physically and economically, to develop effective national research systems.

In chapter 5 B. L. Turner II and Patricia A. Benjamin address the issue of expansion and intensification of agricultural production on lands that are now regarded as sensitive to deterioration under intensive systems of cultivations. They use a four-level classification scheme based on two types of response of land to agricultural use: (1) *sensitivity* refers to the ease with which land deteriorates biophysically under intensive use; and (2) *resilience* is the ability of the land to reproduce those biophysical qualities important to use and to respond to human inputs.

Type 1 land, characterized by low sensitivity and low resilience, is resistant to biophysical deterioration, but once a critical threshold is reached it is difficult to restore. It is clearly fragile. Type 2 land, characterized by low sensitivity and high resilience, is resistant to deterioration and recovers readily from damage. These are robust or prime agricultural lands. Type 3 land, characterized by high sensitivity and low resilience, is highly susceptible to biophysical deterioration and does not readily recover. These are the most fragile lands. Type 4 land, characterized by high sensitivity and high resilience, deteriorates easily with intensive use but is responsive to restoration. It is potentially fragile. No one has attempted to classify or map the lands of the world in terms of the characteristics—sensitivity and resilience—that determine fragility or robustness. Much of current research implicitly assumes that lands occupied by poor people are inherently fragile—that fragility is the source of poverty.

Turner and Benjamin insist, drawing on a set of ten case studies in sub-Saharan Africa, that intensive agricultural systems have demonstrated long-term sustainability under a wide variety of environments, including some that are considered to be ecologically fragile, even under conditions of extreme land pressures. Sustainability is typically associated with access to inputs and markets. Access is associated with the development of institutions and organizations that permit households to balance subsistence needs with agricultural and economic diversification.

Turner and Benjamin also draw on a second set of case studies being conducted by the George Perkins Marsh Institute at Clark University, studies designed to examine the sustainability of agricultural production in a series of new critical environmental zones. In these studies particular attention is given to the impact of environmental changes associated with intensification of agricultural production on the material well-being of human life in the critical zones. These zones include areas in Amazonia, the Himalayas, the Ordos Plateau in Inner Mongolia, and the Aral Sea in Kazakhstan and Uzbekistan. They find that land degradation has typically resulted from excessively intensive cultivation associated with inappropriate technology.

They also find that while such areas cannot, even under the most appropriate technology, achieve levels of production comparable to more robust resource areas, there are usually substantial opportunities to achieve higher levels of agricultural production and higher levels of incomes for farm families than under the exploitation systems currently in use.

My own interpretation of the findings reported by Turner and Benjamin is that, while most of the increases in agricultural production in the next century must come from intensification on the more robust (low-sensitivity and high-resilience) lands, there are substantial opportunities for expanding production on lands that have come to be regarded as highly fragile (high sensitivity and low resilience). While the production from such lands will not add large amounts of agricultural production to global food supplies, the development of more productive and sustainable systems of cultivation sources can contribute substantially to improving the material well-being of farming families and communities in the fragile resource areas.

But if sustainability is to be achieved, on either fragile or robust lands, it is clear that the institutional environment in which agricultural production is carried out must be compatible with the interests and ambitions of the farm families and the community organizations that influence the production decisions of farm families.

In chapter 6 Judith Tendler addresses the complex issue of dissemination of agricultural technology. Discussion of the problem of dissemination has been burdened by two extreme viewpoints. One is the *technocratic policy* that planners, technicians, and experts possess the knowledge and wisdom needed to achieve development and that the poor should be responsive and grateful beneficiaries. The other is the *populist fallacy* that the poor themselves possess all that is needed for their own advancement—that if the technocrats and the bureaucrats would just get out of the way, progress would ensue. For Tendler the world is more complex. She presents case studies of successful dissemination of new crop varieties and methods of plant protection. When she traces the history of these successful adoption experiences, she finds that the institutional arrangements differed from the conventional models of technology diffusion. Demand-side factors, particularly the efforts of the users of the new technologies and their organizations, played a much more significant role than expected. The entrepreneurial activities of technocrats, local elites, and small producers combined to generate rural dvelopment even under highly unfavorable environmental circumstances.

CHAPTER 4

BUILDING PRODUCTIVE NATIONAL AND INTERNATIONAL AGRI-CULTURAL RESEARCH SYSTEMS

Carl K. Eicher

This chapter analyzes a number of strategic issues in revitalizing national and international research systems. We take the long view because technology generation takes an average of 10 years for crops and 15 to 20 years for livestock. Because so many national agricultural research systems (NARS) in the third world are weak, we shall address the fundamental question: What can be done to help NARS acquire the capacity to generate new technology, political support, and financial stability, primarily from national sources? The Consultative Group on International Agricultural Research (CGIAR) will be given special attention because of the recent addition of five new international agricultural research centers (IARCs) during a period of reduced donor support in real (inflation-adjusted) terms for the system.

1. The Problem

The green revolution was launched in India, Pakistan, and the Philippines some 25 years ago, dramatically increasing rice and wheat output on irrigated land and generating political and financial support for a major expansion of global agricultural capacity. Today, modern varieties add at least 50 million tons of grain each year to third-world grain output, which is enough food to feed an additional

500 million people (Lipton and Longhurst, 1989). The visibility of Asia's green revolution encouraged donors to support research. The World Bank initiated its support for agricultural research with a loan to Spain in 1972. The bank invested $2.1 billion in agricultural research projects in the 1981-87 period. The bank is now the second largest donor (after the United States) supporting the CGIAR network of IARCs.

The first problem that we shall examine is what can be done to strengthen NARS—the weak link in the global agricultural research system. This problem is best understood in historical perspective because the rapid buildup of NARS in the third world since 1970 has been punctuated by cycles of growth and erosion of research capacity in NARS (Ruttan, 1982). This expansion and erosion has occurred in many NARS in Asia, Latin America, and Africa. In India, for example, a task force recently recommended sweeping changes to revitalize the Indian Council of Agricultural Research (ICAR), the NARS of India (ICAR, 1988). In Africa the annual outlays on agricultural research increased dramatically in real terms from $103 million in 1970 to $380 million in 1984 (Lele, 1988:215). In Nigeria, the number of agricultural researchers increased from 100 at independence in 1960 to 1,000 in 1985 but then declined to around 800 by 1990 (Pardey and Roseboom, 1989; Idachaba, 1991). Despite this increase in financial support from donors and the parallel increase in the number of scientists, the productivity of many NARS in Africa has declined since the mid-1980s because of ineffective management, the lack of donor coordination, political unrest (some 75 coups in 30 years of independence), and the lack of government support for research.

The global agricultural research system is dominated by two major public research organizations—the CGIAR system of 18 international agricultural research centers and CIRAD, the French Center for Cooperation in International Agricultural Research. CIRAD was established in 1985 through the consolidation of various research institutes specializing in tropical agriculture.[1]

The second problem addressed in this chapter is the quiet crisis in the CGIAR system. The CGIAR system is faced with increasing bureaucratization, an outmoded management structure, and an expanded mandate. The CG system was under fire from environmentalists in the 1980s because of their concern that the IARCs had not devoted enough attention to natural resources (fisheries, forestry, and agroforestry) and the environment (Ravnborg, 1992). At its 1990 annual meeting, the CGIAR agreed to marry its traditional commodity research orientation with research on natural resource management and to add four new centers. In March 1992 a decision was made to add a fifth center, International Center for Living Aquatic Resources Management (ICLARM), to the system. But increasing the number of CG centers from 13 to 18 comes at a time of donor fatigue.

The challenge facing the CGIAR system basically revolves around whether the system has the required scientific leadership, a feasible mandate, a management structure capable of making hard decisions, and an assurance of stable financial resources to address the strategic issues facing global agriculture in the first quarter of the 21st century. The scientific leadership issue has been well articulated by a veteran scientist who commented on a draft of this chapter: "Perhaps the number one challenge is to determine how one attracts, recruits the world's top scientists to the limited number of posts that will be open in the CG over the coming decade. The sense of urgency and excitement that energized the system 1965-1980 needs somehow to be rekindled" (Hardin, 1992).

The balance of the paper addresses two problem areas: revitalizing NARS and the CGIAR system of international agricultural research centers. Section 2 presents an overview of the growth of the NARS of Asia, Latin America, and Africa. Section 3 discusses revitalizing NARS with special attention to Africa. Section 4 discusses the expansion of the CGIAR system by adding natural resources to its mandate and five new IARCs from 1990 to 1992. Section 5 discusses revitalizing the CGIAR system. Section 6 looks ahead and discusses implications for the agricultural research community and donors.

2. The Expansion of National Agricultural Research Capacity, 1960-90

Global agricultural research outlays are running about $9 billion per year. The global research system should be examined in comparative terms because of the historical role of international technology transfer, spillovers, research networks, and the increasing ease of scientific communication. The real expenditure per agricultural researcher has moved in opposite directions in industrial countries and the third world over the past two decades. The average expenditure per scientist in industrial countries increased from $54,200 in 1961-65 to $85,400 in nominal terms in 1981-85, but it declined in the third world from $55,400 to $46,700 per researcher over the same period (Pardey, Rose-boom, and Anderson, 1991a).

Asia and the Pacific

The 17 countries in the Asia and Pacific region are marked by sharp variations in the size of research establishments. With over 55,000 scientists and nearly 30,000 technical support staff in the late 1980s, China's NARS dwarfs the NARS in the rest of Asia (Fan and Pardey, 1992). Excluding China, seven NARS in Asia had more than 1,000 agricultural researchers in 1981-85 (India, Indonesia, the Republic of Korea, Pakistan, the Philippines, Taiwan, and Thailand), while nine had more than 500 researchers. On the other hand, the 11 countries in the Pacific collectively employed only 260 agricultural researchers (Pardey, Roseboom, and Anderson, 1991a:242).

In Asia, there was little institutional innovation in agricultural research from the end of World War II until 1960. The story of the spread of the green revolution of the sixties and seventies is common knowledge. One of the legacies of the green revolution is the conventional wisdom that future research in Asia should concentrate on plant breeding to achieve higher use of fertilizer and other inputs and higher yields (Byerlee, 1990). But plant breeding research on basic food crops is well advanced in many countries in Asia relative to research on livestock and secondary crops, such as grain legumes and crop management (for example, seeding rates, planting dates, pest management, weed control, and resource management). Traxler and Byerlee (1992) recommend increased attention to crop and resource management research on rice and wheat, the two food staples in the Asia and Pacific region, in order to improve the efficiency of input use and address emerging problems in sustaining the quality of the resource base. Although hybrid rice is grown on about 40 percent of the area planted to rice in China (Fan and Pardey, 1992), it is expanding slowly in other Asian countries. Biotechnology research on stabilizing rice yields against pests is being supported by the Rockefeller Foundation.

There are no standard prescriptions for strengthening NARS in Asia in the 1990s because of the wide differences in per capita incomes and because of institutional problems in low-income agricultural economies (Bangladesh, Burma, and Nepal), low-income transitional economies (India, Sri Lanka, and Indonesia), and middle-income countries (Malaysia and Thailand). But even in mature NARS there are problems. For example, a recent evaluation report described India's NARS as a "mature" system ill prepared for the 21st century because of the erosion of its human capital, poor research-extension linkages, and lack of adequate research on basic science to sustain the applied research of the early 21st century (ICAR, 1988).

Latin America and the Caribbean Region

Three NARS (Argentina, Brazil, and Mexico) employ two-thirds of the region's agricultural researchers (Byrnes, 1991). The majority (12 of 21) of the NARS fall in the medium-sized range of 100 to 999 researchers. Because colonial rule had ceased in Latin America prior to the era when European governments established agricultural research systems in Asia (1870-1930) and Africa (1900-1930), the legacy of colonial rule is not an issue in agricultural research policy debates in Latin America. However, in many Caribbean islands, fragile national research systems bear the colonial imprint.

The major expansion of public agricultural research in Latin America occurred in three phases over the past 60 years. The first phase started around 1930 with the establishment of NARS within ministries of agriculture. But these national systems did not flourish because of overcentralization, poorly trained scientists, and unstable financial and institutional support (Piñeiro and Trigo, 1983). The second phase, starting in the 1960s, concentrated on the introduction of semiautonomous NARS, including the National Institute for Agricultural Technology (INTA), Argentina, in 1957; the Columbian Agricultural Institute (ICA) in 1962; the National Institute for Forestry and Agricultural Research (INIFAP), Mexico, in 1963; and the Brazilian Public Corporation for Agricultural Research (EMBRAPA) in 1973. The semiautonomous model promoted the decentralization of research and upgrading of human capital through massive overseas training programs in the 1960s and 1970s. The short-run results of the semiautonomous model were impressive. Hundreds of scientists were trained, but many NARS were unable to generate stable domestic financial support. For example, in Mexico the research system was frequently reorganized, and the budget of INIFAP declined 50 percent in real terms in the 1980s (Traxler and Byerlee, 1992). Research foundations are now in various stages of development in the Honduras, Jamaica, Peru, the Dominican Republic, and Ecuador (Byrnes, 1991).

Despite decades of experimentation with alternative research models, many NARS in Latin America and the Caribbean are under stress. In Latin America and the Caribbean, the small country problem is being tackled by two regional research institutions: CATIE, which provides assistance to researchers in Central America, and CARI, which has the lead research role in the Caribbean. An important question is: Can regional research networks in Latin America and Africa survive without foreign aid?

Latin America's experience reveals that a succession of new models of organizing agricultural research is sidestepping the need to return to the basics of strengthening and sustaining agricultural research capacity in Latin America: improving the macroeconomic policy environment, developing human capital, increasing the relevance and productivity of research, improving research-extension linkages, and mobilizing political and financial support for research from domestic clientele groups. After all, as James Bonnen observes,

> One cannot, after setting off on an institution-building path, reverse directions or reorganize every few years to let some politician "put his stamp on things" or to test some new theory of public accountability. Unilateral changing of the rules in the middle of the game of long-term institutional development breeds suspicion and conflict instead of cooperation and leads to a breakdown in the linkage between separately governed institutions. (Bonnen, 1990:277)

Agricultural Research in Sub-Saharan Africa

In 1885, the great western powers met in Berlin and decided how to carve up Africa. In the intervening years until 1912, Africa was colonized, with the exception of two independent nations, Liberia and Ethiopia. The main colonial research period covers the years 1900 to 1960. From 1900 to 1930, fledgling research institutes were established in most colonies to carry out research on export commodities. No major changes were introduced in the 1930-45 period. Following World War II, the colonial research system was greatly expanded. The colonial research experience embraced many failures, such as chronic underinvestment in the training of African scientists and the pursuit of inappropriate research strategies in land-abundant countries. Nevertheless, several important colonial institutional innovations in organizing, financing, and executing research from 1900 to 1960 have relevance for contemporary agricultural research policy in Africa (Eicher, 1989).

The independence movement started in 1956 when the Sudan won its independence. Namibia's independence in 1990 brought colonial rule to an end. Today sub-Saharan Africa consists of 47 independent nations. In 30 years of independence (1960-90) many African nations gave premature attention to industrialization, neglected agriculture, and increasingly relied on food imports to feed their people. Today the continent faces an enormous food production gap, a loss of world market shares of some of its traditional agricultural exports, and pervasive rural poverty. With 3 percent annual population growth, Africa's population will increase by roughly 100 million over the next 6 years. Although many African countries can rely on expanding the area under cultivation for another 10 to 30 years, science-based agricultural research is needed to meet the annual 3 to 5 percent projected increase in food demand, especially in the land-short economies such as Kenya, Rwanda, Malawi, and Senegal, where yield-increasing technology is the pathway to the 21st century. Today many of the NARS of Africa are weak and overstaffed and spend virtually all of their budget on salaries. Also, staff turnover is high, donor assistance is poorly coordinated, and there is tension between NARS and African universities. Given Africa's early stage of institutional development, the NARS and faculties of agriculture should be strengthened incrementally over the next 25 to 50 years. However, this 25- to 50-year time frame is studiously avoided by virtually every African nation and every donor. And in the interim, donors, CG centers, and the new African Capacity Building Initiative stress the training of individuals while they virtually ignore the greater challenge of strengthening Africa's human capital institutions.

3. Revitalizing NARS

The International Service for National Agricultural Research (ISNAR) was established in 1979 to strengthen the weak link in the global agricultural research system—NARS. More than a decade later, NARS are still the weak link in the system. This is not surprising, because ISNAR has a small budget relative to the problems of NARS in the third world. What is disturbing is the modest amount of solid research by social and technical scientists and management specialists on the political, financial, and managerial issues that influence the productivity of NARS. During the 1980s much of the research on NARS focused on how to organize and manage a NARS, how to carry out on-farm experiments (farming systems research, or FSR), and how to develop master plans. Over the past decade there has been little in-depth research on the political economy of the size and the financing of research and on how NARS fare in the political process, including the art of building grass-roots support from farmers and commodity groups. Likewise, after a decade of structural adjustment programs, why is there still no definitive study of the impact of structural adjustment programs on NARS? Turning from research on NARS to strengthening NARS over the past 10 to 15 years, many donor agencies, consulting firms, and universities designed projects that were too large in size, too overloaded with hardware (buildings, vehicles, and equipment), and too little concerned with the factors that shape the scientific discovery process and the productivity of NARS. Donors should assess this experience and design a new mode of assistance that concentrates on strengthening the productivity of NARS, mobilizing financial support from national sources, increasing farmer participation in research priority setting, and developing new modes of public-private cooperation in research. Research is needed on the politics of NARS, including studies on the size, financing, and productivity of research programs and systems.

Six topics form the core agenda for strengthening NARS over the next 10 to 15 years. We begin with the two most important issues: the size and financing of NARS.

1. *Size of NARS*. This is the most fundamental issue that is plaguing NARS. We should admit straightaway that there is a paucity of information on the optimal size of a NARS. Over the past 30 years many research managers in the third world have assumed that larger NARS (in terms of number of scientists) were necessary in order to achieve a critical mass of scientists to pursue research on multiple commodities and problems. But many NARS have inflated the number of scientists, technicians, and support staff to the point where they are spending 90 to 100 percent of their budgets on salaries (the recommended guide is 70 to 75 percent). This, of course, leaves a paucity of funds for operating expenses. The critical issue of financing research is closely related to the size, financing, and productivity of research programs and NARS. Most commentators on the size or financing of research fail to tackle these issues as a common problem.

ISNAR's recent study of 152 countries reported that 39 NARS had fewer than 25 agricultural researchers. For the next generation it is almost certain that the countries with small (less than 25 scientists) and medium-size (50 to 250 scientists) NARS will constitute about half the nations in the world. What can donors do to assist small-to-medium-size NARS? The agricultural research management literature lacks guidance on the relationship between the size and productivity of research organizations. Ruttan's guideline that "even a relatively small country, producing a limited range of commodities under a limited range of agroclimatic conditions, will require a cadre of 250 to 300 agricultural scientists" (Ruttan, 1991:404) requires further examination and debate. While this guideline may be valid for some countries in Asia and Latin America, it is an inappropriate guideline over the coming 10 to 20 years for most African nations, half of which currently have fewer than five million people. In my judgment, most nations in Africa with fewer than five million should strive for a NARS of 25 to 150 researchers. Many African NARS should pursue a decompression strategy to reduce the number of scientists and concentrate instead on increasing operating budgets per scientist.

2. *Financing NARS.* Currently little is known about the art of mobilizing political support from farmers and farm organizations in the third world for NARS. After a century of institution building in U.S. agriculture, it is clear that mobilizing *stable* financial support has been critical to the success of the research system (Bonnen, 1990). The art of building political support for agricultural research is a high-priority topic for social scientists. Yet it should not be pursued in isolation from an analysis of the role of farmers and farm clientele groups in advising on research priorities. The farming systems research thrust has stressed the need to incorporate the voice of farmers in on-station research priorities (Tripp, 1991; Merrill-Sands, Biggs, et al, 1991). Parallel research is urgently needed on how to mobilize farmers and farm organizations in making the case for public support for agricultural research in the national political process.

3. *Mature NARS.* In the mid-1980s there was great optimism in donor circles that some of the mature NARS in the third world would be able to take over some of the research programs of the CG centers as the centers shifted to more strategic research and upstream linkages with biotechnology centers in industrial countries. But one by one, the mature NARS (Brazil, India) experienced budget constraints, poor conditions of service, high staff turnover, and inadequate operating budgets in the 1980s. More time and resources will be necessary before mature NARS in the third world will have the capacity to generate technology that can be of use to NARS in the same ecoregional zone. For example, the 1988 evaluation of the ICAR (Indian Council of Agricultural Research) urged the ICAR to intensify its research in frontier areas such as tissue culture, genetic engineering, computer

modeling, environmental education, and energy management (ICAR, 1988). There is a need for donors to rethink the whole question of mature NARS, including their likely capacity to gain adequate financial support from national sources and their willingness to share technology with other countries in the same ecoregion.

4. *NARSs-IARC Scientific Partnerships.* One of the factors that has historically inhibited IARC-NARS cooperation is the superordinate-subordinate scientific hierarchy. Embedded in this hierarchy is the view that the generation and transmission of science is basically a one-way flow of knowledge from the north to the south. An example of this is the IARC practice of mobilizing local scientists in NARS to carry out variety trials for scientists in some far-off IARC headquarters. Without question, there is a need for a radical restructuring of the IARC-NARS relationship to one that is based on *jointly* developed ecoregional partnerships.[2] Critical to this reformulation is bringing NARS, universities, and private research organizations into the new ecoregional planning process to ensure that common national problems will drive the ecoregional research agenda.

5. *NARS—University Relationships.* The uneasy marriage between NARS and universities throughout the third world is a quandary in light of the worldwide trend of raising the entry requirement for a new agricultural research officer from a bachelor of science to a master of science degree or equivalent. While two-thirds of the third-world nations have local graduate programs in agriculture, most programs are weak and lack funds for rigorous field research. To date, there is a high degree of tension and competition rather than cooperation between NARS and local universities—both in research and in graduate training. And donors have been slow to support long-term human capacity programs in agriculture. For example, the World Bank has included a small research fund in agricultural research projects in several countries in Africa that can be tapped by local university researchers. However, this approach is flawed because it sets up a superordinate-subordinate relationship rather than building a scientific partnership between NARS and university researchers. Since postgraduate training must be research based, there is an urgent need for third-world universities, NARS, and donors to figure out how to strengthen NARS-faculty of agriculture relationships in both research and postgraduate training.

6. *Special Problems of NARS in Africa.* There is growing evidence that scientific, political, bureaucratic, and donor interests have interacted to inflate the size of many NARS in Africa to the point where they

operate like government departments performing routine experiments with a changing cadre of underpaid scientists. The ready availability of foreign aid in the 1980s served as an "escape valve" for many administrators of NARS who were reluctant to make hard scientific and financial decisions on the number of scientists and support staff, number of commodities, size of commodity research teams, number of research stations, and so on. Many African countries are repeating some of the same mistakes of Asian and Latin American countries in the 1960s and 1970s, when emphasis was placed on expanding the size of NARS to the extent that there were many research facilities and researchers "without programs" (Ruttan, 1987:78). The NARS of Mali is a case in point. Mali increased the number of scientists in its NARS from an average of 9 in 1965-69 to 275 by the mid-1980s! To summarize, the size of NARS and the politics of financing research should be the subject of vigorous debate in ministries of agriculture and finance, in NARS, and among donors in the 1990s. Unless the issues of size, political support, and financing of NARS are addressed simultaneously, the sustainability of many NARS in Africa will turn out to be a mirage.

4. Expansion of the CGIAR System

The first four international agricultural research centers that were established between 1960 and 1967 received scientific guidance and financial support from the Rockefeller and Ford foundations. In 1971, the Consultative Group on International Agricultural Research (CGIAR) was established to oversee the international centers then in operation and other centers as they were added to the system. Eight more centers were added between 1971 and 1976. In 1979, the addition of ISNAR (International Service for National Agricultural Research) to the system increased the number of centers to 13 and acknowledged that NARS were the weak link in the global research system. The mission of ISNAR was to help strengthen NARS in the third world.

Today the CGIAR (CG for short) has a secretariat headquartered in the World Bank, 18 international centers, and 1,700 scientists of the master's degree level and above.[3] The CGIAR is currently receiving annual core funding of around $250 million from 40 donors in the form of independent pledges (See Table 4.1). Even though Africa's total population of 500 million is only a small fraction of that of Asia, the CGIAR spent 45 percent of its budget on Africa in 1990.

Table 4.1. CGIAR core funding by center: 1972-92
(in U.S. $ millions)

Center	1972	1980	1990	1992[a]
1. CIAT	4.32	14.99	27.73	26.50
2. CIFOR[b]	_[c]	–	0.00	3.19
3. CIMMYT	5.04	16.56	27.10	25.60
4. CIP[d]	0.49	7.73	16.92	15.20
5. IBPGR[e]	–	3.03	7.02	9.00
6. ICARDA[f]	–	11.81	18.69	17.18
7. ICRAF[b]	–	–	0.00	11.90
8. ICRISAT	0.34	12.27	31.46	27.70
9. IFPRI[g]	–	2.46	9.09	8.30
10. IIMI[b]	–	–	0.00	7.30
11. IITA	6.40	15.50	22.54	22.20
12. ILCA[h]	–	9.79	20.20	19.03
13. ILRAD[i]	–	9.14	13.60	12.95
14. INIBAP[b]	–	–	0.00	2.40
15. IRRI	2.96	15.90	29.79	28.75
16. ISNAR	–	1.13	7.03	6.60
17. WARDA[j]	–	2.48	6.24	6.20
18. ICLARM[b]	–	–	–	–
Total	19.54	122.78	237.41	250.00

Source: CGIAR Secretariat, June 1992.
Note: Figures for 1972-80 are total core expenditures (operations/capital).
[a]1992 data are incomplete; figures include projected core contributions as of June 30, 1992.
[b]New centers: CIFOR—Center for International Research on Forestry; ICRAF—International Council for Research in Agroforestry; IIMI—International Irrigation Management Institute; INIBAP—International Network for the Improvement of Banana and Plantain; and ICLARM—International Center for Living Aquatic Resources Management.
[c]Center not in operation.
[d]International Potato Center
[e]International Board for Plant Genetics Research
[f]International Center for Agricultural Research in Dry Areas
[g]International Food Policy Research Institute
[h]International Livestock Center for Africa
[i]International Laboratory for Research on Animal Disease
[j]West African Rice Development Association

CGIAR System: Staffing and Budget

Despite the high visibility of the CGIAR system, its annual budget of $250 million is only about 3.5 percent of global agricultural research expenditures of $9 billion. The CGIAR centers have surprisingly limited budgets compared with state agricultural research stations in the United States. For example, in 1989, each of the five largest state ag-

Table 4.2. Comparison between the size of the ten largest CGIAR
centers and agricultural research stations in the United States, 1989

CGIAR Center	Total core & special project expenditures 1989 (million $)	CGIAR rank by total expenditures	State	State appropriations, FY 1989 (million $)	Rank by state appropriations
IRRI	36.2	1	California	111.5	1
ICRISAT	35.7	2	Florida	61.0	2
CIMMYT	33.3	3	New York	53.8	3
CIAT	32.2	4	Texas	52.5	4
IITA	31.8	5	Georgia	40.0	5
ICARDA	28.5	6	North Carolina	35.9	6
CIP	22.1	7	Minnesota	35.7	7
ILCA	21.4	8	Nebraska	25.6	8
ILRAD	12.7	9	Louisiana	24.8	9
IFPRI	11.1	10	Ohio	24.6	10

Sources: CGIAR 1989 financial report and 1991 CGIAR funding requirements, and state agricultural experiment stations, annual reports.

ricultural research systems in the United States (California, Florida, New York, Texas, and Georgia) had a larger state budget for agricultural research than any of the five largest IARCs. Table 4.2 shows that even the $40 million budget for the fifth largest state system (Georgia) in 1989 was larger than the core *and* special project expenditures of the five largest CG centers: International Rice Research Institute (IRRI), $36 million; International Crop Research Institute for the Semi-Arid Tropics (ICRISAT), $36 million; International Center for the Improvement of Maize and Wheat (CIMMYT), $33 million; International Center for Tropical Agriculture (CIAT), $32 million; and International Institute of Tropical Agriculture (IITA), $32 million. Although the larger IARCs each have 80 to 120 scientists and annual budgets of $32 to $36 million, these resources are modest relative to the regional and global mandates of the centers. This is a strategic issue for donors to keep in mind as they pressure the CG system to pay more attention to issues such as gender, nutrition, and the environment. It should also be noted that the Pioneer Seed Company's $70 million research budget in 1991 was twice as large as CIMMYT's annual budget for maize and wheat research combined (*New York Times*, 1991).[4]

CIAR Decision-Making Structure

The CGIAR takes pride in its management structure, which promotes considerable autonomy for each center, in the belief that scientists should not be hamstrung by rules and regulations. Each center has its own executive staff and board of directors. The CGIAR Secretariat in the World Bank offers formal and informal advice to the system, but the CGIAR is not a hierarchical organization. The CGIAR "has no legal identity, written charter or formal requirements for membership" (Anderson, Herdt, and Scobie, 1988:2). It operates as a "forum for discussion" among 40 "members" from bilateral and multilateral donors, foundations, and international organizations such as the FAO. In 1992, 40 members of the CG provided funds to support the system. The "members" make the general policy decisions on the CGIAR, including the overall mandate, number of centers, and so on. "Contrary to the practice in most international organizations, each of the 40 members (donors) decides how to apportion its annual contribution among the CGIAR Centers. Most members pay the Centers directly rather than through the CGIAR Secretariat" (Anderson, Herdt, and Scobie, 1988:4).

On technical issues, the CGIAR is guided by a Technical Advisory Committee (TAC), a group of 18 agricultural scientists from around the world.[5] TAC's Secretariat is based in the Food and Agriculture Organization (FAO) headquarters in Rome. When the distinguished Australian agricultural economist, Sir John Crawford, proposed setting up a Technical Advisory Committee to provide "scientific" guidance to the CG system, he envisioned a group of eminent scientists who would spend their time "thinking" about long-range global problems that required research attention, continuity of effort, and a possible research payoff 15 to 20 years down the road. Today, TAC is a committee of 18 scientists that meets three times a year. TAC is having difficulty, in my judgment, in providing leadership on the critical long-term issues that the CG system should be working on over the next 25 years. TAC members are overburdened with preparing priority papers, special studies, and medium-term plans and quinquennial reviews. TAC members seem to have little spare time to reflect on the big issues facing global agriculture 10 to 25 years down the road.

Without question, the independence of each center is one of the strengths of the CGIAR system because it helps protect centers from political pressure by host governments and donors. But there is clear evidence that the independence of each center hinders collective decision making on the hard global issues facing the system. The CG members (the donors) understandably fear that an overly bureaucratic and centrally directed CG system will end up "sliding down hill," as the FAO has done over the past two decades. It is also well known that center directors and governing boards cherish their independence. Nevertheless, there is an urgent need for a new management model that can make hard decisions more quickly. This view is forcefully stated by Hans Binswanger, a former ICRISAT scientist and one of the most respected and influential economists in the World Bank: "Some international centers have never become productive or have gone through prolonged periods of crisis. Neither the Boards nor the quinquennial review processes seem capable to take the required hard decisions quickly, despite the multiple review processes. But poor institutional performance is very costly, not just to the client countries but also to the reputation of the system" (Binswanger, 1991:4).

Expansion of the CGIAR in 1990: Donor Pressure and Niggardliness

In 1988, TAC was charged with assessing the possible expansion of the CGIAR to incorporate some of the nonassociated international agricultural research centers[6] into the CGIAR system. The 1990 annual meeting of the CGIAR was a watershed that culminated in the resolution of a number of issues, including natural resource management and the addition of several nonassociated centers to the system. TAC presented its "expansion report" at the 1990 annual CG meeting, and CGIAR members reached three major decisions:

1. The concept of natural resource management was added to the mission of the CGIAR system. The twin pillars of the system are now commodity research and research on natural resource management.

2. The concept of ecoregional research activities was added to the mission of the CGIAR in order to increase research on agroecological zones, regionally defined. This approach brings applied and strategic research to bear on the ecological foundations of sustainable production systems. This approach will require intercenter cooperation with subregional organizations and mature NARS in various subregions of the world.

3. Three of the nonassociated research centers and one new center for forestry research were added to the CG system to carry out the CG's expanded mandate in natural resources, forestry, agroforestry, and fisheries. The following four new centers were added to the CG system in 1990:

IIMI (International Irrigation Management Institute). IIMI was established in Sri Lanka in 1985.

ICRAF (International Council for Research in Agroforestry). ICRAF was set up in Nairobi in 1978.

CIFOR (Center for International Research on Forestry). This is a new center in the process of being established in Indonesia.

INIBAP (International Network for the Improvement of Banana and Plantain). Although this network was not endorsed by TAC, it was approved by CGIAR members and hailed as an innovative model that will be carefully monitored.

The addition of these four centers in 1990 was followed by a March 1992 decision to add the Philippine-based fisheries center ICLARM (International Center for Living Aquatic Resources Management) to the system, bringing the total to 18 centers.[7] Unfortunately, the CG members (the donors) increased the number of CGIAR centers from 13 to 18 without adding the necessary resources to implement the expansion and maintain the scientific momentum of the system. It is hard to fathom the niggardly collective behavior of donors unless one understands the powerful role of individual donors in lobbying for the addition of a particular nonassociated center to the system. Over the past decade, many of the same donors that financed the CG system set up centers outside the CG system to address research gaps in areas such as fisheries, agroforestry, and insects. Because these ten nonassociated centers never had assured (core) funding from donors (like the CG centers), they experienced high transaction costs in mobilizing funds from individual donors each year. This explains why some of the same donors who helped launch and fund a particular nonassociated center for a number of years lobbied in 1990 to have "their" center added to the CG system to ensure that it would receive core funding from the system each year. The CG members rejected TAC's sound recommendation to set up one center to carry out an integrated approach to agroforestry and forestry research.[8] Instead, two CGIAR centers were agreed upon: one for agroforestry and one for forestry research.

In short, the 1990 and 1992 decisions to add five new centers to the system were driven by a combination of scientific, political, and technical forces. The expansion is controversial among some scientists and administrators in the 13 old centers because they have been forced to downsize their programs. Table 4.1 reveals that the core funding for almost all of the old centers declined over the 1990-92 period.

5. Revitalizing the CGIAR System

The CGIAR system is facing a quiet crisis of confidence. The CG has added centers, scientists, commodities, and new challenges, including natural resource management, while retaining an outmoded management structure that is unable "to take the required hard decisions quickly." Because donor support is not growing in real terms, it is already proving difficult to finance the old centers and implement the expansion plan.[9] In short, the CG system is moving toward a gridlock.

The CGIAR is now at a stage of maturity comparable to many large research universities in the United States. The president of the University of Chicago, Hanna Gray, recently described the dilemma of U.S. research universities so vividly that she could have been describing the CGIAR system in the early 1990s: "At this time our universities have arrived at a stage of maturity burdened by too many tasks and too many demands and too great a confusion of expectations, by the consequences and distortions of excessive growth and over-dependence on sources of support that may come to exercise too large an influence, and by the illusion that comprehensiveness is necessary for institutional distinction."[10] President Gray calls for drastic action to revitalize U.S. research universities. The following action is needed, in my judgment, to revitalize the CGIAR system:

1. *New management model.* The CG's loose, decentralized management model is clearly inappropriate to manage 18 centers in the 21st century. A high-level commission of eminent scientists and CG members should be established to study alternative management models and prepare a white paper on a management model for the CGIAR in the 21st century. The commission should be entirely foundation financed and should be given 24 months to carry out its study. The new management model should reward excellence in research, retain donor flexibility, and have the ability to make hard decisions on a wide range of systemwide issues such as the CG's agenda for the next 25 years, size of the system, CG-NARS relationships, generating

political support for long-term funding, commodity versus resource-management focus, the relationship between the CG and mature NARS, CG–multinational seed company relationships, and rewarding scientific and managerial excellence in CG centers.[11] A new management model should be in place by Centers Week in 1994.

2. *Protecting the proven centers*. The second step in revitalizing the CGIAR is to protect the real (inflation-adjusted) budgets of the proven centers such as CIMMYT, IRRI, and IFPRI. Despite the growth of private seed companies and mature NARS, global commodity centers have a vital global role to play in germ plasm and information exchange and in complementing the CG's expanded research agenda on natural resource management. The cutback in core funding for some of the global commodity centers from 1990 to 1992 is disturbing (see Table 4.1).

3. *Applying the poverty test*. The world's poverty is centered in Africa and South Asia. If the CG were to enforce the poverty test (annual per capita incomes of less than $600) more rigorously, it could phase out *some* of its activities in the Middle East and Latin America and restrict the urge of CG centers to help large farmers in Africa.[12]

4. *Merging and phasing out centers, and cutting out programs in the old centers*. One can envision generating annual savings of 10 to 15 percent ($20 to $30 million) of the present total core funding of the 13 old centers by phasing out several old centers, merging others, and cutting out programs in the remaining centers. These savings could be achieved gradually over the next five years, allowing due time for review, negotiations, and implementation.

a. The International Center for Agricultural Research in Dry Areas (ICARDA) was set up, in part, to attract oil money from the Middle East to the CG system. But today ICARDA receives less than 5 percent of its budget from sources within the region. Given the funds available in the Middle East, the relatively high incomes of the ICARDA countries, and the difficulties of attracting scientific staff to Syria (its headquarters), the CG contribution should be sharply reduced by requiring ICARDA to generate 80 to 90 percent of its budget from within the Middle East.

b. ICRISAT has now largely fulfilled its basic mission in India. There are several mature NARS in Asia, many competent national scientists, and growing private-sector research that can gradually assume the work of ICRISAT programs in India. For example, Pray and Echeverria (1991) report that Indian private research firms are spending almost as much on breeding pearl millet and sorghum as is the government of India. ICRISAT could phase out its program in India over a five-year period and shift its headquarters to Africa.

The CG system could break new ground by bequeathing ICRISAT's administrative and scientific infrastructure in India to an independent organization to establish a new basic biological science center for Asia. The center could focus on basic science research and postdoctoral training on rice because it is the lifeblood of billions of people in Asia. The research agenda could be drawn up with the participation of scientists in universities and government research centers in Asia to ensure that the agenda reflects the needs of the region rather than duplicating the agenda of basic research labs in temperate climates in industrial countries. The center could be managed by a four-way partnership between the state agricultural universities in India, the Indian Council of Agricultural Research, and universities and private research institutes in Asia and in industrial countries.

c. CIMMYT's wheat program in Latin America can be scaled back to a bare-bones germ plasm exchange program because much of the wheat in the region is produced by large wheat farms in Argentina, Brazil, and Chile. The large-scale farmers can help make the case for expanded wheat programs in their own NARS.

d. CIAT's rice research program benefits many large farms in Latin America. Although one can make the case that poor consumers may indirectly benefit from this type of research through lower rice prices, this issue warrants careful scrutiny. It seems logical for the NARS in Latin America to assume more responsibility in serving large rice farms.

e. The 1990 TAC expansion report suggested that a merger

of WARDA with IITA would be "an attractive possibility particularly if IITA takes on the ecoregional responsibility for the subhumid warm tropics" (TAC, 1990:188). A merger should be explored, but the savings of such a merger might be offset by the loss of political support that WARDA enjoys from African member states.

f. IITA should be restricted to work in western and central Africa for the next 25 years. All IITA programs outside of western and central Africa should be terminated. IITA's cowpea program should be turned over to ICRISAT. In the humid tropics of West Africa, food crops (for example, cassava) are grown along with tree crops. The IITA should develop scientific partnership with tree crop research centers in the NARS in West Africa in order to generate improved technology for both food and tree crops.

g. The two CG livestock centers in Africa should be reviewed, along with the nonassociated livestock centers in Africa, with an eye on mergers, streamlining of programs, and savings.

5. *Improving the scientific integrity of the system.* The CGIAR system needs to improve the scientific integrity of its external reviews, elevate the quality of the scientific staff of the TAC Secretariat in Rome, and open up the system to a "new generation" of international talent and expertise. One way to achieve the latter goal is to limit an individual's membership to a total of six years of service on CG boards. Next, there is a need to lift the veil of silence surrounding the unproductive centers and some of the whitewashed quinquennial reviews. Finally there is a need to address the banal nature of some of the TAC reports.[13]

6. *Human Capital.* The lifeblood of the CG system is its human capital—its scientists, technicians, and support staff. It is well known that 5 to 10 percent of scientists in a research center, department, or institute set the tone of a research program, give a particular center its momentum, and establish the reputation of a center for scientific leadership in a commodity or problem area. There is evidence that the CG system is experiencing difficulty in reproducing itself in terms of the quality of its scientific staff, especially among the top 5 to 10 percent of its scientists. One basic reason is that career prospects in some areas, such as

the social sciences, biotechnology, and plant breeding, are more attractive in the private sector and in universities in the north than in many of the CG centers.[14] One constructive way to deal with the human capital problem is for the CG centers to develop more active partnerships with universities in industrial countries. This would enable academic staff from overseas universities to be seconded on two-to-four-year periods to a CG center. These visiting scientists could help carry out the center's research agenda, guide doctoral and postdoctoral students, and the like. The CG scientists could then spend their sabbatical leaves at the overseas university or at other universities and research institutes.

6. Looking Ahead

Global agricultural research is a complex undertaking representing $9 billion of investments by public and private research organizations each year. Six major research systems make up the global agricultural research system:

1. Public international agricultural research organizations such as CGIAR and CIRAD.

2. Private multinational seed, chemical, and biotechnology firms engaged in conventional plant breeding and/or biotechnology research and the sale of proprietary products.

3. Universities in industrial nations engaged in graduate training and research on conventional plant breeding, biotechnology, and the sale of proprietary products and services.

4. Mature NARS in the third world (China, India, Malaysia, Brazil) with strong national research capacity in conventional plant breeding and some biotechnology capacity.

5. NARS, with 50 to 250 scientists, that generate and import technology.

6. Small NARS (with 25 to 50 scientists) in countries with 1 to 5 million people who import the bulk of their agricultural technology.

The fundamental direction of global agricultural research over the coming 25 years is clear. The big growth areas will be biotechnology and the privatization of research. Multinational firms will be aggressive competitors in conventional plant breeding and seed sales in the third world. Mature NARS in the third world will be unable or unwilling to generate the required technology for "developing" NARS over the next 20 to 30 years. This explains why the CGIAR and CIRAD will continue to play an important role in international germ plasm and information exchange for both high-income and third-world nations.

The identification of institutional innovations to revitalize NARS and the CGIAR system should flow from a deep understanding of the historical process of technology generation and diffusion, an assessment of strengths and weaknesses of research systems in place, a keen awareness of the politics of donors' decision making in the CG centers and the nonassociated centers, and a vision of future challenges for the global system. This historical and comparative review points up the sharp differences in the size, quality, and productivity of national agricultural research systems throughout the world. Nevertheless, there is also much common ground in terms of the major issues facing NARS, regional research organizations, and public and private international agricultural research organizations. Asia is the region with the most mature NARS, followed by Latin America. Africa brings up the rear. The problems facing NARS in Latin America and the Caribbean are strikingly similar to those in Africa: the debt problem, structural adjustment, rapid staff turnover, unstable and/or declining funding, and the special problems of small countries. Moreover, there is substantial variation in the productivity of NARS within continents, especially in Africa, where there are 47 nations.

One compellingly unavoidable conclusion that emerges from this assessment is that the NARS are the weak link in the global system. We have devoted special attention to the NARS in Africa because they are much weaker than their counterparts in Asia and Latin America. It is going to take decades and decades of persistent effort to develop productive and locally financed NARS in Africa. The current system of project assistance to NARS and faculties of agriculture should be replaced by a long-term institution-building strategy that is pursued over the next 25 to 50 years.

The CGIAR model of organizing and funding international research represents a remarkable institutional innovation that has delivered useful technology to millions of farmers around the world. The CG model has given donors hands-on access to funding a particular center or program rather than forcing them to channel funds into a "black box," the approach that donors use for contributing to the

FAO or to an International Development Agency replenishment for the World Bank. The CG model generates core funds by pooling donor contributions at the center level. This, in turn, generates positive expectations among scientists about the continuity of their appointments and funding for research projects with a 5-, 10-, or 15-year gestation period. But in an era of cutbacks in foreign aid and signs of donor fatigue for agricultural research, it remains a puzzle why donors added five new centers to the CGIAR system over the 1990-92 period without concurrently eliminating or merging some of the unproductive centers. This illustrates how difficult it is for CG's present management model to reconcile the scientific, financial, and political factors that influence the size, scientific focus, and performance of the system.

Five states in the United States have more total state funding for agricultural research than the total core budget for all 18 CGIAR centers, many of which have global commodity mandates. The environmentalists should take note of this as they unwisely press the CG system to expand its mandate. TAC's recommendation to set up one center for agroforestry and forestry was sound. But in 1990 the CGIAR members (the donors) rejected this recommendation and set up two new centers: one for agroforestry (ICRAF) and one for forestry (CIFOR). Part of the current stress in the CG system is caused by donors, the financial patrons of the system, as they commit the CG to a broader array of activities without adding the required financial resources to maintain the esprit de corps of the system. Part of the stress, in my judgment, is caused by overburdening TAC with routine tasks instead of "protecting" TAC and enabling it to concentrate on long-run strategic issues. Part of the stress is caused by the CG's decentralized management model, which is unable to make the hard systemwide decisions quickly. These factors do not bode well for the CG in the 1990s and into the first quarter of the 21st century. It is an open question whether the CG can regain its institutional distinction and the luster it had in the 1970s and 1980s, when it had a narrower mandate and increasing real resources.

What flows from this discussion is the inescapable conclusion that a new management structure is needed for the CGIAR system in the 21st century. The CG should move quickly on this issue because it needs to "protect the proven centers" as they are forced to lay off scientific and support staff as their core budgets are being trimmed in real terms. The alternative is to continue to make marginal changes in the present system, allow some of the proven centers to bleed to death, and wait until the world economy improves and donor support for research is increased. This course of inaction is clearly unacceptable. There is an urgent need for the chairman of the CGIAR system to appoint a high-level commission of four eminent scientists and four CGIAR members to study alternative management structures for the 21st century. The commission should be financed by a foundation (or foundations) and given 24 months to prepare a white paper with a recommended management structure. A new management model should be in place by Centers Week of 1994.

Notes

1. CIRAD recently expanded its geographical coverage beyond Francophone Africa by posting agricultural researchers in China, Indonesia, Malaysia, and the Philippines, as well as in Latin America, mainly in Brazil. CIRAD currently employs 1,025 senior scientists and administrators in about 50 countries (CIRAD, 1991).

2. Peter Matlon (1992) of WARDA has much light to shed on this important issue.

3. About 1,200 of the 1,700 are internationally recruited.

4. Of Pioneer's current research budget, 90 percent is spent on traditional plant breeding and 10 percent on biotechnology.

5. The number will be reduced to 16 in 1993 and 14 in 1995.

6. TAC evaluated the ten nonassociated international research centers: *Natural Resource Management*, International Board for Soil Research and Management (IBSRAM), ICRAF, International Fertilizer Development Center (IFDC), IIMI, and International Union of Forest Research Organizations—Special Program for Developing Countries (IUFRO-SPDC); *Crop Protection*, International Center for Insect Physiology and Ecology (ICIPE); *Banana and Plantain*, INIBAP; *Vegetables*, Asian Vegetable Research and Development Center (AVRDC); *Fisheries*, ICLARM; *Livestock Diseases in Sub-Saharan Africa*, ICIPE and International Trypanotderance (outer) (ITC).

7. The CG agreed to add the Taiwan-based Asian Vegetable Research and Development Center to the system in the future.

8. "TAC felt that the creation of a separate forestry research center would be inconsistent with the evolution of the CGIAR system towards more integrated approaches to natural resource management research at the ecoregional level" (CGIAR, 1991:6).

9. The CG system is under financial stress because of the cutbacks in some foreign aid programs, the world recession, and shifting domestic priorities of donors.

10. Abelson (1992), quoting Gray.

11. For a discussion of some of these issues see Dillon (1991) and Binswanger (1991).

12. Applying the poverty test is a complex process that must address variations in land ownership patterns and the direct and indirect effects of new technology on both producers and consumers.

13. Examples include the 1987 report on priorities (TAC, 1987), the expansion report (1990), the report on relationships between the CGIAR centers and NARS (TAC, 1991b), and the recent report on CGIAR priorities (TAC, 1992). The banality of TAC reports is captured in the following dialogue on the CGIAR-NARS interface. The 1992 TAC priorities report notes that the achievement of the CGIAR's vision for year 2025 (calling for

a smaller CG system) will "depend heavily on improvements in the capacity of national research systems and the development of effective regional and transnational mechanisms of cooperation" (TAC, 1992:253). Yet the same report notes that "currently, there is no comprehensive statement on CGIAR policy on the relationship between CGIAR Centres and national research systems in the developing countries" (TAC, 1992:200).

14. The critical issues included in favorable career prospects in industrial countries include the following: easier access to jobs for two-career families, higher salaries, sabbatical leaves, and better medical support systems.

References

Abelson, Philip H. 1992. Scientific research in universities. Editorial. *Science* 256 (April 3): 9.

Anderson, Jock R., Robert W. Herdt, and Grant M. Scobie. 1988. *Science and Food: The CGIAR and Its Partners*. Washington, D.C.: Consultative Group on International Agricultural Research (CGIAR) Secretariat, World Bank.

Binswanger, Hans P. 1991. Summary remarks. Paper presented at the Conference on Agricultural Technology, Airlie House, Virginia, October 21-23.

Bonnen, James T. 1990. Agricultural development: Transforming human capital, technology and institutions. In *Agricultural Development in the Third World*, edited by Carl K. Eicher and John M. Staatz, 2d ed., 262-79. Baltimore, Md.: Johns Hopkins University Press.

Byerlee, Derek. 1990. Technological challenges in Asian agriculture in the 1990s. In *Agricultural Development in the Third World*, edited by Carl K. Eicher and John M. Staatz, 2d ed., 424-33. Baltimore, Md.: Johns Hopkins University Press.

Byrnes, Kerry J. 1991. *A Cross-Cutting Analysis of Agricultural Research, Extension, and Education in A.I.D.-Assisted LAC Countries*. Vol. 1, *Technical Report*, and Vol. 2, *Annexes*. Report prepared for the Bureau for Latin America and the Caribbean, USAID. Washington, D.C.: Chemonics International and USDA.

Centre de coopération en recherche agronomique pour le developpement (CIRAD). 1991. *The CIRAD Strategic Plan*. Paris: CIRAD.

Consultative Group on International Agricultural Research (CGIAR). 1991. *CGIAR Mid-Term Meeting 1991, Paris: Summary of Proceedings and Decisions*. Washington, D.C.: CGIAR Secretariat, World Bank.

Dillon, John. 1991. Summary remarks. Paper presented at the Conference on Agricultural Technology, Airlie House, Virginia, October 21-23.

Eicher, Carl K. 1989. *Sustainable Institutions for African Agricultural Development*. Working Paper no. 19. The Hague: International Service for National Agricultural Research (ISNAR).

_____. 1990. Building African scientific capacity for agricultural development. *Agricultural Economics* 4(2): 117-43.

Fan, Shenggen, and Philip G. Pardey. 1992. Research, productivity and output growth in Chinese agriculture. The Hague: ISNAR.

Hardin, Lowell S. 1992. Letter to author, August 26.

Idachaba, F. S. 1991. Building institutional capacity for agricultural research in sub-Saharan Africa. *Discovery and Innovation* 3(1): 16-28.

Indian Council of Agricultural Research (ICAR). 1988. *Report of the ICAR Review Committee*. New Delhi: ICAR.

Lele, Uma. 1988. Comparative advantage and structural transformation: A review of Africa's economic development experience. In *The State of Development Economics: Progress and Perspectives,* edited by Gustav Ranis and T. Paul Schultz, 187-221. Oxford: Basil Blackwell.

Lipton, Michael, with Richard Longhurst. 1989. *New Seeds and Poor People.* Baltimore, Md.: Johns Hopkins University Press.

Matlon, Peter J. 1992. Collaboration among NARS in a regional systems approach: A potential role for IARCs. Paper presented at the Special Program for African Agricultural Research Workshop on the Humid and Sub-Humid Zones of Africa, Abuja, Nigeria, October 5-9.

Merrill-Sands, D. M., S. D. Biggs, R. J. Bingen, P. T. Ewell, J. L. McAllister, and S. V. Poats. 1991. Institutional considerations in strengthening on-farm client-oriented research in national agricultural research systems: Lessons from a nine-country study. *Experimental Agriculture* 27:343-73.

New York Times. 1991. Wonder seeds now yielding profits. July 17.

Pardey, Philip, and Johannes Roseboom. 1989. *ISNAR Agricultural Research Indicator Series: A Global Data Base on National Agricultural Research Systems* (Cambridge: Cambridge University Press for ISNAR.

Pardey, Philip G., Johannes Roseboom, and Jock R. Anderson. 1991a. Regional perspectives on national agricultural research. In *Agricultural Research Policy,* edited by Philip G. Pardey, Johannes Roseboom, and Jock R. Anderson, 197-264. Cambridge: Cambridge University Press.

_____. eds. 1991b. *Agricultural Research Policy: International Quantitative Perspectives.* Cambridge: Cambridge University Press for ISNAR.

Piñeiro, Martin, and Eduardo Trigo, eds. 1983. *Technical Change and Social Conflict in Agriculture: Latin American Perspectives.* Boulder, Colo.: Westview Press.

Pray, Carl E., and Ruben G. Echeverria. 1991. Private-sector agricultural research in less-developed countries. In *Agricultural Research Policy,* edited by Philip G. Pardey, Johannes Roseboom, and Jock R. Anderson, 343-96. Cambridge: Cambridge University Press.

Ravnborg, Helle Munk. 1992. *The CGIAR in Transition: Implications for the Poor, Sustainability and the National Agricultural Research Systems.* London: Overseas Development Institute.

Ruttan, Vernon. 1982. *Agricultural Research Policy.* Minneapolis: University of Minnesota Press.

_____. 1987. Toward a global agricultural research system. In *Policy for Agricultural Research,* edited by Vernon W. Ruttan and Carl E. Pray, 65-97. Boulder, Colo.: Westview Press.

_____. 1991. Challenges to agricultural research in the 21st century. In *Agricultural Research Policy,* edited by Philip G. Pardey, Johannes Roseboom, and Jock R. Anderson, 399-411. Cambridge: Cambridge University Press.

Technical Advisory Committee (TAC). 1987. *CGIAR Priorities and Future Strategies.* Rome: TAC Secretariat, FAO.

_____. 1990. *A Possible Expansion of the CGIAR.* Rome: TAC Secretariat, FAO.

_____. 1991a. *An Ecoregional Approach to Research in the CGIAR.* Rome: TAC Secretariat, FAO.

_____. 1991b. *Relationships between CGIAR Centers and National Research Systems: Issues and Options.* Rome: TAC Secretariat, FAO.

_____. 1992. *Review of CGIAR Priorities and Strategies—Part I and Part II*. Rome: TAC Secretariat, FAO.

Traxler, Gregory, and Derek Byerlee. 1992. The economic returns to crop management research in a post-green revolution setting. *American Journal of Agricultural Economics* 74(3): 573-82.

Tripp, Robert, ed. 1991. *Planned Change in Farming Systems: Progress in On-Farm Research*. Chichester, U.K.: Wiley.

CHAPTER 5

FRAGILE LANDS: IDENTIFICATION AND USE FOR AGRICULTURE

B. L. Turner II and Patricia A. Benjamin

The global demand for agricultural production, especially for food, has reached an unprecedented magnitude and promises to continue to escalate well into the next century. Much of the growth in agricultural production will continue to come from increasing yields. However, growth in demand, combined with unequal access to land and food, has extended the frontiers of agricultural production inexorably outward, raising concerns about the environmental wisdom and sustainability of major agricultural land expansion. Much of this concern follows from the belief that the "prime"agricultural lands of the world have long been utilized, that little such land, if any, remains, and that most expansion will involve "nonprime" lands that are agriculturally fragile, marginal, or vulnerable.

Such concerns have generated interest in determining the quantity, location, and quality of new agricultural lands. Most of the increase in arable land is expected to come from forests and grasslands in the high-rainfall areas of Latin America and Africa, including seasonally flooded alluvial zones, slopes (Hrabovsky, 1985), and lands with marginal soils (Alexandratos, 1988; Lele and Stone, 1989). Although these reserve lands are often assumed to be of poor quality, a preliminary estimate by the Food and Agriculture Organization (FAO) (1981) did not find them to be inherently poorer, except in Latin America. Putting this land into production would be so costly, however, that the

FAO (1981:63) recommended that land-reform policies aimed at intensifying use of land already in production be instituted in preference to "expensive schemes to settle remote and ecologically sensitive zones." Other perspectives point to the potential for technology to alter the relative productivity of reserve lands (Hrabovsky, 1985), while still others (for example, Brown and Wolf, 1984) emphasize the possibility of resulting land degradation.

These observations raise a number of issues about notions such as fragility and sustainability—conceptualizations that are intuitively useful, but extremely difficult to define and delimit with any precision beyond the extremes. What characterizes fragile, as opposed to prime, agricultural land? Is fragility an inherent, biophysical quality? Or is it a relative concept, intimately linked to a land management context? If management is instrumental in determining "fragility," then the socioeconomic and technological contexts of land use are significant to the discussion. As befits any discussion of the central issues of nature-society relations, however, these social concerns must remain firmly anchored in their biophysical context.

This chapter addresses several issues surrounding fragile agricultural lands, based on the assumption that global-scale land stress will result in the expansion and intensification of use on these lands during the next century. First, we examine the conceptual basis of "fragility," arguing that the concept is grounded in a nature-society relationship and that the notion of "fragile land" is meaningful only in a specific biophysical-management context. Constrained by the paucity of comparable data with which to identify and assess fragile lands, we next draw on two recent sets of case studies that address some of the land-use dynamics of several areas or regions of the world reputed to be fragile. From this comparison, we develop several broad lessons about the circumstances associated with fragile lands and institutional policy directed to them and their users.

The Meaning of Fragility and Fragile Lands

The concept of fragile lands usually implies a biophysical trait. For example, the term *fragile* is commonly applied to areas of steep slopes and arid or semiarid lands with scarce or irregular rainfall (see Jodha, 1990b; Blaikie, 1985; Hrabovsky, 1985; Brown and Wolf, 1984; Brown, 1981). Other characterizations are similar: dry, cold, and steep (Ayyad and Glaser, 1981); "too dry, too steep, lacking in nutrients" (World Commission on Environment and Development [WCED], 1987:12); mountains, polar regions, and tropical rainforests (Hewitt, 1984); "drylands, highlands and forests—with fragile soils" (WCED, 1987:122); highlands and islands (diCastri and Glaser, 1980; Glaser, 1983); small island ecosystems (Fosberg, 1963; Brookfield, 1981); high latitudes (Bach, Pankrath, and Schneider, 1981); and tropical rainforests (Farnworth and Golley, 1974; Golley and Hadley, 1981). Large literatures have been generated around the putative fragility of drylands, highlands, and, more recently, tropical forests. An inadequate reading can lead to the view that fragility is a solely biophysical concept.

A dictionary definition of fragility is the quality of being "easily broken, shattered, damaged, or destroyed." This is not a trait exhibited by natural systems without human intervention, except perhaps in geological time scales. In this sense, biophysical "fragility" is not inherent in ecosystems or land, but is rather a latent biophysical quality that is realized through human use. Thus, fragility refers to ecosystems or lands that have the potential for significant deterioration under human use (Denevan, 1989:11). This meaning, allowing some regions or ecosystems to be described as more or less fragile than others—under some particular management—also underlies the common uses noted above. In agricultural terms, any ecological system may become fragile under some type of use; all lands are fragile if mismanaged (Little and Horowitz, 1987). Thus, fragility implies a mismatch between human use and biophysical conditions.

Fragility and Ecology

The science of ecology does not appear to have a precise and accepted definition of fragility. The concept is used by ecologists—and others—to indicate a system at risk, and risk is linked to ecological concepts of stability (or instability) and resilience. It is through this chain of linkages that fragility obtains its ecological base.

The standard definitions of stability and resilience are provided by Holling (1973, 1986). Stability is "the propensity of a system to attain or retain an equilibrium condition of steady state or stable oscillation," and resilience is "the ability of a system to maintain its structure and patterns of behavior in the face of disturbance" (Holling, 1986:296). Although these definitions are widely used, there does not seem to be consensus among ecologists, either about terminology (see Murdoch, 1975; Odum, 1983; Gigon, 1984) or the degree to which an equilibrium-centered approach is taken (see Pimm, 1984). Appropriated for use beyond the confines of ecology (see Glaser, 1983; Messerli, 1984), stability and resilience are commonly redefined, often with confusing effects.

One treatment of fragility (as systems at risk) in ecological theory was the exploration of the relationship between stability and diversity. The observation that some ecosystems are more susceptible or vulnerable to disturbance than others led to the proposition that complex systems must be inherently more stable than simple ones. This proposition made intuitive sense in that systems with multiple energy pathways and feedback loops would be less subject to breakdown and more resistant to perturbation (Farnworth and Golley, 1974; Murdoch, 1975; Pimm, 1984), but it did not stand up under theoretical or empirical scrutiny. Not only did alternative explanations exist (Goodman, 1975), but by the late 1970s some scientists were even proposing the opposite—that "complex ecosystems will tend either to be more fragile or to have weaker interspecific interactions than simpler ones" (Yodzis, 1980:544). Pimm (1984) argues that both propositions fail to capture the complexity of real systems, while others offer up alternatives such as Odum's suggestion (1983) that it is the functional complexity of ecosystems, not species diversity, that is correlated with stability.

Ideas about ecosystem disturbance, succession, and recovery have provided another connection to the notion of systems at risk. Ecological theory has moved away from equilibrium and linear views of stability and recovery to a more dynamic perspective, with implications for fragility. Holling (1986), for example, sees ecosystems as functioning in cycles of exploitation, conservation, connectance, and renewal. Other recent work emphasizes the cyclic nature of ecosystem change and the spatial and temporal heterogeneity of landscapes and ecosystems (for example, Turner, 1987; Kolasa and Pickett, 1991). Views of succession have broadened to include disturbance as integral to the system, rather than as an exogenous force (for example, Pickett and White, 1986; Turner, 1987). Research into ecosystem recovery (for example, Cairns, Dickson, and Herricks, 1977; Cairns, 1980; Berger, 1989) has questioned whether restoration necessarily implies the reattainment of a preexisting condition (Thorhaug, 1980) or the reestablishment of system stability or integrity (Cairns and Dickson, 1977; Cairns, 1980) and whether human intervention is required to subsidize natural processes (Platt, 1977). Ecological fragility has also been linked to biophysical process rates; Farnworth and Golley (1974), for example, linked the presumed fragility of tropical lands to their relatively high process rates, while Denevan (1989) noted that it may be low process rates that make cold lands fragile.

Ecotones have been advanced as ecologically defined zones that may be intrinsically fragile (International Geosphere-Biosphere Program [IGBP], 1990). An ecotone is a "zone of transition between adjacent ecological systems, having a set of characteristics uniquely defined by space and time scales, and by the strength of the interactions between adjacent ecological systems" (di Castri, Hansen, and Holland, 1988:60). Certain ecotones, such as "the tundra-boreal forest, the temperate grassland-shrubland forest, the subtropical-tropical woodland-savanna, and the wet tropical-seasonal forest transition zones" have been suggested as "likely to be highly sensitive" to global environmental change (IGBP, 1990:6.1-5) or to human activities (Rasool and Ojima, 1989; Holland, 1988).

It is not clear, however, that ecotones are necessarily fragile. Much of the claim that they are seems to stem from the acceptance of Holland's (1988) "plausible hypotheses" about their sensitivity, only one of which implies fragility: species in ecotones are at their margin of distribution and therefore under stress, making them particularly sensitive and unstable. Strong empirical support for this hypothesis is apparently lacking (see Naiman et al., 1988; Hansen, di Castri, and Risser, 1988; Rasool and Ojima, 1989; IGBP, 1990). Indeed, some work suggests that it may not be correct. Ives and Hansen-Bristow (1984), for example, found at least one mountain ecotone that was quite stable, although under environmental stress.

Although ecology explores the general contours of biophysical fragility, consistent and systematic links between ecological theory and the concept of fragility are tenuous. This does not indicate a failing on the part of ecologists but rather indicates that ecology has never claimed the concept of fragility as its own or intended it to have a solely biophysical meaning. The problem of definition remains.

The Evolution of the Concepts

Fragility has been widely discussed in the realms of development and land-use studies. Although these are predominantly social rather than natural sciences, fragility is usually treated as a primarily biophysical phenomenon. As Little and Horowitz (1987:5) have noted, the "fragility of certain environments has widely been assumed" without a rigorous analysis of the exact meaning of degradation or a clear identification of human—as opposed to biophysical—impacts.

In relation to the developing world, the emergence of the concept of fragile lands can be seen as an extension of colonial land-classification and planning policies, beginning with early carrying-capacity studies (see, for example, Allan, 1965) and carried forward today in agroecological and land-suitability assessments (for example, FAO, 1978; Bernard, Campbell, and Thom, 1989; see Young, 1986, for a review). While classifications of this sort are invariably based on land suitability within given technological or economic contexts, the demarcation of land into suitability classes reinforces a tendency to interpret the classes as mainly biophysical phenomena.

The FAO's Agro-Ecological Zones Study (1978-81) serves as a recent example (Alexandratos, 1988). Its methodology explicitly states that land suitability is meaningful only in relation to a specified use, that the use must be sustainable, and that technological and economic factors must be considered as part of suitability (FAO, 1978). Since the integration of all of these factors would have been extremely complex, the initial system simplified the task by considering only rainfed cultivation, major food crops, basic economic conditions, and two input levels associated with subsistence and commercial activities (FAO, 1978). The result is the association of particular types of agriculture with specific agroecological zones and the designation of zones as suitable for certain uses. This association becomes problematic when practitioners ignore or forget the assumptions on which the land classes are based, implicitly attributing the classification to qualities inherent in the land alone. It then becomes all too easy for the use-suitability class itself to be used as an indicator of fragility.

Because of these tendencies, biophysical concepts of fragility and fragile lands have been severely criticized. For example, Hewitt (1984:32) claims that qualities such as fragility are "not intrinsic to mountain ecosystems in some absolute sense that separates them from the rest of the world." Rather, these qualities reflect the instability of mountain ecosystems in relation to human activities. In some contexts, mountains are actually less fragile and more central than the surrounding lands (Hewitt, 1984). These concerns, combined with a lack of baseline data and disagreements about the severity of degradation and ecosystem recovery capacities, have led to a similar dynamic in the literatures of desertification, islands, and tropical rainforests.

While some environments are clearly more susceptible to human-induced deterioration than others (given the same use), it is increasingly recognized that the choice of human use is instrumental in determining the onset of degradation processes. In the context of soil erosion, for example, Brown and Wolf (1984) imply that fragility is a function of soil depth, but also of economic pressure to produce and lack of awareness about erosion hazards. In another context, the FAO (1981:7) refers to fragile areas as those with "easily disrupted ecologies" and implies that the disruption is human induced. Golley and Hadley (1981:13) make the same point in reference to tropical forests, which they describe as "well adapted to persist in the relatively predictable environment in which they have evolved . . . [but] less resistant to the disturbances wrought by man."

The recent literature demonstrates that there is "a resurgent awareness of the pertinence of socioeconomic and political processes" at work in the creation of fragility (Little and Horowitz, 1987:1; see also Bebbington, 1990). This awareness is evident in a large number of works that portray fragile land as the product of a nature-society relationship. As with stability and resilience, however, this recognition does not imply common or standard definitions or applications of the concept. The literature is more apt to provide examples of fragile lands than to give definitions or measures. The emphasis placed on nature-society integration varies. Most authors agree that fragility is the function of a mismatch between human use and biophysical qualities of land. In some cases this process is portrayed as the pairing of two independent and rather static variables—land capability and human use systems—with a tendency to treat humans as an external, disturbing factor impinging on nature. Others take a more interactive view, conceding that fragility can be created or removed by human use activities. For example, inappropriate mechanization of agriculture on sloping land (Hrabovsky, 1985) or certain soil types can initiate rapid environmental deterioration, creating fragility in that use-environment relationship. The same land, however, with appropriate "landesque capital" (Blaikie and Brookfield, 1987) or other inputs, may sustain land use.

Denevan (1989), following a long-held tradition in geography, is a strong proponent of the second view. He argues that agricultural potential is nonexistent independent of use (culture), and views environmental fragility as a function of the availability of knowledge and technology, which in turn reflect social conditions. Denevan (1989:23; see also Bebbington, 1990:205-6) further claims that social fragility—economic, political, and social factors—may be more critical and harder to manage than environmental fragility.

Defining the Concepts

Several nature-society-based definitions of fragility and fragile lands have been proposed. A 1978 National Science Foundation study defined fragile land as "an ecosystem in which present or future human use may cause disruptions of the natural system structure and functions and impair the stability of the system" (Avery et al., 1978). Important attributes of such an environment include a delicate balance of ecosystem structure and processes (in which disruption of critical structure or process will impair system stability), susceptibility to loss of species critical to system stability, low carrying capacity, and low capacity to respond to inputs.

Ayyad and Glaser (1981) defined fragile lands as landscapes in which "vegetation and soil cover degrade much more quickly . . . than in favored regions, if unsuitable land use practices are adopted." Furthermore, once these lands are degraded, it may be more difficult to "restore fertility and productivity" than in other regions (Ayyad and Glaser, 1981:20).

The project on Development Strategies for Fragile Lands (DESFIL) expanded this reasoning to define fragile lands as "highly subject to deterioration under common agricultural, silvicultural and pastoral use systems and management practices" (Bremer et al., 1984). This deterioration is signaled by declining short-term production, a decrease in the long-term production potential of the resource base, off-site impacts due to environmental degradation, and the slow recovery of soil, water, plant, and animal resources after human disturbance.

This definition, with some minor modifications (Moran, 1987; Gow, 1989), has gained acceptance among the community working on fragile lands and fragility (see, for example, Denevan, 1989; Jodha, 1990b) and provides the base for the definitions used here:

> *Fragility* refers to the sensitivity of land to biophysical deterioration under common agricultural, silvicultural, and pastoral systems and management practices, where *biophysical deterioration* refers to declines in those physical elements of the environment required for the land use in question, and *common* refers to most forms of agriculture except exotic, high-technology-based practices such as hydroponics or greenhouse agriculture.

> *Fragile lands*, in contrast, are those that are so sensitive to biophysical deterioration that common uses cannot be sustained and the land does not readily recover.

In these meanings, fragility is an attribute of all land or ecosystems under use, while fragile lands constitute a subgroup of lands that deteriorate to common levels of use and types of inputs. With these meanings, the terms are potentially measurable and afford the possibility of identifying several levels of fragile lands. More important, they narrow considerably the range of candidate lands under consideration.

A useful conceptual tool for classifying fragile lands is that provided by Blaikie and Brookfield (1987) in the course of their analysis of land degradation. Degradation is viewed as a function of both natural and human processes in which natural degrading processes and human interference are mitigated by natural reproduction and restorative management; thus the match between capability and use may be attained either by a focus on land potential or by a focus on its capacity for recovery. The emphasis is not on maintaining a particular biophysical condition or level of use value; rather, it is on the maintenance of stability in the relationship between biophysical characteristics and use. Implicitly, fragility is viewed as the introduction of instability into the relationship.

Ironically, in view of our earlier discussion, Blaikie and Brookfield use ecological concepts to provide a framework for an integrated human use–biophysical capability classification. They classify land in terms of its sensitivity and resilience under use. We employ slightly modified versions of their definitions:

> *Sensitivity* refers to the ease with which land biophysically deteriorates under a given use.
>
> *Resilience* is the ability of the land to reproduce those biophysical qualities important to use and to respond to human inputs.

In this usage, sensitivity and resilience refer only to those biophysical attributes that are significant to human use. This mode of classification integrates the "natural" qualities of the land with its human alterations and provides the possibility of placing bounds on an otherwise elusive concept. It is not concerned with all biophysical changes in the land, only those critical to the land use in question. Of course, use may also be dynamic; the type, magnitude, and rate of land use change will affect the sensitivity and resilience characteristics of the land.

These two land and use qualities form the basis of our classification scheme and its four possible categories (see Figure 5.1; adapted from

Blaikie and Brookfield, 1987:11). Type 1 land (low sensitivity, low re-silience) is resistant to biophysical deterioration (and hence loss of use productivity), but once a critical threshold is reached it is difficult to restore. Type 2 land (low sensitivity, high resilience) is resistant to de-terioration and recovers readily from damage. Type 3 land (high sen-sitivity, low resilience), in contrast, is highly susceptible to biophysi-cal deterioration and does not readily recover. Finally, Type 4 land (high sensitivity, high resilience) deteriorates easily with use, but is responsive to restoration efforts. To reiterate, sensitivity and resil-ience, in our meaning, refer to human actions—use and management as both a cause of biophysical deterioration and a means of restoration—and to biophysical impacts important for the use in question.

In this classification Type 3 lands are clearly fragile, while Type 2 are prime lands; the other types are more problematic. Type 1 may become fragile only through long-term environmental mismanage-ment, while Type 4 may become fragile under immediate abuse. In principle, all four categories of land can be identified. Lacking ade-quate measures and assessments of them, however, qualitative as-sessments typically infer only two categories, Type 2 and Type 3, seen as polar extremes (prime and fragile lands) along a one-dimensional axis. The literature tends to focus on the prime land–fragile land axis (see Figure 5.1).

Concepts, and classifications based on them, are one matter; their utility is another. The approach outlined here appears viable for the task of geographical identification of fragile lands, helping to define what they are and where they occur. Identification of fragile lands by merging biophysical land-quality data with land-use data, however, poses difficult problems; the data required to make such determina-tions are sparse and poor. Indeed, determinations of such lands have tended to focus on criteria other than fragility, regardless of the un-derlying emphasis—biophysical or nature-society.

Comparative Studies of Agriculture on Fragile Lands

Although a large number of individual studies explicitly or implicitly claim to deal with fragile-land agriculture, most assert rather than document the fragile-land claim and generally fail to address the is-sues raised above. As a result, there is substantial variability among claims of fragility. The lack of clear definitions inhibits comparative

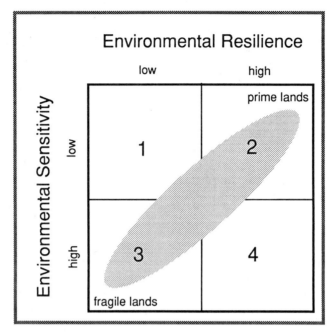

Figure 5.1. Environmental attributes of fragility and fragile land types. (Adapted from Blaikie and Brookfield [1987], *Land Degradation and Society*, 11. Reproduced by permission.)

assessments from which institutional and organizational lessons might be drawn.

We focus below on two recent comparative studies that approach nature-society relations by examining the match between use and environment (not always explicitly). From these studies, we have selected the particular cases concerned with agriculture and occurring in settings commonly described as "fragile." The first study is a survey of agricultural change in very densely populated regions of sub-Saharan Africa. The second is an ongoing comparative study of "critical environmental zones" around the world. The institutional lessons that may be drawn from these studies are limited by the fact that neither of the studies was specifically aimed at institutional and organizational issues per se.

Sub-Saharan Africa Assessment

This study examines population density–agricultural intensity relationships in densely populated areas south of the Sahara (Turner, Hyden, and Kates, forthcoming). By careful consideration of the recent history and current circumstances of selected regions, the study seeks to understand why large populations and intensive cultivation have developed in some areas of the subcontinent and whether environmental conditions play a dominant role in their location. Some scholars (for example, Lele and Stone, 1989) consider a significant portion of sub-Saharan Africa to be dominated by environments that are fragile or marginal for cultivation. They suggest that this may account for the inadequate growth of food production over the subcontinent as a whole.

The topic is approached through ten case studies—five each in eastern and western Africa—of areas with rural population densities approaching or exceeding 200 people per square kilometer, each prepared by experts with extensive field experience. In four of the cases, population densities exceed 500 people per square kilometer. Two studies address areas that have few major physical constraints for agriculture—Kisii District in Kenya and Bushenyi District in Uganda. Eight cases, however, occur on lands commonly classified as "fragile" on the basis of purely ecological criteria such as steepness of slope, soil quality, aridity, or some combination thereof.

The Case Studies. The steep slopes of Ruhengeri Prefecture in Rwanda (Ford, forthcoming) and the Usambara Mountains of Tanzania (Feierman, forthcoming) have led to the common application of the label "fragile" to these regions. Ruhengeri, with its fertile volcanic soils, has long been noted for intensive smallholder cultivation on very steep slopes under conditions of high population density. Colonial policy measures supported smallholder production in an effort to retain population in rural areas. More recently, however, continued high population growth has led to extreme land pressures; deforestation, combined with a policy shift toward promoting annuals instead of perennials, has exacerbated erosion problems, even on terraces (Clay and Lewis, 1990). Large-scale deterioration of the resource base has not yet occurred, thanks to traditional cropping practices, a patchwork landscape, widespread soil conservation measures, relatively supportive policies, expansion of cultivation into wetlands, and the safety valve of migration. Statistics even show an increase in production—the result of labor-based intensification—that is just staying ahead of population growth. Farmers perceive a decline in land productivity, however, perhaps indicating soil mining, and households are no longer completely self-sufficient. At some point degradation may become so severe as to inhibit cultivation.

The Usambara Mountains of northern Tanzania are relatively well watered and have historically supported large populations. Prosperous farms used terracing and other methods to impede erosion and improve soil moisture. Resentment toward coerced terracing under colonialism, coupled with current socioeconomic conditions, has altered cultivation practices dramatically, including lack of emphasis on conservation structures and, presumably, accelerated soil loss (Feierman, forthcoming). Increasingly, males migrate to urban and other areas to seek employment, but retain access to their homelands through their wives and families, who remain on the land. These female-headed households do not have the labor or capital to make needed land improvements, nor do the women allow other farmers access to these lands. To do so would threaten the women's security; under current usufruct rules, a person who makes land improvements then has a claim to that land. As a result, cultivation on most farms throughout the mountains has disintensified, despite mounting land pressures, and soil erosion, on average, has increased. In contrast, male-headed farms appear to be intensifying production.

Aridity, like slope, is a common criterion for labeling a region as fragile. Two of the case studies deal with farming on the arid margins of African agriculture; these are Meru District, Kenya (Bernard, forthcoming), and the Kano close-settled zone of northern Nigeria (Mortimore, forthcoming). In Meru District, Kenya, the well-watered environments at the midelevations of Mount Kenya have traditionally supported dense rural populations by taking advantage of the complex ecological zonation and by integrating crops, trees, and livestock. In the lower, dry regions of southeastern Meru, known as Tharaka, low population densities were supported by agropastoral strategies. A breakdown of the upland system in the 1950s was temporarily halted by a lifting of the colonial prohibition on territorial expansion, combined with new crops, improved seeds, fertilizer use, and urban migration. By the 1980s, however, continued population growth created highland densities of up to 500 people per square kilometer, and renewed land pressure brought declining soil fertility and accelerated erosion to the midelevation zone. These upland pressures resulted in heavy rural-to-rural migration down the altitudinal and ecological gradient to the highly erosive drylands of Tharaka, where upland production methods are ineffective. The results for Tharaka include devegetation, erosion, violent land conflicts, chronic food shortages, and continued peripheral status in policy and the economy. Despite these problems, overall agricultural production is not declining, although it is perhaps becoming more variable and less reliable.

The Kano close-settled zone of northern Nigeria (Mortimore, forthcoming; also Mortimore, 1989) is a semiarid area of variable precipitation and poor soils that has nonetheless supported a dense, rural smallholder population and intensive cultivation for over 100 years (with no reports of fallowing since 1913). With a growing population, attaining local densities of over 500 people per square kilometer by the 1980s, agriculture has intensified largely through high labor inputs. An integrated upland system of crops, livestock, and trees is complemented by small areas of irrigated market gardening. Urban proximity allows the local marketing of agricultural produce as well as economic diversification into alternative income sources. Despite claims to the contrary (see, for example, Watts, 1983a, 1983b), Mortimore regards the upland land-use system as environmentally stable with no evidence of declining outputs, decreased soil fertility, or recent erosion, although fertility is declining on the irrigated lowlands. Agricultural output has not, however, kept up with population growth, partly due to environmental constraints. Household needs have been met by a progressive shift to nonfarm sources of income, which farmers have found to be more economically advantageous than investment in agricultural technologies.

The other four cases, all from Nigeria, may, to varying degrees, be commonly classified as fragile areas on the basis of poor and infertile soils. These soils are marginal in the sense that they require large labor and organic inputs to sustain more than extensive fallow cultivation, and many are fragile because of the processes (nutrient loss and erosion) that follow from intensive use without proper inputs.

The Jos Plateau (Netting, forthcoming) is only occasionally classified as fragile land. The soils of the plateau homelands are fairly good, but major agricultural expansion is under way in the adjacent Benue Valley for commercial food production; this valley has variable soils, from good to poor quality for cultivation. The past 50 years have seen a shift from intensive, permanent cultivation on the plateau and migrant shifting cultivation in the valley frontier to dense permanent cultivation in both areas, in the context of a modern economy and infrastructure. The plateau system was able to maintain soil fertility; it is not clear that the valley system will be able to do so. At present there is no evidence of significant erosion in the valley, but depopulation of the hills and the resultant lack of terrace repair have led to an increase in erosion there. Voluntary labor intensification for the purpose of earning cash income enabled the addition of cash food crops to the traditional subsistence crops, but market involvement has been buffered by food self-sufficiency and has not required the sacrifice of subsistence production or economic autonomy.

Virtually all commentators refer to the Ibo forest belt of southeastern Nigeria as fragile. In the three case studies from this region (Goldman, forthcoming; Okafor, forthcoming; Martin, forthcoming), farmers are confronted with tropical soil conditions that are both highly marginal for cultivation and highly susceptible to degradation, especially nutrient depletion and, in some cases, erosion. Despite the unfavorable agricultural potential of the region, large populations—far above anything that would be predicted from carrying-capacity or land-capacity measures emphasizing physical attributes alone—have been sustained in the area for more than a century, if not longer, full settlement having been attained before 1900.

Most of the tropical forest has been converted to oil palm, bush-derived savanna, and farmland mosaic, with a resulting loss of biodiversity (Okafor, forthcoming). The soils of these lands are primarily sandy, heavily leached, and highly acidic ultisols—low in organic matter and infertile, but easy to work. Much of the region is relatively uniform and flat with little erosion (Martin, forthcoming; Goldman, forthcoming), but the escarpments of the Awka-Nnewi region are dominated by erosion (Okafor, forthcoming). Degradation has followed from extreme land pressures, resulting both from population growth and commercialization (Martin, forthcoming; Martin, 1988). Population densities in one region, Imo State, are estimated to average 430 to 520 people per square kilometer, perhaps reaching 1,400 people per square kilometer in the Ibo heartland (Goldman, forthcoming). For much of this century the farming system was based on long-fallow yam cultivation combined with oil-palm production, but this has changed with the collapse of the oil-palm market and a switch from yam to cassava. At present, the population is sustained by labor-intensive infield or compound gardening and male off-farm employment, supplemented by outer-field swiddening. Fallows in these fields have been declining at least since the 1920s, and today the soils are degraded and infertile. As a result, yields are generally declining or stagnant, and there is a perception of soil mining.

In their analysis of all ten case studies, the editors (Hyden, Kates, and Turner, forthcoming) noted a number of common trajectories. In all cases, growing populations were supported by high and increasing agricultural intensities attained by major labor inputs, especially female labor, supplemented by economic diversification, usually through male outmigration. Other responses to rising demands included increased cropping frequency (nine cases), new cultigens, and land expansion (six cases), resulting in increased production in eight of ten cases. A number of cases recorded increased marketing of food crops, often replacing export crops. Production increases did not necessarily lead to improvements in human welfare or food availability, but the changes associated with them increased social differentiation in seven cases and resulted in changing gender roles that placed more pressure on women.

Lessons

This comparative study indicates that sustained, intensive agriculture under conditions of extreme land pressures has developed in a variety of sub-Saharan environments, some of which are commonly considered to be ecologically fragile lands. Even the poor soils of the Nigerian forest belt have sustained intensive cultivation for generations. This is not to say that prime agricultural lands are not preferred or do not sustain intensive cultivation. Rather, the physical quality of the land alone does not account for the current distribution of sustained, intensive cultivation and extreme population size.

These cases are unusual for the subcontinent in general, due to the level of land pressures that they sustain. The pressures are so high, in some cases, that current practices cannot be intensified further without large-scale environmental damage, especially to soils, or a qualitative change in the system of cultivation (for example, from swidden fields to compound gardens). Given high rates of rural-to-rural migration and the very high rates of population growth in the subcontinent, it is most likely that intensive agriculture will spread further into reputedly fragile environments. But these cases indicate that this spread of cultivation need not necessarily lead to destructive agricultural practices or major environmental degradation.

The question then becomes, Under what circumstances can or will this expansion be sustainable—environmentally, economically, and socially? The comparative study drawn upon here does not systematically examine the institutional or organizational mechanisms influencing this development. The project did glean several broad lessons, however, and some of them may be relevant here (Hyden, Kates, and Turner, forthcoming).

A number of factors seemed to enhance community and household livelihoods in the face of mounting land pressure. These include (1) locational advantages facilitating market access and providing alternative economic opportunities, both of which promote farm household diversification (the presence and maintenance of roads is an important corollary); (2) maintenance of inputs and landesque capital investments so that a culture group retains access to its homeland; and (3) supportive socioeconomic organization and structures.

Locational advantages do not, of course, guarantee the development of sustainable agriculture on fragile lands. But, under mounting land pressures, it is difficult to diversify economically and to improve per capita rewards from cropping without access to markets. Diversification alone is also problematic; it is typically associated with male outmigration, which has variable impacts on agriculture (see, for example, Mazambani, 1990).

The maintenance and upgrading of inputs is an obvious requirement for intensive agricultural use of reputedly fragile lands, but the specific conditions that promote this are quite variable. Land entitlement, for example, supported sustainable agriculture in some cases (for example, in Ruhengeri) and did not in others (for example, in Usambaras). It would appear that those mixes of institutions and organizations that permit households to balance subsistence needs with economic diversification are those that promote sustainable use of fragile lands.

Factors considered to be constraints on agricultural intensification included lack of access to technology, inadequate market development, customary resource allocation, and labor withdrawal. In the cases studied, however, these factors were not always constraints; the protective role of spatial isolation from excessive external interference (for example, in Jos) and of customary resource allocation (which protected smallholder agriculture in Ruhengeri and Kano) were seen as positive in some cases. In response to the heterogeneity of conditions, the authors also note the need for variable and flexible policies, including noneconomic ones. These categories are necessarily broad because of the variability of conditions encountered in the study. Comparative studies directed at the specific issues identified are required to tease out more specific details (see, for example, Pingali, Bigot, and Binswanger, 1987).

Critical Environmental Zones

The Project on Critical Environmental Zones also offers comparative case studies that lend insights into the use of yet another set of reputedly fragile lands. The primary objective of this ongoing work is to assess "environmental criticality" from an anthropocentric perspective. Specifically, it addresses the relationship between environmental degradation and socioeconomic well-being through studies of regions that are assumed or declared to be in environmentally critical condition leading to socioeconomic deterioration.

Like fragile lands, the concept of environmental criticality has been dominated to date by a geocentric perspective in which ecological degradation (such as loss in biomass or soils) alone is used as the criterion for declaring an area critical or endangered. In contrast, the premise of this project is that all human occupance involves some degree of ecological change and that the critical issue from a human perspective is the impact of this change on long-term human affluence and well-being. Thus, the study seeks to determine if extensive environmental change is necessarily related to deterioration in the material conditions of human life—especially in a world in which human well-being is increasingly becoming a function of an open system beyond the immediate region of habitation. It seeks further to identify the causes of environmental change and the perceptions of and responses to it.

Toward these ends, nine case studies, representing a broad range of socioeconomic and environmental conditions from around the world, are under development and evaluation through a common protocol. In six of these cases, the agricultural development of reputedly fragile lands is an important factor in the region's criticality. Common assumptions of fragility in these cases are based on problematic rainforest soils (Amazonia); steep slopes (the Nepalese Himalayas); aridity without major irrigation (the eastern forelands of Kenya, the Ordos Plateau of Inner Mongolia); and aridity with major irrigation (the Aral Sea, the southwestern Great Plains of North America).

The Case Studies. Amazonia (Smith et al., forthcoming) is an oft-studied tropical forest case, in which the proximate sources of environmental change are complex, involving the development of the tropical forest zone for agriculture, pasture, mining, and hydroelectric power. The ongoing environmental degradation and unsustainability of frontier development through land clearance for pastures, cultivation, and land speculation have been well documented (Hecht, 1985, 1989; Salati et al., 1990; Smith, 1982). Problems of severe environmental degradation are particularly acute on the "classical" acidic oxisols and ultisols where deforestation results in the loss of ecosystem nutrients. The soils of Amazonia are not homogeneous, however, varying considerably over relatively small spatial units (Moran, 1990). Historically, portions of the region have sustained large populations (Denevan, 1976; Roosevelt, 1980) based on local production, although these populations concentrated in areas of better soils. There are indications that well-managed forestry — perhaps including extractive reserves (Peters, Gentry, and Mendelsohn, 1989) — pasture recuperation, and perennial crop-based agriculture may provide sustainable and profitable forms of intensive land management (Smith et al., forthcoming). And some research suggests that combining biotechnic with traditional inputs may offer the possibility for sustainable continuous cultivation (Sanchez et al., 1982; Nicholaides et al., 1985; Sanchez and Benites, 1987; but see also Fearnside, 1987).

Ignoring the biodiversity-deforestation problem — which itself may have long-term global consequences for agriculture (Smith et al., forthcoming) — studies from Amazonia indicate that sustained cultivation in tropical forests hinges on the socioeconomic conditions present as much as the questionable marginality and fragility of the soil. Current Amerindian cultivation is sustained through long-fallow techniques and selection of more intensive agriculture on prime soils, often riverine locations (for example, levees; see Hames and Vickers, 1983), as well as subtle knowledge and intricate manipulation of heterogeneous ecosystem patches (Posey, 1985). Migrant cultivation in Amazonia, on the other hand, has been characterized by frontier farming with poor agroecological knowledge and conditions that favor land expansion rather than land improvements. In addition, a series of external sociopolitical and economic forces have not weighed in favor of environmentally sound agriculture (for example, Hecht, 1985, 1989; Sanderson, n.d.). Although disagreement over the precise impacts and relative weights of these forces exists, it is generally agreed that they include poor and marginalized migrants, insecure land tenure and resource access, rewards for mining the forest and land, lack of environmental controls, and coercion, often violent, against smallholder development. The assumption is that if the social and economic circumstances were corrected, then it would be possible to carry out sustained cultivation in many parts of Amazonia, although the costs might be quite high. Smith and colleagues conclude that while Amazonia may contain lands that are marginal or even fragile for agriculture, sustained and, in some cases, economically viable cultivation and livestock rearing are developing in many locales, including those thought to be fragile.

In the Himalayan case study region (Jodha, forthcoming), steep slopes make the area sensitive to land pressures, which, if inappropriately managed, lead to environmental degradation. The study focuses on the middle mountain region of Nepal, particularly the Bagmati Zone in the center of the country. This zone has a long history of cultivation (see, for example, Bishop, 1990), but suffers from increasing land pressures, resulting in deforestation and erosion. Although much of the mass wasting in this region may be attributed to tectonic forces (Ives, 1987), human intervention also has a major impact. The case documents the co-occurrence over the last several decades of a number of environmental changes that reduce the productive capacity of the land; these include soil loss and declining soil fertility, declining fuelwood and fodder resources, declining or unstable water flows, and stress-induced changes in cropping patterns. The result for villagers is a foreclosure of options resulting in the necessity to accept those perceived as inferior, especially short-term strategies such as overextraction of natural resources. People are aware of the situation but lack the resources to respond, and alternative options such as off-farm activities or migration are not sufficiently available.

Mountain characteristics, such as inaccessibility, fragility, marginality, diversity, ecological niches, and human adaptability, contribute to the sensitivity of the land to human interventions. Factors increasing pressures in the area include population growth; commercialization of agriculture that reduces the diversity of production by kind and niche; timber extraction, hydropower development, tourism, and, generally, external market linkages that have promoted an extractive mentality; and public interventions that are inappropriate in the local context, in both content and scale.

These pressures tend to reinforce one another with such socioeconomic results as disruption of the production base and of linkages at various scales resulting in reductions in flexibility, reliability, and collective risk sharing. Specific results include food deficits, seasonal migration, and resource degradation. All of these changes affect different regions and different groups variably. At the national level, the ability to respond is constrained by lack of resources, the real needs of production, financial pressures to generate immediate revenues, and an exclusive emphasis on supply-side responses to the neglect of demand management.

This environment, while easily degraded by erosion, is not necessarily hostile to cultivation, having been the site of a long-term history of landesque capital investments and integrated farming systems sensitive to local environmental and social conditions. The weight of multiple pressures, internal and external, is driving a negative and mutually reinforcing process of natural and humanly induced degradation.

The Kenyan study (Rocheleau, Benjamin, and Diang'a, forthcoming) examines Machakos and Kitui districts in the eastern part of the country. This region, known as Ukambani, homeland of the Kamba people, is widely reputed to be fragile due to its aridity and to the practice of agriculture on erodible soils of mixed fertility, sometimes on steep slopes. Overall, the region is semiarid, but dotted with "islands" of higher elevation and higher-quality lands. It provides a microcosm of the Kenyan context of scarce medium-to-high-potential land, extremely skewed land distribution, and high population growth (3 to 4 percent per annum).

Ukambani is adjacent to Meru District (noted above) and shares many of the same environmental and socioeconomic characteristics. As in Meru, land scarcity, population growth, poverty, and lack of alternatives are forcing large numbers of cultivators onto drier lands formerly used for agropastoralism, resulting in devegetation and erosion. Also like Meru, both food production and vulnerability are increasing, and male urban migration and altered gender roles are profoundly changing social structures.

The traditional farming system was based on microenvironmental exploitation, crop-livestock integration, and an expanding frontier. Today, the tradition of mobility as a strategy for exploitation of frontiers has been retained, but colonial restructuring, social differentiation, and population growth have combined to transform the strategy's content. The urban job market has become a frontier for men, whose mobility has increased. Land adjudication has confined rural households to a fixed space, changing the regional-scale land frontier from a place of fluid expansions and contractions across multiple ecological niches to a set of discrete chunks of land. As a result, agroecological niches are lost to communities or farmers, agricultural expansion is increasingly into drier areas or extremely steep slopes (in areas already densely settled), and the household needs once obtained across the landscape are now sought from a single plot.

Machakos has been defined as a crisis zone for decades, but the type of crisis has varied through time and by defining group. Currently, land pressure is bringing continued deforestation, soil erosion, and soil fertility declines. Yet, migrants bring with them knowledge of soil and water conservation, agroforestry techniques, and the intent to produce and market high-value crops, all of which are implemented as investment resources and labor become available. The environmental factor of aridity is severely constraining, however, and there is a sense of ever-constricting options in increasingly confining spaces.

The Ordos Plateau is located in the great bend of the Huang Ho, Inner Mongolia, China. The historical home of nomadic herders, the sandstone plateau is a semiarid to arid, windy place, with a low-level agricultural economy and weak links to other regions (Hong et al., forthcoming). Although Chinese (Han) farmers began a slow but steady immigration into the region as early as the late 1600s, this movement exploded during the mid-20th century. Populations increased by 225 percent from 1949 to 1973 as government policy (particularly during the "grain-dominated" periods of the Great Leap Forward and the Cultural Revolution) encouraged immigration and the rapid conversion of grassland into cropland, even in the most dry areas of the plateau. State policies for regional development have the intent of intensifying land use and economic activity in the region and of supporting a much larger population there than could be sustained from traditional livestock activities alone.

Although overgrazing and overuse of woody species for firewood have become serious environmental problems since the late 1950s, the wholesale conversion of high-quality pasture into poor-quality cropland, undertaken without conservation controls, has been the main source of the widespread land degradation in the Ordos. Devegetation and soil surface disturbance—in an area of sandy soils and high winds—has resulted in massive erosion. The area affected by dune mobilization nearly doubled between 1957 and 1977, as some regions became 50 percent "sandified." Through combined aeolian and water transport, the Ordos is estimated to contribute 10 percent of the total silt and one-third of the coarse sand load of the Huang Ho. Results include catastrophic flooding, loss of fertility, and degraded vegetation. Large segments of the plateau remain scarred from the erosion that has taken place.

The national government recognized the environmental problems of the plateau, at least in terms of the loss of soil, but government-sponsored schemes (for example, planting trees) met with little success. Since the late 1970s, new policies favoring household and local government control may be slowing and, in some areas, even reversing environmental degradation. Large areas have been taken out of cultivation and put back into pasture or forest, and measures for pasture rehabilitation, dune stabilization, cropland soil conservation, and integrated watershed management have been introduced. Nevertheless, large reaches of plateau remain scarred with erosion.

Although most of the Ordos is a marginal and sensitive environment for agriculture and would better remain uncultivated, a large farming population now lives in the area and, short of an environmental collapse, will continue to farm. To some extent, the classical frontier circumstances that promote low input and nonsustainable systems of cultivation and that have existed in the recent past may be giving way to more skilled and apparently sustainable systems; for example, labor-intensive plots using opaque plastic covers to retain water and heat can be found. This shift is, however, impeded by material and knowledge poverty that limits people's options as well as societal resources for environmental mitigation and restoration. Failures to intensify cultivation in a sustainable manner appear to hinge on the prevailing economic circumstances (for example, access to land, cost of inputs, low labor-to-land ratio by Chinese standards, retention of lands on which improvements might be made) and the ability to obtain inputs.

The Aral Sea of Uzbekistan and Kazakhstan is a highly visible environmental disaster (Glazovsky, forthcoming). The shrinking sea itself poses significant local climatic, health, and economic problems that threaten not only the near-sea area but the greater central Asia region (see, for example, Micklin, 1988; Precoda, 1991). The cause of this disaster, however, does not lie in the use of the sea itself, but in reduced inflow caused by water withdrawals from the Syr Darya and Amu Darya. Although these two rivers have been used since antiquity for irrigated agriculture, the magnitude of that use grew drastically in the 1950s and 1960s. The fertile floodplains of the two rivers have been extensively irrigated, but canals have also been built to take river water to surrounding arid lands. The 1,300-kilometer-long Karakum Canal, for example, which takes 14 cubic kilometers of water per year from the Amu Darya to the Karakum Desert, has been the most important factor in the reduction of inflow to the Aral Sea (Micklin, 1988).

The proximate causes of desiccation of the sea are well understood—even if difficult to alter. The agricultural system is massively overextended and inefficient in terms of technology and management. The irrigated area has expanded rapidly since the early 1960s to a current total of more than 7 million hectares (Precoda, 1991; Kotlyakov, 1991). Large areas of this land are undergoing secondary salinization—up to 40 percent of the irrigated land in Turkmenia; over 900,000 hectares were brought into irrigation in Uzbekistan from 1975 to 1985, and more than 550,000 hectares were lost (Precoda, 1991). The technology of irrigation is highly inefficient, using open, earth-lined canals and inappropriate delivery techniques. Perhaps 65 percent to 70 percent of the irrigation water is lost before it reaches the fields (Precoda, 1991:112). Water-demanding cotton is the principal crop, and rewards and abuses in the system promote excessive use of water. In addition, antiquated management techniques include the use of defoliants to harvest cotton, further contaminating soil and water.

The underlying causes of this circumstance are not so well documented, although the candidates that must be considered in detail are well known. They begin with centralized decision making from afar—Moscow—in which critical decisions (on cultigens, amount of harvest, and managerial techniques) were made based on the need for foreign exchange, not local needs or environmental suitability. Management of the system is corrupt and impeded by inadequate irrigation and cropping technologies, as well as disputes among neighboring political units over the use of water in the two drainages. In addition, the Central Asian region has witnessed an enormous growth in population, which demands employment through agriculture and water use independent of cultivation needs.

The lesson from the Aral Sea case, then, is that agricultural fragility can be linked to a critical resource that is abused (see the next case). The important issue, of course, is the cause of this abuse. If these abuses were corrected and the productive efficiency was improved, the size of the system might still turn out to be too large, but its decline might be stabilized. A retrenchment of irrigation may be required to save the sea and the local environmental consequences of its loss (for example, less precipitation, salt storms, and toxic dust and water).

Agriculture on the American Great Plains is the subject of an extensive literature because of the region's role as an international breadbasket and a model to be emulated elsewhere. Of additional interest are the history of its settlement; the boom-bust cycles of its agriculture, including the Dust Bowl; and the depletion of the Ogallala aquifer (Riebsame, 1990; Späth, 1987; Worster, 1979). This case study (Brooks and Emel, forthcoming) examines the southwestern Great Plains—particularly the Llano Estacado of eastern New Mexico and the Panhandle of Texas. This region shares with most of the Great Plains high-quality agricultural soils, but suffers from more serious water shortages than most of the western plains. The key to agriculture in this arid environment is water.

Government policy in the late 19th century was directed at the expansion of agriculture onto the southern Great Plains during a period of above-average rainfall, using cultivation techniques and practices unsuitable for the environment. Inappropriate cultivation combined with the droughts of the 1930s to devastate field and farmer alike. Agriculture rebounded, however, with the use of a bevy of conservation techniques to protect soil from wind and water erosion. New technologies permitted widespread irrigation, drawn from the Ogallala aquifer, which promoted a switch to cotton production for its high market values, especially in Texas. Cotton has sustained the region economically for the past five decades. At present, however, as the aquifer empties and the cost of pumping water increases, the amount of land taken out of production has been on the rise. Despite the advanced level of technology, effective water-management institutions, college-educated farmers, and the 1980s "shake-out" of poor managers, the viability of agriculture here is fading, and no other economic activities are available to replace it.

The region may be nearing present technological limits for current cultivation practices. Several decades of investment in water conservation technologies and well-developed institutions for management and well spacing have reduced total pumpage and increased efficiency; these measures have slowed but cannot reverse the inexorable loss of groundwater, given current demands. A more extensive and biotechnically integrated mode of cropping might be sustained indefinitely, but this has not proven to be economical at this time. Without massive external subsidies—for which there appears to be no economic or political will at the moment—or a shift in the market value of crops that would make alternative agriculture profitable, cultivation and the social infrastructure built on this land use will inevitably decline.

Lessons. While still under formulation, the lessons of the critical zones study are similar to those of the African study:

Human use of any region is invariably marked by environmental change.

The degree of this change is strongly associated with the level of land pressures in place; those pressures may be economic, demographic, or a combination.

Degradation in terms of agricultural land use is exacerbated when inappropriate cultivation is practiced under environmentally sensitive conditions.

Inappropriate cultivation usually follows from inappropriate technology, management, or level of expected production; these typically follow from some combination of ambition (for example, immediate profits), constraints (for example, poverty), coercion (for example, external force), and inadequate environmental knowledge (for example, frontier migrants).

Environmental sensitivity to exploitation or intensification is the immediately critical element of fragility.

Environmentally sensitive areas (including Type 3) will increasingly be subjected to land pressures promoting cultivation.

These areas probably cannot be cultivated in the manner of "prime" agricultural lands (Type 2) or be expected to replicate similar levels of input-output over the long term.

It is technologically feasible to use these areas for higher levels of agricultural or economic rewards than in the past.

Political, economic, and demographic factors are likely to prevent this from happening in an appropriate manner.

The matrix of human factors driving inappropriate human use leads to conditions of environmental criticality and, sometimes, economic criticality (see Lee, 1986). For many areas that qualify as environmentally critical, these factors promote extractive agricultural activities in frontier settings where environmental knowledge or controls may be poor or carry little weight in decision making, or where alternative opportunities are highly constrained. In no case examined was improved and sustained output not possible over the long run, given proper management, although it is doubtful in some cases that the level of output will necessarily be sufficient to meet the extreme levels of demand. Many, if not most, of the critical zones examined do not appear to have the appropriate sociopolitical or economic conditions that will lead to appropriate management in the immediate future.

Understanding the Use of Fragile Lands: Summary and Contents

Concerns about fragile lands and the environmental impacts of agriculture have gained prominence with increasing interest in two interrelated problems: the need to meet the enormous demand for food and other agricultural products that will continue to rise well into the next century, and concern about the health of the biosphere in response to the expansion of land transformations to meet these needs. This concern is not uniform, however. In practice, so-called fragile lands have been viewed as reservoirs of untapped wealth and as a home for the landless. Because of the environmental damage that has often ensued, the "opening" of such lands has sometimes been criticized on purely ecological grounds; such criticism has sometimes displaced reasoned assessments about the pros and cons of intensifying land uses in such environments. Reasoned assessments must not only define and identify fragile lands, they must draw upon a wide range of studies that have examined the environmental and agricultural outcomes of their use.

Fragile lands and fragility are loosely defined concepts that are commonly but inappropriately intermingled with the concept of marginality. Marginal lands for agriculture are those that respond less well to human inputs than do other lands. In contrast, fragile lands for agriculture are those seen as easily degraded—and thus unproductive. Fragile lands are commonly, but not always, marginal as well.

This view of fragile lands acknowledges the centrality of "nature's endowment" in determining the consequences of use. Repeated studies indicate, however, that long-term, intensive cultivation has taken place on lands that must be considered fragile in terms of environmental criteria alone, and that lands considered prime for cultivation have been severely damaged from misuse. Fragile lands must, therefore, be understood in terms of the uses applied to them.

Identification and Demarcation

Fragility is the sensitivity of land to biophysical deterioration under common uses; in this relational perspective, all lands are ultimately fragile if sufficiently misused. A *fragile land* is one that is so sensitive to environmental deterioration that common uses cannot be sustained and may even lead to irreparable damage. It is important to understand what conditions promote or inhibit the appropriate match of use with environment.

This more complex view does not necessarily inhibit the identification of fragile lands, but it does demand information of a kind that is not readily available, particularly in any standardized form. This information includes environmental sensitivity (propensity to deteriorate) and resilience (ability to retain productive qualities), but in the context of a set of common land uses. Prime agricultural lands (Type 2 in our scheme) have low sensitivity and high resilience, and almost invariably respond well to inputs. These lands have historically been favored by farmers. The other three types have high sensitivity or low resilience or both. Type 3—high sensitivity and low resilience—are the most fragile lands and are, presumably, the most difficult or costly to match with proper intensive use.

Some of the existing efforts directed at mapping the risk of environmental degradation come close in stated principle to the measure suggested here for fragile lands. In practice, however, these efforts almost invariably rely on the environmentally biased measures of agricultural potential or degraded environments. The former typically rely on environmental quality alone as the determinant of fragility, irrespective of use; the latter is a tautology, defining as fragile environments that are degraded. More fruitful approaches are those that seek overlaps between environmental characteristics and socioeconomic circumstances, such as the International Food Policy Research Institute's attempt to match agroecological zones with poverty in the less developed world (IFPRI, 1991). Unfortunately, data to measure the sensitivity-resilience criteria of fragility proposed here are not available.

Relational Perspective: Lessons

While fragile lands cannot be adequately delineated and mapped at this time, case studies provide broad but useful insights about the conditions that create mismatches between land and use, and about the probable future use of Type 3 environments or fragile lands. Lands characterized by aridity, steep slopes, or soils prone to nutrient loss or erosion are commonly classified as fragile. Comparative studies of agriculture on such lands, however, do not yield consistent outcomes. In some cases, traditions of long-term sustainable use, even under intensive cultivation, exist. Land management and landesque capital compensate for environmental constraints. In other cases, such traditions are not evident or have been disrupted, leading to environmental degradation and the disintensification of agriculture.

These studies highlight some conditions under which environment-use mismatches are most likely to occur (but may not). These include

> aridity,
>
> rapidly changing land uses,
>
> frontier,
>
> poverty,
>
> extreme land pressures,
>
> external resource or decision-making control, and
>
> conflicting incentives.

In general, those lands with the greatest propensity to degrade under increasing agricultural intensification or land pressures are those that are arid and without a dependable (renewable) water supply. Environments such as the Ordos Plateau or eastern Kenya require unusual kinds and levels of inputs to overcome these constraints. Even under conditions of affluence, as in the southwestern Great Plains, the long-term viability of the system in place is questionable, based as it is on the mining of groundwater.

Rapidly changing land uses follow from rapid changes in demand, either from population change—migration or natural growth (the Ordos Plateau, Amazonia, eastern Kenya, the Ibo forest belt, the Aral Sea)—or external demands (Amazonia, the Aral Sea). The confusion and conflict that typically accompany rapid change increase the potential for mismatching use and environment. Frontier conditions (Amazonia, the Ordos Plateau, eastern Kenya, the Jos Plateau) also promote mismanaged or inappropriate agriculture through inadequate resource controls, spatial isolation from inputs, and lack of familiarity with the environment. Frontiers typically attract speculators as well as people with no other options.

Farmer poverty and state poverty are linked to mismatches because of the often severe constraints they place on farming options. For the farmer, poverty restricts the application of critical inputs (Kenya), the upkeep of landesque capital (Nepal), the shift to superior systems of cultivation (Usambaras), or the power to change policies. State poverty restricts the scale and kinds of inputs and services that can be provided, and encourages policies that lead to a mining of resources for immediate revenue (the Aral Sea).

External controls vary in kind, ranging from markets to governments and international agencies, but can lead to the same results— decisions or policies that create mismatches. Markets may promote the cultivation of crops that are not well suited to the environment and may not adequately reward those cultigens that are appropriate (Ruhengeri, the southwestern Great Plains). Government and nongovernment organizations (NGOs) may push policies that lead to excessive use demands. Nationally defined needs may conflict with local needs (Amazonia, the Aral Sea); larger policies are often not coordinated within a local context (eastern Kenya, the Himalayas). Activities intended to reduce problems in one locale may displace them to another (for example, migration to the Ordos Plateau and Amazonia). In most cases, these controls make it immediately unprofitable or physically impossible to practice environmentally sustainable agriculture.

Conflicting incentives occur when farmers have the ability to employ appropriate cultivation but fail to do so because this choice is at odds with another, more important consideration. Perhaps the most common such conflict occurs in market agriculture between high but short-term economic rewards and longer-term environmental consequences. This conflict has often been resolved in favor of the short-term rewards, and soil and water mining have followed (for example, the southwestern Great Plains). Other forms may be more localized, as when tenure or usufruct rights are lost with land improvements (Usambaras).

Degradation on fragile lands may be most severe where several of these factors coalesce. Even relatively good environments, including Type 2, can be taxed to their limits where these conditions proliferate (for example, the river valleys entering the Aral Sea). Degradation of fragile lands cannot be avoided by affluence alone, although the capacity to avert large-scale social catastrophes is usually higher with affluence.

It is more difficult to identify a specific set of factors that seem to prevail where fragile lands are used in a sustainable but intensive manner. Most examples of sustainable use are those based on long-term adaptations, either of an extensive kind involving movement and rotation of land use (for example, pastoralism, agropastoralism) or an intensive labor-based kind (for example, irrigated terracing). Higher production can be obtained from extensive systems. With heightened pressure, however, these systems may shift to more intensive forms of land use. Extant intensive systems are generally found in contexts of severe land pressures, where increased outputs cannot necessarily be obtained simply by adding more of the same inputs to the same system.

The conditions that promote a shift to systems that are sustainable are not obvious. It is a truism that the appropriate sociopolitical and economic conditions must exist, but—if the African cases discussed here are any guide—these can take a variety of forms and can be generated under diverse circumstances. Some key elements appear to include sufficient rewards for the investment in intensification; security of this investment; a level of well-being sufficient for the exercise of choice; access to services, appropriate inputs and technology, and markets; sufficient local autonomy to make decisions seen as beneficial to the producing unit; rules and regulations that reward sustainable intensification (for example, subsidies or taxes); and long-term attachment to and investment in a place.

Institutional Considerations

From an ecocentric perspective, most Type 3 lands should probably not be cultivated; all else being equal, these lands would serve humanity better in other capacities (for example, aquifer recharge areas, biodiversity reserves, soil carbon storage, forests, rangelands). Ideally, policies aimed at agricultural intensification on prime lands and the protection of fragile lands should be favored. All else is not equal, however, and experience indicates that agriculture will continue to expand, and probably intensify, on fragile lands into the next century, regardless of developments on prime lands. The agricultural and environmental responses to these pressures will vary. In some cases degradation and agricultural collapse may follow from use of fragile lands; in other cases, the productive capacity of fragile lands may increase without serious environmental degradation. Indeed, this capacity may be undervalued. The key to positive changes will frequently be the enhancement of traditional intensive systems. Intensification of fragile land agriculture, however, will involve high marginal cost, and its productivity will probably never rival that of prime agricultural lands. Given these considerations, certain facets of agriculture on fragile lands require careful consideration.

The institutional framework that has undergirded the industrialization of agriculture in the developed world and the creation of green-revolution technologies is not appropriate to the development of fragile land agriculture, because so much of fragile-land cultivation is and will continue to be that of resource-poor small farmers. Existing institutional frameworks focus on the production of a few select commodities by large-scale and homogeneous systems in which capital is substituted for labor and land tenure is based on private ownership by males. The supporting research structure has tended to be centralized, employing a top-down system of "package" dissemination while deemphasizing local knowledge and management. Moreover, the larger social, environmental, nutritional, public health, and genetic diversity contexts and consequences of this framework have been inadequately considered.

This particular institutional framework has important implications because, as we have argued, the sustainability of cultivation on fragile lands is a product of the way in which the land is used. Fragile lands (with high sensitivity and low resilience) cannot be used in the same manner as prime lands; the framework that has dominated the agricultural development field to date has been directed at prime lands. For most fragile lands, as Jodha (1990b) has argued, optimal development should focus on local comparative advantage and complementarity to the larger system; it should not require inappropriate replication of that system or exploitive resource extraction in the service of the larger system but without local benefit. In addition, residents of resource-poor areas derive the most benefit when multipurpose rather than single-purpose production systems are in place; this may often require the protection of indigenous common property management systems (Jodha, 1990a).

Several critical institutional changes must be made to improve the prospect for viable future use of fragile land. The case studies discussed above indicate that simple rules generalizable across contexts are difficult to derive; it is apparent that different consequences are associated with any single variable or sets of variables (for example, land tenure). But if firm institutional rules cannot be formulated with confidence, other near-term institutional considerations can be. Examples follow:

Most fragile lands will be cultivated by resource-poor farmers

engaged in "dual" (subsistence and market) production. Therefore, policies should be directed at enhancing labor-based,
small-scale cultivation systems and integrating multiple crops,
trees, and livestock.

Many farming units, particularly female-headed households in
Africa, may face ongoing or seasonal labor constraints. Therefore, technology, management, and infrastructure enhance-
ments must be attuned to the local labor schedule.

Use of fragile lands requires a high level of sensitivity to those
biophysical elements that contribute to the high sensitivity and
low resilience of the environment. Finely tuned adjustments to
local conditions, based on hands-on experience, are most effectively developed by local farmers. Institutions should support
innovative technologies and managerial designs based on local
knowledge of (for example) microclimates, soils, farming techniques, and crop varieties.

Institutional considerations of this type have sometimes been addressed by existing "farming systems" research, including research
units housed within NGOs and major agricultural policy and research
organizations (Jones and Wallace, 1986). The benefits of this type of
research have not been fully realized for a number of reasons: extremely low levels of funding, an apparent lack of respect from the
biological science community, and, perhaps, its use by social scientists to pursue topics considered tangential to the central role of the
sponsoring organization (Bebbington and Carney, 1990). Because the
farming systems approach works within the socioeconomic and environmental diversity noted throughout this chapter, its results are expensive on a per capita or per project basis. In any case, both the sustainability and the productivity of agriculture on fragile lands are
likely to be enhanced by an increased emphasis on innovative research in the farming systems tradition and by its explicit incorporation into the design of the larger agricultural research and extension
system.

Beyond these institutional considerations, broader concerns are
raised by the case studies examined here:

Resource-poor farmers, like all farmers, respond to production
opportunities when and where their investments are secure.
These farmers will not pursue sustainable agricultural practices
if the rewards for doing so are insufficient, or if the costs are be-

yond their means, or if their landesque capital investments are insecure. Institutions must, therefore, promote such opportunities and security. The case studies suggest that appropriate institutional arrangements will vary considerably by context. In different contexts, apparently opposite arrangements may lead to the same result, and similar arrangements to opposite results.

Resource-poor farmers are often isolated from most forms of assistance and beneficial opportunities. This has long been recognized and has generally led to calls for increased transportation infrastructure, superior access to markets, and other expensive means of improving communication and contact. It may prove beneficial and economically efficient to invest in extant institutions that serve these functions, such as local trade organizations or merchants. (Bebbington, 1991)

It is difficult to offer more specific insights. Little is known about the level of specificity attainable beyond the local or regional scale. We simply do not have sufficient comparative work to inform us if specific common institutional arrangements will work panregionally. Much evidence, in fact, points up the value of locally specific strategies for managing fragile lands; research policy must explicitly acknowledge and embrace the complexity and the heterogeneity of local cultures, environments, and farming systems.

Finally, it is noteworthy that the social and policy sciences remain locked in controversy over the relative importance of different institutional frameworks for increasing overall food production, for using fragile lands sustainably, and for enhancing the well-being of rural households. Few doubt the importance of technological innovation. Much more contentious are the social and environmental consequences of these innovations and their propensity to dominate development policies and obscure the potential value of complementary strategies.

With this in mind, we argue that research into conventional methods of cultivation should not be abandoned in favor of an exclusive pursuit of high-technology or biotechnology innovations. Little is really known about how much conventional methods and cultigens can produce. With appropriate support, indigenous farming systems may be capable of high production levels. Minimal investments here might produce very high rewards, especially on fragile lands. Moreover, the social and ecological implications of biotechnology development must be taken seriously, and ways must be found for biotechnology research to serve local needs (Juma, 1989).

Agricultural production on fragile lands forms only a small part of the overall global system for producing food and fiber. There is no reason for the search for innovation to focus only on supply and to ignore the demand side. Defining the agricultural problem as the need to increase aggregate production can obscure other important issues, such as the distribution of that production and the well-being of producers. Disaggregating demand—analyzing what is being produced, and for whom—may serve to suggest new priorities or to redefine the problem in new ways. It may be possible for agriculture to learn from the recent experience of the commercial energy sector in the United States, where a gradual shift is occurring from an exclusive focus on increasing supply to an emphasis on managing demand and serving the specific needs of users.

Finally, we return to the broader concerns of nature-society relations to note that long-term ecological well-being is difficult to separate from economic and social well-being. Ecological sustainability cannot be adequately addressed in isolation from economic and social sustainability. And, as implied throughout this chapter, environmental fragility cannot be adequately understood without considering socioeconomic "fragilities." The use of fragile lands only serves to highlight the degree to which nature and society are intimately intertwined.

Notes

The authors thank the participants of the conference for which this paper was prepared for their comments. We also thank Anthony Bebbington, Roger E. Kasperson, and Michael Mortimore for helpful criticisms. Heather Henderson assisted in the production of the paper.

1. This project is being conducted by the George Perkins Marsh Institute, Clark University, in cooperation with the Institute of Geography, Russian Academy of Sciences, and is sponsored by the National Science Foundation (United States) and the United Nations University. The principal investigator is Roger E. Kasperson.

References

Alexandratos, N. 1988. World Agriculture: Toward 2000. Rome: Food and Agriculture Organization (FAO); New York: New York University Press.

Allan, W. 1965. The African Husbandman. New York: Barnes and Noble.

Avery, D., et al. 1978. Science and Technology for Managing Fragile Environments in Devel-

oping Nations. Ann Arbor: Office of International Studies, School of Natural Resources, University of Michigan.

Ayyad, M., and G. Glaser. 1981. Marginal lands. *UNESCO Courier* 34(4): 18-22.

Bach, W., J. Pankrath, and S. H. Schneider. 1981. *Food-Climate Interactions*. Dordrecht: Reidel.

Bebbington, A. 1990. Farmer knowledge, institutional resources and sustainable agricultural strategies: A case study from the eastern slopes of the Peruvian Andes. *Bulletin of Latin American Research* 9:203-28.

——. 1991. *Farmer Organization in Ecuador: Contributions to Farmer First Research and Development*. Gatekeeper Service, no. 26. London: International Institute for Environment and Development.

Bebbington, A., and J. Carney. 1990. Geography in the international agricultural research centers: Theoretical and practical concerns. *Annals of the Association of American Geographers* 80(1): 34-48.

Berger, J. J. 1989. *Environmental Restoration*. Washington, D.C.: Island Press.

Bernard, F. E. Forthcoming. Increasing variability in agricultural production: Meru District, Kenya, in the twentieth century. In *Population Growth and Agricultural Change in Africa*, edited by B. L. Turner II, G. Hyden, and R. W. Kates. Gainesville: University Presses of Florida.

Bernard, F. E., D. J. Campbell, and D. J. Thom. 1989. Carrying capacity of the eastern ecological gradient of Kenya. *National Geographic Research* 5(4): 399-421.

Bishop, B. C. 1990. *Karnali under Stress: Livelihood Strategies and Seasonal Rhythms in a Changing Nepal Himalaya*. Geography Research Paper, 228-29. Chicago: University of Chicago Press.

Blaikie, P. 1985. *The Political Economy of Soil Erosion in Developing Countries*. New York: Longman.

Blaikie, P., and H. Brookfield. 1987. *Land Degradation and Society*. New York: Methuen.

Bremer, J., A. Babb, J. Dickinson, P. Gore, E. Hyman, and M. Andre. 1984. *Fragile Lands: A Theme Paper on Problems, Issues and Approaches for Development of Humid Tropical Lowlands and Steep Slopes in the Latin American Region*. Washington, D.C.: Development Alternatives.

Brookfield, H. C. 1981. Man, environment, and development in the outer islands of Fiji. *Ambio* 10(2/3): 59-67.

Brooks, E. and J. Emel. Forthcoming. The Llano Estacado of the American Southern High Plains. In *Critical Environmental Regions: International Comparisons*, edited by J. X. Kasperson, R. E. Kasperson, and B. L. Turner II. Tokyo: United Nations University Press.

Brown, L. R. 1981. *Building a Sustainable Society*. New York: Norton.

Brown, L. R., and E. C. Wolf. 1984. *Soil Erosion: Quiet Crisis in the World Economy*. Worldwatch Paper no. 60. Washington, D.C.: Worldwatch Institute.

Cairns, J. 1980. *The Recovery Process in Damaged Ecosystems*. Ann Arbor, Mich.: Ann Arbor Science.

Cairns, J., and K. L. Dickson. 1977. Recovery of streams from spills of hazardous materials. In *Recovery and Restoration of Damaged Ecosystems*, edited by J. Cairns et al., 24-42. Charlottesville: University Press of Virginia.

Cairns, J., K. L. Dickson, and E. E. Herricks. 1977. *Recovery and Restoration of Damaged Ecosystems*. Charlottesville: University Press of Virginia.

Clay, D. C., and L. A. Lewis. 1990. Land use, soil loss and sustainable agriculture in Rwanda. *Human Ecology* 18(2): 147-61.

Denevan, W. M. 1976. *The Native Population of the Americas in 1492*. Madison: University of Wisconsin Press.

———. 1989. The geography of fragile lands in Latin America. In *Fragile Lands of Latin America: Strategies for Sustainable Development*, edited by J. O. Browder, 11-24. Boulder, Colo.: Westview Press.

di Castri, F., and G. Glaser. 1980. Highlands and islands: Ecosystems in danger. *UNESCO Courier* 33(3): 6-11.

di Castri, F., A. J. Hansen, and M. M. Holland. 1988. A new look at ecotones: Emerging international projects on landscape boundaries. *Biology International*, special issue 17. Paris: International Union of Biological Sciences.

Dregne, H. E. 1983. *Desertification of Arid Lands*. New York: Academic Press.

Farnworth, E. G., and F. B. Golley. 1974. *Fragile Ecosystems: Evaluation of Research and Applications in the Neotropics*. New York: Springer.

Fearnside, P. M. 1987. Rethinking continuous cultivation in Amazonia. *BioScience* 37(3): 209-14.

Feierman, S. Forthcoming. Agriculture in the West Usumbara Mountains, 1920-80. In *Population Growth and Agricultural Change in Africa*, ed. B. L. Turner II, G. Hyden, and R. W. Kates. Gainesville: University Presses of Florida.

Food and Agriculture Organization (FAO). 1978. *Report on the Agro-Ecological Zones Project*. Vol. 1, *Methodology and Results for Africa*. Rome: FAO.

———. 1981. *Agriculture: Toward 2000*. Rome: FAO.

———. 1984. *Food, Land and People*. Rome: FAO.

Ford, R. E. Forthcoming. Marginal coping in extreme land pressures: Ruhengeri, Rwanda. In *Population Growth and Agricultural Change in Africa*, edited by B. L. Turner II, G. Hyden and R. W. Kates. Gainesville: University Presses of Florida.

Fosberg, F. R. 1963. *Man's Place in the Island Ecosystem*. Honolulu: Bishop Museum Press.

Gigon, A. 1984. Typology and principles of ecological stability and instability. In *Mountain Ecosystems: Stability and Instability*, edited by B. Messerli and J. D. Ives. N.p.: International Mountain Society, 1984.

Glantz, M. H. 1977. *Desertification: Environmental Degradation in and around Arid Lands*. Boulder, Colo.: Westview Press.

Glaser, G. 1983. Unstable and vulnerable ecosystems: A comment based on MAB research in island ecosystems. *Mountain Research and Development* 3(2): 121-23.

Glazovsky, N. F. Forthcoming. The Aral Sea. In *Critical Environmental Regions: International Comparisons*, edited by J. X. Kasperson, R. E. Kasperson, and B. L. Turner II. Tokyo: United Nations University Press.

Goldman, A. Forthcoming. Population growth and agricultural change in Imo State, southeastern Nigeria. In *Population Growth and Agricultural Change in Africa*, edited by B. L. Turner II, G. Hyden, and R. W. Kates. Gainesville: University Presses of Florida.

Golley, F., and M. Hadley. 1981. The tropical forest, a rich but fragile resource. *UNESCO Courier* 34(4): 13-16.

Goodman, D. 1975. The theory of diversity-stability relationships in ecology. *Quarterly Review of Biology* 50(3): 237-66.

Gow, D. 1989. Development of fragile lands: An integrated approach reconsidered. In *Fragile Lands of Latin America: Strategies for Sustainable Development*, edited by J. O. Browder, 25-43. Boulder, Colo.: Westview Press.

Hames, R. B., and W. T. Vickers. 1983. *Adaptive Responses of Native Amazonians*. New York: Academic Press.

Hansen, A. J., F. di Castri, and P. G. Risser. 1988. A new SCOPE project: Ecotones in a changing environment: The theory and management of landscape boundaries. *Biology International* 17:137-63.

Hecht, S. B. 1985. Environment, development and politics: Capital accumulation and the livestock sector in eastern Amazonia. *World Development* 13(6): 663-84.

———. 1989. The sacred cow in the green hell: Livestock and forest conversion in the Brazilian Amazon. *Ecologist* 19(6): 229-34.

Hecht, S. B., and A. Cockburn. 1989. *The Fate of the Forest*. London: Verso.

Hewitt, K. 1984. Ecotonal settlement and natural hazards in mountain regions: The case of earthquake risks. In *Mountain Ecosystems: Stability and Instability*, edited by B. Messerli and J. D. Ives. N.p.: International Mountain Society, 1984.

Hill, P. 1977. *Population, Prosperity and Poverty: Rural Kano, 1900 to 1970*. Cambridge: Cambridge University Press.

Holland, M. M. 1988. SCOPE/MAB technical consultations on landscape boundaries. *Biology International* 17:47-106.

Holling, C. S. 1973. Resilience and stability of ecological systems. *Annual Review of Ecology and Systematics* 4:1-23.

———. 1986. The resilience of terrestrial ecosystems: Local surprise and global change. In *Sustainable Development of the Biosphere*, edited by W. C. Clark and R. E. Munn, 292-316. Cambridge: Cambridge University Press.

Hong, J., Z. Peiyuan, Z. Du, and W. Fenghui. Forthcoming. Ordos Plateau. In *Critical Environmental Regions: International Comparisons*, edited by J. X. Kasperson, R. E. Kasperson, and B. L. Turner II. Tokyo: United Nations University Press.

Hrabovsky, J. P. 1985. Agriculture: The land base. In *The Global Possible*, edited by R. Repetto, 211-54. New Haven, Conn.: Yale University Press.

Hyden, G., R. W. Kates, and B. L. Turner II. Forthcoming. Beyond intensification. In *Population Growth and Agricultural Change in Africa*, edited by B. L. Turner II, G. Hyden, and R. W. Kates. Gainesville: University Presses of Florida, 1993.

International Food Policy Research Institute (IFPRI). *IFPRI Report 1990*. Washington, D.C.: IFPRI.

International Geosphere-Biosphere Program (IGBP). 1990. *The International Geosphere-Biosphere Programme: A Study of Global Change: The Initial Core Projects*. IGBP Global Change Report, no. 12. Royal Swedish Academy of Sciences Core Project no. 6. Stockholm: International Council of Scientific Unions/IGBP.

Ives, J. D. 1987. The theory of Himalayan environmental degradation: Its validity and application challenged by recent research. *Mountain Research and Development* 7(3).

Ives, J. D., and K. Hansen-Bristow. 1984. Stability and instability of natural and modified upper timberline landscapes in the Colorado Rocky Mountains, U.S.A. In *Mountain Ecosystems: Stability and Instability*, edited by Messerli and Ives. N.p.: International Mountain Society, 1984.

Ives, J. D., and B. Messerli. 1990. Progress in theoretical and applied mountain research, 1973-1989, and major future needs. *Mountain Research and Development* 10(2): 101-27.

Jodha, N. S. 1990a. *Rural Common Property Resources: Contributions and Crisis*. Foundation Day Lecture, May 16. New Delhi: Society for Promotion of Wastelands Development.

_____. 1990b. *Sustainable Agriculture in Fragile Resource Zones: Technological Imperatives*. Mountain Farming Systems Discussion Paper no. 3. Katmandu: International Center for Integrated Mountain Development.

_____. Forthcoming. The Nepal Middle Mountains. In *Critical Environmental Regions: International Comparisons*, edited by J. X. Kasperson, R. E. Kasperson, and B. L. Turner II. Tokyo: United Nations University Press.

Jones, J. R., and B. J. Wallace. 1986. *Social Sciences and Farming Systems Research*. Boulder, Colo.: Westview Press.

Juma, C. 1989. *The Gene Hunters: Biotechnology and the Scramble for Seeds*. Princeton, N.J.: Princeton University Press.

Kasperson, R. E., K. Dow, D. Golding, J. X. Kasperson, W. Meyer, R. C. Mitchell, S. Ratick, and B. L. Turner II. 1990. *Endangered and Critical Environmental Zones: Concepts and Distinctions*. ET Publication 90-03. Worcester, Mass.: Earth Transformed Program, Clark University.

Klages, K. H. W. 1949. *Ecological Crop Geography*. New York: Macmillan.

Kolasa, J., and S. T. A. Pickett. 1991. *Ecological Heterogeneity*. New York: Springer.

Kotlyakov, V. M. 1991. The Aral Sea basin: A critical environmental zone. *Environment* 33(1): 4-9, 36-38.

Lee, R. D. 1986. Malthus and Boserup: A dynamic synthesis. In *The State of Population Theory: Forward from Malthus*, edited by D. Coleman and R. Schofield, 96-130. London: Basil Blackwell.

Lele, U., and S. B. Stone. 1989. *Population Pressure, the Environment, and Agricultural Intensification: Variations on the Boserup Hypothesis*. Managing Agricultural Development in Africa (MADIA) Symposium. Washington, D.C.: World Bank.

Leonard, H. J. 1989. Environment and the poor: Development strategies for a common agenda. In *Environment and the Poor*, edited by H. J. Leonard, 3-45. New Brunswick, N.J.: Transaction Books.

Little, P. D., and M. M. Horowitz. 1987. Introduction: Social science perspectives on land, ecology, and development. In *Lands at Risk in the Third World*, edited by P. D. Little and M. M. Horowitz, 1-16. Boulder, Colo.: Westview Press.

Martin, S. M. 1988. *Palm Oil and Protest: An Economic History of the Ngwa Region, Southeastern Nigeria, 1800-1980*. Cambridge: Cambridge University Press.

_____. Forthcoming. From agricultural growth to stagnation: The case of the Ngwa, Nigeria, 1900-1980. In *Population Growth and Agricultural Change in Africa*, edited by B. L. Turner II, G. Hyden, and R. W. Kates. Gainesville: University Presses of Florida.

Mazambani, D. 1990. *Labor Migration Impacts on Communal Land Agriculture: Case Studies from Manicaland, Zimbabwe*. Ph.D. diss. Clark University, Worcester, Mass.

Messerli, B. 1982. The concept of stability and instability of mountain ecosystems derived from the Swiss MAB-6 studies of the Aletsch area. In *Mountain Ecosystems: Stability and Instability*, edited by B. Messerli and J. D. Ives. N.p.: International Mountain Society, 1984.

Micklin, P. P. 1988. Dessication of the Aral Sea: A water management disaster in the Soviet Union. *Science* 241:1170-76.

Moran, E. F. 1987. Monitoring fertility degradation of agricultural lands in the lowlands tropics. In *Lands at Risk in the Third World*, edited by P. D. Little and M. M. Horowitz, 69-91. Boulder, Colo.: Westview Press.

_____. 1990. *Ecosystems Approach in Anthropology*. Ann Arbor: University of Michigan Press.

Mortimore, M. 1989. *Adapting to Drought: Farmers, Famines and Desertification in West Africa.* Cambridge: Cambridge University Press.

———. Forthcoming. The intensification of Peri-Urban agriculture: The Kano Close-settled zone, 1964-1986. In *Population Growth and Agricultural Change in Africa,* edited by B. L. Turner II, G. Hyden, and R. W. Kates. Gainesville: University Presses of Florida.

Murdoch, W. W. 1975. Diversity, complexity, stability and pest control. *Journal of Applied Ecology* 12(3): 795-807.

Naiman, R. J., et al. 1988. A new UNESCO programme: Research and management of land/inland water ecotones. *Biology International* 17:107-36.

Netting, R. M. 1985. *Hill Farmers of Nigeria.* Seattle: University of Washington Press.

———. Forthcoming. Agricultural expansion, intensification, and market participation among the Kofyar, Jos Plateau, Nigeria. In *Population Growth and Agricultural Change in Africa,* edited by B. L. Turner II, G. Hyden, and R. W. Kates. Gainesville: University Presses of Florida.

Nicholaides, J. J., D. E. Bandy, P. A. Sanchez, J. R. Benites, J. H. Villachica, A. J. Coutu, and C. S. Valverde. 1985. Agricultural alternatives for the Amazon Basin. *BioScience* 35(5): 279-85.

Odum, E. P. 1983. *Basic Ecology.* Philadelphia: Saunders.

Okafor, F. C. Forthcoming. Agricultural stagnation and economic diversification: Awka-Nnewi Region, Nigeria, 1930-1980. In *Population Growth and Agricultural Change in Africa,* edited by B. L. Turner II, G. Hyden, and R. W. Kates. Gainesville: University Presses of Florida.

Oram, P. A. 1986. Combining socio-economic data with biophysical environmental data. In *Agricultural Environments, Characterization, Classification and Mapping,* edited by A. H. Bunting, 261-70. Wallingford, England: Commonwealth Agricultural Bureaux International.

———. 1988. Building the agroecological framework: Moving toward sustainability. *Environment* 30(9): 14-17, 30-36.

Papadakis, J. 1966. *Climates of the World and Their Agricultural Potentialities.* Buenos Aires: Papadakis.

Peters, C. M., A. H. Gentry, and R. O. Mendelsohn. 1989. Valuation of an Amazonian rainforest. *Nature* 399:655-56.

Pickett, S. T., and P. S. White. 1986. *The Ecology of Natural Disturbance and Patch Dynamics.* New York: Academic Press.

Pimm, S. L. 1984. The complexity and stability of ecosystems: Review article. *Nature* 307:321-26.

Pingali, P., Y. Bigot, and H. P. Binswanger. 1987. *Agricultural Mechanization and the Evolution of Farming Systems in Sub-Saharan Africa.* Baltimore, Md.: Johns Hopkins University Press.

Platt, R. B. 1977. Conference summary. In *Recovery and Restoration of Damaged Ecosystems,* edited by J. Cairns et al., 526-31. Charlottesville: University Press of Virginia.

Posey, D. A. 1985. Indigenous management of tropical forest ecosystems: The case of the Kayapo Indians of the Brazilian Amazon. *Agroforestry Systems* 3:139-58.

Potter, L., H. Brookfield, and Y. Byron. Forthcoming. The Sundaland region of Southeast Asia. In *Critical Environmental Regions: International Comparisons,* edited by J. X. Kasperson, R. E. Kasperson, and B. L. Turner II. Tokyo: United Nations Press.

Precoda, N. 1991. Requiem for the Aral Sea. *Ambio* 20(3-4): 109-14.

Ragaz, C. 1991. Food as a human right. Paper presented at the Second International Geophysical Union International Famine Workshop, Famine Vulnerability and Most Critical Regions/Places, October 28-November 3, 1991, El Minia, Egypt.

Rasool, S. I., and D. S. Ojima. 1989. *Pilot Studies for Remote Sensing and Data Management.* International Geosphere-Biosphere Program Global Change Report, no. 8. Royal Swedish Academy of Sciences. Stockholm: ICSU/IGBP.

Richards, P. 1985. *Indigenous Agricultural Revolution.* London: Hutchinson.

Riebsame, W. E. 1990. The United States Great Plains. In *The Earth as Transformed by Human Action: Global and Regional Changes in the Biosphere over the Past 300 Years*, edited by B. L. Turner II et al., 561-75. Cambridge: Cambridge University Press.

Rocheleau, D. E., P. A. Benjamin, and A. Diang'a. Forthcoming. The Ukambani region of Kenya. In *Critical Environmental Regions: International Comparisons*, edited by J. X. Kasperson, R. E. Kasperson, and B. L. Turner II. Tokyo: United Nations University Press.

Roosevelt, A. C. 1980. *Parmana: Prehistoric Maize and Manioc Subsistence along the Amazon and Orinoco.* New York: Academic Press.

Salati, E., M. J. Dourojeanni, F. C. Novaes, A. E. de Oliveira, R. W. Perritt, H. O. R. Schubart, and J. C. Umana. 1990. Amazonia. In *The Earth as Transformed by Human Action: Global and Regional Changes in the Biosphere over the Past 300 Years*, edited by B. L. Turner II et al., 480-93. Cambridge: Cambridge University Press.

Sanchez, P. A., et al. 1982. Amazon basin soils: Management for continuous crop production. *Science* 216:821-27.

Sanchez, P. A., and J. R. Benites. 1987. Low-input cropping for acid soils of the humid tropics. *Science* 238:1521-27.

Sanderson, S. N.d. Institutional dynamics behind land-use change. In *Global Land-Use/Cover Change*, edited by W. B. Meyer and B. L. Turner II. Boulder, Colo.: Office of Interdisciplinary Earth Studies.

Smith, N. J. H. 1982. *Rainforest Corridors: The Trans-Amazonian Colonization Scheme.* Berkeley: University of California Press.

Smith, N. J. H., P. Alvim, E. A. S. Serrão, and I. C. Falesi. Forthcoming. Amazonia. In *Critical Environmental Zones in Global Environmental Change*, edited by J. X. Kasperson, R. E. Kasperson, and B. L. Turner II. Tokyo: United Nations University Press.

Späth, H.-J. W. 1987. Dryland wheat farming on the central Great Plains: Sedgwick County, Northeast Colorado. In *Comparative Farming Systems*, edited by B. L. Turner II and S. B. Brush, 313-44. New York: Guilford Press.

Thorhaug, A. 1980. Recovery patterns of restored major plant communities in the United States: High to low altitude, desert to marine. In *The Recovery Process in Damaged Ecosystems*, edited by J. Cairns, 113-24. Ann Arbor, Mich.: Ann Arbor Science.

Turner, B. L., II, G. Hyden, and R. W. Kates, eds. Forthcoming. *Population Growth and Agricultural Change in Africa.* Gainesville: University Presses of Florida.

Turner, M. G. 1987. *Landscape Heterogeneity and Disturbance.* New York: Springer.

United Nations Conference on Desertification (UNCOD). 1977. *World Map of Desertification.* Nairobi: United Nations Environmental Program.

United Nations Educational, Scientific, and Cultural Organization (UNESCO). 1970. *Vegetation Map of the Mediterranean Zone: Explanatory Notes.* Paris: UNESCO; Rome: FAO.

———. 1973. *International Classification and Mapping of Vegetation.* Paris: UNESCO.

United States Council on Environmental Quality. 1980. *Global 2000.* Washington, D.C.: Government Printing Office.

Watts, M. J. 1983a. *Silent Violence: Food, Famine and Peasantry in Northern Nigeria.* Berkeley: University of California Press.

———. 1983b. Social theory and environmental degradation. In *Desert Development*, edited by Y. Gradus, 14-32. Dordrecht: Reidel.

Whittaker, R. H. 1975. *Communities and Ecosystems.* 2d ed. New York: Macmillan.

World Commission on Environment and Development (WCED). 1987. *Our Common Future.* Oxford: Oxford University Press.

Worster, D. 1979. *Dust Bowl: The Southern Great Plains in the 1930s.* New York: Oxford University Press.

Yodzis, P. 1980. The connectance of real ecosystems. *Nature* 284:544-45.

Young, A. 1986. Methods developed outside the international agricultural research system. In *Agricultural Environments: Characterization, Classification and Mapping*, edited by A. H. Bunting, 43-63. Farnham Royal, U.K.: CAB International.

CHAPTER 6

TALES OF DISSEMINATION IN AGRICULTURE

Judith Tendler

Sustainable agricultural development (SAD) seems to pose new challenges to agricultural research and extension. But much of what is required is really not that different from what was asked of these institutions 20 years ago, when they were expected to turn their attention to small farmers and small-farmer crops. Although there are, indeed, some important new twists—reduced use of chemical inputs, increased use of soil-conserving techniques—the "old" challenge is probably a more serious one because, in certain ways, it still hasn't been met. This is particularly the case in rainfed as opposed to irrigated agriculture, and in poorer regions—precisely those places where SAD has the most work to do.

Twenty years ago, under the name of agricultural and rural development, donors challenged research and extension agencies to be more responsive to applied problems, to get out of their offices and into the fields, and to work on the crops and problems of small farmers. Better collaboration between research and extension was deemed essential to these tasks, based on the plausible assumption that adoption and dissemination of improved agricultural varieties, inputs, and practices would not happen without such collaboration. Small farmers occupied center stage in these concerns—as they do today in SAD—because they produced a significant share of food supply in many regions and countries, particularly in the poorer ones. Just as they were seen to be key to reducing rural poverty and unemployment in the old version, they are seen today by SAD as key to reducing environmental degradation. SAD also goes one step beyond the "old" small-farmer focus by adding, as David Bell, William Clark, and Vernon Ruttan stress in chapter 14, a user-centered approach to service delivery in which the farmer rather than the extension worker stands at center stage.

There is nothing wrong with giving a new name—sustainable development—to something that is old, at least in some of its institutional implications. Indeed, renaming an old cause is a good way to provide new excitement and energy for working on difficult institutional problems for which disappointment and boredom have already set in. But the advantage of such a fresh start goes along with the danger of neglecting what was learned about these institutional challenges in their previous incarnation. Put more constructively, the task of SAD is not as daunting as it might seem, as long as we recognize that there is a rich 20-year history to draw upon in trying to understand how to do things right. A cautionary note, however, is in order. The past experience with agricultural and rural development shows that the standard approaches now being relied upon to build good institutions are not necessarily the right ones. Nor can it be assumed that we have correctly diagnosed exactly where the problem of poor institutional performance lies. Anyone doubting these judgments need simply look at the vast amount of evaluation work by donors and governments on agricultural research and extension projects in rainfed and poorer regions, as well as the even greater amount of unpublished material contained in monitoring reports on the various projects.[1] With respect to extension, moreover, no one can say that the problem is one of inadequate spending: by the beginning of the 1980s, low- and middle-income countries were already spending more on extension, as a proportion of their agricultural output, than high-income countries (Judd, Boyce, and Evenson, 1986).

All this is not to say that extension and research have not had some notable successes. The much-heralded dissemination and adoption of green-revolution technologies are testimony to this. And although the past 20 years of work on agricultural development in poor and rainfed regions may not add up to impressive aggregate increases in output, yields, and incomes, there are myriad minor successes coming out of this experience. But lackluster performance of extension and research seems to be more the rule than the exception in countries and regions most in need of SAD attention—where poverty predominates, where small farming is significant, and where environmental degradation is high.

Although the minor successes may not have produced dramatic and sustained impacts, they are numerous enough to add up to something significant in terms of institutional lessons. These should be of considerable use in thinking about the institutional form that SAD programs should take today. With just such a purpose in mind, I have studied a 15-year experience with nine rural development projects targeted on small farmers in Northeast Brazil—a poor, semiarid region of 45 million people.[2] The projects represented an investment of U.S. $3.1 billion, jointly funded by the Brazilian government and the World Bank.[3]

From this history, I identified roughly a dozen cases in which large numbers of small farmers had adopted an improved variety or agricultural practice with significant impacts on productivity and microregional output. I traced back in time the story of each particular case—from adoption to dissemination, field testing, and research—and looked at the patterns that emerged across this set of cases. Asking researchers and informants about the most significant instances of dissemination in their memory, of course, brought forth some cases and some earlier periods in time that did not belong to that particular set of nine projects.

The results of this exercise were surprising in three ways. First, the paths that led from research to adoption, and the institutional arrangements they reflected, differed significantly from the way we currently design agricultural extension and research programs—or think they should be designed. Second, some of the intractable problems often identified as impeding successful research and extension—like ongoing lack of coordination between extension and research—still existed in the success stories and, hence, did not apparently stand in their way. Third, the dissemination stories reported below show that demand-side factors—particularly "user" agencies—played major roles in driving research and extension to do better. But agricultural programs generally take a "supply-side" approach to improving the quality of research and extension, focusing mainly on building up the capacity of these organizations with direct funding and technical assistance. And to the extent that user perspectives are now of concern to SAD planners, they have focused on final farmer-users rather than intermediate users like other public agencies.

Although the results of my research in Brazil are not necessarily conclusive or generalizable, they certainly show that there is still a lot to be learned by simply looking for patterns in what has already worked well. Many other third-world countries, moreover, designed agricultural research and extension institutions in ways quite similar to Brazil, mainly because of the homogenizing influence of years of technical assistance and funding from first-world countries. Finally, much of what is reported below relates to the behavior of organizations, whether in agriculture or other sectors and whether in poor countries or rich. Indeed, some of the findings might not be surprising to a student of the literature of organizational behavior who didn't know much about agriculture or underdevelopment.

On the one hand, then, we cannot assume that SAD presents a largely new task for which we have to devise new institutional models. On the other hand, we cannot assume that the way we think about agricultural research and extension today—at least as embodied in the current crop of agricultural and rural development projects—is adequate to carry us into the era of sustainable agricultural development.

The Trouble with Research and Extension

The problems facing agricultural research and extension systems in Northeast Brazil, as well as the explanations given for disappointing results, sound quite similar to those reported for many other countries.[4] Namely, and to start out, observers of the research and extension experience in rainfed and poorer regions have been disappointed with the performance of agriculture and the lack of productivity increases over the last 10 to 20 years. When increases in output did occur, they were said to result "only" from increases in acreage planted rather than from the increases in yield that extension and research were supposed to make possible.

More often than not, the finger of blame for these disappointing outcomes has been pointed at the state agencies in charge of agricultural extension and research. Research was said to be "too academic," not concerned about small-farm crops and practices, not sufficiently engaged in field testing and adaptation of its findings, and not interested in collaborating with the extension service in the interests of dissemination. Extension agents, in turn, "had nothing to extend," and their experience and in-service training were deemed inadequate; they spent more time in their offices than in the field, often processing the paperwork for credit applications for their clients. They "didn't know anything" about what research was doing. And they were chronically short of what they needed in order to do extension—vehicles, funds for fuel and vehicle maintenance, and per diems to travel. These essential latter expenditures were more vulnerable to fiscal crises and shortfalls than were payrolls for extension personnel.

The exceptions reviewed here did not fit the model of agricultural innovation and diffusion implicit in some of the critiques and concerns listed above. First, extension was not necessarily the agency that carried out the dissemination or caused it to occur. Second, research was not necessarily the institution that carried out the field trials and the adaptation that facilitated widespread adoption. Third, some of the agencies involved in the successful disseminations had actually received consistently poor grades on their overall performance in both ex ante and ex post evaluations by donor agencies. Fourth, the forward movement that carried research from basic findings to field testing, adaptation, and dissemination was not necessarily the result of "collaboration" between research and extension; when it was, the collaboration often occurred only around that particular successful episode, and was not the working style of those two agencies. Fifth, and finally, the two widely disseminated mechanical innovations discussed below—the cistern and the animal traction implements—turned out to be unsuitable for adoption when first released by the research agency; only the last-minute and makeshift adaptive work by the frustrated user agencies made these innovations adoptable.

What did bring about these dissemination successes, if it wasn't good research and extension agencies doing what they were supposed to do? If the same agencies that didn't collaborate, didn't field test, and didn't have anything "to extend" could suddenly change their character, this suggests that part of the problem had to do with something outside the agencies rather than with their inherent capacity. Common to all the exceptions, as the cases presented below demonstrate, was a quite different set of demands and incentives that surrounded these better-performing episodes.

The cases illustrating these points fall into two categories: (1) those that involved campaigns against crop disease and pests and (2) those that did not.

Diseases, Pests, and Other Scourges

Several of the successes in the dissemination of improved varieties resulted from an attempt to control disease or pests in existing plantings. During these episodes, the way extension and research customarily operated changed radically. Two cases are used for illustration here—oranges in the state of Sergipe and cotton in several of the Northeast states.

In all these cases, the successfully disseminated new varieties had desirable productivity-increasing traits beyond their resistance to disease, but the extension service had not been successful at promoting them earlier or had made only half-hearted attempts. The new orange variety ("pear" orange) was not only disease-resistant, for example, but was a juice variety ("Bahia" orange), as opposed to the eating variety that was the only one cultivated previously; this facilitated the establishment of a juice-processing industry in the region, which, in turn, ended up exporting frozen orange juice to Europe and the United States—a first for this very small state.

The new cotton variety was desirable not only for its resistance to the boll weevil, but also for the switch it required from perennial to annual cotton. The perennial plant had been associated with a tradition of low-productivity joint production with extensive livestock (which fed on the leavings of the cotton tree after the harvest) and sharecropper production of interplanted annual subsistence crops. Prior to the campaigns against disease or pests, the productivity of these crops had been stagnant or even declining. Producers were in a kind of low-productivity equilibrium, with state governments not able or worried enough to do anything about it.

The successful disseminations resulting from the disease and pest campaigns all achieved their results in a relatively short period of time. In Sergipe, almost all orange growers switched from the disease-prone eating variety to the disease-resistant juice variety within three to four years. Cotton production, after falling drastically in the mid-1980s, regained its earlier production levels within four or five years, although only in some states. Most of these cases, in addition, involved cash crops that were already being produced by small farmers, but not exclusively by them. That is, the successful cases did not involve the introduction of new crops, as is frequently attempted by extension programs. Finally, the agricultural agencies of the state governments—agricultural planning, extension, research, credit, input supply, seed production and supply—all played a strong role in mounting the disease- or pest-combating campaigns. They acted with a remarkable degree of coordination and dynamism—exactly what they were faulted for lacking in prior evaluation reports.

The Mysterious Case of the Good Credit Subsidy

Just as striking as the findings laid out above, these interventions involved an unusual combination of high subsidy and high discipline, which forced the adoption of the new variety. First, farmers received credit at low or negative real interest rates—although no lower than the prevailing rates on official agricultural credit—to buy certified seeds, rootstock, or seedlings and fertilizer and pesticide applicators, and to eradicate diseased plants and put in new ones. Second, the banks, the extension service, and the research agency carefully monitored the uses to which the credit could be put. Borrowers had to show certificates proving they had purchased the approved variety and applied the requisite fertilizer, or they received credit only in kind, in the form of the recommended inputs. Third, in several cases, the state held monopoly control over inputs. In Sergipe, for example, the agricultural experiment station was able to control the quality of seedlings available in the state's private nurseries by virtue of the fact that (a) the station was the sole source of the rootstock used to make the graft (from a lemon tree), and (b) the station itself had been responsible for the development of a private nursery sector in the state, previously nonexistent, in that it had selected and trained 60 small farmers to produce the certified seedlings. Fourth, the subsidy had automatic "sunset" provisions—to be terminated when the disease problem was overcome.

In the above stories, in sum, subsidized credit (1) focused on a campaign to solve a problem with a particular crop and over a fixed time period; (2) forced changes in cultivation practices and input use that would be automatically self-sustaining, once the subsidy and strong control were dropped in a later period; and (3) came with a strong controlling presence from the state's agricultural agencies—a kind of carrot-and-stick approach. These features contrast sharply with the way agricultural credit and other inputs have been typically subsidized in Brazil and many other countries—namely, indefinitely, across the board, and with little or no performance demands placed on those receiving the subsidy. The more typical agricultural-credit subsidies have tended to be all carrot, in other words, and no stick.[5] More generally, these attributes of success also contrast sharply with some of the current policy wisdom against the use of subsidies in agriculture. The distinction made here between carrot-only and carrot-and-stick, however, is critical. It is not usually taken into account in the current versions of policy advice, which point to subsidized credit as the culprit for much of agriculture's problems.

Negative Externalities, Self-Targeting, and Sheer Mission

Unlike most programs focused on small farmers, the disease and pest campaigns were also of great concern to medium and larger farmers, to the extent that they produced the same crop. This resulted, of course, from the negative externalities of contagious crop disease and pest infestation: if small farmers were not included in the public assistance efforts, infestation in their crops would ultimately spread to the larger farmers. This meant that the campaigns were backed by stronger interest-group support and, hence, greater political power than the typical program focused exclusively on small farmers. At the same time, the campaigns did not follow the course of many untargeted agricultural programs, in which subsidized services and inputs had ended up largely in the hands of larger farmers.

Although the negative externalities of crop infestation helped to keep larger farmers from looking after only their own interests, this outcome was also clearly influenced by an increasing awareness of small-farmer issues and economics among the Northeast's agricultural technocrats. In particular, the disease campaigns took into account the fact that small farmers faced higher prices for purchase of small volumes of pesticides and medicines (these higher prices often prevented small farmers from adopting disease- and pest-eradicating measures) and that they had little access to information about pesticide-applying equipment and its proper use. In the state of Pernambuco, for example, the state organized small "brigades" to distribute a weevil-fighting package to groups of small farmers, paying one farmer to be trained as a brigade leader in the proper use of the pesticide applicator. In Sergipe, the state worked partly through two cooperatives of small orange-growing farmers, also using "brigades." In all these cases, the state agencies made special efforts with small farmers because, as they said, they had to do something more aggressive—if they were to control the weevil—than "simply let the word out" through the extension system. The externalities of disease and pest infestations, then, provided these particular episodes with the best of both worlds: they garnered public support from small *and* larger farmers and, hence, from important political actors—while at the same time keeping larger farmers away because of a project design that was of practical use only to small farmers. And small farmers could be "self-targeted" without all the costs and problems of administrative targeting inherent in many such projects.

Finally, the public figures and agency managers who led the disease campaigns had a strong sense of mission because the problem threatened to undermine the economy of certain microregions, regions, or even whole states. Sergipe's experiment station in Boquim, which spearheaded the dissemination of the disease-resistant orange variety, wanted Sergipe to "beat the competition"—namely, the large and neighboring state of Bahia, at that time a significant producer of oranges, and from whence the improved orange variety had originally come. The small group of agricultural researchers who managed the station referred to themselves as "sons of Boquim"—proud of their region, wanting it to progress, taking responsible positions in the local orange-producer association and in town government. They also wanted to "show up the Bahians"—whom they considered to be "lazier" than Sergipans. Adding to this sense of mission around disease eradication were two small-farmer cooperatives, discussed below, that were eager to act as agents of dissemination for the new variety. The experiment station, in turn, saw its interest in dissemination served by working hand in hand with the cooperatives.

The Boquim station's sense of strong regional identification and developmental mission drew it out of its experimental plots and into the fields of growers—in a way that was unusual for agricultural researchers. Similarly, although on a wider scale, concern for the fate of "Northeast cotton" provided drama to the boll-weevil eradication campaign, since cotton production was an important part of the agricultural economy of several Northeast states.[6] *Not* doing anything about the boll weevil or orange disease, in other words, involved high costs to the state or microregional economy—or it meant foregoing attractive market opportunities for agricultural growth. Much of the work of agricultural research and extension agencies—multifaceted and dispersed—is not blessed with the driving force of this kind of strong regional identification and high-level worry about a particular crop.

The Transformation of Work

The disease campaigns transformed the system of incentives and penalties under which agricultural agencies typically work. The characteristics of this transformed work style and work environment, it turns out, were quite similar to those of the successful dissemination episodes not related to disease.

Extension and research typically work on several fronts at once — many crops, many inputs, many special programs, and many different specializations. Given all this choice between crops and activities at any particular time, the agencies pay more attention to one crop or problem than another, depending on the circumstances of the moment — or, simply, on the preferences and expertise of the head of a particular local extension office. Often, the agencies do not have clear and confident proposals about dealing with "low productivity," nor do they have firm control over the supply of inputs that is usually required to get a "modernizing" technology to be adopted widely. The performance of agricultural agencies, moreover, is customarily judged in terms of inputs rather than outputs — number of farmers visited, farmers attending courses, field trials, and demonstration plots, rather than rates of adoption of new varieties, observed yield increases, or transformations of the local agricultural economy. The agencies suffer no particular penalties for failure to perform in these latter areas, nor is their behavior driven in any way by fear of the consequences of poor performance.

Disease campaigns change all this. The epidemic dictates the crop, the problem, the region, the package of inputs and practices that *have* to be applied, and these are dependent on the cooperation of the input-supply network — temporarily narrowing down the work agenda to one crop and to a specific problem with that crop, and assuring adequate funding for recurrent expenditures. The disease problem itself stipulates an activity with a clear beginning and an end — eradication or substitution of the diseased plants with the improved ones. And the end can be reached, usually, within a period of time shorter than the five-to-eight-year life span of many agricultural or rural development projects. The antidisease package also takes a more concrete form — seeds, rootstock, or seedlings and fertilizer, pesticide, and pesticide applicators — than the changes in cultivation practices that often dominate the recommendations made by extension agents to small farmers.

The disease problem itself is more clearly measurable than the problems research and extension usually work on, and the "end" is marked by an ascertainable event that involves outputs rather than inputs — namely, the number of diseased trees eradicated, the number of acres planted in the new variety, reduced incidence of the pest in the region, or increases in output of that crop. Conversely, failure to perform is measurable and conspicuous—continued high levels of disease or pest incidence and continued declines in production.

The costs of bad performance are also clear, as is their incidence. Growers suffer losses of income, and, just as important for mobilizing state action, the state or the region suffers from the decline of an important economic activity—declining tax revenues, declining employment and its attendant social problems, and declining incomes for an important constituency. Civic leaders fear the loss of a sense of regional self in places where economic, social, and cultural traditions are defined by long association with a particular crop, like cotton in the Northeast states. Regions that find themselves on a roll with a relatively new crop—like oranges in Sergipe—see their visions of a dynamic future dashed if they don't act rapidly.

All this adds up to a more compelling force to bring about changed farming practices than a promise of "increased yields" by the extension service. Whereas the yield-increasing package promises to improve income, the antidisease package promises to cut impending losses and thereby keep income from *falling*. The subsidies built into the disease package, and the reduction in transaction costs to adopting farmers brought about by the temporarily heavy presence of the state in the disease-stricken zone, reduce the costs of adoption significantly in comparison with more normal times. This helps explain why states and growers who had done little for years about low productivity in certain crops could be jolted into highly effective action that, among other things, succeeded in transforming agriculture.

The literature of induced innovation stresses the importance of powerful grower groups in determining the paths taken by agricultural research.[7] But in the epidemics of disease and pests, the independent concern of state and regional actors about the fate of the regional economy and declining tax receipts seemed at least as important as grower demands themselves. Granted, the literature of public choice also shows how third-world states have acted independently of farmer interests in order to raise revenues. But this literature focuses exclusively on how such state actions *penalize* agriculture.[8] With the disease campaigns, in contrast, the state's worries about raising tax revenues led to actions that *favored* agriculture.

Up from Mediocrity

The disease campaigns reveal successful performance coming from mediocre institutions. This mystery requires explaining. Just as perplexing, although not presented here, is the sudden fall into dark times of public agencies that seemed to have finally arrived at responsible and effective behavior. These kinds of reverses, apparent in almost any set of monitoring reports that covers many years of an agency's performance, belie some of our thinking about institution building in the public sector of developing countries. The thinking assumes, understandably, that many years of patient support will translate gradually and cumulatively into permanent competence.

The implicit "cumulative" model behind institution-building programs is clearly visible, among other places, in the project documentation for many agricultural and rural development projects. It surfaces particularly in the frequent requests for longer implementation periods—from five to eight years, for example, in rural development projects—and for follow-up projects. Institution building, these justifications typically state, takes more time and care than we thought; things are proceeding slowly, but they are not yet there. In contrast to this slow-building picture, however, the disease stories involve abrupt jolts from mediocrity into success, not linear upward progress—as well as some periodic lapses back into mediocrity. Similarly, and from a different part of the world, the extension agencies that participated in the highly successful dissemination of green-revolution varieties in South Asia looked listless and mediocre immediately *before* that period.[9]

One possible explanation of successful performance coming from mediocre institutions is that the task during the successful episode is somehow different from what the organization was usually doing. This kind of success would be less the result of a change in the capacity of the agency or its leadership than of a change in the nature of the demands made on it. Correspondingly, mediocre performance might also be explained in these terms—at least partially. The distinction is an important one because it suggests that we need to rethink the model of institution building that assumes steady cumulative growth.

If all that was necessary to produce the dissemination successes of the disease campaigns was the final "pull" of a state concerned about disease, does that mean that Northeast research and extension were doing fine all along, the poor grades notwithstanding? Another possible explanation of sudden good performance, in other words, is that the agencies were actually doing something right all along, including during the mediocre period. Without the benefit of hindsight arising from the successful episode, this "something" wouldn't get noticed and evaluators would have no reason to interpret anything about the generally mediocre agency as "right." In order to fully understand the lessons of the dissemination successes, then, it is as important to understand what was being done right during these longer, quieter periods as during the more dramatic episodes.

The point of looking for the antecedents to success in prior mediocre times is not to say that what looked mediocre was actually excellent—although that is one conceivable result of such a retrospective exploration in any particular case. Although the successful episodes may all exhibit a distinct pattern of short duration, narrowing, concreteness, high penalties for failure, and easily measurable output, this may be only half the story. The more difficult part to discern, and program for, may be the ongoing qualities of an organization that allow the flares of success to occur in the first place. Laying so much stress on the nature of these episodes, then, is not to argue that an enduring agency can be built only by arranging a long string of such episodes—although that might not be a bad way to start.

It is not obvious, in sum, how to integrate the successful with the mediocre, and the episodic with the ongoing, in a viable institution-building strategy. More could be learned about the issue, as a start, by asking evaluation officers and researchers to routinely identify at least one antecedent to a current success in a former period of mediocrity. This would help us to construct a model of institution building that is closer to reality than the linear model underlying our project designs today.

Dissemination without Disease

Ideally, of course, we would not want to wait for crop disease and pest infestations before mounting successful programs of agricultural assistance to small farmers, although focusing on disease and pests in this way would certainly not be a bad start. But it turns out that infestation was not always necessary to achieve these kinds of results. The patterns running across the *non*disease cases of successful dissemination share certain similarities with the disease cases and help explain what causes widespread dissemination of research findings to occur. In brief, the experience reported below suggests that—as in the disease episodes—the problem of agricultural research and extension lies partly *outside* these institutions: they have not been subjected to enough demands for results from users and others who do care about dissemination. Note, again, the difference of this perspective from the typical approach to institution building and technical assistance.

The latter devotes considerable time and energy to convincing the institutions *themselves* to care more and spend more on field testing and adoption—rather than seeking out and supporting those already so inclined.

Several examples are drawn on for illustration in this section: (1) the development and dissemination, by an experiment station in Belém do São Francisco in the state of Pernambuco, of an industrial tomato suitable for irrigated cultivation in the Petrolina-Juazeiro region of the São Francisco River Valley (Bahia-Pernambuco), a region that is now considered to be one of the only agricultural growth-pole successes of the Northeast; (2) the development and widespread dissemination throughout the Northeast of an early-maturing dwarf cashew variety by the state research agency in Ceará; (3) the development of a fungus-resistant black bean by an experimental station of the state research agency of Pernambuco, widely adopted in the nearby black-bean-growing Irecê region of Bahia; (4) the widespread dissemination in Sergipe of research findings of the Boquim experiment station on the interplanting of cassava and passion fruit with orange trees; (5) the field testing and adaptation of improved varieties of vegetables by the Limoeiro experiment station in an area of Pernambuco between the humid coast and the semiarid interior, widely adopted in that region by small farmers, and most dramatically represented in the intensive cultivation of lettuce, green onions, and cilantro in the Natuba Valley; (6) the dissemination throughout the Northeast of a cistern for holding rainwater, developed by the Center for Research on Dryland Tropical Agriculture (CPATSA) in Petrolina, Pernambuco—part of the national system of agricultural research centers (EMBRAPA) specializing in particular crops; (7) the field testing and adaptation by the Pernambuco project unit of implements for animal traction, also developed by CPATSA; and (8) the modification, field testing, and adaptation of the standards used for transformers connecting small-farmer irrigators to the electric power net, carried out by the Brazilian National Development Bank (BNDES) in conjunction with a local organization in the southern state of Rio Grande do Sul; this led to a transformation of small-farm agriculture in that region from dryland to irrigated cultivation and a nationwide change in official standards used by power utilities, making connections easier and less costly for small irrigators.

As with the disease episodes, the "pull" of demanders stands out in these stories. In the case of the industrial tomato, large food-processing firms in São Paulo contributed, along with the university there, to financing an industrial-tomato research project at the Belém do Sao Francisco experiment station. The Arcoverde experiment station in Pernambuco, which came up with one of the most applied small-farmer-oriented research agendas in the state, did so only after being invaded by a group of peasant farmers of the area; they would not leave the station, they said, until the station's management would hammer out a research agenda that was more relevant to small-farmer needs. The project-coordinating unit in Pernambuco, under heavy pressure from the governor to "do something for small farmers," put together a set of teams to do "quick-and-dirty" assessments, county by county, of crop problems and potential bottleneck-breaking interventions; out of these assessments came a set of applied, miniresearch tasks—with dissemination and "short-term results" within a crop cycle or two being the specified end products.

The most influential demanders behind the successful disseminations were (1) other public agencies themselves, or individuals or groups of individuals within them; (2) medium-size commercial farmers who produced the same crop as the small farmers (oranges in Boquim, black beans in Irecê, cotton in various states) and who, as local elites, had a strong influence on experiment stations in their region and other field offices of state agencies; (3) elected leaders— governors, legislators, mayors—who increasingly viewed small farmers as an important constituency and who were looking desperately for "productive" approaches to rural poverty, which was becoming more and more of a fiscal and political burden on their administrations; (4) the World Bank, which, by insisting on a small-farmer orientation in a large investment program over many years, had empowered a generation of government technicians sympathetic to these concerns and had given them considerable project experience in this area; *and* (5)—last and, unfortunately, least—small farmers. The rest of this chapter treats these different forms of demand—from other public agencies, from local actors other than farmer-users, and from small-farmer groups themselves. It closes with a discussion of issues of "supply."

The Case of the Inadequate Innovation

The dissemination of the CPATSA cistern originated in a visit by the governor of Sergipe, shortly after his election, to the CPATSA research center. What did they have "on the shelf," he asked, that would have the biggest impact on the semiarid region? CPATSA strongly recommended its cistern, yet to be disseminated. The governor enthusiastically adopted the cistern and embarked on a program to install it throughout his small state—an effort that was subsequently picked up by other Northeast states to the point that CPATSA now considers its cistern to be its most widely disseminated innovation. But when the state's rural water agency started installing the cistern, it turned out to be technically flawed. CPATSA had clearly not done the field testing and adaptation. Caught in the middle of a highly publicized program to supply water to poor rural households, the Sergipe governor and his water agency could not simply retreat. So the water agency itself carried out the testing and adaptation that CPATSA should have, and came up with an improved model that was also only two-thirds the cost of the CPATSA version.[10]

A similar chain of events with another mechanical innovation of CPATSA occurred in Pernambuco. One of the project-unit managers took the latest in animal-traction implements from CPATSA. But when the unit tried to introduce this innovation to the small farmers of the region (where CPATSA was actually located), they rejected it because it was too cumbersome to use and was designed for two animals rather than one; this doubled the requirements for capital and grazing land, a significant burden for poor farmers. The project unit, anxious to get results and not go back to the drawing board at CPATSA, consulted with farmers in the region about the necessary adaptations, and then contracted out iterations of the suggested changes to a local blacksmith. This kind of field testing and adaptation is, of course, what the research center should itself have done before releasing the implement package.

If the user agencies had known that the package they carried away from CPATSA was inadequate, they may not have taken it in the first place. Only because they were caught in a process of having to show results, and were intensely interested in doing so, did they finish what CPATSA had left undone. They valued the returns to be had from testing and adaptation more highly than did the research agency, whose performance was not judged by standards of adoption and dissemination.[11]

When Research Disseminates

There is nothing like a major research breakthrough to make research more interested in dissemination. In these cases, in a sense, research itself becomes a "demander" of dissemination. The research agencies and individual researchers who made significant breakthroughs—like Ceará's dwarf cashew and disease-resistant banana, Boquim's improved orange, and Belém do São Francisco's industrial tomato—were fiercely proud of them. They wanted to get their due credit and show their results off as much as possible—and hence to be conspicuously present in the dissemination effort. At these moments, and around these particular breakthroughs, research lost its reclusive character. Word of its breakthrough spread rapidly in the informal research and extension networks throughout the entire region—not just inside the state—and extension agents appeared from all over with requests for the new variety.

Examples are not difficult to find. When some of Bahia's extensionists heard about Ceará's breakthrough in cashew, they rented a truck out of their own money and drove there to buy as many of the new seedlings as they could; extensionists from the Irecê region in Bahia swarmed around the Belém do São Francisco research station in Pernambuco to acquire its new fungus-resistant black bean variety, about which word had also spread quickly; and when the Paraíba project unit was looking for something to improve productivity among the small banana producers of the project region, they heard about Ceará's disease-resistant variety and contacted that center directly.

Many of the stories about successful research findings and their dissemination started, actually, with a telephone call by a researcher or extensionist to a colleague in a sister institution *outside* the state. And a majority of these calls even went outside the Northeast region to Piracicaba in São Paulo, where the country's most prestigious state research institute, ESALQ (Escola Superior de Agricultura Luíz Queiróz), was located. This latter pattern, by the way, suggests that there are strong institutional "spread effects" from the richer part of the country to the poorer, contrary to the common portrayal of the Northeast as stagnant and isolated from the dynamism of the more developed part of Brazil.

The cross-state paths of dissemination also revealed a pattern of implicit specialization by state research agencies—Ceará for dwarf cashew and banana, Boquim in Sergipe for oranges, Belém do São Francisco in Pernambuco for black beans and industrial tomatoes. But the model of agricultural extension and research behind the typical agricultural development project does not go with this grain. As occurred in the Northeast, each project tries to build up a self-contained research-and-extension establishment within each state or region, with a broad agenda of crops and activities, and each project tries to forge a collaborative link between extension and research within that area. But in these cases, successful dissemination involved intense episodic interaction between extension and research (or research and research) across states and even outside the region. This went along with, or was a result of, a kind of informal specialization in certain crops or varieties by particular state research agencies.

These cross-state collaborations and disseminations represent moments when research wants to be more applied and open and when extension is enthusiastic about collaborating. SAD planners should try to support these kinds of moments and wants. But the current form of institutional support to research and extension agencies usually does not build on comparative advantage that develops among state research agencies. It does not assist state research centers to spill their most impressive successes beyond state borders, and it does not encourage the informal exchanges of information between states, and particularly between poorer regions and richer regions, that were crucial to many of the dissemination successes studied here. Instead, project designers might make funds available to research agencies for choosing one or two of their *already proven* successes and doing more applied and dissemination work with only them. This would amount to funding research centers for particular tasks in which they already had a strong interest.

The Local Connection

Local actors and institutions played an important role in the cases of successful dissemination—mayors and municipal governments, vocational schools, Rotary clubs, cooperatives. In many cases, the important local actors were researchers at experiment stations who were born or raised in the area, or who had lived for many years there. They also played important civic roles in their towns—they were perhaps small commercial farmers themselves, officers in local civic associations, or even mayors. They worked to promote the development of their municipality or region in general, and their interest in disseminating improved varieties and practices came out of a larger passion for bringing "development" to where they lived.

The director of the Boquim experiment station, for example, came from an orange-grower family, organized and headed the regional association of orange growers, and ultimately became a dynamic mayor of the municipality of Boquim. He was born and raised in Boquim and was fiercely loyal to the region. Similarly, the president of a successful cooperative in the Irecê region of Bahia came from a prominent commercial farming family in the region; he had a university degree in agronomy from the state capital, but had moved back to the more provincial Irecê to teach at the agricultural vocational school there, rather than at a university. He used the school and his classes as a miniexperiment station for testing varieties and practices that he then disseminated to small farmers through the cooperative.

Finally, the success of the Brazilian National Development Bank (BNDES) in coming up with workable standards for the transformers for small irrigation pumps, and in getting them accepted by the state utility, depended on the enthusiastic participation of engineers teaching at the *local* vocational school, far from the capital city and its prestigious engineering university. They viewed the small-farmer irrigation project as having the potential to significantly improve agriculture in their region, as well as the incomes of landless farmers. The BNDES had previously tried in vain to interest the engineering department of the state university to do this work under contract; it ended up, as a "second-best" approach, contracting the engineering teachers of the local vocational school instead, who were keen to work on the problem because of its significance for agricultural development in their region.

The local institutions of these stories were less sophisticated and prestigious than the institutions through which donor-funded agricultural programs usually fund and try to influence research in a more dissemination-oriented direction—state and federal research centers, universities, state extension services. The more modest local actors were eager to do the work because they were interested in the fortunes of their region and because their prestige and status came from making things work where they lived. Applied work was not secondclass for them, as it was for research institutions.

Another variation on the theme of strong local actors and strong demanders comes from the Boquim experiment station in the Tabuleiros Sul region of Sergipe. That station played a central role not only in developing and disseminating improved varieties of oranges and the crops interplanted with it, but also in lobbying to bring juiceprocessing firms into the region and securing public subsidies for them. Ultimately, this made it possible for the region to tap into the lucrative export market for frozen orange juice.

In contrast to most experiment stations in the Northeast, the origins of the Boquim station were in dissemination, and not in research—a fluke of that region's particular history. The station was set up in the early 1970s as a mere "promotion station" for the new improved orange variety developed in the 1960s by the citrus research center at Cruz das Almas, in the neighboring state of Bahia. (At that time, the region around Cruz das Almas also grew oranges.) As a result of these applied beginnings, and the central role played by oranges in the dynamic expansion of the Tabuleiros Sul region, Boquim's subsequent research always had an applied style.

The Boquim station's sequence of institutional growth—"backing into" research from promotion—is just the opposite of the approach taken by those designing agricultural research and extension programs. The latter try to push research agencies to move "forward" into more applied work. But whereas Boquim's origins and concerns caused it to place a high value on moving from application to research, there is nothing about the origins of most agricultural research centers that would draw them from research toward promotion.

The Boquim story, together with those told above of the CPATSA cistern and animal-traction implements, contains two lessons. The *first* is that supporting the more applied agencies to do field testing and adaptation may be a more effective way of bringing about the promotion and dissemination of research results than trying to cajole research institutions themselves into being more applied. The *second* is that researchers are more likely to be interested in applied work the more they identify with and are involved in local development struggles. Researchers like these become the "demanders" of applied work because of their combined roles as researchers and civic leaders, promoters of local development, and local growers.

Local Elites Revisited

The importance of local boosterism in some of these stories of agricultural dissemination raises another set of issues. The "boosterists" who drove the search for better agriculture and its dissemination were local elites—university-trained agronomists who were sons of medium farmers in the region, locally born and bred agricultural professionals working in the field offices of state agricultural agencies, teachers in local vocational schools, and mayors. But project designers concerned about poverty have often shied away from local elites for two reasons: (1) given the chance, local elites have tended to appropriate the benefits of targeted projects and often act against the interests of small farmers and the poor, and (2) local government, as run by these elites, has tended to use such programs for political purposes and to be technically and administratively weak. Central and state government agencies carrying out agricultural and rural projects, therefore, often talk of bypassing local government and local elites in order to work "directly with the poor"—cooperatives, farmers' associations, and rural labor unions.

The fear that local elites and better-off farmers will divert programs away from the target group is well founded. The evaluation literature is replete with case studies documenting this problem.[12] The lesson to be learned from the presence of local elites in the dissemination success stories, then, is not simply that important local actors should be allowed to occupy more space in these projects. A closer look at the successes shows that, in addition, two other factors pushed them in a small-farmer direction. Briefly, (1) although the activity benefited large farmers, it also automatically benefited small farmers, sometimes even to the point that larger farmers could not benefit *without* the participation of small farmers (examples follow), and (2) the more centralized state-level programs offered strong incentives to local actors to move their activities toward small farmers.

The kinds of cases in which small farmers can benefit from interventions that help medium farmers who are also local elites, as illustrated in the cases discussed so far, fall into the following categories: (1) small and medium farmers produced the same crop and in the same way—oranges in Boquim (interplanted rather than monocropped by small *and* medium farmers), cashews in Ceará, black beans in Irecê; (2) disease or pest problems became epidemic and, as discussed previously, could not be wiped out without the participation of *all* farmers—as in the cases of the cotton boll weevil and orange disease in Sergipe; (3) public-good type investments (particularly roads) were undertaken that benefited all, and, because of their reduction of transport costs, local elites often voluntarily contributed financing; and (4) better-off farmers actually contributed assets because they were offered something by the state that they could not get on their own.[13]

What made the stories of successful dissemination work for small farmers, in sum, was not just the prominence of civic-minded local elites. There are too many stories to the contrary to draw that conclusion—namely, cases where local elites appropriated benefits or acted against the interests of small farmers. Rather, the interests of the local elites and small farmers in these particular cases partly overlapped, due to the nature of the problem, the crop, or the activity. More important, certain public programs at the state or central-government level offered financing to developmentalist local actors on condition that they include small farmers, much as the U.S. poverty program of the 1960s offered matching grants to cities that invested more in poor neighborhoods (Marshall, 1982). The coparticipation of local actors in these centralized initiatives, in turn, made the outcomes better than they would have been if the state had been working on its own: the local actors had a certain kind of experience, understanding of local markets and production systems, and intense desire for their regions to prosper that state and central-government agencies did not.

The last decade of literature on decentralization, local participation, and privatization has done an excellent job of focusing our attention on the importance of the kind of local action described above. The stories of this section, however, are saying something more. All the local initiatives reported above were elicited by something that more central levels of government were doing—in the form of conditional finance, technical assistance, arm-twisting, and sheer inspiration. And this more centralized presence *changed* what local actors would have done by themselves. My rendition of what works better, in other words, involves more than a unidirectional movement of activity from central to local, as recommended by much of decentralizationist policy advice. It requires, instead, a particular *combination* of central and local that changes the role of the more central government unit— regardless of whether it reduces that role—to elicit a form of local action that is different from business as usual. This means paying more attention to that combination, and what it requires of state or central government, than is paid by the current enthusiasts of local action.

Users as Demanders: Coops and Other Associative Ventures

In general, small farmers themselves were conspicuously absent as demanders in these tales of "induced" dissemination. This is not an unusual finding. Despite the considerable attention paid to this issue in recent years, there is still little participation of small farmers in the agenda-setting of research and extension offices, and little contracting of research and extension by farmer groups—partly because of the ominous implications this has, as explained below, in the eyes of agricultural professionals. The findings reported in this section, then, raise some questions about the ability of research and extension establishments to, as Ruttan says, put the farmer rather than the extension agent at the center of the adaptation process.

In certain ways, the "user-centered approach" recommended by SAD can be seen as a renaming of the older "participatory" approach to development. Participation, of course, has been extolled for many years in the development field, and with a particular vengeance by many groups and reformist technocrats in Brazil from the early 1980s on, because of the transition of that country from a military to a democratic government.[14] Indeed, "civic society" in Northeast Brazil demanded and partly succeeded in gaining a major redesigning of the region's rural development projects, precisely on the grounds that they were not participatory enough. With this background of longer-standing concern about participation and the more recent emphasis of SAD and others on "user-centered" approaches, it is important to understand why there have been so few cases of user-centered extension by government agencies and what there is to be learned from them.

As noted above, the only two cases of user participation found in this study were (1) the small-farmer orientation of the Boquim experiment station in the state of Sergipe, influenced partly by the clamorous presence in the region of two relatively successful cooperatives of small growers of oranges and associated crops, and (2) the story of the Arcoverde research station in the state of Pernambuco, where small farmers invaded the research station and threatened to remain there if it did not come up with a "relevant" research agenda.

Starting in the 1950s, the Brazilian government, like many other governments in the third world, promoted agricultural cooperatives as a way of stimulating agricultural modernization, channeling public-sector services to rural areas, and winning over rural elites in vast areas virtually untouched by the central government. As in many other poor regions, cooperative successes are so few that "the cooperative path" is certainly not the lesson to be learned from these stories. In addition, although the two Sergipe coops might seem to be the result of genuine and "autonomous" grass-roots action—the kind everyone wishes there would be more of—they were in some ways no more "indigenous" or "grass roots" than many of the failed coops promoted by the state. They had received years of highly subsidized public-sector funds (including funds from the Inter-American Development Bank and the World Bank) and a constant presence of the state in the form of technical assistance. As cooperative enterprises, moreover, even these exceptions to the rule had quite checkered histories, interrupted with bouts of mismanagement and financial crisis. Finally, and most relevant for SAD strategy, the history of these two groups and some others in the Northeast reveals a strong alliance between the small farmers in the area and reformist state technicians, who sometimes even goaded small-farmer members to take over cooperative leadership from a large-farmer/trader elite.[15]

Creating cooperative enterprises that successfully supply agricultural services is a more difficult task than organizing farmers to take control of an organization to which they belong. In order to benefit small farmers, that is, farmer associations should not always have to perform the difficult task of becoming successful as enterprises providing agricultural services. They can also, more simply, serve as a focus for the organized expression of small-farmer needs and demands and as a forum at which sympathetic technicians from the public sector can work out a useful agenda of service. The Arcoverde incident is a good example. The farmers were organized enough to threaten invasion of the research station and present and negotiate a list of the pressing problems for which they wanted help from research. To accomplish this end, it was not necessary that they be capable of providing themselves with agricultural services. The failure of many of the efforts to form small-farmer coops, in other words, is partly a result of the neglect of this "easier" task of stimulating and supporting the organized expression of small-farmer needs and demands.

Improving Supply through Demand

Today, some Northeast states are experimenting with a new arrangement that comes closer to a "user-demand" approach and, more generally, to a variation on "performance contracting." At the county level, the project agency works out an agenda for research and extension with a farmer association, which then contracts those agencies for a fixed period to carry out the tasks specified therein; in some of these cases, farmers even specify the particular extension agent they want. These experiments represent one way of funding extension and research through the demand side.

The current interest in "participation," on the one hand, and improving public-sector performance through "performance contracts" and charging for services, on the other, can be seen as user-driven processes. But performance contracting by users is not easily carried out in poor regions and with small farmers. This is because the very public agencies that operate in the agricultural sector have to play a significant role in bringing farmers together and in funding the contracts, as occurs in the Northeast experiments noted above. This means that public agencies have to sponsor what they see as a disturbing transfer of decision-making power from themselves to their clients. In order to achieve the user-centered approach to SAD, in other words, agricultural agencies have to provide the funding for their own "demise," as well as the institutional support that helps the farmers organize for these nefarious purposes! Not surprisingly, the agricultural extension agencies of Northeast Brazil have not welcomed this idea, although one frequently encounters individual agronomists and extension agents who support it.

The problem of resistance by agricultural extension and research to user-farmer contracting might well diminish if funding and organizing assistance could be provided to the farmer groups through *different* agencies—nongovernment organizations or other public agencies operating in rural areas, such as public works, health, and disaster relief. Such an approach would not be so novel as it appears. Anyone who does fieldwork in rural areas knows that an informal version has already been taking place for some time in many countries. Namely, groups of farmers ask particular extension agents to visit and advise them in return for payments for gasoline for the agent's vehicle, food, and lodging, or for other side payments. Although farmers sometimes pool their own money to fill the extension agent's gasoline tank, more often than not they use funds provided by *other* parties—nongovernmental organizations, public-sector "community development" programs, and so on.

The "informal contracting" described above is partly a result of the chronic lack of funds for operating expenditures suffered by extension agencies in many countries. But it is rarely acknowledged—let alone suggested as a basis for improvement—because it reduces the control of extension agencies over what they work on and what farmers they visit. Although agricultural agencies can be expected to resist a program design that forces them to aid a process by which they lose some power, however, they do not necessarily resist when other agencies offer them contracts. As the examples throughout this chapter show, agricultural agencies were perfectly comfortable doing contract work for other public agencies from time to time when this was not part of a strategy to delegate some of their decision-making power to others. A more fruitful way to think about a strategy of performance contracting by user-farmers, in other words, would be as a strategy not for the agricultural agencies themselves, but rather, for outside funders to aid and abet the emergence of outside demand for such contract services from other agencies and farmer groups. This takes us back to the nonparticipatory stories of induced dissemination told above.

The dissemination stories of this chapter show user *agencies*—rather than farmer-users—playing major roles in driving research agencies to do field testing, adaptation, and dissemination. The "demander agencies" either contract research agencies to do applied work on specific crops, varieties, or other inventions—as with the São Paulo food-processing firms and the industrial tomato, and the Bank of the Northeast and improved sheep varieties—or the demander agencies actually do the applied work themselves, as with Sergipe's water agency and the cistern, Pernambuco's project unit and the animal-traction implements, and the Boquim experiment station in Sergipe. This suggests that more attention should be paid to such user agencies—namely, state development banks, water-supply agencies, and extension offices—as a way of improving the performance of agricultural extension and research. Channeling part of the funding meant for applied research and extension to the "demander" agencies, that is, may be easier or less politically costly than getting extension and research to subject themselves to performance contracting with farmer groups.

Strong agricultural research capacity obviously cannot be treated simply as the by-product of better-designed agricultural development projects. But SAD programs and projects do provide an excellent opportunity to make research and extension more responsive, and agriculture more productive, by administering strong doses of user demand to these institutions.

Conclusion

This detailed look at the institutional history of several small successes in agricultural extension and research provides some grounded suggestions for thinking about how to design institutions for sustainable agricultural development. It also raises serious questions about the way we currently design programs and dispense policy advice.

We tend to see institution building, for example, as a linear process of cumulative growth, requiring long patient support on a variety of fronts. But these stories show marked episodes of good performance arising out of seemingly hopeless agencies and stellar performance followed by relapses into mediocrity. Although these episodes may add up to cumulative growth over a long enough period of time, something caused them to happen that was not cumulatively and patiently administered to them over that long period.

First, they were subjected to "benign" shocks from demanding users—not necessarily from the final users, the farmers, but often from more powerful "intermediate" users like governors looking for something to deliver to their rural constituents; or from other more zealous agencies who needed research and extension inputs to get their job done and simply took the task over from these agencies and did it themselves; or from proud researchers, enthusiastically mounting their own campaigns to disseminate one of their successes. Second, circumstances changed so as to impose very short time horizons on these agencies, in contrast to the more tolerant timing of institution-building projects—epidemics of crop disease or pests, impatient governors wanting "results" before their term of office was over, or simply excitement in a particular locality about making development "happen" at that moment. These pulls and pushes seemed more effective in eliciting good performance than the permissive tolerance of long-term support. *Third*, these "demand-shocks" resulted in a temporary transformation of the work of research and extension agencies from a diverse and wide-ranging menu of activities—something for every crop and every type of farmer—to a narrow, highly time-bound agenda of work on one crop, one problem, and/or one microregion.

All this seems to go against the grain of what we think of as wise practice—assigning tasks to the agencies specialized in doing them (field testing to the research agency, dissemination to the extension agency, and so on); protecting agencies from "meddling" by governors; and developing a long-term plan of work that includes a variety of crops and initiatives, partly to take into account the very complexity of the small farm. Clearly, short bursts of performance, and the demand shocks that bring them on, may not be enough to build an institution. But the success stories of institution building in agriculture—like that of Brazil's research parastatal, EMBRAPA— tend to result from lavish and long support of a single agency, not from support embedded in an area development project in which more than one agency is involved. Put more constructively, SAD projects will indeed present opportunities to build institutions in research and extension, but not in the expected ways.

Much of the recent thinking and policy advice about the role of agricultural institutions in development stresses the importance of decentralization, privatization, and performance contracting as a way of improving performance. Even though no such policy changes were introduced in the cases reviewed here, some of the desirable traits associated with decentralization and so on were present anyway. The demand pulls underlying the bursts of performance, for example, resulted in a wholesome change in the nature of the task and the work environment similar to that sought by performance contracting—namely, clearly specified tasks, closed time periods, conspicuous indicators of results, and clear penalties for nonperformance.

These characteristics help explain the surprisingly important role played by credit subsidies in the stories of successful performance—disturbing to anyone familiar with the lack of discipline associated with subsidized agricultural credit. Localized credit subsidies—according to the bankers, researchers, extensionists, and other observers of the agricultural history of particular microregions—played a crucial role in bringing about rapid and widespread adoption by small farmers in a short period of time. On closer examination, moreover, these cases show a combination of high subsidies *and* high penalties for nonperformance, not unlike the East Asian countries' successful use of credit as a tool of industrial policy. If you didn't eradicate diseased rootstock, for example, you didn't get your next credit disbursement.

Operating in a larger world awash in undisciplined subsidized credit, moreover, these particular cases of subsidy stood out in that they carried built-in sunset clauses. When the new variety was widely adopted by small farmers, for example, the subsidy ceased. This judicious use of disciplined subsidized credit—along with our new understanding of such discipline in the successful industrializations of East Asia—suggests that the unanimous contempt in which agricultural credit subsidies are held may require some reconsideration. At the least, it is worth understanding the conditions under which credit can be so disciplined, if only because governments often subsidize credit whether policy advisers like it or not.

Decentralization and participation enthusiasts will take heart from the unforeseen importance of local actors and initiatives in these stories of above-average performance. The stories seem to reinforce the current view that the more you decentralize, privatize, and participate, the better. But standing behind each strong local actor was a more centralized government agency—offering financial incentives, talking up the desired new approaches, providing technical assistance, and rewarding the good performers. Although the local actors were more colorful, surprising, and novel than the central ones, it would be a mistake to interpret these stories as tales of unidirectional decentralization and "freed-up" local energies. Rather, they represent a particular combination of central and local, in which it is just as important to recognize what the central government did as to recognize the character and strength of the local contribution.

Although decentralization and participation are in vogue today—and with good reason—a raft of evaluation studies in the 1970s and 1980s raised considerable concern about what happens when targeted project funding falls into the hands of "local elites." Namely, services and inputs meant for the poor often did not reach them. My research revealed a process that is not quite consistent with this earlier concern or the current lack of it. Local elites, surprisingly and contrary to the earlier view, were often major contributors in these stories of disseminating benefits to small farmers. But they did not necessarily behave this way without some prodding; at the same time, they were not hemmed in by administrative regulations that forced them to do so. In part, the incentives emanating from state and central government agencies helped induce them to behave this way; state agencies turned down the requests of civic-minded local elites for funds to serve their own purposes, for example, while at the same time dangling the possibility of funding before their eyes if they served more broadly defined social purposes. This forcing of a broader definition of local interests by elite actors was helped along by the taking of action in areas where there was some overlap between the interests of the poor and the elites. Campaigns against contagious crop diseases are an example, given that larger farmers will still be vulnerable if small farmers are not reached by eradication campaigns.

Although farmer-users were less important in these stories of demand-driven performance than one would have hoped, there are still some lessons to be drawn from these cases. One is that in order for groups of farmers to successfully demand attention from research and extension, they do not have to be organized in cooperatives or engaged in other activities first. Indeed, presenting a list of demands to an experiment station is a much simpler activity than becoming a business enterprise, as cooperatives have to do—and simpler, even, than buying inputs collectively, as the less formal farmer associations do. Proponents of participation and local action, however, often promote the organizing of farmers to carry out their own activities—like seed banks, community grain mills, or input-supply stores—rather than, more simply, organizing in order to express their demands to research and extension. Although the business ventures of farmer groups may sometimes be successful, they represent more difficult tasks, and they do not necessarily lead to pressure on research and extension—partly because the extension service itself usually has the responsibility for creating and servicing these groups.

The findings presented here represent a different way of thinking about program design and institution building, rather than a list of dos and don'ts. First, they suggest a "demand-side" approach to institution building, to supplement the supply-side approach normally taken. Part of the problem of research and extension, that is, often lies outside these very institutions: they are often not subjected to enough demand from powerful users and others who do care, for example, about dissemination or farmer-centered work processes. Second, they suggest that project design and cycling try to mimic the distinctly episodic and narrowed character of the achievements recounted here, instead of providing open-ended, ever-present support on a variety of fronts for a permissively long period of time.

Third, project designers should be less catholic about the activities they fund, and should look first at crops and crop problems in any particular country or region that promise easy first successes. This does not necessarily mean shorter projects or rigid work agendas for research and extension agencies; it can simply mean the breaking up of a project into shorter segments, the subsequent segment being decided upon after completion of the first one and the experience and learning that it provided. Fourth, projects should try to elicit the powerful support that is often available from "good politicians" by choosing interventions that promise conspicuous results within short time periods. Although these four perspectives may seem difficult to translate into concrete recommendations, a few suggestions can be drawn from the above text as illustrations.

Instead of exclusively funding agencies directly and treating them as self-contained entities to mold and shape—the supply-side approach—projects can influence these agencies by channeling funding through their users. Although attention has recently turned to the importance of small farmers as users and of contracting extension work through them, agricultural agencies tend to resist this reduction of their power. Hence, there are not yet many examples in the public sector of user-centered extension and research. But the well-founded enthusiasm over farmer-centered approaches has perhaps obscured the politically easier and more powerful intermediate users of research and extension who, in pursuing their own agendas, can exert healthy pressures for performance on these agencies. At certain moments, for example, development banks, irrigation and water-supply agencies, extension offices, and dynamic governors will care much more about field testing, adaptation, and dissemination than will research agencies. Given the funding, they will aggressively contract it out or do it themselves, as the above stories show. In turn, no matter how immune research agencies are to direct pleas from institution builders to become more field oriented, they can change their character on a moment's notice when they are contracted to do so by users for specific tasks, as the cases presented above also show.

Research agencies themselves become interested in field testing and adaptation at certain moments when they think they are onto something really successful. Projects could therefore make funding available to research agencies or experiment stations to adapt and disseminate the most promising variety emerging in, say, the last two or three years. They might use the funding for field testing or, at a later stage, for seed production or, even later, for trucking in extension agents from a variety of places for a special previewing. Normally, however, we fund these activities generically through time, not only on particular occasions and for one particular variety, and they are assigned once and for all to the relevant agency—seed production, for example, to the unit that always does seed production. Finally, and also mimicking the episodic process of the stories recounted above, projects could be timed to fall within the election cycle of governors, to take advantage of the dynamic push that such politicians often bring to intervention campaigns involving particular crops, regions, or problems.

Notes

Support for this research and writing was generously provided by the World Bank, the Department of Urban Studies and Planning, and the Humanities, Arts and Social Sciences Fund of the Massachusetts Institute of Technology, the government of the Brazilian state of Ceará, and the Harvard Institute of International Development. None of these institutions is responsible for the information or opinions reported here. For research assistance, I am grateful to Hugo Eduardo Beteta. The findings discussed in this paper were first reported, along with several other findings, in Tendler (1991).

1. E.g., World Bank (1987). For a cross-country review of evidence of the economic impact of agricultural extension, see Birkhaeuser, Evenson, and Feder (1989).

2. For treatments of Brazilian and Northeast poverty, see Fox and Morley (1990), Denslow and Tyler (1984), Hoffman (1986), Hoffman and Kageyama (1984), and Thomas (1987). For treatments of Northeast agriculture, see Homem de Melo and Canton (1980), Johnson (1971), Katzman (1984), Kutcher and Scandizzo (1981), and May (1986).

3. Fieldwork for the study was carried out in Brazil during three five-week periods

in the late 1980s, in addition to a one-month period in the state of Ceará in the summer of 1992.

4. For agricultural extension and research issues in Brazil and the northeast, see World Bank (1983), Alves (1988), Evenson (1989), and Homem de Melo (1986).

5. This distinction parallels that between Latin America's import-substitution policies and those of East Asia. Contrary to earlier interpretations, the East Asian countries were as lavish as Latin America with tariff protection and credit subsidies for industry. But they were also highly selective about the sectors and firms to which protection was granted, and very demanding of performance; if a firm's output or exports did not increase within a year or two, the subsidies were abruptly withdrawn (Amsden, 1989). Latin America, in contrast, offered protection more across the board, with less selectivity and fine tuning and no demand for performance (Sachs, 1985).

6. In the first quarter of the 20th century, the southern branch of the U.S. extension service originated in a similarly dramatic campaign against the cotton boll weevil. In fact, Baker (1939) attributes the "good start" of the southern branch to the "easiness" of that campaign, in terms of its highly standardized and homogeneous mission. She contrasts this with the more "difficult" evolution of the northern extension service, where each state developed its own particular multifaceted work agenda, partly because of the greater heterogeneity of agriculture in the north.

7. E.g., Binswanger and Ruttan (1978).

8. The state marketing boards for export crops in sub-Saharan Africa are the most commonly cited example of the state's squeezing of agricultural producers in order to raise revenues. Bates (1981) contributes the seminal work in this literature.

9. Vernon Ruttan, personal communication.

10. The water agency's various iterations of the cistern finally ended up with the "chinese-hat" form, which was superior in that (1) its conical shape avoided the stress points in the corners of the previous rectangular version, which had caused leaks and required difficult repairs; (2) the concrete, conical roof was maintenance-free, in contrast to the tin sheeting or wooden beams of previous forms, which were also frequently stolen for roof repairs; (3) the concrete "hat" eliminated the need for plastic sheeting, subject to tearing, which was used to cover the brick-walled-rectangular and tin-roof-covered versions and to seal their interior; and (4) it held significantly more water than CPATSA's cistern. See Beteta (1990).

11. A remarkably similar success story comes from a recent evaluation by the U.S. Agency for International Development of its long-term support to institution building in agricultural universities in Brazil. After pointing to the difficulty of getting the universities to do more applied and "relevant" research, the case study on the Center for Agricultural Sciences at the federal university in the Northeast state of Ceará presents an important exception to this rule: the applied research on (1) improved sheep varieties, leading to a widely disseminated improved variety (Morada Nova Branca), and (2) improving the carrying capacity of the native range in the semiarid zone of Ceará for beef cattle, goats, and sheep. Unlike the rest of the university's agricultural research, the study pointed out, these more applied results came out of research programs that were contracted for by the Development Bank of the Northeast (BNB), a regional development banking parastatal. The BNB's contracts with the university required and financed the extension work necessary to field test and disseminate results (Sanders et al., 1989, 1986 [annexes D and E]).

12. See, e.g., Peek (1988) and the evaluation studies cited therein.

13. For example, the Irecê coop in Bahia asked the state government for access to irrigation funds for financing individual tubewell purchases by its medium-farmer members. But the agency, as agreed to with the World Bank, had insisted that financing for tubewells could be granted only in a way that served groups of smaller farmers, and not just individuals. Although the coop was disappointed at this stricture, it nevertheless enthusiastically oriented its irrigation program in a smaller-farmer direction: this was the only way it could obtain funds for irrigation, as well as help it to attract new members.

14. The following works analyze some of these changes: Falcão Neto (1985), Guimarães Neto (1988), Lavaredo and Pereira de Sá (1986), Muda Nordeste (1985), Sales (1988), Santos (1988), and Stepan (1988).

15. In a study of an agricultural program in Mexico, Fox (1986) analyzes a similar process, which he calls a "sandwich strategy," whereby reformist technocrats in the public sector facilitate the formation of "autonomous" peasant groups to take over these programs from the local elites who have appropriated and managed them in their own interests.

References

Alves, Eliseu. 1988. The challenges facing rural extension in Brazil. Translation from the Portuguese. LATAC (Latin America and the Caribbean), World Bank, no. 88E0410, February 12. Photocopy.

Amsden, Alice H. 1989. *Asia's Next Giant: South Korea and Late Industrialization*. Oxford: Oxford University Press.

Baker, Gladys. 1939. *The County Agent*. Chicago: University of Chicago Press.

Bates, Robert H. 1981. *Markets and States in Tropical Africa: The Political Basis of Agricultural Policies*. Berkeley, University of California Press.

Beteta, Eduardo. 1990. Supporting newly created agencies: A case study from Sergipe, Brazil. Department of Urban Studies and Planning, Massachusetts Institute of Technology, for the Studies and Training Design Department, Economic Development Institute, World Bank. Photocopy.

Binswanger, Hans, and Vernon W. Ruttan (1978). *Induced Innovation: Technology, Institutions and Development*. Baltimore, Md., and London: Johns Hopkins University Press.

Birkhaeuser, Dean, Robert E. Evenson, and Gershon Feder. 1989. The economic impact of agricultural extension: A review. Photocopy.

Denslow, David, Jr., and William Tyler. 1984. Perspectives on poverty and income inequality in Brazil. *World Development* 12(10): 1019-28.

Evenson, Robert E. 1989. Agricultural technology and market failures: A review of issues with reference to Brazil. Draft prepared for the World Bank Conference on Agricultural Development Policies and the Theory of Rural Organization, Yale University, June 14-16.

Falcao Neto, Joaquim de Arruda, ed. 1985. *Nordeste: Eleições*. Recife, Pernambuco: Editora Massangana.

Fox, Jonathan. 1986. The political dynamics of reform: The case of the Mexican food system, 1980-1982. Ph.D. diss., Massachusetts Institute of Technology.

Fox, Louise, and Samuel A. Morley. 1990. Who paid the bill? Adjustment and poverty in Brazil, 1980-1985. February 23. Photocopy.

Guimarães Neto, Leonardo. 1988. *Notas sôbre os impactos sociais da evolução econômica recente do Nordeste.* Recife, Pernambuco: Agôsto.

Hoffmann, Helga. 1986. Pobreza e propriedade no Brasil: O que está mudando? In *A transição incompleta: Brasil desde 1945.* Vol. 2, *Desigualdade social, educação, saúde e previdência,* edited by Edmar L. Bacha and Herbert S. Klein. Rio de Janeiro: Editora Paz e Terra.

Hoffmann, Rodolfo, and Angela A. Kageyama. 1984. Distribuição da renda no Brasil entre famílias e entre pessoas, em 1970 e 1980. Trabalho apresentado a XII Renunião da ANPEC, São Paulo, December 5-7.

Homem de Melo, Fernando. 1986. *Brazil and the CGIAR Centers: A Study of Their Collaboration in Agricultural Research.* Consultative Group on International Agricultural Research (CGIAR), Study Paper no. 9. Washington, D.C.: World Bank.

Homem de Melo, Fernando, and Adolpho Walter P. Canton. 1980. Risco na agricultura brasileira: Nordeste "versus" Sul. *Revista econômica do Nordeste* 11(3): 471-83. Fortaleza, Ceará.

Johnson, Allen W. 1971. *Sharecroppers of the Sertão: Economics and Dependence on a Brazilian Plantation.* Stanford, Calif.: Stanford University Press.

Judd, M. Ann, James K. Boyce, and Robert E. Evenson. 1986. Investing in agricultural supply: The determinants of agricultural research and extension investment. *Economic Development and Cultural Change* 35(1): 77-113.

Katzman, Martin T. 1984. The land and people of Northeast Brazil: Is geography a useful guide to development policy? *Economic Development and Cultural Change* 32(3): 633-38.

Kutcher, Gary P., and Pasquale L. Scandizzo. 1981. *The Agricultural Economy of Northeast Brazil.* World Bank Research Publication. Baltimore, Md.: Johns Hopkins University Press.

Lavareda, António, e Constança Pereira de Sá. 1986. *Poder e voto: Luta política em Pernambuco.* Recife, Pernambuco: Editora Massangana.

Marshall, Dale Rogers. 1982. Lessons from the implementation of poverty programs in the United States. In *Institutions of Rural Development for the Poor,* edited by David K. Leonard and Dale Rogers Marshall, Research Series no. 49, 40-72. Berkeley: Institute of International Studies, University of California.

May, Peter H. 1986. Northeast Brazilian agriculture: An overview. Final Report to Agriculture Operations Division, Brazil Country Department. Photocopy.

Miranda, Maria do Carmo Tavares de, ed. 1985. *Desenvolvimento Brasileiro e Trópico.* Série Cursos e Conferàncias, 17. Recife, Pernambuco: Editora Massangana.

Muda Nordeste. 1985. *Projeto Nordeste: Programa de Apoio ao Pequeno Produtor Rural — Debate Regional.* Convênio SUDENE/Clube de Engenharia de Pernambuco. Recife, Pernambuco: Movimento Muda Nordeste.

Peek, Peter. 1988. How equitable are rural development projects? *International Labour Review* 127(1): 73-97.

Sachs, Jeffrey D. 1985. External debt and macroeconomic performance in Latin America and East Asia. *Brookings Papers on Economic Activity* (Washington, D.C.) 2.

Sales, Teresa. 1988. Movimentos sociais no campo frente à ação do Estado. Trabalho apresentado ao XII Encontro Anual da ANPOCS, Águas de São Pedro. Photocopy.

Sanders, John H., Jerome H. Maner, Daniel R. Gross, and Jose de Souza. 1986. *Northeast Brazil: The Center of Agricultural Sciences of the Federal University of Ceará.* U.S. Agency for International Development. Photocopy.

Sanders, John, Richard L. Meyer, Roger W. Fox, and Fernando C. Peres. 1989. Agricultural university institution building in Brazil: Successes, problems, and lessons for other countries. *American Journal of Agricultural Economics* 71(5): 1206-10.

Santos, Jose Maciel dos. 1988. "Política rural e trabalho assalariado: Uma análise a partir de POLONORDESTE. In *Congresso da Associação Nacional de Pós-Graduação em Economia (ANPEC)*. Belo Horizonte, Minas Gerais: ANPEC.

Stepan, Alfred, ed. 1988. *Democratizing Brazil: Problems of Transition and Consolidation*. London: Oxford University Press.

Tendler, Judith. 1991. *New Lessons from Old Projects: The Dynamics of Rural Development in Northeast Brazil*. Operations Evaluation Department, Report no. 10183. December 16. Washington, D.C.: World Bank.

Thomas, Vinod. 1987. Differences in income and poverty within Brazil. *World Development* 15(2): 263-73.

World Bank. 1983. *Brazil: An Interim Assessment of Rural Development Programs for the Northeast*. World Bank Country Study. Washington, D.C.: World Bank.

_____. 1987. *World Bank Experience with Rural Development, 1965-1986*. Report no. 6883. Operations Evaluation Department, October 16. Washington, D.C.: World Bank.

Part IV
Health Research and Health Systems

The health problems faced by many developing countries are more burdensome than those faced by many presently developed countries at comparable stages in their development. In the developed countries the historically important infectious diseases have declined to very low levels. These health problems have been replaced by the chronic and degenerative diseases of adult life, such as cancer, stroke, lung and heart disease, arthritis, and impairment of the central nervous system.

Many developing countries have been denied the luxury of experiencing this epidemiological transition. Infectious and parasitic disease, nutritional deficiencies, and reproductive health problems are still responsible for a substantial share of sickness and death in the developing world. As life expectancy rises, many developing countries are also beginning to experience the burden of the chronic and degenerative diseases usually considered as problems of the developed countries. They are also beginning to share with the developed countries the health effects of agricultural and industrial pollution and the global AIDS pandemic.

In chapter 7 Adetokunbo O. Lucas addresses the issue of the appropriate objectives, structure, and support for international and national health research. He classifies tasks that must be carried out by essential national health research under four headings: (1) epidemiological situational analysis, (2) enhancing the impact of health interventions, (3) searching for new and improved technologies, and (4) broadening the basic knowledge of biology and human behavior with specific references to human health. Lucas places much greater weight on the importance of social science research in each of the four tasks than is conventional in developed-country health research.

Lucas also brings his substantial experience and scholarship to bear on the appropriate role of international collaboration in strengthening national health research. He is critical of both the donors and the recipients of external assistance for health research for failure to design such collaboration to assure institutional sustainability. He appreciates the role of internationally supported institutes such as the International Centre for Diarrhoeal Disease Research (Bangladesh) and the International Center for Insect Physiology and Ecology (Kenya). They have provided a mechanism for generating a critical mass of investigators and have had more stable funding than many national health research organizations. But he is skeptical that a system of international health research centers could play as significant a role in health research as they have in the case of agricultural research.

In chapter 8 Godfrey Gunatilleke provides a historical overview of the role of health in agricultural and rural development in Sri Lanka. The Sri Lanka experience is particularly important because Sri Lanka is one of the few low-income countries that has been able to achieve levels of health indicators, such as birthrate decline, low infant mortality, and high life expectancy, comparable to high-income countries. Sri Lanka has also been relatively successful in expanding the production of basic food commodities, although it has pursued policies toward traditional export crops (tea, rubber) that have weakened their position in world markets. It is of interest that during the colonial period a tradition of concern with the health status of plantation workers, and the implications for their productivity, led to the implementation of a relatively strong rural health program. Since independence, the focus of rural health programs has focused more on the smallholder sector.

In spite of its impressive accomplishments, Gunatilleke is critical of what he regards as excessive centralization in the management of the Sri Lankan health system and related programs directed at meeting basic human needs. He argues that the next step in the development of the Sri Lankan health system is to move away from an approach that views the mother and the child as passive recipients of health care to enhancing the capacity of the family to perform as the primary unit of health care.

The central role of the family in the health system is addressed more directly by Dan Kaseje in chapter 9. Kaseje reports on the effort in Kenya, an effort in which he played an important design role, to implement a health program that provides direct support to the family, particularly the mother, as the primary health provider. In this program the family is provided, through provincial and community organization, the knowledge, the technology, and the materials to carry out its function as the primary health provider. Kaseje regards the family, and the mother in particular, as the most important health agent. She is the analyst, planner, and decision maker. Placing primary emphasis on the family taps into powerful motivations for family welfare that are not available to the physician, the nurse, or the community health worker. In discussion at the Bellagio conference, Kaseje emphasized that practice has not yet caught up with policy. In many community-based health care organizations, the government or the nongovernmental organizations provide inputs and people passively accept them. Full community involvement and control have yet to be achieved. Family-based health care can, and often does, do without health care professionals and institutions, but the institutions and professionals cannot do without the family-based providers.

CHAPTER 7

THE INSTITUTIONAL INFRA-STRUCTURE FOR HEALTH RESEARCH IN DEVELOPING COUNTRIES

Adetokunbo O. Lucas

Scientific research has made major contributions to the health of people throughout the world, as shown by the steady decline in morbidity and mortality and the increasing expectation of life in both developed and developing countries. Recognition of these benefits has stimulated efforts to build and strengthen research capabilities in developing countries. National governments, in collaboration with private foundations and bilateral and multilateral agencies, have designed and implemented a variety of programs aimed at strengthening the capacity of their scientists and institutions to undertake health research.

In some developing countries, these efforts have led to a steady growth of institutional capacity to undertake relevant research; their scientists are conducting meaningful health research within their own countries and are also making significant contributions internationally to the global fund of knowledge about health and disease. Other efforts have been less successful; the investments of resources in some projects have shown little appreciable returns in terms of enhancing research capabilities of the target institutions and countries; in other cases, the gains have been short-lived and have not survived beyond the period of major external support. In sub-Saharan Africa, some of the capabilities that were established and thriving soon after independence are crumbling and decaying under the pressure from the current economic crisis.

Some of the sponsors of research-strengthening programs have analyzed their experience and applied its lessons in modifying their approaches with the hope of increasing the effectiveness of their inputs. This chapter reviews some of the strategies that have been adopted in attempts to strengthen research capability in developing countries and attempts to identify the most useful lessons learned, especially those that can be applied widely.

Developing countries show a wide range of variations, and most generalizations would not accurately apply to many of them. At one end of the scale, research institutions in some of the developing countries have achieved recognition for scientific contributions in their field. At the other end, some of the least developed countries cannot mobilize a critical mass of scientists to tackle research issues of high priority in their countries. Many developing countries fall in the middle range; they have acquired some research capability but with marginal impact because the institutions lack expertise in key disciplines; they are subject to uncertainties about funding and they are handicapped by other constraints.

Why Build and Strengthen Research Capability?

Developing countries have many urgent competing demands for limited resources. Allocation of financial and human resources to any activity must therefore be justified on the basis of the expected benefits and actual performance. It is necessary therefore to identify precisely what tasks need to be performed and the expected outcomes from investments in health research (Golden, 1988). In a recent report, an independent Commission on Health Research for Development (1990) identified research as an important mechanism for accelerating health development on the basis of equity and social justice. The specific tasks to be performed by research institutions can be conveniently classified under four headings:

Situation analysis is needed to define the patterns of health and disease and to identify their determinants. It also monitors the major causes of disease, disability, and death in various segments of the population and searches for biological, behavioral, social, economic, and environmental risk factors associated with the frequency, distribution, severity, and outcome of these diseases and conditions.

Enhancing the impact of health interventions means designing the most effective strategies for interventions aimed at improving health. The process involves the evaluation and selection of technologies and the assessment of alternative approaches, including various combinations of medical, social, and other nonmedical interventions.

Searching for new and improved technologies can produce new biomedical tools such as drugs, vaccines, diagnostic tests, and environmental measures to control chemical, physical, and biological hazards. For example, in some developing countries, malaria and other parasitic and infectious diseases remain major causes of disease and death; the available technologies are inadequate to bring these diseases under control, and with the emergence of drug-resistant strains of parasites and pesticide-resistant strains of vectors, there is a need to develop new prophylactic and therapeutic agents.

Broadening the basic knowledge of biology and human behavior with particular reference to human health enables us to understand biological processes in health and disease. It informs our knowledge of the biology of infective agents and their vectors and of the role of genetic factors in causing disease or modulating the effects of other pathogenic agents. At a basic level, it will serve to advance fundamental knowledge of human behavior.

The four groups of research tasks outlined above call for scientists from many different disciplines:

> epidemiology and statistics;
>
> social and behavioral sciences, economics, and policy analysis;
>
> management and communications sciences and operational research;
>
> clinical and biomedical science;
>
> biology, biochemistry, immunology, molecular biology, and other biomedical disciplines; and
>
> engineering and environmental science.

This list is not exhaustive but indicates the range of skills and expertise required to meet the various needs of health research. It is necessary to train scientists in the relevant disciplines and, more important, to make institutional arrangements that would permit them to communicate, interact, and collaborate effectively.

Historical Perspective

In order to understand the current status of research capacity in individual developing countries and in regions of the world, it is useful to examine the historical development of these institutions.

Of particular interest are the developing countries that have recently become independent nations after a period of colonial rule. Most of the countries in sub-Saharan Africa fall into this category. During the preindependence period, the colonial medical services established research institutions, but these were mainly staffed by expatriate staff. These institutions and research groups made major contributions to knowledge of health issues in developing countries. This was the age of discovery, when major diseases, especially the parasitic and infectious diseases in the tropics, were described, the causal agents and their vectors identified, and their life cycles defined. In the least developed countries, little effort was made to train and involve national scientists and technologists other than the lowest grade of field and laboratory staff—the bottle washers and the fly catchers.

After independence, many of these colonial research institutions crumbled and decayed; others continued to function as colonial enclaves, staffed and managed by expatriate staff, financed and sustained from external sources (Lucas, 1989).

Some of the more advanced developing countries have established a significant research tradition. For example, in Brazil, there is a long history of health research stretching back to the beginning of this century. In the first decade of this century, Carlos Chagas, the distinguished Brazilian scientist, made the discovery of the disease that eponymously bears his name. He made the unique contribution of also identifying *Trypanosoma cruzi* as the causal agent and reduviid bugs as the vector. More recently, Brazil, Mexico, Thailand, India, and other more advanced developing countries have strengthened their research capabilities to the point where their institutions are making important contributions to scientific knowledge (Martinez-Palomo and Sepulveda, 1989). But even in these more advanced countries, the growth and fortunes of national institutions have traced uneven courses, with significant ups and downs. On the whole, in Asia and in Latin America, there have been significant advances in research capabilities, but progress in sub-Saharan Africa has been less impressive and more unstable.

Major Issues and Lessons

In reviewing the experiences gained in strengthening capacity for health research, it would be useful to examine and analyze seven major issues and to identify the important lessons from these experiences:

1. National commitment

2. Institutional base for health research

3. Human resources

4. International collaboration

5. Strategies for capacity strengthening

6. Setting priorities for capacity strengthening

7. Financing capacity strengthening

National Commitment

National commitment refers to the extent to which a national government is convinced of the value of health research and is willing to support it.

Allocation of Resources. What priority does the government accord to research? How much investment has the government made in building and maintaining the infrastructure for health research? What allocations of funds are made from public funds to support research and to what extent does the government protect the research budget in times of financial stringency? Some developing countries treat research expenditure as a luxury item on the basis of "last in, first out" — it is the last item to be included when funds are available and the first item to be cut when money is short.[1]

Development of Human Resources. In addition to financial allocations, national commitment is indicated by other specific actions of government to promote health research. These include programs for developing relevant human resources for research, including an appropriate reward system to attract and retain good scientists and other workers. For example, in Mexico, the government has established a competitive salary scheme that recognizes excellence in research in terms of salary and compensation (Commission on Health Research, 1990). In addition to this official program, a new private initiative, the Mexican Health Foundation, has introduced complementary programs aimed at stimulating and supporting the repatriation of Mexican scientists (Santos and Soberon, 1990).

Utilization of Research Results. Perhaps the most subtle indicator of national commitment is the respect shown by a government and its agencies for science and research in policymaking and in action. The interest that government shows in the products of scientific analyses and research results provides the most enduring reward and the most powerful incentive to greater achievement to the scientific establishment. In an ideal situation, the government can show its commitment to science by paying serious attention to research findings and promptly using relevant results in policymaking, in planning strategies, and in monitoring and evaluating the performance of health services.

Political Interference. Some governments show their lack of commitment to health research by their treatment of scientific findings and research results, ranging from benign neglect to active suppression of research results and open hostility to the scientists. Some governments try to prevent the publication of research findings that may reflect adversely on their performance or may show the existence and gravity of some health problems. For example, governments may wish to deny the existence of certain communicable diseases that may adversely affect economic activities like tourism, food exports, and other commercial activities. In the early stages of the epidemic of human immunodeficiency virus (HIV) infection, some governments adopted a policy of denial; research findings were actively suppressed and, in extreme cases, individual scientists were harassed to discourage them from disseminating their findings and from conducting further research. Even in less sensitive matters, politicians react with hostility to research findings that conflict with their plans and policies. For studies carried out by international agencies, governments sometimes exercise their prerogative not to approve the release for publication of research reports and scientific analyses that are at variance with the image they wish to present. In these and other ways, some governments frustrate research scientists by interfering politically with the conduct of research, with the dissemination of results, and with the logical application of the findings.

Lesson 1: National Commitment

National commitment is crucial to the development and strengthening of research capability. It includes stable fi-

nancial support at an appropriate level, demand for and utilization of the results of research, and creation of an environment that attracts, trains, and employs the most able scientists in an atmosphere that fosters objective scientific inquiry.

Institutional Base for Health Research

Research institutes, academic institutions, and health care facilities are the three main types of institutions that conduct health research. Dedicated research institutes represent an important but not exclusive base for conducting health research. Academic institutions, universities, technical colleges, and similar institutions also make important contributions. Relevant research on clinical, epidemiological, and health-services issues are conducted in health care facilities like hospitals, health centers, and dispensaries. All three types of institutions are engaged in research, training, and service but with differing emphasis. This framework for viewing the roles of these institutions is based on identification of their primary functions and their responsibilities in other areas. Thus, research is the primary function of dedicated research institutions, but they also provide opportunities for training, often in collaboration with academic institutions, and for service, in cooperation with health care facilities (see Table 7.1).

National capacity for health research is defined in terms of the combination of efforts of all these institutions. Developing countries often do not exploit the full potential of such institutions. Ideally, there would be an appropriate mechanism for ensuring collaboration among them. Such mechanisms facilitate exchange of information, effective interaction among scientists, and, where relevant, integrated, multidisciplinary approaches.

Research Institutes. Dedicated research institutes are often the most prominent resource for health research. Some deal with specific diseases like leprosy, schistosomiasis, or malaria; others cover a broad range of diseases and conditions. One advantage of dedicated research institutes is the concentration of expertise from various disciplines, thereby creating a critical mass and a critical density of researchers. It also provides the opportunity for scientists to share the use of expensive equipment, making it more cost-effective to acquire and maintain such instruments. There is also the obvious advantage of having teams of scientists who regard research as their first priority and not as an extra assignment, as is often the case for academics or for physicians in the health care system.

Table 7.1. Health research institutions

Type of institution	Primary function	Other functions
Research institute	Research	Training, service
Academic institutions	Training	Research, service
Health care facilities	Service	Training, research

In addition to laboratory work, some medical research institutes have developed community-based clinical and epidemiological programs, often including longitudinal studies over several years or decades. Such community laboratories have proved to be valuable resources linking clinical and epidemiological observations with laboratory-based biomedical studies, thereby enhancing the understanding of the determinants, clinical course, and outcome of disease processes.

In sub-Saharan Africa, in the preindependence era, colonial authorities established research institutes for the study of major tropical parasitic and infectious diseases like yellow fever, malaria, trypanosomiasis, schistosomiasis, and leprosy. These institutions produced outstanding research results, including the identification of some of the disease agents and their vectors and natural reservoirs, as well as providing an understanding of the dynamics of the transmission patterns of these infections. These old institutions and some new ones that were established since independence continue to tackle the problems posed by the major endemic diseases in the region. The challenge has been to train national scientists to replace expatriates who formerly ran these institutions and to generate local resources to ensure their financial stability.

In the more developed countries of Asia and Latin America, there are well-established research institutes that have made significant contributions to medical science. Some of them have earned recognition as centers of excellence in their particular area of interest, especially with regard to locally endemic diseases like amebiasis, Chagas' disease, and malaria.

Most of the research institutes in developing countries are funded by their governments. They are therefore susceptible to fluctuations in the economic situation of the national treasury as well as to changes in fiscal policies. Furthermore, priorities tend to be determined through narrow bureaucratic lines with minimal input from outside official sources. Private foundations are slowly emerging as sources of research support in developing countries; for example, the Mexican Health Foundation, which was established a few years ago as a private initiative, has mobilized resources from the private sector both within the country and from external donors. Multiple sources of funding may provide more stable funding for research, and the involvement of a wider constituency would broaden the base of discussion in identifying priority issues and supporting them.

Academic Institutions. Research based in academic institutions often neglects the priority health problems of the nation. This distortion of research priorities is sometimes determined by the fact that the institutions receive financial support from external sources and hence relate to priorities that are selected without strict reference to the needs of their countries. Another difficulty arises from too narrow a definition of health research in terms of faculties of medicine and, even more narrow, in terms of clinical and medical laboratory sciences.

Creative scientists from various disciplines both within medical schools and in other faculties have demonstrated how their skills can be effectively used in addressing health issues. For example, in the University of Ibadan, Nigeria, scientists in faculties other than health research have made important contributions on health-related issues (De Cola and Shoyinka, 1984). In the Department of Sociology, work has been done on aspects of medical sociology. The Department of Geography is conducting research on the spatial distribution of various health problems and the relationships to environmental factors. Research on financing of health care was conducted by the Department of Economics. The Department of Zoology has developed a program in medical malacology and another on molecular biology. International recognition has been won by the Department of Chemistry for its research on the chemistry of hemoglobins, of particular interest because of the high prevalence of sickle cell disease and other hemoglobinopathies in this part of Africa. Another collaborator is the Institute of African Studies, in their collation of information on traditional medical practices (De Cola and Shoyinka, 1984).

These cases illustrate how the knowledge, skills, and perspectives of scientists from other faculties can make valuable contributions to health research. Often, scientists from other disciplines become involved in such projects through chance and accident rather than from consciously designed programs. But the process can be institutionalized through a deliberate effort to recruit the interests of scientists from other faculties in health issues.

Health Care Facilities. Research within the health care delivery system is often of the most practical kind. It provides the opportunity to investigate the day-to-day problems that confront health care givers, to define the pattern and determinants of health and disease in the communities served, and to study the health care system in order to optimize its effectiveness. This research is exemplified by David Morley's studies on the health of preschool children in Ilesha, Nigeria, which produced several of the elements of the current strategies for promoting child health (Morley, 1983). And from his hospital base at Aro, innovative approaches for community-based care of psychiatric patients were developed by Thomas Lambo, a Nigerian psychiatrist (Lambo, 1964). There are many other examples of such research.

On the whole, the opportunities for research based in health care facilities are underutilized. Many professionals who provide health care have had little training in research, often lack facilities, and are not encouraged by their employers to engage in research. Health workers in the front line of service often complain that they are too busy to do research, but those who have a critical attitude of their own performance make time to undertake objective analyses as well as formal research.

National Networking. These three types of research institutes—academic institutions, research institutes, and health care facilities—often work in isolation. It is not always easy to ensure effective communications among the researchers in such different institutions. Even where contacts are made, the communications are often limited to minimal exchanges. For example, in order to obtain specimens from sick patients, laboratory scientists may make contact with hospitals, which can provide blood and other biological materials from patients; but beyond using the hospital as a source of biological materials, scientists do not often take the opportunity to engage in meaningful collaborative research. Such collaborative effort could enhance clinicians' understanding of the conditions that they are treating and would also assist the laboratory scientists to interpret their findings in terms of human diseases. Ideally, every country should have mechanisms for promoting networking. Some countries have experienced the value of this approach, as, for example, the national network of research on amebiasis in Mexico. This mechanism has intensified the interaction among Mexican scientists who are working on various aspects of the disease, and it has facilitated the rapid exchange of clinical epidemiological and laboratory information.

Lesson 2: Institutional Base for Health Research

Research capability comprises the resources in research institutes, in universities and other academic institutions, and within health care facilities. Developing countries need to expand and strengthen these resources, to make more effective use of indigenous resources, and to coordinate the efforts of the various groups.

Human Resources

The lack of skilled scientists in specific disciplines and other trained personnel is an obvious gap that limits the ability of developing countries to conduct research on priority problems (Kwapong and Lesser, 1990).

Research Training. Attempts at strengthening research capability in developing countries often focus on the training of research scientists and other personnel. National governments, bilateral and multilateral agencies, and private foundations have responded to this need by awarding training fellowships for promising candidates to undertake studies at the master's degree, doctoral, and postdoctoral levels. Such schemes have had varied results. In some cases, such programs have enabled institutions to acquire the critical mass of scientists necessary to undertake meaningful research projects. In other cases, the effort has produced limited results.

Some trainees fail to return to their institutions; in some cases, they remain permanently abroad — the so-called brain drain. Others return to take up positions in which they cannot apply their training in conducting research, or find they have acquired skills and interests that are not of immediate relevance to the situation at home. Others cannot apply their newly acquired skills because of the limited infrastructure in their home institutions.

These and similar problems have prompted many sponsoring agencies to review their fellowship programs and to take corrective measures to deal with these issues. There is some consensus that the strengthening of research capability should not be based solely on the competitive award of training fellowships to the brightest students. In addition to the declared interests of the candidates, the award of training fellowships should be based on the analysis of the projected needs for skilled personnel and the absorptive capacity of the national institutions. Failure to relate the award of fellowships to opportunity and needs often produces graduates who cannot find suitable employment or who become disgruntled with the frustrations in their ill-equipped and underfunded institutions.

Research training programs are now being developed in the context of institutional strengthening. This implies linking training programs to other complementary inputs for strengthening the institutions. First, there should be an in-depth analysis of the institutional profile identifying its strengths and weaknesses, assessing its resources, and presenting a realistic projection. This means ensuring that there are relevant positions and career structures so that candidates can have suitable appointments after completing the training program. Support must be provided through the training of other critical personnel in the institution (for example, technologists, statisticians, and computer programmers), through the infrastructure at the institution, and through filling gaps in equipment, library facilities, and other logistics. These programs need directors and other personnel with strong management skills.

The "Brain Drain." The problem of emigration of trained scientists remains a difficult challenge in many developing countries. It is a complex problem partly related to the poor economic situation in home countries as compared with the opportunities available in developed countries. Scientists who emigrate can obtain much higher salaries than at home, but this is not the only factor determining the "brain drain." Emigration provides access to modern laboratory equipment and to other features that facilitate research efforts.

But massive brain drain is not inevitable. National governments can mitigate the problem by adopting policies that encourage scientists to stay at home. These include devising career structures for scientists with realistic salary scales in terms of the local situation and providing resources for infrastructure and the running costs of research establishments. Strong training facilities at home reduce the demand for training abroad. Where some training has to be undertaken abroad, the research topic should be closely aligned to local needs and, if possible, carried out at home. Another policy to address brain drain is providing incentives for scientists, including a reward system to recognize excellence. Governments must also make effective use of indigenous personnel in carrying out local projects instead of having early recourse to foreign experts. Disincentives are rigid bureaucracies, political harassment, and abuse of civil rights. Research councils, with independent scientific boards, may provide more flexible management of research than the rigid bureaucracy of the civil service.

The brain drain cannot be viewed as a total loss. Emigration of scientists has permitted the matching of skills to resources. Some scientists from developing countries have made significant contributions to knowledge in the course of their doctoral and post-doctoral programs in developed countries (for example, F. Zavala, a postdoctoral student from Chile working at New York University, developed the circumsporozoite test for detecting malaria infection in mosquitos; I. J. Udeinya, from Nigeria, working at the National Institutes of Health in Bethesda, Maryland, discovered the phenomenon of cyto-adherence of falciparum-infected red cells to endothelial cells). One compensation of the brain drain is that some of the productive work of emigrant scientists may benefit humanity as a whole, including, although indirectly, their home countries. It should be noted, for example, that a significant number of American and British Nobel Prize winners were foreign-born. They had emigrated from other countries in search of better opportunities. Their immigration to Britain and the United States provided an opportunity for the world to benefit from their genius that might have been lost had they remained in their home countries.

In addition to the problem of the emigration of scientists from developing countries, losses are also felt through their assignment to administrative posts. This effectively removes them from participation in active research. One suggestion for dealing with this internal brain drain is to create parallel career structures that enable scientists to advance their careers without being side-tracked to administrative posts (Frenk, 1991).

Lesson 3: Human Resources

The development of human resources is the key to strengthening research capabilities in developing countries. It is necessary to create a climate and environment in which the most promising candidates can be identified, trained, and groomed to undertake the challenging tasks of using science to tackle health problems. Appropriate incentives— salaries, rewards for excellence, and adequate funding of projects—should be devised to attract and retain the best scientists.

International Collaboration

Much experience has been accumulated in recent years about the role of international agencies in strengthening health research capability in developing countries. From its regular budget, the World Health Organization (WHO) has operated fellowship programs for the training of health personnel, including researchers. Usually, candidates are identified by national authorities, with selection related to local needs and opportunities. Less successful are cases in which the selection of candidates is not based on objective criteria and is influenced by political considerations.

The World Health Organization. Over the past two decades, WHO has developed several special programs of research and training on human reproduction, tropical diseases, diarrheal diseases, and acquired immune-deficiency syndrome (WHO, 1987). Each of these programs has devised strategies for capacity building, and their approaches have evolved over time. For example, the Tropical Diseases Research Program (TDR) abandoned its open fellowship program at an early stage when it encountered problems in placing scientists who had completed their training. As these WHO special programs have matured, they have developed innovative approaches. They provide training grants only in the context of institution strengthening.

An interesting approach is the promotion of "sandwich" Ph.D. programs in which the candidates undertake their course work in developed countries but carry out the research work under supervision in the home institute. Reentry grants are awarded to scientists on completion of their training in order to enable them to get started on work soon after their return. Priority health problems of the country are linked to training programs and institution strengthening programs. Programs that encourage and enable the strengthened institutions to address such problems demonstrate to national authorities the value of health research. National networks among scientists and institutions within the same country are promoted, carrying out capacity strengthening on a national basis.

These special programs have had some impact in their areas of interest. They have trained many scientists and strengthened institutions that now conduct research at a credible level of performance. For example, by 1989, the human reproduction research program had awarded 1,012 training grants to scientists (WHO, 1990). The impact of the WHO programs has been enhanced where governments have followed up the initiatives, but strengthened institutions have floundered in the absence of national commitment. For example, TDR noted the fact that even though vector-borne diseases are highly prevalent in Africa, training programs for vector biologists are weak. TDR strengthened several national institutions to offer master of science programs in medical entomology and parasitology. In spite of initial success, it is proving difficult to sustain these programs because of indifference on the part of national governments. The factors responsible for this difficulty have not been fully identified. Have the governments in Africa not recognized the need for training entomologists for research and service? Do they prefer to have them trained abroad rather than locally? In a country like Nigeria, with over 20 universities and academic institutions, it seems strange that one master's degree program on vector biology that received support from TDR would wane and die because of lack of national support.

In addition to WHO, many other agencies have provided support for strengthening research capacity in developing countries: the United Nations Development Program and the World Bank jointly cosponsor TDR and other WHO initiatives as well as operating their own programs. Other health-related U.N. agencies—UNICEF and UNFPA—are also engaged in similar ventures. Bilateral and regional agencies—the International Development Research Centre of Canada, the Swedish Agency for Research Cooperation with Developing Countries, and the Commission of European Communities—operate research and strengthening programs that include the health sector. Also relevant to the health sector are recent initiatives for strengthening biotechnology programs in developing countries (Zilinskas, 1989). Private foundations, notably the Carnegie, Ford, and Rockefeller foundations in the United States, the Wellcome Trust in the United Kingdom, and other charitable organizations, have invested extensively in institution strengthening.

International Research Centers. One contentious issue is the role of research centers that are managed by international agencies. Some of these institutions, especially in Asia and in Latin America, have made valuable contributions to knowledge and have provided opportunities for training national scientists. The Kenya-based International Centre for Insect Physiology and Ecology (ICIPE) has contributed to entomology for both agriculture and medicine. In addition to its intramural program, ICIPE is involved in a network of agricultural institutions in Africa; its special contribution has been the training of scientists in modern research methods. The well-known international center on diarrheal diseases research in Dacca has done outstanding work, particularly in the development of oral rehydration—a simple, affordable, life-saving technology. The finances of these institutions tend to be more stable than those of national institutions, and they are less subject to local political pressures. They provide a mechanism for generating a critical mass of investigators, including scientists from many different countries. But these international centers are rather expensive to run and often encounter political and other problems that limit their effectiveness.

International research centers have played a more striking role in agriculture than in medicine. Even though the experiences gained in agriculture cannot be translated directly to health research, some general principles can provide useful guidelines. The agricultural centers, when most successful, have managed to transfer innovations to national programs that have adapted and adopted them. The process has been more successful in Asia and in Latin America than in sub-Saharan Africa. The difference is partly due to the fact that the Asian and Latin American countries, with their existing national research capabilities, were more able to absorb the innovations and apply them in promoting the "green revolution." In Africa, the national research base was much weaker and may have been further weakened by the diversion of external aid from national institutions to international centers. In any case, there has been a steady decline in the per capita production of food in sub-Saharan Africa since the international agricultural centers were founded!

In the early days of their existence, the international agricultural centers were criticized for being too isolated from national institutions. They have responded by establishing linkages with networks of institutions in their region. It would appear that the formula for the success of international research centers is effective collaboration with national centers, a relationship that should be designed to strengthen the national research capabilities, especially in the least developed countries.

Duration of External Support. Of particular importance for successful institution-strengthening programs is the duration of the support. Some sponsors are anxious to obtain rapid results and provide support for a few years, hoping that such input will be sufficient to launch a strong research capability. Experience has shown that some of the institutions require support over a much longer period—a decade or longer before they become firmly established.

Lesson 4: International Collaboration

International programs have provided the means of strengthening research capabilities in developing countries, but their impact has been varied. In part, the success is determined by the strategies adopted by the sponsors but more importantly by the responsiveness and the commitment of national authorities. The various inputs—human resources development, institution strengthening—need to be tailored to the local circumstances. National policies on employment, career structures, salaries and other reward systems, and institutional support influence the tendency for scientists to emigrate from developing countries.

Strategies for Capacity Strengthening

Many factors, both internal and external, influence the growth, development, and success of research institutions. The wide variations in the level of development in different countries and the many differences in opportunities make it impossible to design a rigid strategy for capacity building and strengthening. Each case has to be treated on its own merit with a flexible approach.

Inputs for Capacity Strengthening. Any new initiative for capacity strengthening should be based on a careful analysis of the present situation of the institution, its objectives, and a realistic assessment of internal and external resources, as well as the national priorities for health development. Professional leadership and effective management are important ingredients for success. Potential leaders need to be identified and groomed to take responsibility for directing the institutions. Besides obtaining sound scientific training in their respective disciplines, they should acquire competence in research management.

A variety of inputs are required for capacity strengthening. Financial support for capital development, improvement of infrastructure, supply of reagents and other consumables, and other running costs is essential. Sometimes, a relatively small amount of flexible funds, especially in hard currency, can make a major difference in permitting an institution to obtain crucial supplies. Key personnel must be trained as described above. Programs need to host visiting scientists from developed institutions to bring in new ideas, to stimulate and generate local leadership, to serve as role models, and to show what can be achieved in local circumstances. Capacity is also built through linkages with a developed institution. The most successful linkages were perceived as being mutually beneficial to both institutions, and they were maintained long enough to produce enduring change in the developing institution. The successful models usually involved joint research projects, training of personnel, and two-way exchange of staff.

More Effective Utilization of National Capabilities. Both national authorities and external agencies are sometimes guilty of undermining indigenous capabilities by using foreign experts in preference to national scientists and institutions. The effect is often exacerbated by the enormous differences between the meager salaries of local scientists and the much larger fees and lavish allowances enjoyed by foreign experts. Some of the expenses involved in bringing foreign experts could have been used to strengthen local institutions by meaningfully involving them in national projects. National scientists, well qualified, experienced, and competent, find it galling and frustrating to watch their peers from other countries imported as foreign experts and to see lavish spending on externally funded projects while their institutions flounder and languish from lack of support. National scientists who are bypassed and ignored by their own governments often tackle similar tasks effectively as consultants in other countries. In the worst cases, bilateral aid is tied to the use of foreign experts. In such cases, the governments of developing countries face the difficult choice of accepting the free services of foreign experts from bilateral programs or having to pay for their own nationals from local resources. Some foreign-funded programs are designed so that the external support ends when foreign scientists are replaced by nationals, again discouraging the emergence of local leadership. There is often a strong temptation for cash-strapped governments to accept such foreign aid as temporary expediencies, thereby retarding the development and growth of national institutions.

Lesson 5: Strategies for Capacity Strengthening

Research strengthening is a complex process. Success depends on a careful analysis of the many different factors, both internal and external, that influence the performance and productivity of research workers. Apart from financial support, relevant inputs may include the training of personnel, the use of visiting scientists as catalysts for change, and well-designed linkages with more advanced institutions on

the basis of mutual respect and peer relationships. Such linkages have to be carefully crafted to avoid the appearance of exploitation (Angell, 1988). National governments and external agencies should make the fullest use of indigenous expertise and should avoid actions that would tend to undermine their effectiveness.

Setting Priorities for Capacity Strengthening

No simple formula can be applied for deriving a list of priorities for strengthening research capacity in developing countries. Not only do the countries show significant differences, but in each nation, the situation is dynamic, with the evolution of health problems over time. Some of the more advanced developing countries have now brought under control many of the traditional health problems, characterized by a high prevalence and incidence of communicable disease complicated by malnutrition. They now have to deal with cancers, heart disease, and other degenerative disorders as the dominant health problems. The requirements of each country have to be tailored to local needs and opportunities (Feacham, Graham, and Timaeus, 1989).

The Commission for Health Research developed a framework for reviewing research priorities in developing countries. Recognizing the importance of research for achieving the efficient and equitable development of health services, the commission identified the need for each country, no matter how poor, to establish "essential national health research" (ENHR). ENHR, a new strategy for managing research, comprises two components:

Country-specific research is aimed at informing each nation of the nature, dimensions, and determinants of its health problems and at optimizing the impact of health programs. The results of these studies tend to be locale-specific, and the findings cannot be validly transferred to other countries.

Global health research includes research for the development of new and improved technologies such as drugs, vaccines, and environmental and communications techniques. Many of these elements lend themselves to international and global collaboration, and the results are transferable across borders (Bloom et al., 1989; Task Force on Health Research, 1991; Ramalingaswami, 1989).

Each country should, therefore, seek to build up its capacity to undertake a meaningful ENHR program. This involves acquiring the capacity to carry out epidemiological studies and social and behavioral, health services, and policy research. The information derived from the situation analysis would help to identify the priorities for global health research. Developing countries also need to strengthen their capability to undertake global health research. This would involve investments in biomedical and social sciences.

Lesson 6: Priorities

Developing countries should give high priority to (1) building and strengthening their capability to conduct essential national health research that would provide a situational analysis of the health issues of the nation and direct health policy, and (2) to the operation and management of services in the most effective channels.

Financing Capacity Strengthening

Developed countries derive funding of health research from various sources, both public and private. National governments strengthen research capabilities in public institutions—research institutes, universities and other academic institutions, and health care facilities. Private foundations and public charities also make substantial contributions in some countries, and the pharmaceutical industry makes substantial investments in research.

The research establishment in developing countries is often mostly dependent on public resources. Some of the more advanced developing countries are now building up the tradition of funding through private foundations and public charities, and are building up indigenous pharmaceutical industries that support research and development.

The Commission on Health Research and Development, an independent group of scientists, estimated that out of a global expenditure of some U.S. $30 billion, only U.S. $1.6 billion was spent on the problems of people in developing countries. Out of that $1.6 billion spent on developing country issues, almost half was provided by governments and other agencies in developing countries themselves. Bilateral aid and multilateral agencies and private foundations based in developed countries spent an estimated U.S. $685 million, about 58 percent of the research funds, on developing country problems (Murray et al., 1990). The commission recommended that each developing country should devote at least 2 percent of its health budget for research. This figure establishes the principle that in order to operate efficiently, the health care system needs research and should therefore invest in it. The commission further recommended that externally funded projects should devote 5 percent of their budgets for strengthening indigenous research capability. The implementation of these recommendations would provide much-needed financial resources for health research and in particular for building and strengthening national capacity.

Lesson 7: Financing Capacity Strengthening

The level of financial support is an indication of the degree of national commitment to building and strengthening indigenous research capability. In order to ensure adequate allocations to research, each country should decide what proportion of its national assets would be devoted to health research. This should be stated as a proportion of gross national product or as a percentage of the health budget. Such clear indicators would help to protect research funding during periods of financial stringency.

In conclusion, recent efforts to strengthen research capabilities in developing countries have generated useful experience and models that can guide future initiatives. The various models must be adapted to suit local circumstances.

Notes

1. Some of the issues relating to capacity building in Africa were discussed at a roundtable conference in Dalhousie University in 1989; see Kwapong and Lesser (1990).

References

Angell, M. 1988. Ethical imperialism? Ethics in international collaborative clinical research. *New England Journal of Medicine* 317(16): 1001-3.

Bloom, B. R., P. Salgame, V. Mehra, H. Kato, R. Modlin, J. Convit, L. Lugozi, and S. Snapper. 1989. Vaccine development. On relating immunology to the Third World: Some studies on leprosy. *Immunology* 2 (supplement): 7.

Commission on Health Research for Development. 1990. *Health Research: Essential Link to Equity in Development*. Oxford: Oxford University Press.

De Cola, F., and P. H. Shoyinka. 1984. *Three Decades of Medical Research at the College of Medicine, Ibadan, Nigeria—1948-1980*. Ibadan: Ibadan University Press.

Feacham, R. G., W. J. Graham, and I. M. Timaeus. 1989. Identifying health problems and health research priorities in the developing countries. *Journal of Tropical Medicine and Hygiene* 72:133-91.

Frenk, J. 1991. Balancing relevance and excellence: Organizational responses to link research with decision making. Unpublished manuscript.

Golden, M. H. 1988. The importance of medical research in the Commonwealth Caribbean. *West Indian Medical Journal* 37:193-200.

Kwapong, A. A., and B. Lesser, eds. 1990. *Capacity Building and Human Resource Development in Africa: Report of a Roundtable Convened by the Lester Pearson Institute for International Development, Dalhousie University—September, 1989.* Halifax, Nova Scotia: Lester Pearson Institute.

Lambo, T. A. 1964. The village of Aro. *Lancet* 2:513-14.

Lucas, A. O. 1989. Health research in Africa: Priorities, promise and performance. *Annals of the New York Academy of Science* 569:17-24.

Martinez-Palomo, A., and J. Sepulveda. 1989. Biomedical research in Latin America: Old and new challenges. *Annals of the New York Academy of Science* 569:36-44.

Morley, D. 1983. A medical service for children under five years of age in West Africa. *Transactions of the Royal Society of Tropical Medicine* 57:79-83.

Murray, C. J. L. 1990. A study of financial resources devoted to research on health problems of developing countries. *Journal of Tropical Medicine and Hygiene* 93:229-55.

Ramalingaswami, V. 1989. Perspectives on research and diseases of the tropics: An Asian view. *Annals of the New York Academy of Science* 569:25-35.

Santos, A., and Guillermo Soberon. 1990. *The Undertaking of FUNSALUD after Five Years' Work.* Mexico: Fundacion Mexicana para la Salud.

Task Force on Health Research for Development. 1991. *Essential National Health Research (ENHR): A Strategy for Action in Health and Human Development.* Geneva: Task Force on Health Research.

World Health Organization (WHO). 1987. *Tropical Diseases Research: A Global Partnership. Eighth Programme Report of the UNDP/WORLD BANK/WHO Special Programme for Research and Training in Tropical Diseases.* Geneva: WHO.

———. 1990. *Special Programme of Research, Development, and Research Training in Human Reproduction: Biennial Report 1988-1990.* Geneva: WHO.

Zilinskas, R. A. 1989. Biotechnology and the Third World: The missing link between research and applications. *Genome* 31:1046-54.

CHAPTER 8

HEALTH POLICY FOR RURAL AREAS: SRI LANKA

Godfrey Gunatilleke

At the time Sri Lanka became independent, the health status of the population measured by indicators of life expectancy and mortality had already reached a level that was well above that of most of the developing countries in Asia. In 1953, the crude death rate was 10.9 per 1,000, and the infant mortality rate was 71 per 1,000 live births. Life expectancy at birth was 58 years. Adult literacy was 69 percent. The health situation in the early 1950s was the outcome of a combination of social and economic policies, among which health policies and infrastructure for health care played a major role.

The Health Outcome: 1950-60

The improvements in health have continued at a steady pace over the last four decades (see Table 8.1). Life expectancy is now estimated to be around 70 years, infant mortality has declined to about 18 per 1,000 live births, and the crude death rate is 6.2 per 1,000. Adult literacy has risen to 87 percent. These indicators reveal no significant rural-urban disparities. Furthermore, as the share of the urban population is approximately 21 percent of the total, the national averages are broadly representative of the situation in the rural sector. The only exception is a small segment of relatively higher mortality and ill health in the plantation sector.

Table 8.1. Social indicators for Sri Lanka

Social indicators	1953	1963	1971	1977	1981	1989
Crude birth rate (per 1,000 population)	39.4	34.1	30.0	27.9	28.2	21.3
Crude death rate (per 1,000 population)	10.9	8.5	7.7	7.4	5.9	6.2
Infant mortality (aged 0-1 yr. per 1,000 live births)	71.0	56.0	45.0	42.4	29.5	17.5
Rate of natural increase	2.8	2.5	2.3	2.1	2.2	1.5
Life expectancy at birth (yrs.)	58.0	63.5	65.2		69.0	70.0
Literacy (%)	69.0	76.9	78.5		86.5	87.0
Per capita calorie consumption	1944.0[a]	2118.0	2230.0	2343.0	2200.0	2292.0 (1990)

Sources: Department of Census and Statistics, censuses, 1953, 1963, 1971, 1981; Ministry of Health, annual health bulletins, 1981-90; Registrar General's Department, reports on vital statistics; and Department of Census and Statistics, food balance sheets, 1953-90.
[a]For the year 1950.

The crude birthrate, which had risen to 39.4 per 1,000 of population in 1953 from 35 in the mid-1940s as a result of the steep decline in mortality, has fallen to 21 by the beginning of the 1990s. With the steady and continuing decline in both mortality and fertility, Sri Lanka is well into the demographic transition. On the current projections, the net rate of reproduction would drop to one (one birth per one death, implying no net increase) in the mid-1990s, and the population would eventually stabilize at around 25 million well before it could double.

However, along with these positive health and demographic developments is one disturbing feature: the high prevalence of malnutrition, reflected in the figures for low birth weight (28 percent), stunting (approximately 36 percent), and wasting (approximately 18 percent) for children under five years of age. This outcome in health, in which long life expectancy and declining fertility exist alongside persistent malnutrition, has had a mixed impact on the growth and productivity of the work force, of which the largest component is in agriculture and in the rural sector.

The pattern of morbidity and the causes of mortality have also changed significantly. The prolongation of life at a low level of economic well-being has produced "a double burden" of ill health. Sri Lanka has not yet been able to control and prevent the communicable diseases and diseases of bacterial and parasitic origin, which are associated with low life expectancy, poverty, and a poor physical environment. These include diarrheal diseases, respiratory infections, and malaria. At the same time, the noncommunicable diseases and the organic and degenerative disorders, such as cardiovascular diseases, which are typical of the disease pattern of industrialized societies, have also become major causes of both morbidity and mortality.

Health Policy in a Welfare-oriented Strategy of Development

The term *health policy* itself raises major issues that apply to the management of health in all countries. They become particularly relevant in analyzing the improvement in health that has taken place in Sri Lanka. Health policy could be defined in a relatively restricted sense to limit it to the policies directly concerned with the delivery of health care and health services to the population. In its wider sense, health policy will include the health-related policies in various other sectors that were contributing to the health outcomes. The policies in most sectors—education, transport, industry, agriculture—as well as macroeconomic policies, which affect prices of food and health-related goods, can all have some impact on health, positive or negative. In many cases the impact of these developments, such as in education, can have a more pervasive and far-reaching effect on health than can the delivery of health services themselves. Policymakers seldom attempt to identify and take account of these health impacts when setting and pursuing the goals specific to the sectors with which they deal. Therefore the effects of their policies on health tend to remain outside the ambit of consciously designed, purposive policies.

In the case of Sri Lanka it might be said that the health outcome itself was the product of the interaction of policies in various sectors, particularly education, food, and agriculture. While it would not be correct to argue that there was a conscious effort to formulate and coordinate policies in these other sectors in order to achieve specific health objectives, it is important to recognize that the common objective of satisfying the basic needs and improving the well-being of the population was a primary objective of all these policies. Therefore in discussing "health policy" in Sri Lanka, it is essential to examine two policy components and examine how they interacted and reinforced each other. First, there were the policies relating to the delivery of health services, which was the responsibility of the Health Ministry and other ministries concerned with water, sanitation, housing, and the immediate physical environment directly related to the epidemi-ology of disease. Second, there were the policies that were directed at the satisfaction of the basic needs of the population—particularly food, education, and income generation for the poor.

The implications of health policy for agriculture and rural develop-ment in Sri Lanka must therefore be analyzed in this larger context. The relevant issues have been organized in this chapter in the follow-ing sequence. The first set of issues relates to health goals and objec-tives, how they were conceived and pursued by the policymakers and the extent to which the improvement of the health status of the rural population became an essential part of the welfare-oriented develop-ment strategy, which was aimed at the satisfaction of basic needs and the improvement of the quality of life as a whole. Flowing from this is the second set of issues, which concerns the general state of health of the population and the problems of disease, the development of the health infrastructure, and the delivery of health services. The third set of issues relates to the links between health and agricultural growth and productivity, both in the plantation agriculture and the estate sec-tor, as well as in domestic agriculture and the rural sector. It also in-cludes the specific health problems posed by the agricultural pro-grams that were implemented—both the demands made on health by agriculture and those made by health on agriculture—whether they relate to food and nutrition or to the new health hazards generated by agricultural development.

The importance of good health as the foundation of human capital and as a necessary condition of economic growth was recognized, and the Sri Lankan policymakers made health a primary objective val-ued for itself, a condition of well-being that was an integral part of the development they sought to promote in the country. Sri Lanka's pol-icies were criticized for what was considered to be the excessive weight given to investments in "nonproductive" social sectors at the cost of economic growth. This raises a whole range of issues regard-ing the trade-offs between social and economic objectives that cannot be explored fully within the limits of this chapter. Those that have specific relevance to the subject of the chapter, however, are exam-ined in later sections. In the welfare-oriented approach that was adopted, the availability of food, education, and health to the mass of the population became the primary consideration of policymakers and was accepted as a public responsibility. The health policy was part of this ideology of development.

The Satisfaction of Basic Needs

The state undertook responsibility to make provision for the satisfaction of three basic needs. Health services and education from primary to postsecondary were provided free, and a subsidized food ration was made available to the entire population. With its well-developed plantation sector, Sri Lanka's economy was able to generate substantial state revenues. In 1950 government revenue amounted to approximately 15 percent of gross domestic product. The state therefore possessed the capacity to incur large public expenditures. It used these resources to put in place a benevolent welfare state on a scale that was unusual for a country with its level of per capita income. The sociocultural roots of this ideology of welfare, which found ready acceptance by the indigenous elites, and the political economy that made its application possible require more extensive analysis than can be attempted in this chapter. There are many intriguing features in the Sri Lankan situation, in which substantial income transfers were made by the elites and the processes of accumulation and investment in the private sector were curtailed. For the issues discussed in this chapter, however, what is relevant is the way in which health objectives were integrated in this welfare ideology.

The provision of free health services to the entire population came to be accepted as a public responsibility in the 1930s, after Sri Lanka gained a large measure of self-government in preparation for full independence. Universal adult franchise was granted in 1932, and representatives were elected to a state council that elected a board of ministers who enjoyed limited legislative and financial powers. Elected representatives saw their main responsibility as one of developing the infrastructure and obtaining public services for their electorates. Health and educational facilities figured prominently in their agenda. The ministers of health in the preindependence era laid the foundation of the health services, which were expanded later. The benevolence of the state in the health sector was ideologically close to the Buddhist value system and ethos of the political leaders. The people looked back to a tradition that placed great value on compassion and the alleviation of suffering. One of the few lay activities that Buddhist monks freely undertook was the practice of Ayurveda, the traditional system of medicine. The World Bank Mission (1950), which reviewed the health system and made recommendations, recognized the importance assigned to health services in the social ethos in Sri Lanka. They begin their chapter on health with a saying from the Buddha: "Of all gains, the gain of health is the highest and best." The striving after good health was different qualitatively from the normal desire or "thanha" for material gain.

The budgetary allocation for health amounted to about 9 percent of the total government budget in the 1950s and approximately 1.8 percent of GDP. The government continued to maintain this level throughout the four decades, with minor fluctuations. The state health services covered all aspects of health care, preventive and curative. The state made generous allocations for both investments on the development and expansion of the infrastructure and maintenance of the services. The three main components of the health service were, first, the network of curative institutions; second, the major preventive disease-control campaigns; and third, the primary health care infrastructure. The effort was well distributed among all three components. They reached all parts of the rural sector and provided the rural population with access to free health services. The main elements of primary health care services included family health, antenatal and postnatal maternal health care, infant and child health care, family planning, health education, and nutrition programs. Already in the late 1940s many of these elements were in place in the rural sector. For example, the administration report by the director of Medical and Sanitary Services in 1946 records activities under the following programs, among others:

1. *Maternity and child welfare.* There were 533 health centers in the country. Nineteen thousand clinics were held. Attending and receiving treatment at clinics were 180,000 expectant mothers (approximately 70 percent of all mothers), 96,000 infants, and 144,000 preschool children. Deliveries in hospitals and maternity homes, as well as those by Health Department midwives, numbered 120,000, or about 60 percent of all births. The recorded home visits by public health midwives came to 852,000 for the year, which would give a statistical average of about 4 per pregnant mother.

2. *Health education.* The program included 88 lectures with "lantern" slides, 1,734 lectures, 56 cinema shows, and 106 health exhibitions. The administration report states that 82,468 talks were given in schools, villages, and clinics and that "125,000 copies of health propaganda leaflets on Nutrition, choice of food, malaria, venereal disease and tuberculosis were distributed. The Department of Medical and Sanitary Services also undertook a program

of construction of wells and latrines of improved design as measures for providing a protected supply of water and improving
sanitation."

3. *Nutrition*. The state introduced a program of free milk distribution at the postnatal and antenatal clinics, and the free distribution of biscuits and milk to school children.

The broad framework of health policy and the main components of
health services that were to be provided by the state were already fairly
well articulated by the mid-1940s. It is on this foundation that the health
system was further developed and expanded, both in terms of coverage
of population and special problems of disease control. These aspects will
be examined in greater detail in the section that follows.

The second major component in the integrated welfare program
was free education from the primary to the postsecondary stages. Education had a pervasive impact in improving health. Health education
and far-reaching changes in health behavior were possible, primarily
because of the receptivity and responsiveness of an increasingly liter-
ate and educated population. The critical lever in health improvement
in Sri Lanka has been female education. In the first phase, in the 1950s
and 1960s, this was reflected in improved practices in regard to maternal health and infant and child care. Women were readier to enter
maternity homes for deliveries, to attend clinics, and to acquire
knowledge relating to infant and child care. The capacity to avert infant deaths and respond promptly to ill health increased rapidly and
steadily lowered infant and maternal mortality. In the second phase,
in the 1970s and the 1980s, there was increasing acceptance and use of
contraception and family planning. Education had rapidly increased
the participation of young women in the work force, reinforcing the
motivation for family planning. These behavioral changes have occurred despite the fact that structural changes in the economy have
not been significant. The urban industrial sector has grown slowly,
and the rate of urbanization has been relatively slow. The demographic transition in Sri Lanka has taken place in the rural context and
offers a very different model from that of urbanization and industrial
growth.

The third component in the strategy for improving rural well-being
was the food policy. First, the state provided a subsidy on a food ration. This commenced during World War II to meet the acute food
shortages of the period. It was provided to the entire population regardless of income. The food subsidy underwent numerous changes,

but the subsidy was generally the equivalent of one kilogram of free rice per person per week. In the early stages the ration was 2 kilograms per person per week, with a subsidy of approximately 50 percent. This was reduced to 1 kilogram of free rice in the late sixties. In the late seventies the food subsidy was restructured, converted into a food stamp scheme, and targeted to low-income households, covering almost half the population. At present the food stamp scheme continues to serve slightly less than half the population. The food subsidy scheme, despite its shortcomings, contributed 15 percent to 30 percent of total income in households in the last three income deciles. The current food stamp scheme would amount to about 10 percent to 15 percent of the income of a household at the poverty line, or more, depending on how far below the poverty line the household is situated. On the average, it would be providing a critical margin of purchasing power to the absolutely undernourished households who are unable to satisfy their minimum nutritional needs. The food subsidy would therefore help in meeting at least part of the nutritional deficits of poor households.

Apart from the subsidy, policymakers also followed macroeconomic policies that attempted to stabilize prices of food and essential or "basic needs" goods. The cost of living index increased only 50 percentage points for the entire period 1952 to 1973, until the oil price increase and other international economic developments drastically altered the situation. While these macroeconomic policies had an adverse impact on economic growth and delayed the structural adjustments that were necessary, they protected consumers against international price increases and maintained their current standards of living.

The Development of Peasant Agriculture

The fourth component of this strategy was the program of agricultural development, which was aimed at expanding the cultivation of rice in peasant small holdings. Health policies were an integral part of this four-pronged strategy of rural development. At the outset the rural households were in a matrix of deprivation in which four conditions reinforced each other: (1) the poor state of health, manifested in high mortality, high morbidity, and high fertility; (2) the low level of literacy and knowledge, which deprived them of access to knowledge and information essential for behavioral and attitudinal change, as well as the know-how and technology to increase income-earning capacity; (3) lack of economic resources, income-earning capacity, and

purchasing power; and (4) a general state of powerlessness manifested in the lack of control over decision making related to their own
future well-being. These factors were closely interlinked and mutually reinforced each other to confine these households to a hard core
of deprivation. If the households were to move out of their condition,
it was necessary to attack all four states of deprivation simultaneously. The strategy adopted in Sri Lanka had this integrated character, in which health policy was one major component. The improvement in the state of health and its impact on economic well-
being, including agricultural development, were the outcome of the
interaction of these four elements, including the preventive and curative health services and the infrastructure that went with them.
Health policy in the wider sense included the health-related components of the other elements, which reinforced the conventional
health-care component, resulting in improvement in health. Improvements in health again fed back to the other elements through increased participation in education, improved nutritional status, and
higher productivity.

The Role of Health in Agricultural and Rural Development

The relationship between the health ideology and health expectations of
a society, on the one hand, and its socioeconomic conditions and level of
development, on the other, raises a range of complex issues that cannot
be considered in depth within the limits of this chapter. There are, however, a few observations on the links between health and economic development as perceived in the Sri Lankan context that are relevant for
the themes discussed. The perception of the link between health and
productivity in a developing economy that aims at rapid increases in income and output is significantly different from the health ideology that
pervades a subsistence economy, which is relatively stagnant. In the
former, this link is placed in the context of growth and development.
Health status is related to the energy and physical well-being needed to
promote a sustained increase of output. The subsistence state, on the
other hand, does not possess the same inner dynamic that pushes toward higher productivity and better health.

Health in the Development of the Plantation Sector

The coffee and tea plantations in the central part of the country, which were developed in the 19th century and the early part of the 20th century, relied primarily on immigrant labor from South India. For a variety of reasons, the local population, engaged in traditional agriculture, could not be attracted into the plantations as wage-earning labor. The owners of plantations realized the importance of maintaining their imported human capital in good condition. Given the nature of the agricultural operations in the plantations, particularly tea, interruptions in the supply of labor could have serious economic consequences. The economic returns from a healthy work force became evident to the employers. They made the necessary investments for the provision of health care. They established their own hospitals and hired the staff to provide most of the health services needed. The British rulers, who had a major economic interest in the success of the plantations, supported these efforts by strengthening the health services provided by the state, particularly in dealing with major problems of disease control, such as smallpox and hookworm. The plantation sector therefore became an important factor in the development of health services in the early stages.

The relative efficiency with which the system functioned is exhibited by two outcomes. First, despite a major flow of migrant labor, there were no major outbreaks of disease in the country that could be attributed to the migration. Second, the health indicators for the plantation sector and the basic health services available for the sector in the period preceding independence were superior to those of the rural sector. The crude death rates for the estate population were 22.1 in 1930 and 17.1 in 1945, when the corresponding national averages were 25.4 and 21.9. Infant mortality rates were close to the national average and in some years significantly lower. According to the statistics published in the administration reports of the Health Department in the mid-1940s, there were 161 hospitals in the 2,808 plantations, which were scheduled under the legal enactment governing health care, the Medical Wants Ordinance. The extent of the surveillance of health conditions in the estates was such that the Health Department could report in 1946 that the "sanitary conditions in 6% of the estates was very good, 53 were good, 29% fair, 9% poor and 3% were bad. Of the 66,813 line rooms (housing accommodation) inspected, 56,946 were up to Government standards. . . . 89,981 persons were treated for Ankylostomiasis (hookworm) on 252 estates" (*Administration Report*, 1948).

Campaigns for Disease Control

From the early stages of development, public policies on health showed an awareness that the protection and improvement of health was a precondition of economic well-being. The state assumed the main responsibility for the control of the major diseases affecting the population. The identification of a major disease and a systematic public effort to deal with it through special campaigns formed one crucial element of health policy from a very early period. For example, the hookworm campaign was inaugurated in 1916. This approach to the problems of health—the identification of specific countrywide problems of disease and the mobilization of resources for their solution—placed the delivery of health care and services in a strategy with well-defined objectives and goals. Consequently, the health authorities were able to deal successfully with killer diseases such as plague and smallpox; launch campaigns for the control of tuberculosis, malaria, and leprosy; carry out mass immunization campaigns against diseases such as typhoid and smallpox; and undertake mass treatment campaigns as in the case of hookworm. For example, the administration reports of the director of Medical and Sanitary Services record hookworm treatment for 1.322 million persons in 1945 and 1.37 million in 1946, carried out in schools, villages, estates, hospitals, and dispensaries. Already in the early 1950s Sri Lanka had developed a basic health infrastructure and administration that the International Bank for Reconstruction and Development (IBRD) mission in its report in 1951 described as admirable and that had the capacity to create conditions for the control of disease and ill health that were the foundation for a productive work force.

The Health Needs of Agricultural Programs in the Postindependence Period

The plans for economic development that were formulated soon after the country gained independence reflect a concern with the state of health and the impact it was having on growth and productivity. The IBRD mission in its report, "The Economic Development of Ceylon (Sri Lanka)" (1952), had this to say on the country's health situation:

> In the calculation of a country's resources for economic development, health is a primary factor. . . . Economic improvement or progress will be illusory if the health of the people is not improved. . . . Economic and social progress has always been hindered by the prevalence of disease. . . . Ceylon is far from being at the lowest level. . . . Its people are better off economically than those of most other countries in Asia, and they have a well organized curative and preventive service. But although death rates

have fallen, the same cannot be said of the sickness rate of various diseases.

It remains obvious that there is a great deal of sickness in Ceylon . . . and that the country continues to suffer a grave loss from consequent impairment of productivity.

The strategy of agricultural development had wide-ranging implications for the health sector. On the one hand, there were health needs and preconditions relating to health status that had to be met if the strategy was to be implemented successfully. On the other hand, the strategy had far-reaching effects on the health outcome, due both to the increases in purchasing power and improvement in food and nutrition and to the new health hazards that were produced as a result of technological changes, new human settlements, and irrigation systems.

While it is not possible to quantify the independent contribution that improvement in health made to economic development and to agricultural growth in particular, it is evident that the control of disease and the decline in mortality in the rural population occurred together with the economic development of the rural sector. Improvement in health was one important input into the economic development of the rural sector. It strengthened and sustained the human capital base.

The major program of agricultural development—import substitution in rice—posed a wide range of problems in relation to health. While the infrastructure for health care that had been developed for the country as a whole was able to respond to many of these challenges, several problems of health and health-related productivity persisted in the rural sector. First, the program for import substitution covered the entire country, including both the densely populated wet zone and the sparsely populated dry zone. Second, the import substitution program envisaged the expansion of land for rice cultivation in the dry zone and the transfer of population from the wet zone to the dry zone. The total number of families resettled in this manner during the period 1950-90 is in the region of 350,000, excluding the migration of the nonagricultural population into these areas in the wake of agricultural development. These new settlements were dispersed in all parts of the dry zone. A major constraint for resettlement in the dry zone was the endemic prevalence of malaria. The effective control of malaria therefore became more than a general problem of disease control. It was essential for the successful implementation of the import substitution program in rice.

The malaria control program illustrates the complex problems of coordinating health policies with agricultural policies. The health infrastructure as it had developed in the 1940s had the capacity to mount a major special campaign for the control of malaria when the effectiveness of DDT spraying was discovered and proved. The campaign covered the epidemic-prone areas in the wet zone and the entire dry and intermediate zones. Intensive spraying was undertaken in all agricultural settlements and irrigation schemes, to protect both settlers and the construction workers who were developing new land for future resettlement. The enforcement of spraying required special regulations permitting health personnel to enter household premises and spray DDT. New settlements and clearing of jungle would result in the resurgence of malaria and its transmission to other parts of the country, unless timely control and surveillance measures were taken. For this, there had to be close coordination between the health authorities and the authorities responsible for the development of the settlement schemes. In the recent past, the interests of the health program have come into conflict with those of agriculture in regard to the use of the main insecticide that is used for control of malaria. The use of malathion or malathion-based insecticide by the cultivators has resulted in the malaria mosquito developing resistance to the spray. Agreement on a regime of insecticide use by cultivators and monitoring of such use have posed a variety of problems for both sectors — health and agriculture.

Apart from malaria control, the agricultural development program in rice required the strengthening of the health infrastructure in the rural sector as a whole. It would not be correct to say that this was done specifically or consciously in relation to the development objective. The improvement of the health status of the population was an objective in its own right. Nevertheless, the priority given to the peasant sector and its economic activities gave a rural bias to policies in other sectors as well and strongly influenced the priorities in health. The health infrastructure was systematically expanded and improved to provide the rural population with better and readier access to health facilities and services.

Between 1934 and 1960, the hospital bed capacity had increased from 1.6 beds per 1,000 people to 3.3 per 1,000. In 1934 more than 50 percent of the bed capacity was concentrated in the western and central provinces of the island, which is the most urbanized sector and the area in which the main part of the tea plantation was located. By 1960 the bed capacity was distributed among a wide range of hospitals located throughout the country. In the main urban centers, the provincial and base hospitals had a bed capacity of 9,000, and 103 district and cottage hospitals covered all the districts and provided a bed capacity of 9,300. Another 251 peripheral units, rural hospitals, and maternity homes with a bed capacity of about 5,200 provided closer access to the widely dispersed small rural communities.

For the newly settled areas, the basic health infrastructure was established at the time the families were settled. The infrastructure itself formed part of the larger network of health care facilities to which it was linked as a peripheral unit. Mobile clinics and visiting health staff were therefore deployed from the main centers to serve the settled population. The provision of health facilities to the new settlements was perceived as an entitlement of the newly settled population. Within the national framework, these households had enjoyed free health services in the areas in which they had originally resided. They could not be excluded from those services when they moved into new settlements.

The Health Hazards of Agricultural Development

The discussion so far has focused on the support given by health services to the agricultural development program in rice. The agricultural program in turn created health problems of its own that required attention. First, the settlers selected for the new schemes were from the poorest strata in the rural sector. Preference was given to landless peasants with large families. The new settlements therefore contained a concentration of highly vulnerable groups in terms of health. A study of a recent settlement under the major river diversion scheme— the Mahaweli Development Scheme—revealed high levels of child malnutrition. These conditions probably reflected the low quality of life of these settlers prior to settlement, as well as their incapacity to improve it in the early phase of settlement.

The conditions of settlers in the early phase of the settlement program in the 1950s and 1960s have not been adequately researched and documented to come to any firm conclusions on the health status of the settler population prior to and immediately following settlement. Policymakers, however, often complained that the settlement program was not producing the returns that were expected from the investment and that increase in productivity was not being realized fast enough. Among other factors the poor health and nutritional status of the settlers would have contributed to this performance. The agencies responsible for health were not equipped to deal with this problem in all its aspects, which were multisectoral in character. The nutritional supplementation programs of the health sector were targeted programs, serving only a segment of the population—pregnant and lactating mothers and children under five years. Although this may have had some effect in keeping nutritional levels from worsening, the prevailing high levels of malnutrition do not suggest that they have resulted in any significant reduction of malnutrition.

The expansion of rice cultivation and the implementation of major irrigation projects were accompanied by new health hazards. One major new hazard has emerged from the widespread and intensive use of insecticides and pesticides. There has been a sharp rise in cases of sickness and death due to toxic effects of exposure to these agrochemicals during spraying, contamination of food due to improper storage, and chemical residues in the food marketed. Because of their ready availability, pesticides have become one of the most common methods of committing suicide in the rural sector. Data on pesticide poisoning indicate that the incidence has been highest in the paddy growing areas.

The widely distributed channel system of the major irrigation projects existed alongside conditions in which sanitation was poor. No systematic efforts were made to provide a protected water supply, and the risks of fecal and other forms of pollution and waterborne disease were high. Some types of livestock had specific health hazards (for example, Japanese encephalitis was associated with pig rearing). Mechanization of agriculture increased the incidence of accidents and injuries. The development of agriculture therefore required a program of occupational and health education that dealt with these problems. The health care programs that were available generally failed to incorporate these elements.

The Seasonality of Ill Health and Intersectoral Links

The seasonal nature of paddy agriculture produced conditions in which health hazards, economic hardship, and physical stress were combined during specific periods of the year. The beginning of the cultivation season normally coincided with the commencement of rains. Microlevel surveys indicate that incidence of ill health from diarrheal and respiratory diseases arising from water pollution, poor sanitation, and substandard shelter tends to rise during this season, and household income and food availability tend to be low during this period, which falls between two harvests. The demand for physical effort in agricultural operations is quite high. The low levels of income, undernutrition, and increase in health hazards during a working season that requires sustained physical exertion on the part of adults, both male and female, result in a period of great stress. Microlevel surveys have confirmed the prevalence of these conditions in most parts of the rural and estate sectors.

The problems of seasonal stress in relation to health and nutrition have not received any special attention, and no strategies have been designed to help families pay more attention to the nutritional and health-related aspects of seasonality and manage these periods of stress more efficiently. The long-term solution, however, lies in a more productive and stable agricultural enterprise in which households could generate surpluses to support them comfortably throughout the year and also find off-season income-earning opportunities. A mix of tree crop agriculture, such as horticulture, together with livestock could be combined in the farming enterprise to achieve both income stability and nutritional objectives.

The agricultural development strategy could have been better coordinated with health policy to achieve both agricultural and health objectives. For example, a more determined effort to create favorable market conditions for cultivation of crops such as soya and groundnut, particularly during the season when water availability is low, and the promotion of livestock and horticulture would have produced more calories and protein, as well as income, per unit of land and water. Such a strategy would have had to pay greater attention to health and nutrition criteria within the agricultural programs themselves. Health policies would then have had to look beyond the health services and health care programs to causes of ill health, as well as to opportunities for promoting health and nutrition that lie in other sectors and development activities.

Health Policy and Family Planning

Selection of settlers was biased in favor of large households. Health policy during this period did not pay sufficient attention to family planning. The state policy on family planning remained equivocal, and the health care system did not identify it as an important area of concern. In the new agricultural settlements, the rapid growth of population soon led to second-generation problems. The size of land holdings given to settlers were adequate only to support a single family, and then only if a high level of productivity was achieved. The conditions of land tenure prohibited subdivision of the allotment. The agricultural development program itself was monocultural in its orientation. Rice as a crop did not lead to many forward linkages, which would have become a base for the diversification of the rural economy. The development strategy that was pursued promoted neither agricultural nor nonagricultural diversification and consequently failed to generate adequate nonfarm employment. The focus on the development of the rural sector and the relatively slow growth of the urban industrial sector resulted in a low rate of urbanization.

Meanwhile the expansion of health services had helped to lower mortality, while fertility continued at previous levels. These factors all contributed to conditions that kept the population in the rural sector and rapidly increased the rate of unemployment in the rural work force. While these conditions were generally applicable throughout the country, what was more disquieting was that the new agricultural settlements, which were expected to provide a model for solving the problems of rural unemployment and poverty, were as yet not yielding the expected results. The lacuna in health policy in regard to family planning has to be seen in this context.

Sri Lanka's experience of lowering mortality, with little effort to reduce fertility simultaneously, provides important lessons. Sri Lanka had been able to organize the delivery of maternal and child health services with remarkable effect to lower infant and maternal mortality. This combination of developments in Sri Lanka provided an unparalleled opportunity for a family planning effort of the same magnitude and intensity as the other mass health campaigns (such as hookworm treatment and immunization). The opportunity, however, was missed, with serious adverse consequences for economic development and the well-being of the rural population. The decline in fertility that occurred in the 1970s and 1980s, as a result of freer access to contraception and family planning services, indicated the pent-up and unsatisfied demand for such services.

Health Trends in the Plantations after Independence

The improvements in health in the rural sector can be compared with trends in health of the resident work force in one part of the plantation sector. These trends illustrate the situation in the absence of the integrated inputs described previously. After independence, the health status of the immigrant work force in the plantations fell below the national average and remained significantly below it. The higher rates of morbidity and mortality in the estate sector had their source in a number of interrelated factors. The quality of health care available, which, prior to independence, compared favorably with what was available in the rest of the country, remained at the same level or deteriorated, while health services were rapidly improved and expanded outside the sector. Both political and economic factors contributed to this situation. Immediately after independence, the immigrant laborers, who formed the majority of the work force in the tea plantations, were disenfranchised as part of national policies and therefore lacked the political leverage enjoyed by the rural electorate. Economically, the plantation sector stagnated and declined as a result of both domestic policies and trends in the international market for tea. Consequently, the sector was left with negligible surpluses for maintenance and improvement of the social infrastructure, particularly in health, housing, and education. Infant mortality, which in the period 1930 to 1945 was on the average slightly lower than the national average, quickly rose above it in the three decades that followed. In 1975, the rate of infant mortality in the estate sector was estimated at 83 per 1,000 live births as compared with a national average of 48.

Low economic returns; the relative lack of access to national programs in health, education, and housing; and the consequent poor health status and low level of literacy of the work force all contributed to the declining productivity of the plantation sector. The trends in health have been reversed since the plantations were nationalized and the state assumed responsibility for the provision of health and other services.

Current Strategies and Their Implications for Health Policies

Despite the integrated, equity-oriented strategy pursued by Sri Lanka, levels of malnutrition continue to be high. The rural economy is relatively undiversified in terms of both agriculture and off-farm nonagricultural economic activity. The proportion of rural households in absolute poverty, defined in terms of food insufficiency, is estimated at about 28 percent of the total. Rural unemployment is in the region of 14 percent. This assessment, however, should not overshadow the positive achievements that have been described. These achievements relied on massive state interventions and large-scale public expenditures. The key question is whether Sri Lanka could have achieved a more efficient mix of policies to provide a better balance between the state and the market.

Reappraisal of Past Strategies

Recent reappraisals of the development experience of Sri Lanka have argued that Sri Lanka's performance in terms of social indicators is not the unique case it has been widely claimed to be; some other countries, such as South Korea, starting from similar levels of per capita income in the early sixties, have performed equally well socially, but have far outpaced Sri Lanka economically, with policies that relied minimally on state welfare. Again it is not possible to enter into this controversy within the limits of this chapter, except to comment, parenthetically, that many critical conditions, such as resource availability and strategic considerations, were very different for the two countries. Nevertheless, the question whether Sri Lanka's strategy was excessively dependent on state intervention is a valid one.

The alleviation of poverty and the improvement of well-being for the poorer half of the population could not have been achieved to the extent done without the state's playing a substantial role. Sri Lanka was in the fortunate position of being able to generate large public revenues. These were in the region of 15 percent of GDP in 1950. Neither would these improvements have been possible without simultaneous efforts to deal with deprivation on several fronts: health, education, food, and increase in the incomes of the rural poor. Nevertheless, the universal, untargeted character of the free services and the welfare programs had several adverse outcomes. The people as a whole developed a pervasive attitude of dependence on state intervention. It removed the incentives for self-reliant action on the part of households and communities, and militated against the process of empowerment that was essential for the poor to lift themselves from their condition of deprivation. The state became the omnipresent patron and benefactor. An equitable system of cost recovery would have been both feasible and more sustainable and efficient. It would have provided more resources for better services to the needy and allaround improvement of quality.

The Social Impact of Economic Adjustments

With the economic reforms that were introduced in 1977 and the period that followed, current strategies have moved rapidly in the direction of liberalization and the use of the market in all areas of economic activity. Subsidies and administered prices have been progressively reduced or eliminated. The regulatory system of import controls has been almost entirely dismantled, and trade has been liberalized. The government has embarked on a program of privatization of a large number of state commercial and industrial enterprises. The food subsidy has been restructured and targeted in the form of a food stamp scheme to the poorer half of the population.

Along with this movement toward freeing the market of state controls and intervention, the government has been careful not to reduce the state's responsibility or the level of public expenditure in some of the key social sectors. The government's commitment to free health services and free education remains intact. The government health expenditure as proportion of GDP has been in the neighborhood of 2 percent over the last decade. With the growth of GDP considerably higher than that of population, per capita expenditure has increased in real terms.

The social impact of the liberalization program began to receive the serious attention of policymakers in the mid-1980s. Although the mortality indicators were improving steadily, nutrition surveys showed high levels of malnutrition, reflected in the percentage of low-birth-weight babies and the rates of acute and chronic malnutrition among children under five years. Approximately 25 percent to 30 percent of households were below the absolute poverty line, defined as the income needed to satisfy 80 percent of the minimum nutritional requirements. The restructured food stamp scheme, which had a fixed money value, did not take account of inflation. By the mid-1980s, food stamps had lost more than half their real value. Moreover, the expectation that the opening of the economy would lead to rapid growth that would trickle down and alleviate poverty was not being realized.

The government has responded to this with several initiatives. Those that have particular relevance for the health sector are the Agricultural Food and Nutrition Strategy, the Food and Nutrition Policy Plan, and the Janasaviya Program.

Food and Nutrition Policies

The nutrition plan focused on eight determinants that appeared to be important for the reduction and elimination of malnutrition. They included the mother's education, per capita income, food expenditure, toilets, birth order, and garbage disposal. The strategy supported by the plan attempted to provide a framework that would coordinate the programs and policies of several sectors to achieve nutritional objectives. The planned activities included the production of low-cost starchy staples; the fortification of foods, such as wheat and rice flour with soya, salt with iodine, and low-cost staples with minerals and vitamins; food processing and nutrient conservation; food preservation and storage; preparation of weaning foods; and the development of inland fisheries.

The program envisaged close collaboration between the ministries of agriculture and health, among others. This plan is the first attempt to identify the nature of the intersectoral collaboration needed in the field of health. However, concerned as it is with specific nutritional objectives, it does not extend to all the areas discussed under the section on health policy, particularly the areas relating to new health hazards and the prevention of ill health. The plan relies largely on state machinery for its implementation. An adequate effort has not been made to identify how communities and households could be brought into the program and how local-level institutions could be developed and greater responsibility assigned to them.

The New Poverty Alleviation Program: Janasaviya

With the introduction of the Janasaviya Program the government has attempted to combine the market-oriented, outward-looking strategy of development with a new large-scale intervention for the alleviation of poverty. The eventual objective of the program is one of enabling poor households to raise their incomes and free themselves from dependence on state welfare. But the initial process involves income transfers to households on a scale larger than that of any previous welfare program. The scheme is intended to cover the food stamp beneficiaries, after a further process of screening to exclude households above a specified poverty line. First, monthly grants are made for consumption for a specified period of two years, essentially constituting substantial increases of what is now given as food stamps. Second, loans are given to the same households for investments and income-earning activities. The innovative character of the program lies in the way in which welfare has been integrally linked to the process of income generation and growth. The consumption component is time-bound and limited to a two-year period, on the understanding that these transfers will enable households to make good the nutritional deficits in their current struggle for survival and will provide them with the basic economic security that will release them for greater productive effort. The investment component provides them with access to the economic resources needed to improve their income-earning capacity. There are various aspects of the program that have come under criticism, and in the last two years it has undergone various modifications. It is not possible to examine and evaluate the program in any depth within the limits of the present chapter, but some of the relevant issues are dealt with briefly.

The Janasaviya Program is likely to eventually cover at least the lowest three income deciles of the population, estimated to be living below the poverty line as defined in the Sri Lankan context. In terms of the planned contribution to economic growth and employment creation, the program would therefore be quite significant. Closing the poverty gap would mean in the first instance generating additional income-earning capacity, which, when it eventually covers the entire Janasaviya population, would be equal to at least 6 percent of current GNP. Thereafter this component of the economy would be at a level that could sustain its growth.

The Janasaviya Program is conceived as a multisectoral program. The Health Ministry, supported by the World Health Organization, is contributing to the Janasaviya Program by aiming to strengthen the health outcome of Janasaviya in terms of both nutritional status and higher productivity as an input to Janasaviya, as well as by directing increases in income to uses that will improve the health status and quality of life of the household. While the Janasaviya Program itself is based on state intervention, the intervention is conceived as that of a "change agent," which increases the self-reliant capacity of the households to compete in the market. For this purpose the program attempts to use a broad-based coalition of nongovernment organizations (NGOs), private business, and other agencies to engage in the program. Private business and NGOs would be able to provide technical assistance in various forms. Private-sector firms could help with production and marketing links, with mutual benefit to the Janasaviya entrepreneurs as well as themselves. The Janasaviya Program itself is a recognition of the limitations of the excessive and continuing reliance on welfare in past rural development strategies.

Both the nutrition plan and the Janasaviya Program open up opportunities for the health sector to collaborate closely with agricultural and poverty alleviation programs in a manner beneficial to both the objectives of economic development and those of health. Health policies themselves would need changes and adjustments to take account of past limitations of the welfare-oriented approach as well as the new demands in health. These have implications not only for health policy in general, such as in the case of cost recovery and privatization, but also for agriculture and rural development.

Enhancing Capacity at the Household Level

As stated earlier, the health care system, with its wide range of state services, has been unusually successful in reducing mortality. Nevertheless, the system has not been able to deal effectively with the problems of malnutrition and high rates of morbidity arising out of the diseases associated with poor living conditions, such as diarrheal and respiratory infections.

At present there are several state interventions and health programs to deal with these problems. The "triposha" program—a nutrition program for pregnant and lactating mothers and for children under five years of age—and school midday meals and the food stamp schemes are programs that attempt to provide nutritional supplements and food purchasing power. Janasaviya has a much broader poverty-alleviation objective in its attempt to create conditions that would eventually render these interventions unnecessary. The health services have now identified diarrheal diseases and acute respiratory infections as the areas requiring a special effort analogous to major disease-control programs. However, the delivery of free state health services in the preventive and curative areas, as presently organized, has not been adequate to reach this hard core of malnutrition and ill health.

Improvement in nutritional status and the physical quality of habitat, water sanitation, and housing—which will reduce diarrheal and respiratory diseases—must come primarily from the alleviation of poverty and an increase in the incomes of low-income households. But along with alleviation of poverty, there is still much that can be accomplished in the field of nutrition and quality of life within prevailing conditions, through enhancing capacity at the level of the household and the community. Fuller and more efficient use of nutritional resources available to the household is one area. Microlevel studies reveal how, at the same level of income and wealth, there is still a wide variation in health and nutrition. While part of these may be due to genetic and other factors outside the control of the household, the level of capability for management of household resources, patterns of health behavior and lifestyles, and other critical factors relating to hygiene and environmental sanitation, which are well within the control of households, also account for malnutrition and poor quality of life.

In order to realize the potential that is available, a special effort has to be made to enhance the capacity of households. This requires a major reorientation in current programs of family health, which essentially approach the family unit, particularly the mother and child, as a passive recipient of health care. The family, which has been identified as the primary unit of health care, would need to enhance its capacity for self-care. The concept of increasing the self-reliance of households for protecting health and preventing ill health does not find ready acceptance in a top-down delivery system.

Health-oriented Development

Improvement of health and quality of life, approached in this manner, has a positive impact on stimulating demand for "health goods" appropriate to the rising level of income in the rural sector. These "goods"—nutritional food such as milk, eggs, fruit, and high-protein products like soya—can also help in the greatly needed agricultural diversification. The demand for an improved quality of life, if appropriately promoted, will result in demand for improvements in housing, the construction of protected wells and toilets, and the acquisition of goods—such as smoke-free stoves, consumer durables, and equipment—that render food preparation and storage more hygienic. Most of these goods have a low import content and can be produced within the rural sector, creating new income-generating opportunities and employment within the sector. Designing programs of this nature will foster patterns of consumption and lifestyles that are health promoting, economical, and also likely to be environmentally benign.

Participatory Action at Local Level

Enhancing the capacity of the household in the manner described above is closely linked to the awareness and capacity for collective action at the community level. The latter is critical for improvement of water, sanitation, and the physical environment, and for building institutions at the local level that enable the rural communities to participate more actively in decision making for their health and quality of life and to assume an increasing role of responsibility. Although the political processes in Sri Lanka introduced democratic institutions at a very early stage, including local government reaching to the village, they failed to promote the sharing of responsibility and power at the lower levels. The system remained highly centralized, with the power and resources concentrated in the organs of authority in the central government. The central government budget, which became the main source of funding, and the welfare programs, which made both citizens and local institutions relate to the state as beneficiaries of state welfare, prevented the growth of self-reliant participatory democracy. The recent changes in structure that envisage substantial devolution of power, including revenue-raising power to subnational units—the provincial-level councils and, further down, divisional councils closer to the village level—could reverse the centralizing trends of the past. Health policies could appropriately make use of these opportunities.

The Health Dimensions of Agricultural Policies

In regard to agriculture itself, health policies need to identify more clearly the health-agriculture link and make use of these more efficiently, in conjunction with the ministries directly concerned with agriculture and rural development. These links have already been briefly examined. They include links in the field of nutrition, such as incorporation of nutritional objectives in agriculture, which would also help to stimulate demand and diversify agriculture; health effects of irrigation; health hazards of pesticide use and other technological innovations; health hazards of livestock development; and programs to deal with the special stresses of seasonal agriculture. As stated earlier, there is a whole area of "occupational health" in agriculture that has yet to be adequately identified. It requires more effective health education of the rural population on the entire range of new health hazards. It also calls for more specialized preventive and curative services and systems of monitoring and regulation. Simultaneously there is need to build appropriate capacity to identify, investigate, and research the changing pattern of morbidity specific to agricultural changes.

Health- and Market-oriented Policies

Finally, there is the larger issue of adjusting health policies to the new market-oriented strategies. This raises the question of the future of free health services, although there is a strong, continuing commitment to the provision of such services. Tentative proposals to introduce some form of cost recovery, at least in relation to income, or forms of contributory health insurance schemes, bringing the market more openly into health care, have not yet found acceptance. There has, however, been a considerable measure of "privatization" of state health services. This has been done by granting government doctors the right of private practice. The main criticism of this system is that the government doctors give priority to their private practice to the detriment of their normal duties, and that various forms of discriminatory treatment and abuses are likely to occur. The system has, however, demonstrated that many rural households have the capacity to bear at least part of the cost of their health care. This is confirmed in studies of the utilization of health services at the micro-level. In the case of infants and children, parents prefer obtaining treatment from Western private medical practitioners for most episodes of diarrhea and other illnesses that do not require hospitalization. In cases of acute illness requiring indoor treatment, which cost more than what rural households could afford, they invariably use the state health services.

At the same time the private sector in health care, serving the upper-income groups in the urban sector, has expanded rapidly for outpatient and inpatient treatment, as well as for laboratory services. The demand for private health care by the rural population is likely to grow rapidly with the increase in income. An increasing cadre of general practitioners is required to satisfy this demand. This has been constrained to some extent by the general shortage of doctors owing to the limited annual supply from the existing faculties for medical education. A grade of "assistant medical practitioners" has been available to provide health care at an intermediate level. The expansion of the cadre has been met with some resistance by the higher medical profession, and has been criticized on the ground that it would dilute the quality of services available to the public. Many similar issues need to be resolved to enable the health sector to accommodate the need for an expanding private sector and the demand of the public for wider choice and more consumer-oriented services.

References

Administration Report of the Director of Health Services for 1960. 1961. Colombo: Government Publications Bureau.

Administration Report of the Director of Medical and Sanitary Services for 1936. 1937. Colombo: Government Publications Bureau.

Administration Report of the Director of Medical and Sanitary Services for 1946. 1948. Colombo: Government Publications Bureau.

Central Bank. 1950, 1960, 1970, 1980, 1990. *Annual report.* Colombo: Central Bank.

Gunatilleke, Godfrey. 1985a. *Changing Needs of Children: The Experience of Sri Lanka.* Colombo: Marga Institute.

———. 1985b. Health and development in Sri Lanka—an overview. In *Good Health at Low Cost,* edited by Scott B. Halstead et al., 111-24. Proceedings of a conference held at Bellagio Conference Center, Bellagio, Italy, April 29 to May 3, 1985. New York: Rockefeller Foundation.

———. 1989. *Government Policies and Nutrition in Sri Lanka: Changes during the Last Ten Years and Lessons Learned.* Pew/Cornell Lecture Series on Food and Nutrition Policy. Ithaca, N.Y.: Cornell University.

International Bank for Reconstruction and Development. 1952. *The Economic Development of Ceylon.* 2 vols. Colombo: Government Publications Bureau.

Marga Institute. 1984. *Intersectoral Action for Health: Sri Lanka Study.* Colombo: Marga Institute.

———. 1988. *Seasonality and Health: A Study of the Socio-economic Environment of Ill Health in Five Locations.* Colombo: Marga Institute.

———. 1990. *Economic Policies for Sustainable Development: Country Study—Sri Lanka.* Colombo: Marga Institute.

———. 1991. *Priority Issues and Policy Measures for the Alleviation of Rural Poverty.* Colombo: Marga Institute.

Richards, P., and E. Stoutjesdijk. 1970. *Agriculture in Ceylon until 1975.* Paris: Organization for Economic Cooperation and Development (OECD).

Snodgrass, Donald R. 1966. *Ceylon: An Export Economy in Transition.* Homewood, Ill.: Irwin.

Thorbecke, Erik, and Jan Svejnar. 1984. *Effects of Macroeconomic Policies on Agricultural Performance in Sri Lanka, 1966-82.* Paris: OECD.

CHAPTER 9

HEALTH SYSTEMS FOR RURAL AREAS: KENYA

Dan C. O. Kaseje

Health for All

As the quest for health for all (HFA) continues, much has been written on the subject of primary health care (PHC), which was adopted as the strategy for the achievement of the following global goal: "The attainment by all people of the world by the year 2000 of a level of health that will permit them to lead a socially and economically productive life." This chapter is intended to present and evaluate the Kenyan experience in the quest and to make recommendations for strengthening the system, particularly for the rural areas, as we move into the 21st century. Kenya was a signatory to the Alma-Ata declaration, which adopted the PHC strategy and defined it as

> essential health care based on practical, scientifically sound and socially acceptable methods and technology made universally accessible to individuals and families in the community through their full participation and at a cost that the community and country can afford to maintain at every stage of their development in the spirit of self-reliance and self-determination. It forms an integral part both of the country's health system, of which it is the central function and main focus, and of the overall social and economic development of the community. It is the first level of contact of the individual, the family and community with the national health system bringing health care as close as possible to where people live and work, and constitutes the first element of a continuing health care process. (WHO and UNICEF, 1978)

Implicit in this definition is that primary health care is an integral part of the overall social and economic development of the community and should therefore be community based. The implications of this for agricultural and rural development are clear from the definition.

Improvement in agricultural production in rural subsistence agriculture can also only be achieved through the community-based approach: learning from people, their practices, insights, and knowledge and building on these in such a way that wholesome traditional methods and techniques are not undermined but are enhanced and improved.

The idea of active community participation implied here is key to the development of a health care system that not only focuses on recovery from illness but also on promotion and maintenance of good health through the involvement of individuals, families, and communities. This is the only way to achieve health for all, but it is also the only way that agriculture production can be improved in the rural areas. It is well known that increased food availability is a major contribution to health improvement, which in turn ensures adequate production.

Ill health compromises productivity through direct incapacitation of food producers and through time spent in caring for the sick and attending funerals and related ceremonies. The resulting loss of production eventually undermines health status. Peak agricultural activities tend to coincide with peak transmission of certain diseases, malaria, for example, and thus compromise productivity. These problems must be adequately dealt with by all concerned, the communities and their intersectoral support system.

There are agricultural activities with negative effects on health that would be identified and minimized through the community-based multisectoral approach recommended in PHC. The success of this would be enhanced by appropriate action-oriented epidemiological and participatory research involving agriculture, health, and development. This requires adequate capacity.

Long-lasting food-production and health-improvement practices are based on people's attitudes and behavior. Thus, a system to enhance both must focus more on partnership with those affected than on technology. Availability of technology does not automatically lead to adoption and utilization. Our blunt instruments of technology could be sharpened immensely by people's participation.

The History of the Kenyan Effort

The achievement of health for all has been an objective of the government of Kenya (GOK) since independence in 1963. The government had made several attempts to realize this objective long before the Alma-Ata conference in 1978. In 1965 free medical treatment in government facilities was introduced in accordance with the guidelines of the manifesto of the ruling party to try to make services affordable by and accessible to all. In the year 1970, the central government took over most of the services previously run by local councils, including the rural health services, to ensure effective service delivery. In 1971-72, a Joint GOK-WHO mission formulated the "Proposal for the Improvement of Rural Health Service in Kenya and the Establishment of Six Rural Health Training Centres" (Bennett and Maneno, 1986). The MCH-FP Programme was launched in 1974. In 1982, the Integrated Rural Health and Family Planning Project was launched. A community-based health care unit was subsequently set up within this project in 1984.

Additionally, the number of rural health facilities provided by the government increased from 187 in 1973 to 242 in 1982, while dispensaries increased from 416 to 872 over the same period. Together, this represents a 15 percent increase in rural health facilities between 1973 and 1982.

Despite these increases, more than 57 percent of households in Kenya still travel four or more kilometers to obtain health services, and only about 30 percent of the population lives within two kilometers or less of a health facility. Health status, as measured by selected indicators of coverage by health services, morbidity, and mortality, hardly changed with the improvement of health infrastructure.

The main problem facing the delivery of rural health services continued to be the preferential allocation of resources to urban-based services, where fewer than 20 percent of the people live. Funds allocated in the rural areas for drugs, supplies, and fuel and the maintenance of equipment, buildings, and vehicles remained grossly inadequate.

The concept of community participation in health and development activities, a major cornerstone in the PHC strategy, was attractive to the GOK, as it was seen mainly in terms of the self-help movement that had existed since independence and had greatly contributed to development activities. It was seen as an advantage to have the communities, particularly in rural areas, helping to develop and maintain their own health services.

The Policy for Health for All

The Kenyan government realized that the provision of health services addresses one of the basic needs and is essential as a precondition for overall agricultural and other economic development and social progress. This has been set forth in the Kenyan Constitution and National Development Plans since independence (Bennett and Maneno, 1986).

In line with these provisions, the government's main objectives for the development of health services since independence have been: (1) to strengthen and carry out measures for the prevention and control of diseases; (2) to provide adequate and effective diagnostic, therapeutic, and rehabilitative services for the whole population; and (3) to carry out biomedical and health services research as a means of identifying more efficient and cost-effective methods for delivery of services.

These objectives would be achieved through a multitude of strategies. One is to increase coverage and accessibility of health services in rural areas. Another is the consolidation of urban and rural curative, preventive, and promotive services. A key emphasis is on maternal and child health and family planning services in order to reduce morbidity, mortality, and fertility. The government of Kenya is strengthening the Ministry of Health management capabilities, with an emphasis on the district level and on increasing interministerial coordination. Additionally, a search for alternative financing mechanisms for health care is being conducted. And finally, the GOK has been developing primary health care. In this approach, emphasis has been given to community participation in environmental health activities, prevention of diseases, and establishment of community health funds and income-generating activities. The emphasis on community participation as a strategy for achieving the goals of primary health care marked a major policy shift.

This should have given a whole new dimension and direction to the health system, in contrast to the more conventional approach based on provision of basic health services alone, as Kenya had been attempting for years. Yet it only meant the recruitment and training of community health workers (CHWs) and traditional birth attendants (TBAs) who were to work as volunteers or receive support from their own villages, but were expected to be extenders of basic health services.

The Role of Nongovernmental Organizations

Since the early 1970s many nongovernmental organizations (NGOs) had started a number of health programs that attempted to facilitate community participation in a process in which they were empowered, through dialogue, training, and logistic support, to take health into their own hands. Such efforts were encouraged and enabled by the supportive government policy and political climate. Another significant development was the establishment of a support unit for community-based health care (CBHC) initiatives. The unit was run by NGOs, but the government was represented on its board. The unit set up a coordinating committee to provide a forum for sharing, mutual guidance, and joint planning and for implementation of CBHC programs in the whole country.

The flexible and simple bureaucratic systems of NGOs made it easier for them to be at the forefront of CBHC implementation. They provided invaluable experience for the government to learn from in order to apply it in a nationwide program. Thus, the support unit and its coordinating committee provided a mechanism for scaling up isolated CBHC programs into a national program.

The National Program

To develop the strategies required to meet the quest of health for all, a situational analysis was conducted. This analysis identified four problem areas: population growth, agricultural production, government expenditure and basic-needs policies, and health problems.

Decreasing mortality and high fertility have resulted in a dramatic growth in Kenya's population in the last two decades. Since 1970, Kenya has been among the countries having the world's most rapidly increasing populations. The persistence of high fertility in Kenya (total fertility is around eight children per woman) was mainly caused by a low percentage of couples that used contraceptives. Only 11 percent had ever used a modern method at the time of the baseline surveys, in the early 1980s.

Per capita landholdings have affected agricultural production and adequacy of food. Kenya is an agricultural country, with about 80 percent of the population living in rural areas. Almost all rural dwellers derive most of their livelihood from farming or livestock or both. Agriculture currently accounts for slightly over one-third of the GDP, more than twice the contribution of any other sector. About two-thirds of Kenya's exports—primarily coffee and tea—are agricultural commodities.

During the last two decades, Kenya is supposed to have achieved self-sufficiency in food production, but there are population groups that continue to experience food and nutrition problems. There are still recurring food shortages, especially of maize (the staple food for most Kenyans), due to drought, overemphasis on cash crops, and poor distribution, causing problems for smallholders.

The importance accorded to basic needs and services in government policy was only partially reflected in actual expenditure during the past two decades. Economic constraints and competing priorities have diffused the impact of the basic-needs strategy. A disproportionate share of public spending benefits urban and more favored groups, increasing the disadvantage of the rural populations.

The provision of basic-needs facilities and services has been a long-standing and increasingly prominent development strategy of the government. Development plans affirmed the prime responsibility of the government in the provision of these services, while emphasizing the need to involve local communities through self-help activities and the energies of NGOs.

Health problems are mainly caused by preventable diseases: measles, malaria, acute respiratory infections (ARI), diarrheal diseases, and malnutrition. These take the lead in terms of mortality and morbidity rates.

The Organizational Structure, Key Actors, and Their Roles

Having defined the problems, mechanisms and structures were identified that would permit the development of national guidelines for the implementation of the community-based system. It was understood that such a project requires a strong, clearly articulated policy and political will; a change in the knowledge, attitude, and practice not only of the health personnel but also of the community; and the motivation of the key actors in the health-promotion partnership. Other required conditions include an equitable distribution of available resources, greater decentralization and intersectoral collaboration, community participation, and the use of the most appropriate, available, and affordable technology.

The Family Level

The family (parents, children, and the extended family) is the first level of constant and assured health care regardless of its competence, capacity, or resources. The health care process in the family includes education, nutrition, water and sanitation, disease prevention and control, cure of ailments, handling of essential traditional or medical drugs and other curative agents, antenatal care and delivery, and other health promotive and preventive actions. The process always involves active participation by all family members, immediate and extended. Thus the family must be considered as the nucleus and main focus of any effective system of health care.

The most effective techniques for building family health skills involve information, education, and communication. Demonstrations done in the home setting actively involve all the family members, including schoolchildren, who are an important target for health education. These are best done by the resource persons in the community within reach of every family: the mother, other family members, CHWs, TBAs, traditional healers, and even extension personnel from a variety of sectors and nongovernmental organizations. The context of education and the common experience of learners and resource persons ensure relevance of educational messages, materials, and activities and thus promote the intended change in knowledge, attitudes, and practice. The families participate in protection of springs and wells and in construction and use of latrines. They keep their homes clean and ensure hygienic handling of water and food. The family can be encouraged to discuss their own fertility issues and thus become motivated to take remedial actions and ensure safe motherhood.

The family can also be enabled to monitor the health progress of the children (for example, the nutrition and immunization status based on the child's health card) and take appropriate action. They can identify a number of common conditions and take appropriate actions in terms of prevention and home management. Their capacity to perform this task can be enhanced through training and availability of appropriate technology. "Appropriate" also means affordable, sustainable, and socioculturally acceptable and absorbable.

The Community Level

The health functions undertaken at the community level (CHWs, TBAs, and health committees) include information, education, and communication (IEC); community diagnosis and analysis leading to identification of priority problems and appropriate actions to solve these problems; mobilizing existing resources to respond to health problems; providing organized structures and facilities for health action; and providing resource persons for specific health functions.

For effective IEC at the community level, it is important that health resource persons spend enough time listening to and learning from the community in order to build on what is already known and to integrate any new ideas into the local cultural context. The use of local structures, methods, and materials enhances learning because active participation is assured.

The community is involved in its health care through assessing its members' health status and self-diagnosis and then taking appropriate health actions and through the important interaction between agricultural, health, and other extension workers.

Certain community resource persons can be trained by health and extension personnel at the local level to enhance the capacity of the community for its tasks. The TBA occupies a central place in MCH-FP community-based activities and can train the key health provider at the family level, the mother, to recognize high-risk factors in mothers and children and to seek the necessary assistance, to use essential services available to her, and to take household-based health actions that would promote the health of the family and prevent illness.

The CHWs are able to support the mother, the family, and the community in their health tasks through information, education, and training to provide adequate knowledge and skills needed to maintain or regain good health. They should have a greater capacity to recognize and manage health problems than the family and the community. This management includes appropriate referral of persons to other levels of competent care. Their work would thus require them to visit families and to organize and conduct community meetings.

The CHW has to be trained for these tasks, which have to be tailored to their needs and those of the community. In many programs in Kenya, they are given some basic drugs and other equipment and materials for their functions.

The community health committee (CHC) provides a link between the CHWs, the community, and the health facilities and supports the CHWs in their work, with particular regard to collective community actions.

In general, the activities undertaken by the community are those that are shaped around their lifestyle and in which participation requires only their own skills and resources. Since participation is not cost free, community actions are more effective and sustained if they are appreciably rewarded and if the actions are integrated into other ongoing activities in the community.

The Location and Divisional Level

The locational and divisional level involves health and agricultural extension workers and provides the technical support and management base for all health and agricultural activities. The personnel and infrastructure support and provide backup and oversight for all health and agricultural activities for several communities, covering a population ranging from 20,000 to 60,000 people. They provide the necessary equipment and supplies for effective functions of the community resource persons.

The District Level

The district is the most peripheral fully organized unit of local government administration. In Kenya, the population is well above half a million. It is geographically compact and is small enough for staff to understand the major problems and constraints of socioeconomic and health development. It also is a large enough unit to develop technical and managerial skills essential for planning and management. It is the most appropriate level on which to base intersectoral collaboration and coordination and is an appropriate meeting point for bottom-up and top-down planning.

This level serves as the management base for all the health activities in the district. These management functions are carried out by the district health management team (DHMT), which is responsible for the development of all the health programs in the district, with information from the community and from locational and divisional levels.

They train, orient, and supervise the extension-level personnel, but their own exposure to the communities is limited to brief visits. They channel health information into the district development committee (DDC) and ensure intersectoral action for health. They determine the learning needs of their staff and resource persons at various levels and organize training programs to meet those needs.

The management team produces health learning materials and teaching aids appropriate for the district. They ensure food security in the district. They compile health and related information and thus are responsible for nutritional and other disease surveillance data. They produce reports used for further planning and policy formulation.

They are responsible for infrastructure development and have to ensure availability of all equipment, materials, and supplies necessary for health actions. The personnel and facilities at the district level should be able to meet all the referral and technical needs in the district.

The National Level

This is the highest level of management of health services and decision making. This level has responsibility mainly for policy formulation; guidelines for implementation, resource allocation, and capacity building; and all management functions, particularly intersectoral collaboration, at the national level. This is enhanced by intersectoral coordinating committees at all administrative levels. Such committees enable the participating sectors to identify their specific roles and to share and harmonize their plans affecting health.

Training Required for Community-Based Health Care

Everyone involved in the community-based programs requires some reorientation or training in basic concepts and methods involved. At the national level, this includes policymakers, as well as managers and trainers in government and NGO institutions. At the intermediate level, it involves middle-level managers and practitioners, and at the local level, it involves community leaders, the people in the community, and community-based workers such as CHWs and TBAs.

A crucial element involves *equity and redistribution* of available resources. The focus must be on the community and *community participation*, including its facilitation. An aim is the better balance of all essential elements of health care, which means understanding health in more than just medical terms. Successful training will involve more collaboration with other sectors (for example, agriculture, education, and water) and NGOs. The program and communities also require technical support through increased application of appropriate technology.

The training is carried out by an appropriate intersectoral training and resource team at all the five levels: national, district, locational, community, and family. The training method is consistent with the community-based approach. It is hoped that basic training programs of government and nongovernment institutions will be modified to reflect the requirements and emphasis of the community-based concepts and methodology. A special training program developed by NGOs has been adopted by the government of Kenya to prepare the trainers at each of these levels. The national team was formed following a long process of identifying and bringing together experienced CBHC practitioners, people with skills and experience in facilitating participatory learning and leadership and adult education programs. This group was multidisciplinary, consisting of people with health, adult education, agriculture, and social science backgrounds. Most of these were from NGOs (the African Medical Research Foundation, the Roman Catholic Secretariat, and the Methodist Church) and the medical school's Department of Community Health.

The process of developing this team was spearheaded by the CBHC Support Unit. The team developed a training of trainers (TOT) curriculum for training front-line initiators and facilitators of CBHC at the locational level. The demand for this training increased rapidly and necessitated increasing the number of people at the national level able to conduct TOT training for CBHC. Another course was developed for this level, namely, training of facilitators (TOF), aimed at preparing trainers, facilitators, and managers for the CBHC support system, particularly at the district and national levels. From time to time, external consultants were invited to enrich the training pool by bringing in new ideas, techniques, and methods.

The training process was initiated at all levels (community, locational, district, and national). The experiences from the training courses and from new programs were shared regularly in various forums: CBHC coordinating committees, formed at all the four levels to anchor the partnership, and annual CBHC conferences, attended by all partners from all levels, including CHWs and TBAs. All these experiences, ideas, and skills were channeled into the training process and facilitated effective implementation of CBHC. This process was ensured by both the selection of trainees and the organization of the course.

Those who were responsible for CBHC programs or were already involved in some direct way were given first priority for courses. Involvement in CBHC, and hence opportunity to practice the skills and knowledge from the training courses, was considered more important in the selection of trainees than basic academic qualification.

The course was organized in three phases, with the first phase introducing the *concepts* of health; community of CBHC, community-based distribution, and primary health care; and adult learning and awareness raising. This phase also discussed needs assessment, community diagnosis, and baseline information gathering. Finally, trainees were instructed on community entry and the involvement process. The second phase was aimed at developing skills in assessing learning needs, planning, carrying out and evaluating courses, training workshops and learning sessions, and using participatory methods to facilitate learning. The last phase was designed to review the first two phases and to sharpen management and evaluation skills particularly appropriate to the CBHC approach. Three to six months were allowed between phases to ensure application of new skills and knowledge from the courses. This was enhanced by follow-up visits by resource persons. The follow-up activities continued after the third phase. This process was enhanced by regular conferences and follow-up workshops. These meetings also provided an opportunity to introduce new skills and disseminate new information to strengthen the process of implementing CBHC and to promote continuous growth among the partners.

Scaling Up

The implementation of CBHC in Kenya started in small areas as local projects, but the training program described above set in motion a "scaling up" process. As the number of trainers, managers, and practitioners increased at all levels, it was possible to divide the country and districts among teams of trained resource persons, so that each team had a manageable area of responsibility for training and follow-up and for facilitating the process of development and management of CBHC.

This was to ensure that each district in the country had a core team of competent persons for the activities. Each team was linked up to one national training team member for support and encouragement. The networking and sharing of resources among teams also ensured competence in every major activity in each district.

The scaling up process in Kenya required several elements to be in place. The organizational system and its leaders had to be transformed. The process had to be flexible and community specific, with its implementation focusing on building partnership. The participants also had to share an understanding of the CBHC model. The transformed organizational system had to facilitate and manage the process of participation, not simpy *permit* participation. This was very difficult for the GOK structure. From their experience, the NGOs had an upper hand in forming a structure for CBHC capacity building and implementation. The structure consisted of CBHC coordinating committees at each level. The coordinating committees formed task groups for the training and evaluation activities. The national coordination committee was composed of elected representatives from the district coordinating committees. While the coordinating committees met regularly, the task groups met on an ad hoc basis to plan and undertake specific training courses or evaluation exercises. The coordinating committees ensured that the process was securely anchored at their respective levels of responsibility.

The transformed team of leaders and resource persons had to be a core team with commitment to and a shared understanding of CBHC and how it can be implemented in a given district or community. The team needed to encourage self-reliance in communities, and it had to have the necessary funds, materials, and means of transport for its work at the larger levels. The communities were expected to be responsible for meeting the costs only of their own health actions, not the costs of the support structure activities. These funds had to be obtained from external sources. Cost sharing among the partners was always discussed with sensitivity to the economic realities of the communities. It was critical for all partners to know the terms, regulations, and limitations of the partnership. This process was threatening to the elite, particularly the professionals who now had to share what had formerly been their monopoly: power, benefits, information, and other available resources. It took a strong, committed, and charismatic leadership to ensure the continuation of the process of change until a new system of sharing, delegation of authority, accountability, and mutual correction would emerge to nurture the growth and development of CBHC in a given locality.

The implementation process needs to be community specific, particularly when scaling up. It should be guided by research to identify a course of action in each local setting. The local implementation process can be considered as participatory action research feeding its findings continuously to the implementation process, which should therefore remain flexible. This was the case to a greater or lesser extent in various Kenyan districts.

The implementation process in any new district started with intersectoral awareness and planning workshops at all the levels. The workshops were aimed not only at creating awareness but also at setting in motion the process of building bases for anchoring and supporting partnership with the community, with particular emphasis on the key provider, the mother.

This model of CBHC addresses health issues on the basis of a broader understanding of health and how it can be attended. Seen in the contexts of human dignity, development, and total well-being, health action becomes an entry point to social action and holistic development. The community-based program focuses deliberately on the disadvantaged majority. It assumes that these people would take action to improve their own health if they could. It also aims at addressing existing social and economic injustices, which are the root causes of ill health. Addressing these injustices means the transformation of the whole system. In this model people contribute not only resources and labor but also *ideas*, and they share in power and the decision-making process.

The community is in the forefront, analyzing problems, seeking solutions, and then taking the required individual and collective action. The providers are invited to participate in the community's program.

Avenues of generating local funds are tried, such as drug sales and contribution and insurance schemes, but these are designed and developed by the community in consultation with outside resource people.

The approach is not without its unique problems. It does not immediately deliver health services, which is what people may expect. In fact, the expectation of the people is normally charity, not empowerment. This leads to conflict that can prove costly to both the facilitators and the community—the community expecting care and cure and the providers delivering organization and education. Thus the rhetoric of the facilitators may fail to tally with the people's view of reality—people who have been at the receiving end of packages developed at the top. These are people who are often barely able to feed themselves, let alone afford money and time for health activities. All of these real factors have to be taken into account as the community is enabled to rebuild their self-confidence and move toward self-reliance and community involvement ideals.

This model recognizes the strengths and resources of the community; seeks to facilitate and enhance these strengths; recognizes that communities have always been responsible for their own health, even without the interference or intervention of health professionals; recognizes that the mother is the most important and knowledgeable health provider, present in every home; and thus seeks a mutually supportive, reciprocal relationship among those involved in order to improve health care, agricultural productivity, and holistic development of individuals and communities. As such it becomes a process of self-discovery for all involved, a process of solidarity among partners in which each member is aware of his or her strengths, weaknesses, and limitations and hence of the unique contribution that each can make.

The Strengths of the Conceptual Model

The community is able to address their health problems as a total, integrated, community-directed development package. It is a steady, sustained effort to transform the whole life of the community. This transformation occurs through continuous participatory education, through leadership and skills development, and through the availability of appropriate technology, including the necessary technical support. Ideally the technical assistance would come from several government sectors (health, agriculture, water, and housing) and with complementary assistance from NGOs.

The process unleashes local initiative and mobilizes local resources; it empowers the community, particularly those who are at the fringes and are often excluded from decisions and services: women, children, and particularly the poorest segment of the society. All members of the community are enabled to fully understand the likely benefits of their options so that they can make informed choices.

As a result and as a part of this process, the community can take initiative to work toward its own improvement, including maximum use of its own available resources and appropriate technologies.

This model focuses on the key health care provider, food producer, and user of appropriate technology: the mother. In any community the most important health agent is not the CHW, the nurse, or the doctor, but the mother. It is vital to enhance her capacity for her tasks. This means enabling her to participate effectively in the whole process of care for her family and community. She gathers information, analyzes her situation, makes informed decisions and choices, and takes necessary action for health care, food production, and agrobased economic activities. She is already motivated to carry out her tasks by a powerful incentive, the current and future well-being of her children and family.

Assessment of the Kenyan Experience

Most districts in Kenya now have some form of CBHC-PHC program. More than 800 people from different sectors and professional backgrounds have been trained as facilitators and managers of CBHC programs; more than 15,000 persons at the community level have been trained as Community's Own Resource Persons (CORPS) (Community Based Health Care Support Unit, 1991). Many of these people have been followed up and supported to ensure application of acquired knowledge and skills.

In assessing the Kenyan experience it is not enough to simply look at numbers; it is appropriate to examine the extent to which each of the elements considered essential to CBHC are present in the national or specific programs.

Broad Understanding of Health

The programs in Kenya still tend to portray an overly medical and technological approach to health and to be driven by donors or supporting institutions. It is necessary to reduce the medical emphasis in order to allow not only for greater community participation but also intersectoral collaboration. At the moment, the Ministry of Health tends to dominate the process, causing the other vital ministries— agriculture, education, social services, water development—to shy away. Yet the activities of these ministries may have more to do with health than the Ministry of Health itself.

A Clear Policy Statement

The government of Kenya has made a clear statement and has developed guidelines jointly with NGOs for implementation of the community-based programs. Although the principles, objectives, and strategies are clearly stated and communicated, the required structural changes were not indicated, and hence the implementation process has been slow, patchy, and isolated from the formal government services. The government needs to undertake the necessary structural changes that would facilitate real community involvement with an appropriate support network.

Not only is the freedom NGOs have to initiate and run community-based programs a strength; it may also be the only way that community-based systems could be implemented in Kenya. The policy of "District Focus for Rural Development" has created and strengthened intersectoral and interagency collaboration. While it allows greater community involvement in development issues, it is still dominated by the elite.

Political Will

It is doubtful that there has been adequate political will, at the national level, to break professional and bureaucratic inertia in order to allow the necessary change from the long-standing conventional approaches that benefit the dominant powerful minority. This inadequacy is shown in the allocation of resources. It is clearly not done according to basic needs. The urban elite still enjoy the lion's share of the national "cake." This gives NGOs an upper hand in CBHC implementation and results in its fragmentation and patchiness. This tends to be the experience in other countries, as well (Oakley, 1989). It raises the question of fairness, since these programs are community-participation programs that require a just distribution of resources with due preferential consideration to the poor, underserved, and marginalized majority.

Community Participation

From the policy and guidelines, the Kenyan understanding of the role of community participation appears to be limited to contribution of labor, money, and materials in order to extend and maintain services, based on the "Harambee," a one-time collective effort for development, practiced since independence. At best it may also include compliance and cooperation with what is being provided by the system, but not sharing in decision making, power, and responsibility for health. Other people make decisions, and the community takes the consequences of those decisions. Their ideas, experience, talents, and skills are largely excluded. True participation is only possible when the means to bring about the desired results are in the hands of the people. Maximum use of internally generated resources from within the community would allow them greater scope for involvement and would facilitate the process of empowerment. This should not exclude inputs of needed resources from outside the community. The Kenyan programs tend to overemphasize the objective of effectiveness and the involvement of CHWs and health committees, a phenomenon that has been described in other countries (Paul, 1987).

The level of involvement possible is further determined by the political system, a factor often taken for granted (Midgley et al., 1986).

The district focus for rural development is a method to mobilize people to action, but it is also a method of social control, a problem described by David Werner (1983). Real participation may lead to conflict with the interest of the state, which tends to define the extent to which participation is allowed. One other factor that may affect participation is poverty.

It is best to strengthen and work within the existing leadership and community organization and structures (Kaseje and Spencer, 1987). It is unnecessary and undesirable to reorganize the community by setting up new structures to facilitate participation, as often happened in Kenya.

Equity

Equal access to services, resources, information, and power is important. The whole community cannot have equal power to make important decisions at the same time, but they can all participate in delegating this power to popularly elected members, who are subject to them through established and mutually agreed-upon mechanisms. Those who make decisions would thus be subject and accountable not to some external authority structure, but to the community itself. This does not imply excluding inputs from professionals participating in the partnership.

Appropriate Technology

Fitting use of locally appropriate, available, and affordable technology is another key element. The Kenyan programs have made reasonable progress in this regard, except for the insistence on oral rehydration for prevention and management of dehydration. Oral rehydration solution (ORS) is often neither appropriate nor available to mothers in rural areas when diarrhea strikes. It should be obvious that the local community must participate in selecting technology considered appropriate with the necessary advice from the supporting partners. Technology is appropriate when it takes into account local expertise and resources, and when it enables people to cope better, resulting in self-esteem and encouraging self-responsibility and self-reliance. Professional rigidity stifles the identification, development, and use of appropriate technology.

Intersectoral Coordination and Collaboration

Equal participation of the community in making decisions that affect their lives means that a given community may select a package of services or activities that involves skills and resources not found in one sector, like the Ministry of Health, alone. At a basic level, even the skills of working with the community may not be available in the health sector. It is therefore important that persons from various sectors team up in the process of implementation. Much effort has gone into this, particularly with the district focus, but it is still hampered by the monopoly on health by the health ministry and its overly medical understanding of health. This has given room to the distortion of PHC into fragmented "quick-fix" technical interventions with only lip service to people's empowerment.

Human Resource Development

It has been recognized that the practice of the community-based approach takes knowledge, attitude, and skills that existing providers may possess. The roles of various key actors prescribed in this chapter require careful training. Success requires competence at all levels of leadership, including the technical and pedagogical skills for facilitating, nurturing, and managing the community-based process, at all stages and at all levels in the system presented above. This one element has been extensively implemented, but availability of competent leadership at all levels, particularly the policy levels, is yet to be realized.

Information System for Monitoring and Evaluation

Health and management information gathered and analyzed at all levels is invaluable to the management process of any program. Any appropriate information must be processed and used at every level at which it is gathered, but there should be a two-way flow system that allows comparisons within and between areas and uniform planning, management, and policy development at the central level. Attempts have been made in the Kenyan system, but again they are fragmented and often outside the formal system. Routinely collected service data tend to be passed on to the central level, but feedback is very seldom received. The assessment of outcome and impact of these programs has not been presented here because of inadequacy of data available.

Summary and Conclusions

The health system in rural Kenya has always aimed at bringing services to all people but has met with little success. In spite of a clear policy statement regarding the approach necessary for the achievement of this goal, it has not been backed up by an appropriate structural change or by the needed reallocation of resources in favor of rural communities, where the majority and most needy in Kenya live.

The world community realized more than ten years ago that the present system, providing medical services for recovery from illness, will not deliver health for all to the people since health has to do with much more than medical technology. Thus PHC was adopted as a strategy to respond to this realization. Professionals would no longer have the monopoly for health care, but rather all people would participate in all decisions and activities that affect their lives. In this way people would be fully involved and responsible for achieving and maintaining an acceptable level of health.

Health is a justice issue and is very much influenced by social, political, spiritual, and environmental factors and cannot therefore be improved by medical prescriptions alone, however appropriate. Health care must be part of an overall socioeconomic development plan in which agricultural production is the key. In this case the appropriate system must seek to empower the people affected to take full control of the problem, by analyzing their situation, mobilizing their resources, and taking the necessary individual and community actions to meet their needs (Rogers and Shoemaker, 1971). Such an approach will be slow in achieving desired change, but the change will be permanent once it occurs, as people adopt healthy ways that become assimilated into habitual practice and life.

The end result of a successful CBHC program would be communities that are fully empowered to take control of their own health situation, which they would analyze, plan, implement, and manage in partnership with resource people, both internally and externally. They would take responsibility for the decisions made and also fully share in benefits and failures. The vision is of a steady effort toward transformation and the resulting liberation of all involved—starting with the most marginalized in the community to the most central—the national-level personnel. The focus of this process must be the family, especially the mother, who is the key health agent and who needs adequate knowledge, skills, and support to make informed choices and take necessary actions on the health options available to her. In most cases, she is also the farmer; she must plan, analyze, make decisions, and act in health just as she must do in agriculture, but with the backup support of the public-service system.

References

Bennett, F. J., and J. Maneno. 1986. *National Guidelines for the Implementation of Primary Health Care in Kenya*. Nairobi: Ministry of Health.

Community Based Health Care Support Unit. 1991. *Assessment of the National CBHC Training Programme*. Evaluation report. Nairobi: African Medical and Research Foundation.

Kaseje, D. C. O., and H. C. Spencer. 1987. The Saradidi, Kenya, Rural Health Development Programme. *Annal of Tropical Medicine and Parasitology* 81, supp. 1.

Midgley, J., A. Hall, and N. Navine. 1986. *Community Participation, Social Development and the State*. London: Methuen.

Oakley, P. 1989. *Community Involvement in Health and Development: An Examination of Critical Issues*. Geneva: World Health Organization.

Paul, S. 1987. *Community Participation in Development Projects: The World Bank Experience*. Washington, D. C.: World Bank.

Rogers, E., and F. Shoemaker. 1971. *Communication of Innovations*. 2d ed., New York: Free Press.

Werner, D. B. 1983. Health and human dignity: A subjective look at community-based rural health programmes in Latin America. In *Practicing Health for All*, edited by D. Morley. Oxford: Oxford University Press.

World Health Organization and United Nations Children's Fund. 1978. *Primary Health Care*. A report on the International Conference on Primary Health Care, September 6-12, Alma-Ata, USSR.

Part V
Monitoring Global Change

Capacity to monitor the impacts of global change is exceedingly limited. Even in the most recent studies the complex interrelationship among changes in resource endowments, changes in technology, changes in human resources, and the productivity of land and people rests on an exceedingly weak empirical base.

In chapter 10 Stephen L. Rawlins addresses the problems of developing adequate systems for monitoring changes in soil, water, and genetic resources. During the last decade there have been improvements in the capacity to observe and interpret global land-cover changes. An important start has been made in the estimation and mapping of indicators of soil degradation. But much of the data serving as the basis for the indicators rests on subjective estimates. Even in the United States the data on which to base estimates of the magnitude of soil degradation and of the impacts of soil degradation on land productivity rest on only two sample surveys taken in 1977 and 1982. In most areas of the world the data that serve as a basis for such estimates are based on a limited number of studies that were not designed to serve as a basis for aggregate estimates. Capacity to monitor changes in the availability and quality of water resources and of the erosion of genetic resources is even less adequate than for land resources. In the conclusion to his chapter, Rawlins insists that the emerging global environmental monitoring system needs to more adequately incorporate those elements that are of particular significance for agricultural land use and land productivity.

In chapter 11 Martin Parry, David Norse, and J. A. Lee give particular attention to the capacity to monitor the effects of global climate change on agricultural potential. The climate changes that will impact agricultural production include the changes in global average temperature, differential temperature changes between low and high latitudes, changes in temperature extremes, and changes in the distribution and frequency of rainfall. In addition to the greenhouse-gas-induced changes in climate, increased atmospheric carbon dioxide concentration can also stimulate the growth of crop plants and weeds. But the impact of carbon dioxide under field conditions, as contrasted with the results from growth-chamber experiments, remains highly uncertain.

In chapter 12 David Bradley turns to issues of interpreting the interrelationships between agricultural change and changes in human health. He identified three categories of health consequences of agricultural change. These include (1) the specific effects of agricultural practices such as the trauma and toxins associated with the use of machinery and chemicals; (2) the health effects related to family- and community-level changes in farming systems and income distribution, such as respiratory infection; and (3) the health effects of changes associated with more intensive farming practices, including such diseases as malaria, schistosomiasis, and river blindness. He also notes that earlier concerns about the impact of health in agricultural production, particularly as practiced in colonial plantation settings, have been neglected in recent years. He argues that it is now time to reopen the analysis of the relationships between changes in health and agricultural production.

Bradley is particularly vigorous in criticizing the adequacy of health and illness indicators that are produced as a by-product of medical practice. Effective monitoring systems are dependent on carefully designed and systematically conducted surveys. The establishment of linkages between changes in agriculture and changes in health will require careful interdisciplinary research that relate specific changes in agricultural technology, changes in farming systems, and changes in habitat development and land use to the health status and production activities of rural people.

CHAPTER 10

INSTITUTIONAL CAPACITY TO MONITOR THE SOURCES AND EFFECTS OF ENVIRONMENTAL CHANGE IN AGRICULTURE

Stephen L. Rawlins

Productivity growth in agriculture has more than compensated for the rapid growth in demand in the past few decades, but there is no assurance that it will continue into the future. Many of those sources of past productivity growth are becoming fully exploited, and new sources are not fully apparent (see chapter 2). Anything as important as global food security cannot be left to chance, to blind faith that the market forces that mobilized sources of productivity growth in the past will continue to do so in the future.

Sustainable agricultural production depends not only upon biophysical resources, but also on how intelligently these resources are used (see chapter 5). The stability and effectiveness of social and economic institutions are extremely important requirements for effective resource use. Although this chapter deals primarily with monitoring of the biophysical sources of increased productivity, we cannot ignore the fact that a substantial part of our future agricultural productivity growth will have to come from social and economic sources—from innovations in social institutions that make better use of limited biophysical resources. Monitoring the health and effectiveness of social sources of productivity may be more important in providing the needed intelligence on threats to our future agricultural sustainability than monitoring biophysical sources. Changes in the biophysical system such as climate can adversely affect the social sources of productivity growth.

This chapter is concerned with our institutional capability to monitor those sources of productivity growth to support a sustainable future agricultural system in this changing environment. It deals with monitoring resources and microenvironmental constraints by the terrestrial component of the environment, including land, genetic resources, and terrestrial water supplies, as well as by external inputs, such as energy and minerals.

Holistic Production Systems

Although the primary concern in this chapter is the production component of the food system, we realize that this component is inextricably connected to the processing, storage, transportation, distribution, and consumption components of this system, as well as to the transportation and industrial sectors of the global economy in general. Increased efficiency in any of these sectors will have the same effect as increasing direct sources of agricultural productivity. But because they all compete for the same limited resources, they need to be considered as part of a single holistic system.

Poverty, whether caused by low profits from agriculture or from a deprived nation's need to import expensive items such as petroleum, usually leads to underinvestment in those capital improvements of farmland required to maintain productivity. Whether from a healthy agriculture or from some other sector of the economy, financial resources are important to assure the sustainability of agricultural production. These resources are also needed to support the education and health care of people that operate the agricultural production system. A system to monitor the sustainability of agricultural production needs to take into account the financial well-being of those who must invest in and operate the production system.

Land resources important to agricultural production include not only farmers' fields, but also the watersheds that infiltrate and moderate the supply of water for those fields. Shortage of fuel wood can lead to overexploitation of vegetation on watersheds, which reduces their effectiveness and has a direct effect on agricultural sustainability. Our monitoring system needs to include such indirect threats to agricultural productivity growth. It needs to identify alternative sources of fuel such as bottled gas, or the possibilities for developing biogas generators fed with household or animal wastes, or solar cookers to help alleviate this problem. It must also take into consideration the competition for resources and constraints imposed by the economy as a whole. Agriculture is not an island empire that can be separated from the rest of the global economic system.

Because a secure food supply is the primary reason we are concerned about the sustainability of agricultural production systems, we need to look also at potential sources of food other than those from agriculture. Fisheries, wild game, and nuts and fruit from unmanaged lands, of course, are important existing nonagricultural sources of food.

Some innovative new ideas for producing food biotechnologically from readily available biomass may be less dependent on environmental or depleting nonrenewable resources than our present agricultural system. One such system would produce food or animal feed in vitro in bioreactor vessels. Another would convert the same low-grade biomass to food in vivo by transforming the flora within the gut of animals to permit them to break down cellulose.[1] One of the salient features of these potential technologies is that they would depend on perennial plant products that can exist as a standing reserve of feed-stock requiring no storage and few if any nonrenewable resource inputs to grow, and that would be less vulnerable to the vagaries of weather than annual crops, which supply most of our food.

Resource Monitoring

Some of the resources upon which agricultural production depends are classified as renewable and others are considered to be nonrenewable. Fossil sources of fuels and chemicals, including nitrogen fertilizer; phosphorus reserves; and fossil groundwater reserves; and germ plasm are usually considered to be nonrenewable. Water contained in the hydrologic cycle and carbon dioxide from the atmosphere are considered to be renewable. The distinction between the two categories is mainly a matter of the cycle time. Use of some natural resources does not destroy them, it usually only disperses them, making them less available in concentrated form. Recycling can do a great deal to reduce this dispersion.

Primitive societies produced, consumed, and recycled almost everything on the land, minimizing the draw on stored nonrenewable resources. As societies industrialize, products are shipped from farms to cities or to high-density animal feedlots, where the wastes are rarely returned to the land. Failure to recycle these wastes to the land makes it necessary to exploit additional nonrenewable resources to replace them. The environmental impacts and high costs for disposing of these concentrated wastes is beginning to cause us to rethink the issue of waste disposal, with a trend toward recycling them back to the land. Our monitoring system needs to take this trend into account.

Land resources include not only soil properties, but also slope, elevation, drainage characteristics, and other properties that affect agricultural productivity. A monitoring system capable of evaluating land resources as a source of productivity growth for agriculture will not consist of a set of easily measured indices. Instead, what is needed is specific information related to the productive potential of each land area, including not only in situ resources but also the availability, costs, and reliability of inputs; pest and environmental threats; access to reliable markets; and numerous other factors. Also needed is an analysis system that takes this information into account and computes the integrated agricultural productivity response to all of these factors for each land area. These individual values can then be aggregated, taking into account market and trade factors, to give information on the impact of environmental changes on the stability and sustainability of agricultural productivity for communities, countries, and the world. Fortunately, a technology called Geographic Information Systems (GIS) is emerging as an important computerized information management tool to provide these kinds of analyses.

Geographic Information Systems

Geographic Information Systems technology allows managers to input, manage, analyze, manipulate, and display geographic data and results of analyses. TeSelle (1991) describes the system being developed by the U.S. Department of Agriculture (USDA) Soil Conservation Service to provide decision support to resource managers. It uses tabular data, data-base management system techniques, geographic data bases, and powerful computer models. The resulting graphical displays of the information make relationships, trends, changes, and proposed solutions easily understood.

Typically, GIS spatial information is displayed as a set of individual map layers that can be superimposed to portray individual spatially distributed themes such as climate, soils, land cover, topography, roads and streams, hydrology, electrical power and gas lines, and so on. Analyses can create additional map layers that display computed results, such as cropland with slopes greater than a selected value within a specific distance of a stream, or highly erodible cropland areas by field. Taking into account soil permeability, types of crops to be grown, rainfall patterns, and proximity to groundwater, analyses can be displayed that predict such factors as the probability of pesticides reaching aquifers.

At a larger scale, computed map layers can be displayed that show important economic information, such as lands suitable for growing wheat, with transportation costs to a seaport within a specific range. One of the strengths of GIS is its capability to combine biophysical and socioeconomic information. Another is its capability to integrate information across a wide range of spatial scales.

Soil Resource Monitoring

Because soil is such an important component of the agricultural production system, soil degradation is frequently the focus of monitoring systems concerned with sustainable production. In reviewing international efforts concerned with monitoring soil degradation, Sanders (1991) found the most recent and comprehensive to be the Global Assessment of Soil Degradation (GLASOD), sponsored by the U.N. Environmental Program (UNEP) and carried out by the International Soil Reference and Information Centre (ISRIC).

The project had a duration of 28 months and involved many organizations, including the International Society of Soil Science (ISSS), the Winand Staring Centre of the Netherlands, the Food and Agriculture Organization (FAO), and the International Institute for Aerospace Surveys and Earth Sciences (ITC) of the Netherlands. Altogether some 250 scientists were involved from all over the world. In October 1990 the project produced the first "World Map of the Status of Human-Induced Soil Degradation" at a scale of 1:10 million. The GLASOD map was developed with the aim of demonstrating the seriousness of land degradation to decision and policy makers as well as to the public. Four main "degradation types" were mapped: water erosion, wind erosion, chemical deterioration, and physical deterioration. These types were linked with the "causative factors" of deforestation and removal of natural vegetation, overgrazing, agricultural activities, exploitation of vegetation for domestic use, and (bio)industrial activities. The results were combined to give each mapping unit a soil degradation status, to which was added an indication of the recent past rate of the degradation (over the past 5 to 10 years).

In summarizing this and other international efforts to monitor land degradation, Sanders concludes that over the last 20 years the several attempts made to systematically assess the global extent of land have not included global attempts to monitor changes. Global assessments of land degradation have proved very difficult because sufficient, reliable data are not available to support complex methods of assessment. The three aspects of degradation—status, rate, and risk—are frequently confused. But much valuable experience has been gained, and the recently completed GLASOD study will provide a valuable baseline for future work. According to Sanders, future progress will require the increasing use of GIS to provide much greater capability for the storage and manipulation of data. The lack of reliable, usable, and comparable data is only likely to be fully overcome when properly equipped and manned stations are established in representative areas to monitor land degradation.

Although an extremely important component of the agricultural production equation, soils information alone is insufficient to assess the sustainability of the production system. Where a soil parameter such as depth controls crop production, a map of soil erosion could be closely correlated with changes in agricultural productivity. But if the soil is deep, erosion may have little or no effect on productive capacity for a very long time. How deep a soil needs to be before it limits crop production depends, for one thing, on rainfall distribution patterns. At a location where rainfall is frequent and reliable, less soil depth is needed to store water than where long periods of drought occur.

Soil erosion may, in some cases, result in increased productivity for an entire river system, depending upon the disposition of the sediment. King (1911) describes huge increases in land resources that have resulted in China from the careful husbanding of the enormous volumes of silt carried by rivers and deposited over flooded areas. For example, he found that Chungming Island in the mouth of the Yangtze Kiang River provided homes for a million people on the 270 square miles of newly made land. The city of Shanghai, which originally stood on the seashore, had by the time of his trip grown 20 miles northward and eastward. The town of Putai in Shantung, then 48 miles from the sea, had in 220 B.C. stood one-third of a mile from the shore. He observed:

> Besides these actual extensions of the shore lines the centuries of flooding of lakes and low lying lands has so filled many depressions as to convert

large areas of swamp into cultivated fields. Not only this, but the spreading of canal mud broadcast over the encircled fields has had two very important effects, — namely, raising the level of the low lying fields, giving them better drainage and so better physical condition, and adding new plant food in the form of virgin soil of the richest type, thus contributing to the maintenance of soil fertility, high maintenance capacity and permanent agriculture through the centuries. (106)

Whether the capture of this sediment has increased the productive capacity of the entire river system is open to question. If the eroded sediment came from steeply sloping lands high in the mountains, where low temperature limited production, the loss in productive capacity due to soil loss may well have been more than compensated for by the highly productive soils formed in the delta, where the climate is ideal for crop production. In any case, by careful husbanding of this sediment, the Chinese people have certainly increased the productive capacity of the river basin above what would have been the case had these sediments simply been allowed to wash out to the sea.

Any assessment of agricultural productive capacity needs to consider the possibility that some human actions could lead to increased productive capacity. Assuming that sediment is always a curse limits our vision of some potential opportunities to put it to work for us. What is the potential for building new land areas below dam sites by constructing pipelines to carry dredged sediments, now accumulating and decreasing reservoir storage capacity, to sites where productivity is limited by shallow soils? Our monitoring system needs to take such possibilities into consideration.

At the field scale we also need to take into account possible productivity gains from eroded sediments that deposit farther down the hill slopes. Existing soil erosion assessment equations consider only soil loss. Frequently erosion results more in redistribution of soil on the landscape than in total loss of sediment from it. I've often made the (partly) facetious remark that the only erosion we consider to be positive is that done with a bulldozer during the process of building terraces. Appropriate use of vegetation to capture the sediment in grass hedges at strategic points can build the same terraces by the natural erosion process. This process is occurring to some extent without the purposeful placement of hedges. Our monitoring system needs to consider these potentially positive contributions from deposited sediment. We need to focus our attention on the integral productivity of entire landscapes rather than looking only at the effects on eroding hill slopes.

Water Resource Monitoring

Both the quantity of water available and its quality are important for sustaining agricultural productivity. Some of the most comprehensive studies of global water balance were carried out as part of the United Nations International Hydrological Decade (UNESCO, 1971). Because natural waters are interlinked into a single global water cycle, the study of water balances requires international coordination. The U.N. studies revealed that although the volume of global water is very large, serious environmental and water-supply problems in many parts of the world had been caused "by wasteful exploitation of fresh water, reckless release of deleterious and even dangerous water-borne wastes into rivers, lakes and the ground, and careless management and mismanagement of watersheds, recharge areas and aquifers." Most of these problems could have been forestalled with proper foresight, based on understanding of the hydrological cycle.

But the data required to understand the hydrological cycle were sparse. Less than 60 percent of the water in rivers flowing to the ocean was accurately measured. There was a wide divergence of opinion about the amounts of water in rivers (channel storage), in lakes and swamps, in glaciers and ice caps, in the soil and vadose zones, and in aquifers. Calculations of soil-moisture storage and groundwater differ by orders of magnitude. In compiling information on global water availability and use, van der Leeden (1975) found that data on the use of water resources were the least adequate.

The only systematic attempt to gather water-quality data globally, being carried out by the Global Environmental Monitoring System (GEMS) (Meybeck, Chapman, and Helmer, 1989), has also suffered from the paucity of data, particularly in the developing world. The GEMS water monitoring program, launched in 1977 by the United Nations Environmental Program and World Health Organization (WHO), is based on voluntary contributions of data from 59 countries.

Although assessment of water quality will always require in situ measurements, there is considerable progress being made in remotely sensing many of the variables required to predict stream flows, surface water storage, and even soil water content. Global assessments based on such data, however, require GIS technology to handle the massive quantities of data in a way that makes quantitative analyses possible. In recognition of this, a new division within the International Committee on Remote Sensing and Data Transmission for Hydrology on GIS was recently created, joining the Division of Remote Sensing and the Division of Data Transmission (Rango, 1992). In combination with the international network of ground-, sea-, and space-based observing systems of the World Weather Watch (WWW) system, this technology should make it possible to vastly improve our capability to monitor global water balance.

Genetic Resource Monitoring

Germ plasm is similar to other nonrenewable resource inputs to agriculture. We began with essentially a fixed endowment, which is being eroded by our actions. As reported by the United Nations Environmental Program (1990), of the estimated 50 million species alive today, some 100 species are lost every day. Only 1.4 million species have been identified, and only a small part of these have been evaluated for their usefulness to humanity. For example, of an estimated 265,000 species of plants, only 5,000 have ever been cultivated for food. The world's food supply depends upon only a few of these species. By breeding for high yields we have narrowed down the genetic base of crops, increasing the risk that a single pest or disease could wipe out vast areas. Genes from hardier wild relatives can give back pest resistance, but without a diverse genetic pool to draw from, such improvements will not be possible.

There are two basic strategies for preserving the genetic diversity of plants needed to support agriculture. One is to place the seeds into storage banks, where they are renewed periodically by planting and regrowing them. The International Board for Plant Genetic Resources has established a global network of gene banks in 30 countries, both developed and developing, which house the world's 40 base collections. More than 100 countries collaborate in this, and in 1990 over 500,000 plant samples had been collected, evaluated, and deposited in the base collections. All U.N. member states can access the germ plasm and the information about it for sustainable agricultural development (UNEP, 1990).

Some developing countries, which are the custodians of the major part of the world's genetic resources, are realizing the value of those resources and are beginning to resist giving it up for exploitation by developed countries and private companies. Gibbons (1991) has proposed establishing Swiss-style banks for seeds to allow nations to deposit and withdraw germ plasm in complete privacy to protect against loss. This could be very helpful in overcoming the resistance to germ plasm collection in some developing countries. Providing a means for it to be banked in their name could go a long way toward helping to preserve some valuable resources.

FAO and UNEP are sponsoring pilot projects to conserve endangered animal species as well. Animal descriptor surveys, conservation methodologies, and pilot gene banks and data banks have been developed for animal genetic resources in Africa, Asia, and Latin America (UNEP, 1990).

But gene banks can do only so much. The only way to preserve the vast genetic resources that could potentially be valuable to agriculture is to preserve the ecosystems in which they grow. For existing domesticated species this could be done by encouraging, perhaps through subsidy, the cultivation of traditional varieties rather than the adoption of improved varieties with a narrower genetic base. For wild species, however, the only effective means of preservation is to protect the entire ecosystem in which they exist. Because so many of the world's species have never been described, ecosystem preservation is the only way to assure that they will be here when we need them.

In October 1980, the UNEP, the World Conservation Union, and the World Wildlife Fund launched the World Conservation Strategy—a policy statement of the link between living resource conservation and sustainable development (UNEP, 1990). It calls for ways to maintain maximum genetic diversity for improving agriculture, forestry, health, industry, and environment. The World Conservation Monitoring Centre supported by UNEP supports and assesses the distribution and abundance of the world's species. It has also supported inventories of habitats and their value. In 1983, UNEP and UNESCO convened the First International Biosphere Reserve Congress to take a comprehensive review of biosphere reserves. By 1990, the UNESCO-UNEP network included 286 biosphere reserves in 72 countries.

In February 1992, the World Resources Institute, the World Conservation Union, and the UNEP issued a framework for action to stem the loss of the world's biotic wealth and mobilize its potential for the benefit of present and future generations (World Resources Institute et al., 1992). The strategy led to a convention on the conservation of biological diversity as part of the UNCED held in Brazil in June 1992. It calls for unified actions of governments, nongovernmental organizations, communities, and industry to take steps that will inventory, protect, and ensure that the use of species, genetic resources, and ecosystems is both equitable and sustainable.

Integrated Monitoring Strategies

A strategy described by Dumanski and Onofrei (1990) takes into account the risk associated with the multiple factors affecting agricultural productivity. Production (yield) risk occurs as a consequence of natural factors such as weather, soil variability, diseases, and so forth. Instability of markets and prices adds additional risk to the farming enterprise. They state: "The proper assessment and management of risk is very important today. . . . In many developing countries, soil and other resources have been degraded to the point that small perturbations (in weather for example) may trigger a complete collapse of the farming systems, e. g. the Sahelian disasters."

Risk, which generally is highest in the coldest and driest areas, can often be mitigated to some degree by specific soil and crop management practices. Dumanski and Onofrei propose the use of crop production models to evaluate production risk. These models, based on fundamental physical and biological processes, can be structured to reflect the interaction of soil, weather, management, pests, and diseases in controlling crop yield. Although yield in any one year is uncertain, it can be expressed in terms of variability and probability, and in this way yield can be related to risk. But such risk analyses involve studies in variability and probability that require suites of long-term data. GIS are ideally suited to handle both the major driving variables that control biomass production throughout the growing season and the simulation models required for production risk assessments.

The International Benchmark Sites Network for Agrotechnology Transfer

The International Benchmark Sites Network for Agrotechnology Transfer (IBSNAT), sponsored by the U.S. Agency for International Development (USAID), is based on the strategy of using models to assess risk. The project was established in 1982 to help decision makers take advantage of the "technodiagnostic and problem-solving capabilities of information science and computer technology." The central concept is that the whole system must be understood to evaluate changes in any single component. It brings together existing knowledge of the farming system, identifies major components and processes and their interaction, and seeks to identify constraints hindering improved performance.

IBSNAT attempts to provide the structure and mechanisms to link soil, water, weather, crop, and management elements into a coherent, problem-solving instrument—the Decision Support System for

Agrotechnology Transfer (DSSAT). It has identified 12 major food crops (maize, rice, sorghum, millet, barley, wheat, soybean, peanut, bean, cassava, taro, and potato) for which crop models are to be developed. A "minimum data set" has been defined for soil, crop, weather, and management variables, which all models use. Crop models simulate the effects of weather, soil water, genotype, and nitrogen dynamics on crop growth and yield. Test versions of crop models for wheat, maize, soybean, and peanut have been distributed, along with a genetic-coefficient estimator, modified weather-generator programs, and soils data bases as part of DSSAT. Genetic-coefficient and weather-generator programs are needed to assist the operator to develop daily input files for the crop models from whatever data are available locally. The soils data base consists of all Soil Conservation Service and Soil Management Support Service (USDA and USAID, respectively) international benchmark soils. Working versions of crop models for rice, sorghum, millet, dry bean, potato, and cassava have also been developed.

A prototype network of 45 benchmark experimental sites in developed countries and 16 developing countries has been established to collect the minimum data required to validate the crop models. An international group of systems analysts, modelers, economists, breeders, and plant protection specialists has been mobilized to work with the IBSNAT prototype network of collaborators.

Progress is always painfully slow on any project as comprehensive as this, but signs of successful adoption by other international organizations is promising. Workshops have been held with ICRISAT (International Crops Research Institute for the Semi-Arid Tropics, Hyderabad, India), IFDC (International Fertilizer Development Center, Muscle Shoals, Alabama), and BARC (Bangladesh Agricultural Research Council) to explore collaborative research on model validation for rice and sorghum. Use of DSSAT by national agencies is under consideration in both Bangladesh and Thailand. The South Pacific Commission, with support from DSIR (Department of Scientific and Industrial Research, Lower Hutt, New Zealand) and resources from CIRAD and ORSTOM (Office de la Recherche Scientifique et Technique Outre-Mer), has plans to establish IBSNAT within its member nations. The Rockefeller Foundation has funded scientists from the Edinburgh School of Agriculture and IFDC to work with the University of Malawi to use DSSAT for decision support in managing maize production.

Natural Resource Models

Other natural resource models have been developed by a number of groups, including the Agricultural Research Service (ARS) of the USDA, to provide decision support technology to action agencies such as the USDA Soil Conservation Service for the management of natural resources.[2] Realization is increasing that soil, water, and other resources are limited and vulnerable to degradation resulting from erosion, compaction, waterlogging, excessive salinity, mineral imbalances, root zone pathogens, and other problems. Models provide the means to identify critical problems and assist managers in developing corrective strategies to deal with them.

Agricultural productivity is largely determined by physical, chemical, and biological properties and processes in concert with climate, resource, and management inputs. Productivity also depends on the specific use to which the land is put. Mathematical models based on fundamental processes have broad applicability. These processes are the same everywhere; only the environmental conditions vary with location and time. If the appropriate environmental data are provided, a truly process-based model will accurately predict the desired behavior or response. But compromises always have to be made. Providing the required data to drive any model can be a monumental task. A close working relationship between those building the models and those developing the data sets to drive them is always required. The level of detail that can be incorporated in any model that is to be used is always governed by limitation in available data. In some cases where parameters required to operate a model are not available explicitly, they can be derived from other available data. In other cases where critical data are missing, new observations and monitoring programs must be developed.

Models provide a rational process for determining which data need to be collected by monitoring programs. Because observation sites are expensive to establish and maintain, it is impractical to provide the necessary density of monitoring sites to observe the natural variation in any parameter. Models based on fundamental processes are useful in estimating parameter values between sites by taking advantage of known relationships between the required parameter and available data. As a trivial example, because temperature decreases with elevation, elevation can be used to help extrapolate temperature values at points between monitoring sites along a slope. Monitoring programs should always be designed to collect the most important data that cannot be derived from other available information. Establishing monitoring sites on a uniform grid is seldom the optimum strategy. Monitoring should be used to fill the most critical information gaps that lead to the greatest uncertainty in predictions of future productivity growth.

Soil Conservation Service Monitoring and Assessment

Two Soil Conservation Service (SCS) programs, the National Conservation Program (NCP) (Soil Conservation Service, 1989) and the Natural Resources Inventory (NRI) (Soil Conservation Service, 1991), illustrate the evolving use of process-based simulation models for policy assessment and the shaping of monitoring programs to provide the needed data for these models.

For 50 years SCS has conducted periodic inventories of U.S. soil, water, and related resources. Early efforts were reconnaissance studies—the Soil Erosion Inventory of 1934 and the 1945 Soil and Water Conservation Needs Inventory. The 1958 and 1967 Soil and Water Conservation Needs Inventories were the agency's first efforts to collect data nationally using scientifically selected sample field sites. The Potential Cropland Study of 1975 and the National Resources Inventories of 1977, 1982, and 1987 were extensions and modifications of these earlier inventories. The 1992 NRI will rely heavily on remote sensing and will use modern computer and GIS technology. This will permit comparisons to be made among 1982, 1987, and 1992 values to, for example, examine effects of the 1985 Food Security Act.

This change to reliance on computers and geographic systems technology is the result of new demands for data to facilitate the use of models used in the Resources Conservation Act (RCA) appraisals. The RCA of 1977 (Public Law 95-192) as extended by the Food Security Act of 1985 (Public Law 99-198) directs the secretary of agriculture to make a continuing appraisal of the condition of the soil, water, and related resources of the nation, and to develop and update a National Conservation Program based on that appraisal. The NCP uses the NRI to undergird its appraisal.

To respond to the RCA mandate, in 1980 the USDA formed the National Soil Erosion–Soil Productivity Planning Committee to take a hard look at the impacts of erosion on productivity. Prior to that time only statistical models had been used for this purpose. But the rapid development of computer technology that could make use of digital simulation models to meet the mandates of RCA was seen as a practical solution to a very difficult problem. The Office of Technology Assessment, for example, stated: "Mathematical models are among the most sophisticated tools available for analyzing water resource issues. They can use the capabilities of today's digital computers to perform and integrate, understand and project the consequences of alternative management, planning, or policy-level activities" (Office of Technology Assessment, 1982).

To meet the challenge, the ARS, SCS, and Economic Research Service (ERS) developed a process-based simulation model, the Erosion Productivity Impact Calculator (EPIC; see Williams, Renard, and Dyke, 1983). The activities that took place in the next year to assemble the necessary data bases to validate and run this model to deliver data for the 1985 RCA process stretched the capability of everyone involved. At the end of the process, Putnam (1986) commented: "We have a data base of 90 items for 12 months in each of the 100 years for 12,000 simulations—approximately 1.3 billion numbers. These data are currently backed off on 125 tapes, and 12,000 microfiche. . . . We started with a handful of microfiche; admiring how much data each held. When we started on the second filing cabinet of microfiche we began to realize the magnitude of our problem." As difficult as it was, the team successfully delivered the needed analyses on time. And partly as a result of this success, the specification of data requirements in the NRI are now tightly linked to the data needs of models used to support the RCA appraisals that use a wide range of natural resource models. The same holds true for the SCS Soil Survey Division. Data needs to support natural-resource simulation models drive their priorities for data analyses and new data acquisitions.

The Environmental Monitoring and Assessment Program

At a higher level of integration, the Environmental Monitoring and Assessment Program (EMAP), sponsored by the U.S. Environmental Protection Agency (USEPA), seeks to develop an interagency program to monitor the condition of the nation's entire suite of ecological resources (USEPA, 1990). EMAP hopes to meet the growing demand for information characterizing the condition of our environment and the type and location of changes in our environment. It will simultaneously monitor pollutants and environmental changes to help identify likely causes of adverse changes. When fully implemented, EMAP will answer the following questions:

What is the current status, extent, and geographic distribution of our ecological resources (for example, estuaries, lakes, streams, wetlands, forests, grasslands, deserts)?

What proportions of these resources are degrading or improving, where, and at what rate?

What are the likely causes of adverse effects?

Are adversely affected ecosystems responding as expected to control and mitigation programs?

Assessment of changes over large geographic scales and long periods of time requires continuity of the program. Meeting these needs by simply aggregating data from many individual, local, and short-term networks that are fragmented in space or time has proven to be impossible. EMAP will focus specifically on national and regional scales over periods of years to decades, collecting data on indicators of ecological conditions from multiple ecosystems and integrating them to assess environmental change. This approach, along with EMAP's unique statistically based design, distinguishes it from most existing monitoring programs. This design is being developed cooperatively with the international community in hopes that some aspects of it can be extended more broadly.

The monitoring program has identified eight components: air and deposition, landscape characterization, agroecosystems, arid ecosystems, forest ecosystems, near coastal ecosystems, surface water ecosystems, and wetland ecosystems.

Although USEPA assumes responsibility for the overall project design, the technical leadership for each component is typically delegated to another agency. For example, the technical director responsibilities for the agroecosystems component have been delegated to the ARS, and the USDA Forest Service has primary leadership for the forest ecosystems component. Each of these, in turn, are relying heavily on the existing data collection and monitoring programs in USDA to meet the needs of EMAP. New data collection and monitoring efforts will be mounted only when critical gaps are identified.

One of the primary benefits of this program is the fact that it treats the entire continent as a single system. Treating each ecosystem individually, as we now do, loses track of important processes and fluxes that occur at the interfaces. Because ecosystems often occur as a patchwork on the landscape, outputs from one system are almost always inputs to another. Only by treating the entire landscape as a system can all of the important system properties be evaluated.

This program was initiated in 1990 and is expected to evolve over a period of years. The hope is that it will contribute toward the problem of monitoring the productivity of agricultural systems by giving us a better handle on problems arising at the interface between agriculture and the ecosystems that surround it.

Global Environmental Change Program Opportunities

Monitoring the agricultural production consequences of environmental changes will, as discussed above, require the specification of ranges of variations and scenarios for change for many external as well as internal environmental variables. These include not only the physical environment, but also required external inputs such as water, energy, chemicals, germ plasm, and management. Because any one of these factors may be limiting at a given time or location, all must be incorporated into any assessment system that can infer the capability of agricultural production growth to meet expanding demands. Constructing the data bases containing all the variables on which such a system depends with the resources traditionally available to agriculture is impossible.

Within the last few years an unprecedented international scientific effort has been mounted to address the concern that human activities may have on the earth's environment (Committee on Earth and Environmental Sciences, 1991). Recognizing the profound economic and social implications of global environmental changes, including international food security, the president of the United States has set in motion a comprehensive process to develop a better understanding of the earth as an integrated system, to serve as a basis for review of potential policies and their implications. This includes an accelerated, focused research effort in collaboration with international partners. The president's funding request for the U.S. portion of this program alone exceeds $1 billion for fiscal year 1991.

Food security depends not only upon the resources typically considered to be agricultural, but also upon a myriad of other factors. These include changes and stability of weather patterns, atmospheric chemical composition, stream flow and competition for fresh-water resources, water quality, energy availability, competition for land by expansion of forests to stabilize atmospheric carbon dioxide concentrations, human health, and productivity of fisheries. All are being addressed by the global-change research community. Given all these scientists, with all this money, monitoring programs and providing observations, scientific understanding of processes, development of predictive models, and development of global data bases, agriculture no longer needs to depend upon the limited resources traditionally available in order to assess the capability of agricultural systems to provide a secure supply of food for earth's exploding population. A major question is, Will the agricultural scientific community step forward fast enough, with sufficiently organized strategies, to make certain that these efforts are tailored to meet agriculture's needs?

Data and information management will provide the critical bridge between national and international global-change observations and scientific understanding. One institutional barrier that must be addressed is that existing U.S. statutes inhibit open access by requiring some agencies to charge user fees for data for scientific use. Required data management activities center on three issues: better integration of existing and forthcoming satellite and in situ data sets, higher emphasis on the priority science needs, and enhanced international exchange of data. Agriculture has large in situ data sets that need to be integrated into the global GIS being developed. Agriculture's science needs must be addressed early to assure that they are placed high on the list of priorities. Establishing a global data base with a common framework for sharing of international data will go a long way toward addressing the shortcomings of existing agricultural monitoring programs listed by Sanders (1991).

The U.S. Global Change Research Program is linked to both governmental and nongovernmental international research efforts. The nongovernmental effort is coordinated primarily through the U.S. National Academy of Sciences' membership in the International Council of Scientific Unions (ICSU). ICSU has recently published a report describing details of core projects of the International Geosphere-Biosphere Programme (IGBP) (International Council of Scientific Unions, 1990). Four core projects are of special interest for agriculture: Global Change and Terrestrial Ecosystems (GCTE), Data Information Systems for the IGBP (IGBP-DIS), Needs for Remote-Sensing Data in the 1990s and Beyond, and the IGBP Global Change Regional Research Centres (RRC).

Focus 3 of the GCTE core project, which deals with the global change impact on agriculture and forestry, is particularly pertinent. This program includes assessing the impact of human-induced global change on agroecosystems and possibilities for mitigating the effects or adapting to the changes. The research priorities identified in this focus concentrate on yield of the major crop, forest and livestock species, and key factors that affect harvestable products. The fact that agroecosystems around the world share a number of common characteristics makes practical an integrated research focus on the effect of global change on agroecosystems. Other national and international organizations, such as IBSNAT, the Consultative Group on International Agricultural Research (CGIAR), FAO, and others, are addressing similar questions. This focus is intended to complement these programs while attaining specific IGBP research goals for agroecosystems.

The core activities required involve monitoring, experimental research, and modeling. Monitoring is required for direct assessment of change, in order to test hypotheses about change and to obtain information in order to generate new hypotheses. Modeling will allow prediction of the net effect of several concurrent changes, and will allow understanding to be integrated across levels and between subsystems. The model structure should offer the means for integrating the various impacts of climate change and will be an important guide in the development of research and data needs. Models developed for this focus will differ from others because of the inclusion of management and the importance of production and yield of harvestable products.

The activities listed for this focus include (1) effects of climate and atmospheric change on key agronomic species; (2) changes in pests and diseases of crops and livestock; and (3) changes in on-site properties, redistribution, and net loss of soil.

The governmental component of the global-change research program is coordinated primarily through the United Nations and its associated bodies. Global resource monitoring is a prominent element of their efforts. Without basic measurements of global changes in important environmental and resource variables it is impossible to assess the impact of human activities on critical systems or to develop policies to mitigate their effects.

Although some global monitoring systems exist, most notably the UNEP Global Environmental Monitoring System (GEMS), Mock (1990) concludes that they are seriously handicapped by constrained resources. He suggests that the World Weather Watch (WWW) system, which has existed for years, could serve as a prototype for an effective global monitoring system. The WWW is an international network consisting of ground-, sea-, and space-based observing systems ranging from surface weather stations to sophisticated satellites, along with computers to analyze the data obtained and communication links to make analyses widely available. The guiding philosophy of the WWW is that each member nation contributes services according to its means, while all nations have equal access to the data and forecasts produced.

Any effective global monitoring scheme must make simultaneous observations of the biosphere, geosphere, cryosphere, and hydrosphere on a global basis if the physical, chemical, biological, and social processes that drive environmental change are to be understood. Furthermore, observations must continue over extended time if we are to measure changes. This will require substantial upgrades in both satellite and ground-based stations. Particularly important will be the addition of measurements of soil, hydrologic, and other resources. As stated by Dorfman (1991), we need "an utterly reliable and impartial monitoring system that will keep track of the state of the environment and will report its findings without bias, giving good news as much emphasis as bad."

Conclusions

Our existing institutional capacity to monitor the productivity growth of the agricultural system in the face of global environmental changes is severely limited. A major part of this limitation stems from our failure to treat agriculture as an integral part of a complex and interconnected global system. Substantial growth in our global natural resource and environmental monitoring is being planned. Agriculture needs to become an intimate partner in this planning to assure that its priorities are addressed.

Because land and resources are limited, we have to use them more effectively in the future to obtain the productivity growth needed to keep step with an expanding population. Using them more effectively will require not only better technology, but better education, more reliable sources of inputs as well as capital, and more sophisticated global marketing systems to iron out short-term yield fluctuations and to permit local farmers to grow those commodities best suited to their environment. These sources of productivity growth require social and institutional innovations. Our monitoring system needs to address them as well as biophysical resource constraints if we are to provide the relevant information to those making the decisions that will determine the sustainability of our future agricultural system.

Notes

1. Some ideas have been put forth for future agricultural production systems, including the possibility of nontraditional off-farm, in vitro production components (Rogoff and Rawlins, 1987). Improving our capacity to convert biomass that is already being grown into human food could reduce our dependence on environmentally vulnerable annual seed crops and could lessen the demands we have to place on fragile, eroding land resources. Converting a larger proportion of the biomass that already grows each year into food could also reduce the intensity of agricultural production systems, which could lessen our demand for nonrenewable inputs, needed largely to sustain artificial monocultures in the presence of natural ecosystem pressures.

2. An abbreviated list of models developed by the Agricultural Research Service includes the following:

AGNPS—Agricultural Nonpoint Pollution Source Model

CREAMS—Chemicals, Runoff, and Erosion from Agricultural Management Systems

EPIC—Erosion Prediction Impact Calculator

ERYHM—Ekalaka Rangeland Yield and Hydrology Model

GLEAMS—Groundwater Loading Effects on Agricultural Management Systems

KINEROS—Kinematic Runoff and Erosion Model

MUSLE—Modified Universal Soil Loss Equation

PRMS—Precipitation, Runoff Modeling System

RUSLE—Revised Universal Soil Loss Equation

RZWQM—Root Zone Water Quality Model

SHAW—Simultaneous Heat and Water Model

SPAW—Soil, Plant, Air, and Water Model

SPUR—Simulation of Production and Utilization of Rangelands

SRM—Snowmelt Runoff Model

SWAM—Small Watershed Model

SWRRB—Simulator for Water Resources in Rural Basins

USLE—Universal Soil Loss Equation

WEE—Wind Erosion Equation

WEPP—Water Erosion Prediction Project

WEPS—Wind Erosion Prediction System

References

Committee on Earth and Environmental Sciences. 1991. *Our Changing Planet: The FY 1991 Research Plan, a Report to Congress.* Reston, Va.: Committee on Earth and Environmental Sciences, U.S. Geological Survey.

Dorfman, Robert. 1991. Protecting the global environment: An immodest proposal. *World Development* 19(1): 110.

Dumanski, J., and C. Onofrei. 1990. Evaluating crop production risks related to weather and soils using crop growth models. *Transactions: 14th Congress of Soil Science.* Kyoto, Japan: Commission V.

Gibbons, A. 1991. Saving seeds for future generations. *Science* 254:804.

International Benchmark Sites Network for Agrotechnology Transfer. 1990. *IBSNAT Progress Report, 1 September 1987–30 June 1990.* Honolulu: Department of Agronomy and Soil Science, University of Hawaii at Manoa.

International Council of Scientific Unions (ICSU). 1990. *The International Geosphere-Biosphere Programme: A Study of Global Change.* Report no. 12, *The Initial Core Projects.* Stockholm ICSU.

King, F. H. 1911. *Farmers for Forty Centuries.* Emmaus, Pa.: Rodale Press.

Meybeck, Michel, Deborah Chapman, and Richard Helmer, eds. 1989. *Global Freshwater Quality: A First Assessment.* Oxford: Blackwell Reference.

Mock, Gregory. 1990. Global systems and cycles. In *World Resources: 1990-91.* New York: World Resources Institute, United Nations Environmental Program, and the United Nations Development Program, Oxford University Press.

Office of Technology Assessment. 1982. *Use of Models for Water Resources Management, Planning and Policy.* Washington, D.C.: Government Printing Office.

Putnam, John. 1986. Erosion-productivity index simulator. In *Assessment and Planning Staff Report: Forum on Erosion Productivity Impact Estimators,* edited by James A. Maetzold and Klaus F. Alt. Washington, D.C.: USDA Soil Conservation Service.

Rango, A. 1992. Report on the plenary session of the International Committee on Remote Sensing and Data Transmission, Vienna, Austria, August 1991. *International Committee on Remote Sensing and Data Transmission for Hydrology, International Association of Hydrological Sciences of the International Union of Geodesy and Geophysics, Newsletter.* No. 5 (March). Available from Dr. J. C. Ritchie, Secretary, IAHS-ICRSDT, USDA/ARS, BARC-West, Bldg. 007, Beltsville, MD 20705.

Rawlins, Stephen L. 1988. Systems science and agricultural sustainability. *National Forum: Phi Kappa Phi Journal* 68 (Summer).

Rogoff, Martin H., and Stephen L. Rawlins. 1987. Food security: A technological alternative. *BioScience* 37:800-807.

Ruttan, Vernon W., ed. 1989. *Biological and Technical Constraints on Crop and Animal Productivity, Report on a Dialogue.* St. Paul: University of Minnesota, Department of Agricultural and Applied Economics.

Sanders, D. W. 1991. International activities in assessing and monitoring soil degradation. *International Workshop on Assessment of Monitoring of Soil Quality.* (Emmaus, Pa., July 11-13, 1991). Emmaus, Pa.: Rodale Research Center.

Soil Conservation Service. 1989. *A National Program for Soil and Water Conservation: The 1988-97 Update.* Washington, D.C.: USDA Soil Conservation Service.

——. 1991. *Instructions for Collecting 1992 National Resources Inventory Sample Data.* Washington, D.C.: USDA Soil Conservation Service.

TeSelle, Gale W. 1991. Geographic information systems for managing resources. In *Agriculture and the Environment: The 1991 Yearbook of Agriculture.* Washington, D.C.: Government Printing Office.

UNESCO. 1971. *Scientific Framework of World Water Balance.* Paris: Technical Papers in Hydrology, UNESCO.

United Nations Environmental Program. 1990. *UNEP Profile*. Nairobi: Information and Public Affairs Branch, UNEP.

U.S. Environmental Protection Agency (EPA). 1990. *Environmental Monitoring and Assessment Program: Overview*. Office of Modeling, Monitoring and Quality Assurance, RD-680. Washington, D.C.: EPA.

van der Leeden, Fritz. 1975. *Water Resources of the World: Selected Statistics*. Port Washington, Wash.: Water Information Center.

Williams, J. R., K. G. Renard, and P. T. Dyke. 1983. EPIC: A new method for assessing erosion's effect on soil productivity. *Journal of Soil Water Conservation* 38(5): 381-83.

World Resources Institute, the World Conservation Union, and the United Nations Environmental Program. 1992. *Global Biodiversity Strategy*. Washington, D.C.: World Resources Institute Publications.

CHAPTER 11

MONITORING THE EFFECTS OF ACID DEPOSITION AND CLIMATE CHANGE ON AGRICULTURAL POTENTIAL

J. A. Lee, David Norse, and Martin Parry

Introduction

The purpose of this chapter is to consider our current capacity to monitor the effects of acid deposition and global climate change on agricultural potential. We do not consider at length here the effects per se that these macroenvironmental changes may induce or the potential technological responses to them. These have been discussed elsewhere (for example, IPCC, 1990; Parry, 1990). It should be emphasized that substantial uncertainties are attached to our estimations of likely future change of climate and rates of acid deposition, these stemming both from our imperfect knowledge of the physical and biological processes involved, of the economic and social factors that will affect future emissions rates, of the ability of agriculture to adapt to environmental changes, and of the other changes that will occur in agriculture over the next 50 years due to factors unconnected with environmental change. The fact that we do not dwell on these issues should not be taken to imply that we do not believe them to be important. We do, and they should be treated as working assumptions behind our discussion of the specific question at stake: How can we best monitor the effects of these macroenvironmental changes on agriculture?

Acid Deposition

Acid deposit is taken here to include both the wet and dry deposition of acidic pollutants from the atmosphere to plant and soil surfaces. These pollutants became increasingly important in western Europe during the 19th century, when effects of acidic gases on the growth of crops and trees were first reported (see, for example, Smith, 1872). In the absence of any appreciable pollution-control measures, very high concentrations of sulphur dioxide (SO_2) existed as the result of coal combustion in industrial towns and in adjacent agricultural and horticultural areas. High concentrations of sulphur dioxide were prevalent in these regions for the first half of the 20th century also, but progressive pollution-control measures and changes in fuel usage and combustion technology have resulted in a marked decline in (SO_2) concentrations.

These concentrations in polluted rural regions of the developed world are now below those at which direct toxic effects of sulphur dioxide alone on crop growth can be demonstrated. However, sulphur dioxide is present at potentially phytotoxic concentrations close to urban and industrial centers in some parts of central Europe, China, and South America. The changes in fuel usage and combustion technology have also resulted in the increased importance of nitrogen oxides (NO_x) as a pollutant during this century. The increases in nitrogen oxides and hydrocarbons have, in the presence of sunlight, resulted in the production of secondary pollutants. These photochemical oxidants, notably ozone, have resulted in major crop damages, particularly in parts of North America.

Global Climate Change

The potentially most important changes of climate for agriculture include changes in climatic extremes, warming in the high latitudes, poleward advance of monsoon rainfall, and reduced soil water availability (particularly in mid-latitudes in midsummer and at low latitudes).

Climatic Extremes. It is not clear whether changes in the variability of temperature will occur as a result of climate change. However, even if variability remains unaltered, an increase in average temperatures would result in the increased frequency of temperatures above particular thresholds. Changes in the frequency and distribution of precipitation are less predictable, but the combination of elevated temperatures and drought or flood probably constitutes the greatest risk to agriculture in many regions from global climate change.

Warming in High Latitudes. There is relatively strong agreement among global climate model (GCM) predictions that greenhouse-gas-induced warming will be greater at higher latitudes (IPCC, 1990). This will reduce temperature constraints on high-latitude agriculture and increase the competition for land there (Parry and Duinker, 1990). Warming at low latitudes, although less pronounced, is also likely to have a significant impact on agriculture.

Poleward Advance of Monsoon Rainfall. In a warmer world the intertropical convergence zones and polar frontal zones might advance further poleward as a result of an enhanced ocean-continent pressure gradient. If this were to occur, then total rainfall could increase in some regions of monsoon Africa, monsoon Asia, and Australia, although there is currently little agreement on which regions these might be (IPCC, 1990). Rainfall could also be more intense in its occurrence, so flooding and erosion could increase.

Reduced Soil Water Availability. Probably the most important consequences for agriculture would stem from higher potential evapotranspiration, primarily due to the higher temperatures of the air and the land surface. Even in the tropics, where temperature increases are expected to be smaller than elsewhere and where precipitation might increase, the increased rate of loss of moisture from plants and soil would be considerable (Parry, 1990; Rind, Goldberg, and Ruedy, 1989). It may be somewhat reduced by greater air humidity and increased cloudiness during the rainy seasons, but could be pronounced in the dry seasons.

Estimated Long-Term Effects of Acid Deposition

Effects of Wet Deposition

Many studies have examined the effect of simulated acid precipitation on the growth of crop species. Irving (1990) reviewed the evidence for effects of acidic precipitation on crop foliage and concluded that the majority of species tested were not affected.

Most reports of foliar injury from experimentation occur at pH 3.5 or less, and rainfall as acidic as this is rare in regions where crops are grown. Although it is difficult to simulate rainfall events in experimental conditions, it would seem unlikely that acid precipitation is directly responsible for crop damage.

Long-term indirect effects of acid precipitation on crops could be mediated through effects on soil processes. Among the factors influenced by acid precipitation that have been proposed to affect plant growth in forests are a decrease in base saturation and the mobilization of aluminum, resulting in calcium-to-aluminum ratios decreasing to levels that cause toxicity to roots (Meiwes, Khanna, and Ulrich, 1986). Increases in forest soil acidity that can be related to acidic precipitation input have been observed in Sweden during this century. However, in contrast to forests, most agricultural soils are maintained at soil pHs well above pH 4.5, where the aluminum buffer range is approached.

It is also important to remember that sulphur and nitrogen are essential elements for plant growth, and that effects of acid precipitation can be positive as well as negative. For example, nitrogen uptake rates into arable crops may be of the order of 40 kg/ha^{-1}/yr^{-1}, whereas nitrogen deposition rates in Europe may range from 2 to 50 kg/ha^{-1}/yr^{-1} (Chadwick and Kuylenstierna, 1990). Thus, although many arable soils will be artificially maintained at high available nitrogen through fertilizer application, nitrogen deposition in some areas may contribute significantly to the available nitrogen supply.

The contribution of atmospheric deposition to available nitrogen and sulphur is likely to be greatest in marginal agricultural areas of heaths and rough grazing. Here the available mobile anions as the result of acidic deposition may have a marked effect on soil acidity and aluminum mobilization. The much lower (compared with arable crops) nitrogen removal rate (circa 2.5 kg/ha^{-1}/yr^{-1}) may exacerbate this process, and the increase in nitrogen availability may directly affect the species composition of these pastures and perhaps, therefore, their grazing value over the long term. There may also be indirect effects of acid precipitation on plant growth through effects on soil organisms. The microorganisms responsible for nitrogen mineralization from organic matter may be directly affected by acid precipitation. Soil pH is an important variable apparently affecting nitrification rates, and it is possible that there may be both positive and negative effects of nitrogen and sulphur inputs on the activity of nitrifying and ammonifying microbes.

Dry Deposition

Responses of crops to dry deposited SO_2 and NO_x have been inferred largely from effects of controlled fumigation experiments. These experiments have included the addition of known concentrations of pollutants to ambient air or to air that is filtered to remove any pollutants present. Experiments have also included comparisons between growth in filtered and unfiltered air combined with monitoring of the pollutant concentrations in the unfiltered (ambient) air. Various fumigation procedures have been employed, including closed chambers, open-top chambers, and field-release systems. Open-top chambers allow good control of gas concentrations combined with temperature and humidity conditions closer to ambient air than closed chambers. Thus, open-top chambers have been employed widely in studies of pollutants on crops.

Experiments at high concentrations of NO_2 and SO_2 (more than 40 parts per billion) have generally demonstrated reductions in crop yield (see, for example, United Kingdom Terrestrial Effects Review Group, 1988). However, fumigation with concentrations of the gases more typical of present-day polluted rural atmospheres in Western Europe (less than 20 ppb) have shown little adverse effect and sometimes have appeared to stimulate growth. These experiments have involved fumigation with each gas in isolation or in combination, but a few studies incorporating NO_2, SO_2, and ozone suggest that reduction in yield can occur at concentrations between 20 and 30 ppb (for example, Mooi, 1985).

There is considerable evidence from North America of crop damage by air pollutants, where oxidants have caused a marked reduction in the yield of some crops. There is also evidence from these studies that there are marked differences between cultivars in the sensitivity to oxidants (see, for example, Heggestad et al., 1980). This difference in sensitivity of cultivars has been utilized to monitor the regional distribution of ozone in the United Kingdom and elsewhere by using tobacco varieties. The tobacco cultivar BEL-W3 shows injury symptoms at ozone concentrations above 40 ppb (close to the natural background). Ashmore, Bell, and Reilly (1978) showed, using BEL-W3, that ozone concentrations in the United Kingdom were above the natural background over large areas in the summers of 1977 and 1978, and the degree of ozone injury was related to the hours of sunshine and the wind direction from urban areas. Overall, there is evidence of ozone becoming an increasingly important air pollutant in Europe in recent decades.

Estimated Long-Term Effects of Climate Change on Agricultural Potential

There are three ways in which increases in greenhouse gases (GHG) may be important for agriculture (Parry and Zhang, 1991). First, increased atmospheric carbon dioxide (CO_2) concentrations can have a direct effect on the growth rate of crop plants and weeds. Second, GHG-induced changes of climate may alter levels of temperature (as well as temperature gradient), rainfall, and sunshine, and this can influence plant and animal productivity. Finally, rises in sea level may lead to loss of farmland by inundation and to increasing salinity of groundwater in coastal areas. These three types of potential impact will be considered in turn.

Effects of CO_2 Enrichment

Effects on Photosynthesis. Carbon dioxide is vital for photosynthesis, and the evidence indicates that increases in CO_2 concentration would increase the rate of plant growth (Cure, 1985; Cure and Acock, 1986). There are, however, important differences between the photosynthetic mechanisms of different crop plants and hence in their response to increasing CO_2. Plant species with the C3 photosynthetic pathway (for example, wheat, rice, and soybeans) tend to respond more positively to increased CO_2 because it tends to suppress rates of photorespiration. However, C4 plants (for example, maize, sorghum, sugarcane, and millet) are less responsive to increased CO_2 levels. Since these are largely tropical crops, most widely grown in Africa, there is the suggestion that CO_2 enrichment will benefit temperate and humid tropical agriculture more than that of the semiarid tropics. Thus, if the effects of climate changes on agriculture in some parts of the semiarid tropics are negative, then these may not be partially compensated for by the beneficial effects of CO_2 enrichment, as they might in other regions. In addition, we should note that, although C4 crops account for only about one-fifth of the world's food production, maize alone accounts for 14 percent of all production and about three-quarters of all traded grain. It is the major grain used to make up food deficits in famine-prone regions, and any reduction in its output could affect access to food in these areas (Morison, 1990).

In temperate and subtropical regions, C3 crops could also benefit from reduced weed infestation. Of the world's 17 most troublesome terrestrial weed species, 14 are C4 plants in C3 crops. The difference in response to increased CO_2 may make such weeds less competitive. In contrast, C3 weeds in C4 crops, particularly in tropical regions, could become more of a problem, although the final outcome will depend on the relative response of crops and weeds to climate changes as well (Morison, 1990).

Many of the pasture and forage grasses of the world are C4 plants, including important prairie grasses in North America and central Asia and in the tropics and subtropics. The carrying capacity of the world's major rangelands are thus unlikely to benefit substantially from CO_2 enrichment (Morison, 1990). Much, of course, will depend on the parallel effects of climate changes on the yield potential of these different crops.

The actual amount of increase in usable yield rather than of total plant matter that might occur as a result of increased photosynthetic rate is also problematic. In controlled environment studies, where temperature, nutrients, and moisture are optimal, the yield increase can be substantial, averaging 36 percent for C3 cereals such as wheat, rice, barley, and sunflower under a doubling of ambient CO_2 concentration. Few studies have yet been published, however, of the effects of increasing CO_2 in combination with changes of temperature and rainfall.

Little is also known about possible changes in yield quality under increased CO_2. The nitrogen content of plants is likely to decrease, while the carbon content increases, implying reduced protein levels and reduced nutritional levels for livestock and humans. This, however, may also reduce the nutritional value of plants for pests, so that they need to consume more to obtain their required protein intake.

Effects on Water Use by Plants. Just as important may be the effect that increased CO_2 has on the closure of stomata. This tends to reduce the water requirements of plants by reducing transpiration (per unit leaf area), thus improving what is termed *water use efficiency* (the ratio of crop biomass accumulation to the water used in evapotranspiration). A doubling of ambient CO_2 concentration causes about a 40 percent decrease in stomatal aperture in both C3 and C4 plants, which may reduce transpiration by 23 to 46 percent (Morison, 1987; Cure and Acock, 1986). This might well help plants in environments where moisture currently limits growth, such as in semiarid regions, but there remain many uncertainties, such as to what extent the greater leaf area of plants (resulting from increased CO_2) will balance the reduced transpiration per unit leaf area (Allen, Jones, and Jones, 1985; Gifford, 1988).

In summary, we can expect that a doubling of atmospheric CO_2 concentrations from 330 to 660 ppm (projected to occur around 2040 under the Intergovernmental Panel on Climate Change (IPCC) business-as-usual scenario) might cause a 10 to 50 percent increase in growth and yield of C3 crops (such as wheat, rice, and soybean) and a 0 to 10 percent increase for C4 crops (such as maize and sugarcane) (Warrick, Gifford, and Parry, 1986). Much depends, however, on the prevailing growing conditions. Our present knowledge is based on experiments mainly in field chambers and has not yet included extensive study of response in the field under suboptimal conditions. Thus, although there are indications that, overall, the effects of increased CO_2 could be distinctly beneficial and could partly compensate for some of the negative effects of CO_2-induced changes of climate, we cannot at present be sure that this will be so.

Effects of Changes of Climate

Changes in Thermal Limits to Agriculture. Increases in temperature can be expected to lengthen the growing season in areas where agricultural potential is currently limited by insufficient warmth, resulting in a poleward shift of thermal limits of agriculture. The consequent extension of potential will be most pronounced in the Northern Hemisphere because of the greater extent there of temperate agriculture at higher latitudes. There may, however, be important regional variations in our ability to exploit this shift. For example, the greater potential for exploitation of northern soils in Siberia than on the Canadian Shield may mean relatively greater increases in potential in northern Asia than in northern North America (Parry, 1990).

A number of estimations have been made concerning the northward shift in productive potential in mid-latitude Northern Hemisphere countries. These relate to changes in the climatic limits for specific crops under a variety of climatic scenarios, and are therefore not readily compatible (Newman, 1980; Blasing and Solomon, 1983; Rosenzweig, 1985; Williams and Oakes, 1978; Parry and Carter, 1988; Parry, Carter, and Porter, 1989). They suggest, however, that a 1° C increase in mean annual temperature (projected by about 2030 under the IPCC business-as-usual scenario) would tend to advance the thermal limit of cereal cropping in the mid-latitude Northern Hemisphere by about 150 to 200 kilometers, and to raise the altitudinal limit to arable agriculture by about 150 to 200 meters.

While warming may extend the margin of potential cropping and grazing in mid-latitude regions, it may reduce yield potential in the core areas of current production, because higher temperatures encourage more rapid maturation of plants and shorten the period of grain filling (Parry and Duinker, 1990). An important additional effect, especially in temperate mid-latitudes, is likely to be the reduction of winter chilling (vernalization). Many temperate crops require a period of low temperatures in winter to either initiate or accelerate the flowering process. Low vernalization results in low flower bud initiation and, ultimately, reduced yields. A 1° C warming has been estimated to reduce effective winter chilling by between 10 and 30 percent, thus contributing to a poleward shift of temperate crops (Salinger, 1989).

Increases in temperature are also likely to affect the crop calendar in low-latitude regions, particularly where more than one crop is harvested each year. For example, in Sri Lanka and Thailand a 1° C warming would probably require a substantial rearrangement of the current crop calendar, which is finely tuned to present climatic conditions (Kaida and Surarerks, 1984; Yoshino, 1984).

Shifts of Moisture Limits to Agriculture. There is much less agreement between GCM-based projections concerning GHG-induced changes in precipitation than there is about temperature—not only concerning changes of magnitude, but also changes of spatial pattern and distribution through the year. For this reason it is difficult to identify potential shifts in the moisture limits to agriculture. This is particularly so because relatively small changes in the seasonal distribution of rainfall can have disproportionately large effects on the viability of agriculture in tropical areas, largely through changes in the growing period when moisture is sufficient and thus through the timing of critical episodes such as planting. However, recent surveys for the IPCC have made a preliminary identification of those regions where there is some agreement among $2 \times CO_2$ (doubling of CO_2) experiments with general circulation models concerning an overall reduction in crop-water availability (Parry, 1990; IPCC, 1990). It should be emphasized that coincidence of results for these regions is not statistically significant. The regions are as follows:

Decreases in soil water in December, January, and February

Africa: northeastern Africa, southern Africa

Asia: western Arabian Peninsula; Southeast Asia

Australasia: eastern Australia

North America: southern United States

South America: Argentine pampas

Decreases in soil water in June, July, and August

Africa: North Africa, West Africa

Asia: northern and central China, parts of the former Soviet central Asia and Siberia

Australasia: western Australia

Europe: parts of Western Europe

North America: southern United States and Central America

South America: eastern Brazil

Regions Affected by Drought, Heat Stress and Other Extremes. Probably most important for agriculture, but least understood, are the possible changes in climatic extremes, such as the magnitude and frequency of drought, storms, heat waves, and severe frosts (Rind, Goldberg, and Ruedy, 1989). Some modeling evidence suggests that hurricane intensities will increase with climatic warming (Emanuel, 1987). This has important implications for agriculture in low latitudes, particularly in coastal regions.

Since crop yields often exhibit a nonlinear response to heat or cold stress, changes in the probability of extreme temperature events can be significant (Mearns, Katz, and Schneider, 1984; Parry, 1976). In addition, even assuming no change in the standard deviation of temperature maxima and minima, we should note that the frequency of hot and cold days can be markedly altered by changes in mean monthly temperature. To illustrate, under a $2 \times CO_2$ equilibrium climate the number of days in which temperatures would fall below freezing would decrease from a current average of 39 to 20 in Atlanta, Georgia, while the number of days above 90° F would increase from 17 to 53 (EPA, 1989). The frequency and extent of area over which losses of agricultural output could result from heat stress, particularly in tropical regions, is therefore likely to increase significantly. Unfortunately, no studies have yet been made of this. However, the apparently small increases in mean annual temperatures in tropical regions (about 1° to 2° C under a $2 \times CO_2$ climate) could sufficiently increase heat stress on temperate crops such as wheat so that these are no longer suited to such areas. Important wheat-producing areas such as northern India could be affected in this way (IPCC, 1990).

There is a distinct possibility that, as a result of high rates of evapotranspiration, some regions in the tropics and subtropics could be characterized by a higher frequency of drought or a similar frequency of more intense drought than at present. Current uncertainties about how regional patterns of rainfall will alter mean that no useful prediction can at present be made. However, it is clear in some regions that relatively small decreases in water availability can readily produce drought conditions. In India, for example, lower-than-average rainfall in 1987 reduced food grains production from 152 to 134 million tons (mt), lowering food buffer stocks from 23 to 9 mt. Changes in the risk and intensity of drought, especially in currently drought-prone regions, represent potentially the most serious impact of climatic change on agriculture at both the global and the regional levels.

Effects on the Distribution of Agricultural Pests and Diseases. Studies suggest that temperature increases may extend the geographic range of some insect pests currently limited by temperature (EPA, 1989; Hill and Dymock, 1989). As with crops, such effects would probably be greatest at higher latitudes. The number of generations per year produced by multivoltine (that is, multigenerational) pests would increase, with earlier establishment of pest populations in the growing season and increased abundance during more susceptible stages of growth. An important unknown, however, is the effect that changes in precipitation amount and air humidity may have on the insect pests themselves and on their predators, parasites, and diseases. Climate change may significantly influence interspecific interactions between pests and their predators and parasites.

Under a warmer climate at mid-latitudes there would be an increase in the overwintering range and population density of a number of important agricultural pests, such as the potato leafhopper, which is a serious pest of soybeans and other crops in the United States (EPA, 1989). Assuming planting dates did not change, warmer temperatures would lead to invasions earlier in the growing season and would probably lead to greater damage to crops. In the U.S. Corn Belt increased damage to soybeans is also expected due to earlier infestation by the corn earworm. In Western Europe a 1° C warming is estimated to lead to a northward shift in the limit of the European corn borer (currently a pest in southern but not in northern Europe) by about 300 to 500 kilometers (Porter, Parry, and Carter, 1991).

Examination of the effect of climatic warming on the distribution of livestock diseases suggests that those at present limited to tropical countries, such as Rift Valley fever and African swine fever, may spread into the mid-latitudes. For example, the horn fly, which currently causes losses of $730.3 million in the U.S. beef and dairy cattle industries, might extend its range under a warmer climate, leading to reduced gain in beef cattle and a significant reduction in milk production (Drummond, 1987; EPA, 1989).

In cool temperate regions, where insect pests and diseases are not generally serious at present, damage is likely to increase under warmer conditions. In Iceland, for example, potato blight currently does little damage to potato crops, as it is limited by the low summer temperatures. However, under a $2 \times CO_2$ climate that may be 4° C warmer than at present, potential crop losses to disease may increase to 15 percent (Bergthorsson et al., 1988).

Most agricultural diseases have greater potential to reach severe levels under warmer and more humid conditions (Beresford and Fullerton, 1989). Under such conditions, cereals would be more prone to diseases such as septoria. In addition, increases in population levels of disease vectors may well lead to increased epidemics of the diseases they carry. To illustrate, increases in infestations of the bird cherry aphid (*Rhopalosiphum padi*) or grain aphid (*Sitobian avenae*) could lead to increased incidence of barley yellow dwarf virus in cereals.

Effects of Sea-Level Rise on Agriculture

GHG-induced warming is expected to lead to rises in sea level as a result of thermal expansion of the oceans and partial melting of glaciers and ice caps, and this in turn is expected to affect agriculture, mainly through the inundation of low-lying farmland but also through the increased salinity of coastal groundwater. The current projection of sea-level rise above present levels is 20 centimeters ± 10 by about 2030, and 30 centimeters ± 15 by 2050 (Warrick and Oerlemans, 1990).

Preliminary surveys of proneness to inundation have been based on a study of existing contoured topographic maps, in conjunction with knowledge of the local "wave climate" that varies between different coastlines. They have identified 27 countries as especially vulnerable to sea-level rise, on the basis of the extent of land liable to inundation, the population at risk, and the capability to take protective measures (UNEP, 1989). It should be emphasized, however, that these surveys assume a much larger rise in sea levels than is at present estimated to occur within the next century under current trends of increased GHG concentrations. On an ascending scale of vulnerability (1 to 10), experts identified the following most vulnerable countries or regions: 10, Bangladesh; 9, Egypt, Thailand; 8, China; 7, western Denmark; 6, Louisiana; and 4, Indonesia.

The most severe impacts are likely to stem directly from inundation. Southeast Asia would be most affected because of the extreme vulnerability of several large and heavily populated deltaic regions. For example, with a 1.5-meter sea-level rise, about 15 percent of all land (and about one-fifth of all farmland) in Bangladesh would be inundated and a further 6 percent would become more prone to frequent flooding (UNEP, 1989). Altogether, 21 percent of agricultural production could be lost. In Egypt, it is estimated that 17 percent of national agricultural production and 20 percent of all farmland, especially the most productive farmland, would be lost as a result of a 1.5-meter sea-level rise. Island nations, particularly low-lying coral atolls, have the most to lose. The Maldive Islands in the Indian Ocean would have one-half of their land area inundated with a 2-meter rise in sea level (UNEP, 1989).

In addition to direct farmland loss from inundation, it is likely that agriculture would experience increased costs from saltwater intrusion into surface water and groundwater in coastal regions. Deeper tidal penetration would increase the risk of flooding, and rates of abstraction of groundwater might need to be reduced to prevent recharge of aquifers with seawater.

Further indirect impacts would be likely as a result of the need to relocate both farming populations and production to other regions. In Bangladesh, for example, about one-fifth of the nation's population would be displaced as a result of the farmland loss estimated for a 1.5-meter sea-level rise. It is important to emphasize, however, that the IPCC estimates of sea-level rise are much lower than this (about 20 centimeters by 2030 and 50 centimeters by 2090 under the IPCC business-as-usual case).

Summary of Plant, Pest, and Sea-Level Effects

Potential impacts on yields vary greatly according to types of climate change and types of agriculture. In general, there is much uncertainty about how agricultural potential may be affected.

In the northern mid-latitudes where summer drying may reduce productive potential (for example, in the U.S. Great Plains and Corn Belt, the Canadian prairies, southern Europe, and the south European region of the former Soviet Union), yield potential is estimated to fall by about 10 to 30 percent under an equilibrium 2 x CO_2 climate (Parry, 1990). However, toward the northern edge of current core producing regions (for example, the northern edge of the Canadian prairies, northern Europe, northern regions of the former Soviet Union, northern Japan, and southern Chile and Argentina), warming may enhance productive potential, particularly when combined with beneficial direct CO_2 effects. Much of this potential may not, however, be exploitable, owing to limits placed by inappropriate soils and difficult terrain, and on balance it seems that the advantages of warming at higher latitudes would not compensate for reduced potential in current major cereal-producing regions.

Effects at lower latitudes are much more difficult to estimate, because production potential is largely a function of the amount and distribution of precipitation and because there is little agreement about how precipitation may be affected by GHG warming. Because of these uncertainties, the tendency has been to assert that worthwhile study must await improved projection of changes in precipitation. Consequently very few estimates are currently available of how yields might respond to a range of possible changes of climate in low-latitude regions. The only comprehensive national estimates available are for Australia, where increases in cereal and grassland productivity might occur (except in western Australia) if warming is accompanied by increase in summer rainfall (Pearman, 1988).

The effects just described relate to possible future changes in *potential* productivity or yield. How *actual* production alters would, of course, be a function of how agriculture develops in response both to these influences and to a host of other factors not related to climate changes, such as demand and technological development.

Current Efforts to Monitor Agricultural Sustainability

Monitoring Acid Deposition Effects

Acidic deposition has been shown to have damaging effects on some seminatural ecosystems, and the need for reductions in emissions of sulphur and nitrogen has been recognized by scientists in both Europe and North America. Currently there is an attempt to link emission-abatement strategy with the capacity of ecosystems to withstand the effects of acidic deposition. This approach assumes that there is a threshold concentration of pollutant gas and/or total deposition of an element below which damage to ecosystems does not occur. For total deposition of an element this is called a *critical load*, which has been defined as "the highest load that will not cause chemical changes leading to long-term harmful effects in the most sensitive ecological systems" (Nilsson, 1986). The equivalent term for gaseous concentrations is *critical level*. Critical loads and levels are estimates of the maximum deposition and gaseous concentration at which harmful effects on ecosystems are unlikely to occur. They will vary from ecosystem to ecosystem and from organism to organism within any one ecosystem. In practice, target loads may be set that may or may not be equal to the critical loads.

Chadwick and Kuylenstierna (1990) describe a target load approach in which the relative sensitivity of ecosystems to acidic deposition is derived from a number of site variables (bedrock lithology, soil type, land use, and rainfall). Among the most sensitive ecosystems with a target load set at 20 kg $H^+/km^{-2}/yr^{-1}$ are rough grazing and heathland vegetation on slow-weathering rock types with poorly buffered soils in high-rainfall areas. This vegetation provides the most marginal of agricultural areas, and it follows therefore that any abatement strategy set to protect these areas of more or less seminatural vegetation would automatically protect more productive agricultural ecosystems. Similarly, bryophytes and lichens are among the most sensitive plants to SO_2 and NO_2. Any target level set to protect these organisms within ecosystems will automatically protect crop species.

Monitoring of acidic deposition has occurred spasmodically since the middle of the 19th century, and there were early attempts (see, for example, Smith, 1872) to link measured deposition to effects on crops. In the last few decades several monitoring systems have been developed, including (1) the use of sensitive plants as phytometers (for example, the tobacco cultivar BEL-W3 as an indicator of ozone concentrations); (2) bulk deposition measurements at local, national, and international levels; (3) wet-only collection networks; (4) daily mean measurements of sulphur dioxide concentrations; and (5) continuous measurement of NO_x, SO_2, and O_3 concentrations. The most sophisticated networks contain wet-only collectors and may also contain continuous gas measurement equipment. These networks have been established in Europe and North America. For example, eight major wet deposition networks cover the United States, allowing evaluation on a regional scale of seasonal and annual deposition (see, for example, Irving, 1991). In the United Kingdom a primary network of 9 sites where wet-only collectors are used to make daily measurements is combined with a secondary network of 59 sites involving weekly measurements of bulk deposition. Data from these networks are used to model deposition on a national or international basis (see, for example, United Kingdom Review Group on Acid Rain, 1990).

Measurement and modeling of deposition has also been combined with attempts to monitor effects, most systematically in a series of forest-health monitoring studies (see, for example, Innes et al., 1986). These studies, however, are hampered by the difficulty of distinguishing effects due to pollutants (which are rarely specific) from other stress factors.

Monitoring Climate Change Effects

The detection of climate change impacts on agriculture requires monitoring at two levels—the physical and the biological. The first is concerned with the physical status of the natural resource base, and primarily with sea-level rise and related constraints to agricultural production. A number of monitoring systems are planned for this level, but none are operational yet. The second-level monitoring is of the biological productivity of the resource base. It is concerned largely with the agroclimatic parameters governing crop and livestock productivity and their pests and diseases, for example, temperature and precipitation. These parameters, however, are generally monitored as individual values and not as integrated derivatives, notably potential evapotranspiration or soil moisture, which are more meaningful for crop growth analysis.

Although the first institutional efforts to achieve systematic measurement of a number of the factors governing climate impacts on agriculture date from 1873, when the International Meteorological Organization was established, much of the historic data are irrelevant or unsuitable for climate change impact assessment.

The most comprehensive current monitoring efforts are those conducted as part of the World Meteorological Organization's World Weather Watch System (WWW). This system endeavors to achieve international comparability in measurements of such factors as wind speed and direction, air trajectories, temperature, humidity, precipitation, insolation, cloud cover, and so forth. Minimum standards are set for observing methods and techniques.

The WWW's monitoring data from ground stations are now complemented by global observations recorded by satellites that orbit the earth twice a day and give complete surface coverage. These satellites give additional information, for example, on vertical temperature and humidity profiles and on changing vegetation cover, although the latter is not yet systematically modeled at the global level. The Food and Agriculture Organization of the United Nations, however, has a regional program for Africa, which for the past ten years has been monitoring vegetation cover and biological productivity as part of its Global Early Warning System. This system gives advanced warning of crop failures, low storage production, and potential food shortages. It could provide the methodology and baseline for a global monitoring system for climate impacts.

Monitoring data from the WWW is a major input to another World Meteorological Organization (WMO) activity—the World Climate Programme (WCP). The WCP has four main components, although they are currently under revision to take account of the recommendations of the Second World Climate Conference. The four main components are

> data measurement, collection, and exchange;
>
> application of climate information to improve or safeguard agriculture and other economic activities;
>
> evaluation of the potential socioeconomic impact of climate change; and
>
> research on the climate system (atmosphere, oceans, land, and biota) and on factors such as increased greenhouse gas concentrations that affect it.

The data component of the WCP uses monitoring information from the WWW to establish the means, extremes, fluctuations, and trends for a number of the climatic factors governing agricultural production. In particular, two of its projects can contribute to monitoring macroenvironmental changes: the Climate Change Detection Project (CCDP), as its title suggests, aims to produce high-quality data sets that permit early detection of departures from the normal range of climate variation, while the Climate System Monitoring Project issues monthly reports on the dynamics of the global climate system.

These monitoring projects have been complemented by the WMO's software-development activities, notably the Climate Computer System (CLICOM) project, as part of its WCP, activities that are important in the context of impact assessment. CLICOM is a standardized system for data entry, quality control, storage and retrieval, data inventories, and other basic climatological products, which can be used locally for agricultural planning and water-resource management with respect to climate change, and internationally as a mechanism for data exchange in a common format.

Finally, there is the World Climate Research Programme (WCRP), which aims to improve our ability to predict the future behavior of the global climate system. As with the data component of the WCP, this program builds up the institutional capacity for better monitoring systems and for more effective utilization of the output of such systems. Although the WMO is the lead agency, it is operated in conjunction with the International Council of Scientific Unions (ICSU) to draw on the widest possible scientific community.

Recommendations for Future Monitoring

Future Monitoring of Acid Deposition Effects

Many crop species are grown as annuals, and as such are not exposed to acidic deposition over long periods. There is no evidence that acid precipitation is having an adverse effect on crop growth. The major potential threat to agricultural crops in North America and Western Europe is the secondary pollutant ozone on its own and in combination with SO_2 and NO_2. Monitoring of crop growth in fumigation chambers should, however, continue to be used to set critical levels of this pollutant for different regions.

Long-term effects of acid precipitation could be mediated through effects on soils. Most arable crops are, however, grown on soils resistant to acidic deposition or are grown on soils artificially maintained as such through liming practice. Permanent pasture provides the most likely agricultural system to be affected by acid precipitation, but effects can be positive as well as negative because of the fertilizing effect of atmospheric nitrogen and sulphur deposition. Overall, the effects of wet deposition of acidity on agriculture are likely to be small and difficult to monitor and to quantify, but this should not deter the development of an integrated monitoring scheme (similar to that proposed below for climate change).

Future Monitoring of Climate Change Effects

Recent international activities, notably the Intergovernmental Panel on Climate Change, the Second World Climate Conference, and the ICSU–International Geosphere-Biosphere Program (IGBP) Study on Global Change, have led to an extensive reassessment of monitoring requirements. They have stimulated or proposed the establishment of additional monitoring systems and an overall framework mechanism, the Global Climate Observing System (GCOS).

Nonetheless, important monitoring gaps remain, particularly regarding certain basic features of the natural resource base and its utilization for agriculture. Priority should be given to filling three of these gaps—in soil quality changes, in actual land use, and in certain agroclimatic parameters that govern the functioning of agroecosystems and the range of crops that can be grown at a given location.

Two of these gaps concern essential baseline data for understanding the magnitude of the risk posed by climate change, for monitoring the actual changes, and for determining the impact. They also have an important role to play in monitoring the sustainability of agriculture in the wider context.

Soil Carbon Monitoring. The first recommendation concerns soil organic matter and its high carbon content. The rate of organic matter breakdown is very temperature sensitive and occurs more rapidly at higher temperatures. Consequently, global warming, other factors being equal, will accelerate the rate of breakdown, releasing CO_2 to the atmosphere and intensifying the greenhouse effect. There may, however, be a compensatory mechanism through the CO_2-enhancement effect on plant growth, leading to greater root growth and larger organic residues, and an appropriate monitoring system could clarify the picture.

Climate-change-induced organic matter decay could have three other important negative impacts. First, it could reduce the water-holding capacity of soils, and second, it could increase soil erosion. Thus, if climate change lowers rainfall directly or limits soil moisture levels through greater evapotranspiration, it is likely to intensify vulnerability to drought in arid and semiarid areas. In high-rainfall areas, in contrast, the loss of organic matter would increase the erodability of rainfall, particularly if climate change results in more intense rainfall. Third, since there is a strong link between loss of soil organic matter and loss of soil nitrogen, crop yields will also suffer unless the losses are compensated for by fertilizers.

It is therefore recommended that priority be given to establishing a global monitoring system for soil organic matter and soil carbon. Several of the basic building blocks for such a system are in place. The FAO-UNESCO Soil Map of the World, already available in Geographic Information Systems form, provides a consistent and relatively complete, albeit generalized, data base for the distribution of the main soil types and gives an indication of their organic matter content. Scientists in the United States are close to completing a first-round estimation of global soil carbon levels using these data.

There are well-established and inexpensive methods for the required minimum set of data for determining bulk density and soil carbon content that are within the technical and financial capabilities of almost all countries. Finally, computer models are available, well validated for some soil types and agroclimate environments at least, that can utilize soil organic matter data to predict the rate of decay and CO_2 release.

It is proposed that these inputs be used to establish a monitoring system composed of fixed long-term sites at appropriate locations around the world with a set pattern of land management, repetitive soil sampling, and analysis. A sampling frequency of once every five years would probably suffice.

Monitoring of Actual Land Cover and Land Use. The second recommendation relates to another essential part of the jigsaw, namely land cover and land use. None of the existing monitoring systems gives global coverage of these two items. The available agricultural land-use data provide information on how much land is used for given crops in a particular country, but not where those crops are grown, or in which agroecological environments. It is therefore not generally possible to determine changing cropping patterns in response to climate change, or other forces, at the subnational or agroecological zone level. Moreover, since most of the land-use data are collected by ground-based methods that vary between countries in nature and quality or application, reliable national and regional comparisons cannot readily be made.

Interpretation of remote sensing data with limited ground checks is the key to achieving the required information, possibly first concentrating on land cover changes as in the pilot studies by the IGBP,

FAO, and others. This information is the basis for the ground-based mapping and monitoring of land use. As with the soil carbon monitoring recommendations, the main building blocks exist. The additional requirements are greater financing and closer international collaboration.

Monitoring of Plant Growth Parameters. The final recommendation concerns agroecosystem function and its sensitivity (positive or negative) to climate change. Current monitoring systems cover most of the primary climate factors, but with highly inadequate spatial coverage in some regions. In the case of the Sahel, for example, reliable time-series rainfall data are only available for some 30 or so locations, although the establishment of the Observoire du Sahel should help to overcome this constraint. The other major weakness in primary-factor monitoring that needs to be addressed is the temporal coverage, since many crops are sensitive to diurnal changes and impact analysis requires knowledge of day and night conditions and of extreme events and critical thresholds.

In contrast to the situation with primary variables, the monitoring of derived variables falls far short of global coverage. Yet derived variables have a higher utility in many respects because they integrate some of the key primary variables. Evapotranspiration, for example, integrates temperature, precipitation, humidity, solar radiation, and wind speed. Evapotranspiration and soil moisture content and tension are critical factors for crop growth, and tend to be more reliable parameters for impact analysis than the primary variables because of the possibilities of compensation between the latter, such that a change in one primary variable cancels out another.

It is therefore recommended that priority be given to achieving more comprehensive monitoring of these two derived variables, particularly in the transition zone between certain biomes that are likely to be highly sensitive to climate change.

References

Allen, L. H., Jr., P. Jones, and J. W. Jones. 1985. Rising atmospheric CO_2 and evapotranspiration. In *Advances in Evapotranspiration*, Proceedings of the National Conference on Advances in Evapotranspiration, 13-27. St. Joseph, Mich.: American Society of Agricultural Engineers.

Ashmore, M. R., J. N. B. Bell, and C. L. Reilly. 1978. A survey of ozone levels in the British Isles using indicator plants. *Nature* 276:813-15.

Beran, M. A., and N. W. Arnell. 1989. *Effect of Climatic Change on Quantitative Aspects of United Kingdom Water Resources.* Report for Department of Environment Water Inspectorate. United Kingdom: Institute of Hydrology.

Beresford, R. M., and R. A. Fullerton. 1989. Effects of climate change on plant diseases. Submission to Climate Impacts Working Group, May.

Bergthorsson, P., H. Bjornsson, O. Dyrmundsson, B. Gudmundsson, A. Helgadottir, and J. V. Jonmundsson. 1988. The effects of climatic variations on agriculture in Iceland. In *The Impact of Climatic Variations on Agriculture.* Vol. 1, *Cool Temperate and Cold Regions,* edited by M. L. Parry, T. R. Carter, and N. T. Konijn. Dordrecht: Kluwer.

Blasing, T. J., and A. M. Solomon. 1983. *Response of North American Corn Belt to Climatic Warming.* Prepared for the U.S. Department of Energy, Office of Energy Research, Carbon Dioxide Research Division. DOE/N88-004. Washington, D.C.: Government Printing Office.

Chadwick, M. J., and J. C. I. Kuylenstierna. 1990. *The Relative Sensitivity of Ecosystems in Europe to Acidic Depositions.* York: Stockholm Environment Institute at York, University of York.

Cure, J. D. 1985. Carbon dioxide doubling responses: A crop survey. In *Direct Effects of Increasing Carbon Dioxide on Vegetation,* edited by B. R. Strain and J. D. Cure, 100-116. U.S. DOE/ER-0238. Washington, D.C.: Government Printing Office.

Cure, J. D., and B. Acock. 1986. Crop responses to carbon dioxide doubling: A literature survey. *Agricultural and Forest Meteorology* 38:127-45.

Drummond, R. O. 1987. Economic aspects of ectoparasites of cattle in North America. In *Symposium: The Economic Impact of Parasitism in Cattle,* 9-24. Proceedings of the 23rd World Veterinary Congress. Montreal: World Veterinary Congress.

Emanuel, K. A. 1987. The dependence of hurricane intensity on climate: Mathematical simulation of the effects of tropical sea surface temperatures. *Nature* 326:483-85.

Environmental Protection Agency. 1989. *The Potential Effects of Global Climate Change on the United States.* Report to Congress. Washington, D.C.: Government Printing Office.

Gifford, R. M. 1988. Direct effect of higher carbon dioxide level concentrations on vegetation. In *Greenhouse: Planning for Climate Change,* edited by G. I. Pearman, 506-19. Melbourne: CSIRO.

Heggestad, H. E., A. S. Heagle, J. H. Bennett, and E. J. Koch. 1980. The effects of photochemical oxidants on the yield of snap bean. *Atmospheric Environment* 14:317-26.

Hill, M. G., and J. J. Dymock. 1989. *Impact of Climate Change: Agricultural/Horticultural Systems.* Department of Scientific and Industrial Research (DSIR) Entomology Division submission to New Zealand Climate Change Programme. New Zealand: DSIR.

Innes, J. L., R. Boswell, W. O. Binns, and D. B. Redfern. 1986. *Forest Health and Air Pollution.* Forestry Commission Research and Development Paper 150. Edinburgh: Forestry Commission.

Intergovernmental Panel on Climate Change (IPCC). 1990a. *Scientific Assessment of Climate Change: Policymakers' Summary.* Geneva and Nairobi: World Meteorological Organization (WMO) and United Nations Environmental Program.

———. 1990b. The effects on agriculture and forestry. In *The Potential Impact of Climate Change,* edited by M. L. Parry and P. Duinker. Geneva: WMO.

Irving, P. M. 1990. Acidic precipitation effects on crops: A review and analysis of research. *Journal of Environmental Quality* 12:442-53.

———. ed. 1991. *Acidic Deposition: State of Science and Technology.* Washington, D.C.: National Acid Precipitation Assessment Program.

Kaida, Y., and V. Surarerks. 1984. Climate and agricultural land use in Thailand. In *Climate and Agricultural Land Use in Monsoon Asia*, edited by M. M. Yoshino, 231-53. Tokyo: University of Tokyo Press.

Mearns, L. O., R. W. Katz, and S. H. Schneider. 1984. Extreme high temperature events: Changes in their probabilities with changes in mean temperatures. *Journal of Climatic and Applied Meteorology* 23:1601-13.

Meiwes, K. J., P. K. Khanna, and B. Ulrich. 1986. Parameters for describing soil acidification and their relevance to the stability of forest ecosystems. *Forest Ecology and Management* 15:161-79.

Mooi, J. 1985. Wirkungen von SO_2, NO_2, O_3 und ihrer Mischungen auf Pappein und einige andere Pflanzenarten. *Die Holzzucht* 1/2:8-12.

Morison, J. I. L. 1987. Intercellular CO_2 concentration and stomatal response to CO_2. In *Stomatal Function*, edited by E. Zeiger, I. R. Cowan, and G. D. Farquhar, 229-51. Stanford, Calif.: Stanford University Press.

———. 1990. Direct effects of elevated atmospheric CO_2 and other greenhouse gases. In *The Potential Effects of Climatic Change on Agriculture and Forestry*, edited by M. L. Parry and P. N. Duinker. Working Group II Report, IPCC.

Newman, J. E. 1980. Climate change impacts on the growing season of the North American Corn Belt. *Biometeorology* 7 (2):128-42.

Nilsson, J., ed. 1986. *Critical Loads for Nitrogen and Sulphur*. Report from a Nordic Working Group. Copenhagen: Nordic Council of Ministers, Miljørapport.

Parry, M. L. 1976. *Climatic Change, Agriculture and Settlement*. Folkestone, England: Dawson.

———. 1990. *Climate Change and World Agriculture*. London: Earthscan.

Parry, M. L., and T. R. Carter. 1988. The assessments of the effects of climatic variations on agriculture: Aims, methods and summary of results. In *The Impact of Climatic Variations on Agriculture*. Vol. 1, *Assessments in Cool, Temperate and Cold Regions*, edited by M. L. Parry, T. R. Carter, and N. T. Konijn. Dordrecht: Kluwer.

Parry, M. L., T. R. Carter, and J. H. Porter. 1989. The greenhouse effect and the future of UK agriculture. *Journal of the Royal Agricultural Society of England*, pp. 120-31.

Parry, M. L., and P. N. Duinker. 1990. *The Potential Effects of Climatic Change on Agriculture and Forestry*. Working Group II Report, IPCC.

Parry, M. L., and J. Zhang. 1991. The potential effect of climate changes on agriculture. In *Climate Change: Science, Impacts, Policy*, edited by J. Jafer and Ferguson. Cambridge: Cambridge University Press.

Pearman, G. I., ed. 1988. *Greenhouse: Planning for Climate Change*. Melbourne: CSIRO.

Porter, J. H., M. L. Parry, and T. R. Carter. 1991. The potential effects of climatic change on agricultural insect pests. In *Agriculture and Forest Meteorology*. Oxford: Elsevier.

Rind, D., R. Goldberg, and R. Ruedy. 1989. Change in climate variability in the 21st century. *Climatic Change* 14:5-37.

Rosenzweig, C. 1985. Potential CO_2-induced climate effects on North American wheat-producing regions. *Climatic Change* 7:367-89.

Salinger, M. J. 1989. The effects of greenhouse gas warming on forestry and agriculture. Draft report for WMO Commission on Agrometeorology. Geneva: WMO.

Smit, B. 1989. Climate warming and Canada's comparative position in agriculture. *Climate Change Digest*, CCD 89-01, Environment Canada.

Smith, R. A. 1872. *Air and Rain. The Beginnings of a Chemical Climatology*. London: Longmans, Green.

Study Commission of Eleventh German Bundestag. 1989. *Protecting the Earth's Atmosphere: An International Challenge*. Bonn: Bonn University.

United Kingdom Review Group on Acid Rain (UKRGAR). 1990. Acid deposition in the United Kingdom, 1986-1988. Third report of the UKRGAR. London: Department of the Environment.

United Kingdom Terrestrial Effects Review Group. 1988. *The Effects of Acid Deposition on the Terrestrial Environment in the United Kingdom*. London: Her Majesty's Stationery Office.

United Nations Environmental Program (UNEP). 1989. Criteria for assessing vulnerability to sea level rise: A global inventory to high risk areas. Draft report. NEP and the Government of the Netherlands.

Warrick, R. A., and R. Gifford, with M. L. Parry. 1986. CO_2, climatic change and agriculture. In *The Greenhouse Effect, Climatic Change and Ecosystems*, edited by B. Bolin, B. R. Doos, J. Jager, and R. A. Warrick, 393-473. SCOPE 29. Chichester: Wiley.

Warrick, R. A., and J. Oerlemans. 1990. Sea level rise. In *Climate Change: The IPCC Scientific Assessment*, ed. J. T. Houghton, G. J. Jenkins, J. J. Ephraims. Cambridge: Cambridge University Press.

Williams, G. D. V., and W. T. Oakes. 1978. Climatic resources for maturing barley and wheat in Canada. In *Essays on Meteorology and Climatology: In Honour of Richard W. Longley*, Studies in Geography, Mono. 3., edited by K. D. Haye and E. R. Reinelt, 367-85. Edmonton: University of Alberta.

Yoshino, M. M. 1984. Ecoclimatic systems and agricultural land use in Monsoon Asia. In *Climate and Agricultural Land Use in Monsoon Asia*, ed. M. M. Yoshino, 80-108. Tokyo: University of Tokyo Press.

Yoshino, M. M., T. Horie, H. Seino, H. Tsujii, T. Uchijima, and Z. Uchijima. 1988. The effect of climatic variations on agriculture in Japan. In *The Impact of Climatic Variations on Agriculture*. Vol. 1. *Assessments in Cool, Temperate and Cold Regions*, edited by M. L. Parry, T. R. Carter, and N. T. Konijn, 723-868. Dordrecht: Kluwer.

CHAPTER 12

INSTITUTIONAL CAPACITY TO MONITOR THE INTERACTIONS OF AGRICULTURAL AND HEALTH CHANGE

David Bradley

> *We are not in the business of growing better rice for sick farmers.*
> —Klaus Lampe, director,
> International Rice Research Institute, 1990

It is the message of this conference that all events are interconnected, that agriculture affects health and health affects agriculture, and that both areas are changed by technology; by population needs, wants, and distribution; and by environmental changes, whether they are externally driven or a consequence of earlier agricultural and other human behavior and actions. The scope of discussion therefore must be arbitrarily limited.

This chapter focuses, first, on the measurement of human health at the population level, both directly and as reflected in information from the biased samples who seek medical care or die, both routinely and through specific studies; second, on the interrelation of health variables to agricultural activity; and third, on the effects of habitat change, particularly change for agricultural purposes, on health. The aim in all cases will be to optimize health.

Health and *agriculture*, although formal definitions have been endlessly debated, each have a fairly clear meaning to most people. *En-*

vironment as currently used means quite different things to different people (Redclift, 1987). I use *environment* to mean everything outside a person, even other people, in the manner of ecologists (Andrewartha and Birch, 1954). I use the word *habitat* to describe the environment in a particular place. When a particular set of changes are undertaken for agricultural purposes, such as clearing a piece of forest or building an irrigation scheme, there is a whole group of interlocking environmental changes best thought of as a change in the habitat.

Nutrition remains a Cinderella subject, and although the issues related to it are discussed briefly here, they are likely to be handled in the least satisfactory manner. I also deal with the linkage of scientific understanding to policy in an unsatisfactory way, not only because that relationship *is* unsatisfactory, but also because there are strong forces tending to keep it that way.

The Nature of the Problem: Intractable Issues

In this chapter I discuss the nature of the problem in two ways: in an orthodox analysis, but preceded by a more eclectic illustration of practical difficulties. These come first, as institutional planning is too easily utopian, and we need to be clear that many of the obstructions to progress go deeply into that combination of socioeconomic underdevelopment and human nature that is so easily forgotten and that is overwhelming to the agricultural or health worker in the field.

The Sources of Data at the Periphery

> *The government is very keen on amassing statistics—they collect them, add them, raise them to the nth power, take the cube root and prepare wonderful diagrams. But what you must never forget is that every one of those figures comes in the first instance from the village watchman, who just puts down what he damn well pleases.*
>
> —L. D. Stamp

The beginning of surveillance in all texts and epidemiology courses is the collection of routine data from many sources: from registration of births and deaths, causes of death on certificates, hospital and dispensary returns, and other statutory records. But in most developing countries death registration is erratic, statements of cause of death are either nonexistent or meaningless, and records from health care establishments at the periphery are wildly erratic (Sydenstricker, 1988).

A sudden change in diagnoses usually reflects not an epidemic but a change in the medical assistant or nurse in charge of the dispensary. Attempts to upgrade general reporting are difficult, and they involve use of a significant proportion of health resources. In rural clinics of very poor countries even now the compilation of records and statistics may consume up to 30 percent of health workers' time. There is much opportunity for greater efficiency and effectiveness, but an attempt to simply collect more information may not be productive of health.

The Sources and Use of Data in the District

A step further up, the collection of health data by district medical officers is often no more reliable. While faults may be shared with the village watchperson, there are two other problems to cope with. Time is valuable and seen to be so. If two hours are spent checking the monthly statistics for hospital or district, that is two hours in which a couple of surgical operations could have been done and perhaps saved lives. The officer also knows what happens, or does not happen, to the statistical returns. The heap is left mouldering at medical headquarters, and no feedback is ever received. The medical department's annual report is four years behind, so any analyses done from that cannot be a basis for action. The current president of the Royal Society of Tropical Medicine recalls how, as a district medical officer, he would once a month settle down late in the evening, drink a half bottle of whisky, and then invent the month's statistical return, as he would be reprimanded if he didn't submit a return, even though he knew that nobody ever read it. Policy was made when the director of medical services flew up to Arua for a round of golf, not from statistics. The system is that of a preliterate society, but it is still widely followed!

Communication

The sophistication of any one aspect of human existence, be it agricultural production or health, can only run a limited way ahead of other aspects of society, although health can perhaps progress further than most. Information on health status that can lead to action depends on communications generally. In the early 1950s, a yellow fever epidemic in an area of Ethiopia caused probably 50,000 deaths, although awareness of its happening took some 18 months to reach the central health authorities. The rate at which information and subsequent relief travel are crucial to effective intervention. An example at the other extreme is a rapid survey that was done following a disastrous flood in Bangladesh, with its results ready within 48 hours of the flood. The results enabled officials to modify the pattern of intervention drastically to make it fit the needs of the surviving population (Chen, 1973).

Organization of the Changing Sector

Agricultural resource development on a large scale is expensive. To build a dam and a large irrigation scheme costs so much that international finance is needed. The whole process is heavily structured and organized, and once rules for environment and health monitoring are laid down they can be implemented, health hazards can be predicted, and corrective action can be taken if there is sufficient political will (Stanley and Alpers, 1975). By contrast, where myriad small dams are constructed by a variety of informal and local activities there will be no central recording, no careful monitoring, and no agreed-upon procedures. The consequence may be large-scale health hazards, and a surveillance and action system will be difficult to devise (Bradley, 1977).

A related problem concerns multisectoral activity. There will tend to be a lead discipline: engineering in the case of water resource development, agriculture in the case of land clearance—and there follows an unspoken hierarchy of expenditure. The engineers who built the Volta Dam in Ghana allowed a few percent for social welfare, such as rehousing and looking after displaced people, and settlements. The 20 to 50 percent of the total cost that might have been appropriate would have seemed preposterous to an engineer, and so with other activities in health or agriculture.

Given the difficulty of multisectoral interventions at the policy and the practical level, it is most desirable to formulate the outcome of surveillance of health hazards to keep action needed *within* the separate sectors as far as possible.

Pervasive Problems of Poverty

In the vast majority of communities, mortality and morbidity are inversely related to social class, prosperity, and economic success. Even in developed countries this is the case. Within the United Kingdom, the Black Report (Townsend and Davidson, 1982) showed a marked difference in premature mortality between the highest and lowest of the five broad socioeconomic (employment) categories used by the registrar-general—one was twice the other—and the government has been unwilling to act deliberately to reduce this differential (Whitehead, 1987).

The problem, in absolute even more than relative terms, is even greater within developing countries. If people are at the margin in terms of income, and therefore of nutrition, further reductions in the incomes of the poor will have dire consequences. This may result from changes in agricultural practice that benefit many but penalize some (Weil et al., 1991). It may be part of a wider economic reorganization of which agriculture is but a part. In either case, the problem may be more one of political will than of scarcity of data. Issues of equity need reliable data, but these in themselves will not change the situation.

More broadly, the gap in many developing countries is less between ill health and data than between information and action, for financial and political reasons.

Analysis of the Problem

The greater part of the illness and premature death suffered by those in agriculture in developing (or other) countries will be unrelated to their occupation, but a substantial amount will be determined by the locality in which they live (Feachem, Jamison, and Bos, 1991). The major diseases in most developing countries will be infections, and they will have a large effect on agriculture and productivity. Major changes in agricultural activities will affect health specifically by changing the incidence of particular diseases and nonspecifically by increasing or reducing the disposable income of the farmers (Weil et al., 1991). Superimposed on that pattern of endemic disease, and change resulting from major shifts in land use, often over a long period, are specific hazards due to discrete changes in agricultural methods—a new insecticide or threshing machine—and new diseases that emerge and harm the farming population. AIDS is by far the most important of these in this century. In all cases we need to understand as much as possible about the environmental determinants of the diseases, to prevent, control, or at least minimize the effects of them. Surveillance of disease needs to coexist with surveillance of environmental determinants and, if it is to be of use, with surveillance of plans of society to do things that will change those determinants.

An additional, usually "Cinderella," area concerns nutrition. The objective of agriculture ultimately is not production but good nutrition. Milk lakes and butter mountains are unedifying even if edible, and in practice there is a tension between the nutrition of the world's population and the disposable income of farmers. This is blurred in subsistence agriculture, and the tension is most extreme for those who grow opium poppies and tobacco plants. Surveillance of the effects of agriculture on health therefore needs to extend through economics to nutrition and beyond.

Agricultural Determinants of Health

The relation between agricultural activity and health may be analyzed as a whole or incrementally. Rural life and agriculture are so intertwined in developing countries that specifically occupational hazards are less important than the overall pattern of life in determining ill health. An overall approach therefore looks at the whole of health. An incremental or marginal approach looks at the effects of *changes* in agricultural activity on health. (And conversely, what are the effects of health changes on agriculture?) The overall approach is essential in planning health improvements and is particularly addressed in other chapters of this book. An incremental approach is followed here as most relevant to agricultural effects on health, but this points back to the overall approach.

The agricultural changes that affect health can be grouped into three broad (and slightly overlapping) categories. First are changes in specific agricultural techniques and specific components of agricultural systems. Examples are the introduction of a new piece of agricultural machinery, a new fertilizer or insecticide, or a new crop-drying process. A new implement or pesticide is likely to have a single main potential health effect, which can be studied and surveyed.

The second category consists of changes in farming systems, due to any cause. Here, more complex alterations in many aspects of agricultural life may result. Causes of such changes in farming systems may primarily be economic or climatic or due to a shift from subsistence to cash-crop farming. The effects on health may be slight or they may be multiple and very great. Many will be indirect, and the relations between cause and effect may not be initially apparent; many effects may be mediated by changes in disposable income of different members of the community. Sometimes even what appear to be simple changes in a specific agricultural activity may have the features of a changed farming system. The introduction of short-stemmed cereals in some areas of Bangladesh had complex effects on life and reduced the resources previously available to the poor, with bad consequences for their health and welfare (Briscoe, 1979). While changing a farming system is an incremental or marginal action, it may be necessary to look at

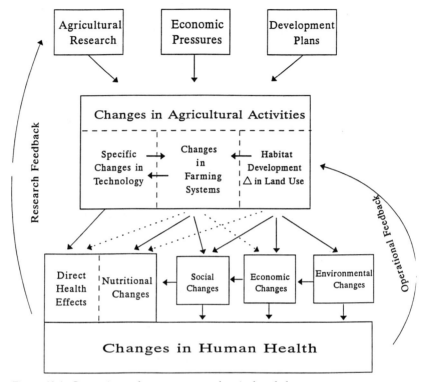

Figure 12.1. Categories and consequences of agricultural change.

the whole system to understand the health effects. It will be argued below that effects of changing farming systems are the most neglected and complex part of agriculture-health interactions and will make the heaviest research demands of an interdisciplinary type.

The third category of agricultural change is habitat development, or land and water resource development. It includes creating irrigation projects, deforestation for agricultural reasons, and similar changes in the habitat of a geographically defined area. Where such changes are large in scale, planned, and funded by international financing, they are already (in theory at least) the subject of environmental impact assessment, which usually involves a health aspect, and the effects will be particularly on vectors of human diseases (Bradley, 1977; Stanley and Alpers, 1975). The three categories are shown in Figure 12.1 and relate primarily to different types of health hazard and also to differing institutional and organizational needs for their amelioration.

Health Processes and Consequences

The health consequences of agricultural change may be also grouped into three categories, which roughly parallel the three groups of agricultural determinants of health. First are the specific consequences of agricultural processes. These will particularly include trauma and toxic effects, due particularly to new implements or machinery and new chemicals, including pesticides, herbicides, and fertilizers. Monitoring such events will require that they first be identified and clinically defined as precisely as possible, usually by a specialist unit, and then the syndrome can be incorporated into a list for routine reporting from health care facilities or it may be the subject of special surveys, which might include laboratory investigations. A particular area needing survey and analysis concerns work-related injuries.

The second group of health conditions are those more broadly related to the local farming systems. The diseases are likely to be qualitatively the same as those seen in the inhabitants of the region generally, but with an increased incidence and prevalence. For example, the frequency of leech bites, insect bites, and upper and lower respiratory infections are all much increased in those who pluck tea at high and wet altitudes (Bradley, Rahmathullah, and Narayan, 1988). Assessment of the hazards due to agricultural activities will require a combination of improved reporting from selected health care facilities and specific surveys or population-based records over time.

When farming systems change, there may be changes in the distribution of disposable income so that some groups become further impoverished while others benefit. This may be reflected in changing distribution of illness patterns, and it will be important to stratify surveys and other inquiries to detect such changes.

The vector-borne diseases will primarily be affected by habitat changes that alter breeding conditions for vectors and intermediate hosts of such diseases as malaria, schistosomiasis, Japanese encephalitis, river blindness (onchocerciasis), sleeping sickness, and leishmaniasis (Bradley, 1977). Methods for population-based surveys for these conditions are well developed and can be carried out most simply on a repeat cross-sectional basis over several years, although true longitudinal surveys provide much additional information (Barker and Hall, 1991). Rapid assessment methods for such diseases as urinary schistosomiasis have also been developed.

There is a tendency for those assessing disease to focus on one of the three groups listed above: occupational health workers concentrate on the first group of diseases, those concerned with primary health care go for the second group, and parasitologists and vector-borne disease units focus on the last category. To get a clear picture of agricultural effects on health requires study of all three groups in the same population. This is even more important in predicting the health consequences of agricultural developments or of resource developments for agricultural purposes (Bradley, 1988). A single problem focus is likely to give a very unbalanced picture.

In addressing the effects of health on agriculture in the next section, the health measurements follow the same pattern as has been discussed here, with a greater emphasis on the role of anemia.

Health Determinants of Agriculture

The perception of the relationship of health to agriculture has changed greatly over the last century, partly as a result of more effective curative medicine but also for vaguer and less satisfactory reasons. The subject is due for reappraisal.

At the beginning of this century there was a clear perception that a tropical climate was bad for health—whether directly or by way of vector-borne or infectious, nutritional, or toxic diseases—and that the resulting ill health was disastrous for work, agriculture, and commerce. Hard-headed businessmen contributed to schools of tropical medicine because they felt that unhealthy workers in the tropics were diminishing their profits. The major vector-borne diseases were of particular agricultural importance. Malaria prevented agricultural settlement of the Nepalese Tarai, sleeping sickness and nagana limited agriculture in parts of tropical Africa (Duggan, 1962), and river blindness prevented the agricultural use of large tracts of the West African savannah and Sahel (Hunter, 1966). Tea planting in South India at certain altitudes critically depended on prior malaria control. Until modern chemotherapy and insecticides became available, environmental methods were needed for transmission control of vector-borne disease as well as for land development, so the agricultural and health measures went together to some extent. In other areas, the use of residual insecticides was a necessary preliminary to agricultural settlement, which in turn modified the habitat and changed the environment for vector breeding.

These heroic periods of organized development, where disease control was a prerequisite, have become less apparent and were followed by a period in which water resource development, partly for agricultural purposes, dominated the scene (Worthington, 1977). This was often accompanied by migration of people down from overpopulated highlands (Prothero, 1965), as well as the increase in surface water that could act as vector-breeding habitats, so the emphasis shifted to agriculture as cause and disease as effect rather than vice versa. While there are a few notable examples of the consequent disease outbreaks leading to abandonment of irrigation schemes, secondary measures have often been used to deal with illness, and its effects on agriculture have often been neglected as the "new" diseases merged with the endemic disease background of the farming community. This constitutes an argument for looking beyond the incremental or marginal approach that is recommended earlier in this chapter and for keeping a balance between marginal and overall approaches to the health of agricultural communities.

Such analyses as were recently made of the effects of ill health on agriculture have been characterized by a relatively narrow economic approach, and sometimes also by an unfortunate choice of either level of endemicity or methodology. The work that showed little effect of schistosomiasis on productivity in Saint Lucia chose an area of low endemicity (Weisbrod, 1973); one that indicated no effect of onchocerciasis on productivity in an East African timber mill went on to show that this was because the recruitment process selected out those who had more than a very light onchocercal infection. A narrow focus on productivity in easily measurable agricultural tasks will tend to miss all the compensatory processes that may operate under conditions of subsistence agriculture involving whole communities.

There is a need to reopen the analysis of health effects on agriculture. Routine monitoring is unlikely to be informative. Two approaches are more relevant. One uses comprehensively studied communities such as are recommended for work on changing farming systems elsewhere in this chapter. The other seizes the opportunities presented by particular agricultural systems. The accurately measured daily productivity of women tea pluckers has been used to show the effects of iron deficiency anemia on the quantity of tea plucked, and can also be used to determine the effects of children's illnesses upon maternal agricultural activity (Bradley, Rahmathullah, and Narayan, 1988). The most powerful design for studies to determine short-term effects of a disease on agriculture is a randomized controlled intervention trial (Smith and Morrow, 1991). But the detailed description of the effects of health problems on functioning of an agricultural community can provide useful information, and collaborative research between medical and agricultural workers can add much.

The formal analysis of health problems into death, morbidity, and disability is clearly relevant to looking at agricultural effects. The tendency in some recent literature (especially in schistosomiasis) to equate infection with morbidity is a backward step. Disability is the easiest aspect of health to link to agricultural productivity. Death, and especially death of young children, is much harder to evaluate in agricultural rather than humanitarian terms, especially as compensatory behavior may be well established and complex. Approaches to improving the health of rural people are dealt with elsewhere in this book.

This chapter has taken the view that health and agriculture are interdependent goods but that in the last analysis agriculture is the means, and the health and welfare of the community, including its farming members, is the objective. However, if we adopt temporarily the narrower, agricultural-production-oriented view, there are seven main health issues for agricultural development whose relative importance will vary locally:

> Health measures can make land habitable and available for agricultural use, as in the settlement of the Nepal Tarai after malaria control and the agricultural use of the West African river valleys only after onchocerciasis had been controlled.

> Sick people may be limiting farming activity. At times when peak work output is needed for cultivation, the effects of hookworm anemia or disability from guinea worm or from earlier injuries may be substantial.

> Indirectly, a lowered infant mortality rate may be a necessary although not sufficient requirement for birth control and consequent limitation of population growth.

> As discussed above, agricultural habitat developments should avoid having an adverse effect on health, which would in turn impede proper use of the developments.

> Health improvement has been suggested as an entry point to agricultural institutional change, although on very scanty evidence.

> Better health provides extra time for farmers and their families,

time that can be spent on education, aspects of farm improvement, and activities other than seeking health care.

The substantial use of food for those who are not growing (because of infection) or for those who are about to die will be avoided if growth and survival are the norm.

Approaches

The tools necessary for monitoring health change cover a wide range. They are named and discussed below. Not necessarily created for the particular situations of developing countries, their utility varies depending on the community.

Routine Reporting

In industrial countries, routinely collected health statistics are the basis of surveillance and monitoring of health status. The recording of births and deaths is reliable, and the causes of death as recorded on the death certificate are useful pointers, even though some categories are unreliable. Changes in the infant mortality rate in particular are indicative of the community's state of health, while standardized mortality ratios for different occupations can draw attention to special risks. In the United Kingdom, shepherds have the most long-lived occupation! Occasional major risks may escape the record system: a notorious example was deep-sea fishing, an extremely hazardous occupation that did not emerge as such until Schilling studied it directly, since the majority of deaths occurred at sea, with burial there, so that they were not notified in the regular system (Schilling, 1966; Moore, 1969). Hospitals also keep detailed records of admissions, discharges, and diagnoses. Specific diseases, usually infectious, are notifiable to government, and special confidentiality arrangements may apply for stigmatized diseases to reduce the blocks to reporting.

These sources of information are of very limited value in many developing countries. A reliable reporting system is expensive relative to their budgets. Doctors may be scarce and health staff overworked and sometimes of limited education. Births are now registered in many countries, as the birth certificate is required for subsequent school registration, but death registration is less common and the recorded causes of death are usually meaningless. Morbidity reporting may be good from some centers and peripheral posts, but it will usually depend on the individual more than on the overall system. Some notable successes have been obtained. Cancer reporting in Africa from a chain of mission hospitals has been of a quality to permit detailed research (Cook and Burkitt, 1971). Some commercial plantations reach a high standard of reporting: the larger and better tea gardens of South Asia produce detailed reports on a defined population with very low migration rates across the estate borders. If the chief medical officer remains unchanged, the data quality may permit reliable inferences on changes in disease incidence. This provides opportunities for the equivalent of "sentinel practices" in the United Kingdom—a set of general practices by workers of known competence who keep detailed records of cases that are compiled weekly and provide evidence of beginning epidemics.

The advantage of sentinel communities is that all relevant data can be collected routinely in an unstressed environment. When data are collected as part of a specific campaign, there is pressure to distort the figures: during malaria eradication attempts in South Asia, there was underreporting of residual cases to the government so that control teams appeared in a good light. Health care facilities tend to keep detailed records of cases seen and of diagnoses. In hospitals these tend to be ordinary clinicians' diagnostic categories or the shorter international classification of disease categories. In dispensaries and health centers, a short list of common diagnostic categories is often used. Such data are of value in mapping the distribution of commonly perceived health problems and for assessing needs for the commoner medicines, but they are insensitive for detecting new problems or changes in the relative importance of diseases. A more focused reporting of a very short list of specific conditions is preferable if peripheral facilities are to be used for monitoring.

While there is a clear need to steadily improve routine health-problem reporting, it cannot appropriately be given too high a priority with limited resources. The aim should be simplicity, reliability, and the use of categories appropriate to the diagnostic skills available. In addition, much stronger emphasis is needed on professional (as distinct from administrative) supervision and encouragement to report unusual conditions or apparent disease outbreaks. The most effective incentive to better reporting of health problems from the periphery is an immediate and constructive response from the center. If the report of three peculiar febrile patients is followed by a friendly visit from a member of the epidemiological unit staff that week, an incipient epidemic may be detected and controlled, and certainly that health facility's staff will become much better at surveillance for the future.

Since commercial agricultural operations often have the best health care services in rural areas of developing countries, their development as sentinel reporting systems could be exploited much more. However, owners are unlikely to encourage reporting of insecticide toxicity among workers, for example, and it is notable that tea estates in Bangladesh have been so wary of media coverage that they have been very cautious about release of data and sometimes unenthusiastic about research by their own staff.

Epidemic Investigation

In the last few years the potential of epidemiological work to improve the quality and efficiency of health services has been widely accepted in principle, even if less so in practice, and many ministries of health now have epidemiological units concerned both with the analysis of routinely reported health data and with the investigation and control of reported epidemics. They are essential to the effective operation of a routine reporting system. If an unusual increase in cases of a disease is reported, and especially if a medical officer reports either an unusual syndrome or subjective "epidemic," investigation by the unit is needed. The more regularly and helpfully this occurs, the better will become the reporting system: no one wishes to have a team arrive to study an artifact and, equally, no one will go on reporting outbreaks if nothing happens as a result.

The main relevant value of epidemic investigation will be in relation to new agricultural techniques and outbreaks of toxic effects of pesticides or of vector-borne diseases.

Surveys

In most countries, and especially developing countries with limited resources, reported disease is only a small part of that in the community. Only in the case of well-recognized severe diseases that are not quickly fatal and for which good chemotherapy is known to exist will reporting be at all adequate. To assess endemic diseases and those of a prevalence exceeding about 2 to 4 percent, cross-sectional surveys of the total population of sample villages will provide useful data on infection rates, morbidity, and disability. The markedly seasonal nature of disease incidence, nutritional state, and availability for survey of the population means that very limited reliance can be placed on a single survey. Experience has shown that concentration on a limited number of questions and observations is necessary for accuracy of results. General-purpose questionnaires and examinations achieve little. Where there needs to be heavy reliance on questionnaires, adequate piloting is essential, and the field staff needs careful training in standard ways of raising a topic. Accurate recall is short-lived, and a recall period exceeding two weeks will rarely give reliable results. For dietary surveys, the preceding 24 hours is usual. Surveys therefore can provide quantitative information on previously defined problems.

Methods for nutritional surveillance of children are now well developed and cost little where they focus on growth. Specific micronutrient deficiencies are also detectable clinically. Methods for nutritional surveys and for predicting famine and food shortage are also well developed. Linkage between these aspects of health and agricultural production is the major gap, with problems of economy and of transport coming between them. The mismatch in place, time, and economy between production and consumption of food is probably the main effect of agriculture on health.

Assessing Innovations

If agricultural innovations such as new pesticides are not to generate health problems, the first requirement is proper registration. Legislation needs to be adequate and enforced to ensure that new substances cannot be introduced without the knowledge of the ministry of health (MOH). Commercial products previously used by industrial countries are likely to have full toxicological documentation. If not, it is the manufacturers' responsibility to provide it. Adequate assessment of the material by the MOH is needed, but also some local investigation of toxicity in normal use. Often manufacturers specify precautions that in practice are unfeasible in some developing countries. A local university pharmacology department or research institute should be able to do this practical assessment. It is often feasible to repackage for safety. Insecticide may be dispensed in single sprayer-size containers to avoid problems of mixing and measuring out concentrated chemicals.

Community Studies

To understand changes in farming systems and their effects on health and welfare requires detailed interdisciplinary study. Usually this will only be feasible for a small population—one or two villages—if the necessary detail is to be obtained, and longitudinal studies will usually be needed. The lower the human migration rate into and out of the village, the more readily can such studies be carried out and interpreted. These detailed studies should generate conclusions and specific findings that can then be tested on a wider scale by means of surveys and routine reports. The rural health research units discussed below are likely to find that long-term studies of a few communities will be essential to the degree of understanding needed for their work.

Policy Studies

The objectives of investigating the effect of agricultural changes on health is to change policy and then practice for the better. To this end it is necessary to involve those concerned with agricultural and health policies in the planning of the work and not just at the end. They should help to formulate the questions being addressed in such a way that the sectors involved can utilize the answers in improving policies.

Environmental Impact and Health Opportunity Assessment

At present, a key entry point for preventing effects of habitat and agricultural resource development that may be injurious to health is the environmental impact assessment that has to be made before several of the key international funding agencies, beginning with the World Bank, will finance the development. There are three further needs. The first is to ensure that recommendations are implemented adequately, which requires increasing pressure by and on governments. The second is to broaden the range of projects assessed. Even if international finance is not involved, small water and other resource developments need to be assessed — collectively if not individually — and here legislation is needed to register all such projects and not merely those of huge individual size.

Third, and most important, is to change the perspective to one of health opportunity assessment (Bradley, 1991), instead of the essentially negative and secondary one whose focus is primarily on environment, with health tagging along behind and the aim merely to avoid worsening matters. In any planned agricultural habitat development, the goal should be to explore the opportunities provided for improving health. This will extend beyond the effect of the planned development on vector breeding to an estimate of likely population changes by migration and a review of how to improve the health services and other factors affecting health in the area.

Changing Methodology

The rate of change in the health sciences is great, and new techniques and methods proliferate. This section deals with three types of change that are particularly relevant.

Computers

The development of rapid, low-cost, portable computers with large memories and computing capacities have transformed our ability to record, analyze, and feed back information from health monitoring. There is now extensive, good experience of entering data in the field using staff who have limited formal education but who have been well trained; this also reduces transcription errors. Routine analysis of monitoring data can be handled by prepared programs so that analysis can be prompt and the delays of months or years in manual data analysis from massive returns can be avoided. It is now feasible to turn routine data around in less than a week so that results can help fieldworkers and can also be used as a basis for planning and for instigating field investigations (Barker and Hall, 1991).

Verbal Autopsy

The analysis of mortality in developing countries has been much hindered by the difficulty or, in some cases, impossibility of getting autopsy data on fatalities of interest. In recent years, methods of inquiry about childhood deaths have been developed and tested against clinical data in several countries, and relatively reliable methods of "verbal autopsy" by a standardized questionnaire to relatives of the dead child have been developed. Comparable approaches to adult mortality investigation are being planned.

Molecular Biology

The rate of progress in molecular biological research is now amazingly rapid, and through molecular genetics medicine is being provided with a range of probes of specificities from the individual to the species and beyond. The invention of the polymerase chain reaction as a method of amplifying DNA makes it possible to detect gene sequences from even a single cell, and to amplify material so that a mutation affecting a single amino acid in the corresponding protein can be identified. Diagnostic procedures will be much affected, and many diseases may soon be recognized from analysis of a single drop of blood or other tissue. While issues of cost may keep these to the laboratory in some developing countries, procedures for diagnosis are likely to become much less invasive, far more sensitive, and often more precise.

Processes and Institutional Needs

The measurement of health changes requires a combination of processes, tools, and policies. Such techniques often require an institutional base. This section details these areas.

The Lessons of Experience

Over the last century the interaction of health and development, particularly agricultural development, has been widely but patchily perceived. Initially the view was that better health was essential for agriculture in the tropics, and hard-nosed commercial firms invested substantially in health. More recently the dominant concern has been the other way around, and international concern has been to avoid the health hazards of some forms of agricultural development. What can be learned about health monitoring from this past period?

At the beginning of the century, health problems that were addressed tended to be so obvious that they required no formal monitoring to be detected. The Uganda sleeping sickness outbreak forced its attention on an administration that would have preferred not to know about it, and the more usual problem with endemic disease was that it prevented settlement. The tea gardens of South India and cultivation of the Nepalese Tarai were not feasible until malaria had been controlled. Because the Tarai was little inhabited, any attempts to look at data on human health would have provided little information. Hence the need for also having a broader environmental surveillance as well. In general, the major killing diseases provide their own surveillance, especially if they are in epidemic form. By contrast, those conditions that are endemic and cause less distinct morbidity but that occur on a large or even universal scale in affected populations are much more likely to be missed as major impediments to agricultural development. So action is taken to deal with cholera or sleeping sickness epidemics, but chronic iron deficiency anemia due to hookworm (Bradley, Rahmathullah, and Narayan, 1988) is tolerated to a great degree by the labor and management of tea estates right up to the present. These widespread conditions are best brought to light by sample health surveys, even if on a small scale, rather than by any form of passive surveillance. Problems that are both uncommon and insidious will probably be missed by all feasible surveillance methods, and the vast majority will be of limited public health importance. Vigilance for the unusual and investigation of such reports is the only likely way into such problems. The first prerequisite for better health surveillance of developments is adequate registration. Sensible criteria for what projects and activities need to be registered are essential, followed by several years of thorough recording without further actions. Only then can effective health planning measures be brought in.

Malaria, Schistosomiasis, and Public Health. The great vector-borne diseases have had massive effects on agricultural activity and have also been affected by agricultural water resources development. These processes have involved little monitoring of health: either there was so great an outbreak of illness and death that attention had to be given, or else a possible hazard was foreseen and expert predictions made—often incorrectly—of what might happen.

Malaria illustrates many issues: the massive consequences that environmental changes can have on a vector-borne disease; the changing epidemiology over time, especially in relation to the frequency of chloroquine-resistant malaria; but particularly the importance of geographical and epidemiological heterogeneity on the outcome of agricultural change. This could easily be forgotten. In the initial assessments of the Volta Dam in Ghana, the health advisers to the engineers suggested that an increased malaria risk would follow construction and that this might be prevented by intermittent lowering of the lake with a siphon. This was based on experience in the southern United States. Fortunately, further malariological advice was sought, and Macdonald (1955) pointed out that malaria was already so highly endemic that no significant rise could occur with increased mosquito populations, and that varying the lake level would massively increase, not reduce, mosquito breeding because of biological differences between the African and North American species. For sound prediction of epidemiological changes, the need was for detailed local expertise to be brought in at the planning stage. Once that was done, subsequent monitoring followed without difficulty and in the case of malaria confirmed Macdonald's predictions.

Schistosomiasis was also predicted to be a major problem at the Volta Lake by Macdonald (1955) as well as others, and this indeed was the case. Predictions as to the species and intermediate host snail were less accurate, and only one malacologist successfully identified the snail, *Bulinus truncatus rohlfsi*, that would in fact create the problem. The schistosomiasis hazard was much increased by massive immigration of fishermen, inadequately foreseen, and the lake itself passed through a series of ecological changes that took some 15 years before a relatively stable epidemiological state was reached. Health assessment thus again required specialist expertise, local experience, and also long-term surveillance.

Two Decades of Water-Supply Research in Relation to Health. The relationships between water supply and health have been the subject of research, debate, and some controversy for the last 20 years (White, Bradley, and White, 1972). The relevant conclusions for effective monitoring and corrective action may be summarized briefly. Measuring health impact directly has been very difficult and expensive. The outcome of water-supply improvements has varied greatly, dependent in part on behavioral changes by users so that narrowly focused monitoring is inadequate. It has proved much more feasible to use process and intermediate variables for monitoring change; it has required extensive multidisciplinary research to make progress toward the relevant social science methodology; and progress in getting relevant engineering changes oriented to health needs has in part depended on formulating the health issues in engineering concepts and terminology. This last comment is widely applicable where the results of health monitoring require action by other sectors and disciplines. Engineers now regularly listen to the health monitors; the agronomists would prefer not to know! The differences are instructive. For some 30 years a determined effort has been made to define the health problems that can result from water engineering developments and to teach engineers about them. Courses on diseases and their prevention have been added to postgraduate engineering courses. It has been found possible to reclassify water-related diseases in terms of the engineering interventions required to reduce their incidence rather than by the biology of the pathogen.

Nutritional Monitoring. The measurement of growth and ways of assessing dietary intake have been massively studied (World Health Organization Working Group, 1986). While the focus of much of this work has been the individual disadvantaged child, it has been widely applied in developing countries to assess the need for community intervention and to predict food shortage. It has been more successful in directing and targeting short-term aid than in influencing long-term policy. In the past, experience of famine and drought has led to planting policies, for example, in relation to cassava in East Africa during the colonial period, but such decisions have derived more from practical observation of famine than from ordered health surveillance.

Cyclical and Secular Patterns of Change. Any form of survey-based or intermittent monitoring has to take into consideration the dramatic seasonal variation in many developing countries. In The Gambia, for example, infant mortality regularly doubles for children born at certain seasons as compared with others (Billewicz and McGregor, 1981), and malaria transmission occurs mainly during and just after the rains, when almost every child is infected, and almost disappears in the dry season. Meningitis in the Sahel is markedly seasonal but also varies on a cycle of around 11 years. Annual seasons vary in precise dates between years. Therefore, if monitoring is not continuous, great care has to be taken in interpreting interyear variation. The longer-term changes in maturation of a new reservoir or irrigation scheme have already been referred to. No baseline monitoring system can safely cover less than a year, and longer may be needed.

Health Monitoring Requirements

The process of health monitoring, in itself, is quite complex. There are several components in the process that are necessary to ensure the procuring of good information.

Specific Changes in Technology. It is clear that any new substance or implement introduced to agriculture in an area needs first to be evaluated to ensure that it does not create a hazard. The appropriate place to test the innovation will vary; what is essential is the legislative and regulatory framework to ensure that it does happen. Many such innovations will be chemicals with an obvious toxic potential. There, thorough testing in one country to establish the basic toxicology and safety standards for use may suffice for many purposes, but there needs to be local or national testing for safety under local conditions of use.

Similar criteria will apply to new agricultural implements, machinery for rural use, and so forth. Studies of safety and prevention of injury can also be carried out with studies on durability of the implements, so that the vexing issues of maintenance and repair facilities can be solved prior to widespread use.

The institutions involved in these procedures will include agricultural research stations, university departments of pharmacology and of community medicine, or occupational health as well as international institutions and agencies (the World Health Organization produces good assessments of pesticides and the like).

In addition there is need for postmarketing surveillance. While untoward events may be detectable by routine reporting in developed countries, this poses difficult problems in less developed countries and requires both an epidemiological unit at the MOH, which can investigate reports or rumors of problems, and also vigilance by individual health workers, who need to feel that any observations or concerns they report will be heard and acted on. For new substances with predictable types of toxicity, such as new organophosphorous insecticides, small follow-up surveys of users may be appropriate.

Changes in Farming Systems. These changes may be both complex and subtle, with health effects that would be missed in any short-term survey or routine monitoring of data, at any rate until it was too late for revision of the innovative system. A multidisciplinary research approach will be needed to identify and analyze these problems. Not every country can afford the necessary resources, so it is likely that the institutions proposed will develop in relation either to large developing countries or to international agricultural research institutes.

The preferred organization is a unit, either as part of an agricultural research institute or an institute of public health, with diverse staff and adequate funding.

Agricultural Habitat Development. At least three levels of activity are needed. As with specific innovations, the first need is for adequate and enforceable regulations as to what resource and habitat developments need assessment for environmental and health hazards at the planning stage. At present, coverage is wholly inadequate and largely limited to internationally financed projects of great size. The majority of projects are, however, much smaller — in Nigeria, for instance, for one big Kainji Dam there have been over 500 small dams in one region alone. Some type of generic approach will be essential. Revised national legislation is needed to be much more comprehensive, especially in respect to local authority and commercial developments. Second, in environmental assessments, health needs to be properly covered and not dealt with by someone whose concerns are primarily with wildlife and natural history. Third, there needs to be adequate action taken following assessment, to modify designs for the development. Secondary responses after construction are inadequate and expensive, and the initial project proposals need to contain a realistic proportion of the development costs for health purposes. In the next section, the proposal to separate the issues of health, instead of regarding them as an appendage to the environment, is pursued.

Health Opportunity Assessment

The necessity for an environmental impact statement has had a large effect on the planning of development projects. Since the ultimate goal of agricultural development is human health and welfare—of both farmers and consumers of their produce—we have argued that health should be more overtly included and that a positive approach should be taken. For each agricultural or other development a health opportunity assessment (HOA) should be undertaken. It should usually be quite modest and must involve local health staff, but it would explore the possibilities of a positive improvement in health along with agriculture. The practical problems of defining when the HOA should be required are considerable, but as a start, one should be mandatory whenever an environmental impact assessment is to be carried out. The concept of the health opportunity assessment has been raised several times in recent years (Bradley, 1991), and there is now a plan to develop its content and incorporate it into courses on development and environment.

Policy

All the above approaches, except those in the health opportunity assessment, concern how to avoid agricultural developments that are bad for health—they are essentially negative approaches. Is it possible to have a positive approach? Can we move from health needs to nutritional policy to directions for agricultural research? The present lack of enthusiasm for centrally planned economies will mean such ideas will be viewed with jaundiced eyes, and maybe the main route from health to agriculture will remain that of educating consumer preferences. Certainly, the analysis of changing farming systems should be fed back to the plant breeders. If shortening the rice straw length really does further impoverish the poorest of the poor, ought this to help specify the rice for which the breeders, who are supported by public funds, are aiming? In the same way that drought resistance is now viewed as a quality to be bred into rice, with the potential to save lives from famine, how much further can this be taken into health issues? The use of international financing for so many large development projects gives an opportunity for the lender drafting the terms of reference for any feasibility study or appraisal to pay due attention to health opportunities and so ensure that they will not be ignored.

The institutional arrangements for research on farming system changes, if strengthened from the nutritional and nutritional policy angle, may well be the way into planning farming and plant-breeding changes that will have health as a more overt goal. The task of changing the goals of agriculture in the public sector from simple production toward multiple goals is massive but necessary.

Organizational Arrangements

The institutional, and therefore the organizational, arrangements for monitoring health in relation to agricultural development must be able to meet the changing needs outlined above, but with limited consumption of resources, and any proposals must be conventional enough to be implemented without utopian demands on operational facilities, although at the research level much more may be attempted. Figure 12.2 sets out some of the points to be raised. Problems are most intractable in the poorest countries, especially when they are small countries, since health funding may be so low as to permit little useful activity. But once growth is occurring, there are both opportunities to develop an epidemiological unit and dangers of major development hazards.

National Health Monitoring

The failures of routine health monitoring by medical care facilities are partly due to their inappropriate records but still more to a central failure to respond. In recent years there has been created within the ministry of health in many developing countries an *epidemiology unit*, whose function is to review routine data being collected, to investigate outbreaks, and generally to relate changes in health to the planning process. Such epidemiology units are closely related to any planning unit within the health ministry, or at any rate they should be. Planning units in turn, if they are to be effective, must be concerned with intersectoral action and have close links to ministries of finance and of planning. The best hope of effective monitoring of health in relation to agriculture is therefore with the MOH epidemiology unit, and the best hope of health monitoring leading to useful change is

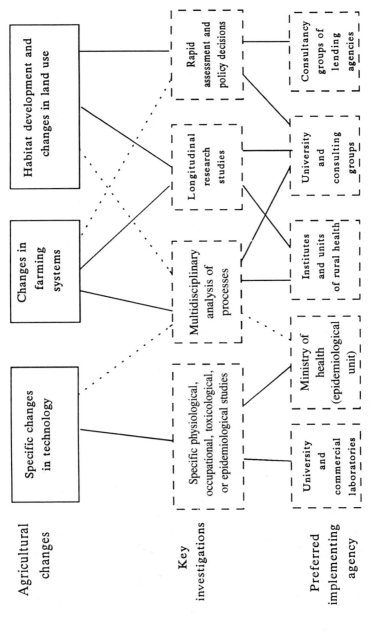

Figure 12.2. Main responses for assessing health aspects of agricultural change.

likely to be in close collaboration with the MOH planning unit and the ministry of finance and planning.

These proposals can only hope to succeed if good relations with the agriculture ministry are built up over several years—not a common activity for the MOH—and if links also have been developed with ministries of finance, water development, and planning, where they exist.

The organizational details will depend greatly on the size of the country concerned. In a country of limited population and resources, such as Mali, Ghana, or Nepal, monitoring health in relation to agriculture may have to be an added responsibility of the limited epidemiology unit staff or of one or two people added to the unit. In a large country such as Brazil or India, a substantial group can specialize in agriculturally related activities.

So far as routine reporting is concerned, the epidemiology unit needs to simplify the amount of data being collected; train relevant professional and particularly subprofessional staff in the definition of conditions to be recorded; provide simple recording procedures, which will increasingly be computer-based in many countries; and provide prompt and comprehensible feedback to the reporting stations. It is at least equally important that personal relations are developed between peripheral reporting staff and epidemiology unit staff so that rare or unexpected events are promptly reported, taken seriously, and investigated. Locally perceived changes in disease frequency should be followed up even though many prove of little consequence. More use should be made of regulations making diseases temporarily reportable. If a new agricultural chemical is suspected of causing toxic effects, it may be useful to make the relevant syndrome reportable for a few years as the new substance becomes more widely used.

The epidemiology unit of the MOH should also be best placed to predict health consequences of habitat development and, even more, to point out the health opportunities (as well as hazards) that this presents. While lending agencies and planning ministries may rightly insist on a health impact assessment of the proposed development, the MOH should both receive the report early and also look at the positive opportunities that the proposed development affords. It is best placed to push the proposals beyond hazard avoidance toward health improvement, but as an operational unit its capacity for really original and imaginative planning is likely to be limited and will depend on specialist groups.

Most of the discussion in this chapter is about local activities, because health is a locally maintained activity. However, there is also a global need for health surveillance to balance the data against global environmental and agricultural information. There is no easy way to get reliable global health data, but prospects are improving. Methods have been developed for rapid assessment of immunization coverage, and there is a trend toward global standardization of epidemiological monitoring that can be built upon. Sadly, it is least effective where most needed, since deliberate national falsification of data on AIDS, cholera, and other major epidemics is commonplace and some of the widely used tabulations of national health indices are based on inadequate information.

Rural and Agricultural Health and Medicine

Attempts have been made to tackle the health problems of farmers. These have started from an occupational medicine, and to some extent an occupational health, viewpoint and so have led to associations and, rarely, departments of rural medicine. On the whole, these have not flourished (except possibly in Eastern Europe, for which I have little information). This is too narrow a position. An approach is needed that will tackle at least the following types of problem:

> What are the health consequences, for all, of changes in farming systems or of new components to farming systems?

> What agriculturally driven habitat changes are likely to occur, how can they be effectively categorized, and what measures are needed to minimize health hazards and maximize health gains?

> What health improvements for farming communities can be effected, and how can this improve agricultural life and productivity?

A university or medical college department of rural medicine, as generally conceived, will not handle such problems adequately, nor are there good models within developing countries of alternative ways to tackle the problem. What is required is a multidisciplinary group of health research workers with a deep understanding of epidemiology and a realistic involvement in policy issues, but linked very closely to agricultural research and development institutions.

Much innovative interdisciplinary work is needed to meet future challenges in the interaction of agriculture and health. This necessitates a few multidisciplinary units in critical locations to influence thinking and practice. Key opportunities are provided by the Consultative Group on International Agricultural Research (CGIAR) centers, which have great prestige and influence and which are rightly already under pressure to take a broader view of their goals and to appreciate that increased agricultural production, regardless of "secondary" consequences, is not a sufficient objective.

Agricultural health research units need to be set up in practical collaboration between such agricultural institutions and either health research institutes or schools of public health or of medicine. Such units need to be multidisciplinary, imaginative, and relatively close-knit. They could well be parts of institutes of occupational health, provided they take a much broader view of their function than is usual in occupational health directed toward urban industry. Linkage to the MOH epidemiology units of the countries where work is being done will of course be essential. Specific proposals are made below.

Such units will be able to examine the three types of agricultural effects on health. The consequences of specific innovations will be the most straightforward to study and can be used for individual study by graduate students and postdoctoral workers. The effects of complex changes in farming systems will require more long-term teamwork by senior staff from health, agriculture, and social science backgrounds, since even the key questions may not initially be apparent. This type of *human ecology of change with an emphasis on health* provides the greatest challenge for new thinking. It must be done really well for a few systems in order to enlarge the way in which such changes are perceived. Third, such units can assess proposals for habitat developments for agriculture, selecting particular examples, where a basic health impact assessment has been carried out, for more detailed study.

Some units of this type will also need to analyze the legislative framework for planning and development for agriculture to ensure that plans are reviewed from a health viewpoint and that opportunities are not missed. In particular, since the first step toward improving any situation is to become aware of the plans for change, notification of plans will need legislation, which will be difficult to formulate if it is not to be cumbersome.

Future Development

The way ahead is to make a good beginning, and this section makes some precise proposals to get the process of relating agriculture and health under way. Many alternatives may be as good or preferable, but to make the proposals general seemed less satisfactory.

Multidisciplinary units should be established in relation to three (or more) of the CGIAR institutes, with the specific remit of studying and improving the interactions of agricultural development and health. One should be concerned primarily with rice farming and could best be associated with the International Rice Research Institute (IRRI) or the West African Rice Development Association (WARDA), one should be concerned with an aspect of relatively-arid-zone farming in the tropics, and the third could be based with another CGIAR institution. The units should be relatively small and would be critically dependent on imaginative and top-quality staff, who nevertheless wish to work in an interdisciplinary way, and on a grouping of parent agricultural and health institutions. Results will not come quickly in the major areas, so a medium-to-long term of initial funding is more important than large size. The third unit could perhaps better be placed in relation to tea-plantation agriculture, as this provides a unique opportunity to analyze health processes. Such a unit would have to overcome substantial resistance to research by the proprietors, who tend to be highly sensitive to such activities.

Each unit should institute a long-term comprehensive study of a smallish community where farming systems are likely to undergo appreciable change, which may or may not involve habitat development. The agricultural research institute involved must be interested in and prepared to devote substantial resources to the agricultural and related aspects of the study community. The analyses must be quantitative, and population differentials within the community need to be studied.

Health needs to be studied both as a dependent variable on agricultural change and as a determinant of agricultural activity, and comparable activity needs to be devoted to these two aspects of the relation between agriculture and health.

Conclusions

The effects of agriculture on health can be usefully divided into three categories: the effects of specific agricultural changes, the effects of complex changes in farming systems, and the consequences of habitat or resource developments undertaken for agricultural purposes upon human health. The last category, habitat development, not only can cause health hazards, but also may provide opportunities for improving health. There is a need to view health impact assessment more broadly and positively and to carry out health opportunity assessment in relation to environmental changes.

Beneficial effects of improved health on agricultural activity, once considered axiomatic, have been much neglected in recent decades and require renewed attention. This could both rectify an imbalance in understanding and create a more receptive agricultural audience than exists at present.

Analysis of the agriculture-health relationship should focus particularly on effects of change in either area. Health monitoring will require better quality and use of routine statistics, monitoring by surveys, and special investigations. The epidemiology units of ministries of health provide the best opportunities for improved routine monitoring and for investigation of reported health incidents. Reduction of health hazards from specific agricultural innovations and from habitat resource developments for agriculture depends on a stronger legislative basis for reporting planned changes, and then competent health impact and opportunity assessment.

The interdisciplinary problems posed by changing farming systems and habitat development require development initially of a few groups linked to major, preferably international, agricultural research organizations who can carry out the necessary medium-term studies needed to understand and change for the better the mutual effects of agriculture on health and vice versa. Suggestions are put forward to achieve effective multidisciplinary work and to broaden the perception of the issues needed for progress in the 21st century.

References

Andrewartha, H. G., and L. C. Birch. 1954. *The Distribution and Abundance of Animals*. Chicago: University of Chicago Press.

Barker, D. J. P., and A. J. Hall. 1991. *Practical Epidemiology*. Edinburgh: Churchill Livingstone.

Billewicz, W. Z., and I. A. McGregor. 1981. The demography of two West African (Gambian) villages, 1951-75. *Journal of Biosocial Sciences* 13:219-40.

Bradley, D. J. 1977. The health implications of irrigation schemes and man-made lakes in tropical environments. In *Water, Wastes and Health in Hot Climate Countries*, edited by R. G. Feachem, M. G. McGarry, and D. D. Mara, 18-29. New York: Wiley.

———. 1988. The epidemiology of ricefield-associated diseases. In *Vector-borne Disease Control in Humans through Rice Agroecosystem Management*, 29-39. Los Baños, the Philippines: International Rice Research Institute.

———. 1991. Malaria—whence and whither. In *Malaria: Waiting for the Vaccine*, edited by G. A. T. Targett, 11-29. Chichester: Wiley.

Bradley, D. J., L. Rahmathullah, and R. Narayan. 1988. The tea plantation as a research ecosystem. In *Capacity for Work in the Tropics*, edited by K. J. Collins and D. F. Roberts. Cambridge: Cambridge University Press.

Briscoe, J. 1979. Energy use and social structure in a Bangladesh village. *Population and Development Review* 5:615-41.

Chen, L. C., ed. 1973. *Disaster in Bangladesh*. New York: Oxford University Press.

Cook, P. J., and D. P. Burkitt. 1971. Cancer in Africa. *British Medical Bulletin* 27:14-20.

Duggan, A. J. 1962. A survey of sleeping sickness in Northern Nigeria from the earliest times to the present day. *Transactions of the Royal Society of Tropical Medicine and Hygiene* 56:439-80.

Feachem, R. G., D. T. Jamison, and E. R. Bos. 1991. Changing patterns of disease and mortality in sub-Saharan Africa. In *Disease and Mortality in Sub-Saharan Africa*, edited by R. G. Feachem and D. T. Jamison. New York: Oxford University Press.

Hunter, J. M. 1966. River blindness in Nangodi, Northern Ghana: A hypothesis of cyclical advance and retreat. *Geographical Review* 56:398-416.

Macdonald, G. 1955. Medical implications of the Volta River project. *Transactions of the Royal Society of Tropical Medicine and Hygiene* 49:13-24.

Moore, S. R. W. 1969. The mortality and morbidity of deep sea fishermen sailing from Grimsby in one year. *British Journal of Industrial Medicine* 26:25-46.

Prothero, R. M. 1965. *Migrants and Malaria*. London: Longmans.

Redclift, M. 1987. *Sustainable Development: Exploring the Contradictions*. London: Methuen.

Schilling, R. S. F. 1966. Trawler fishing: An extreme occupation. *Proceedings of the Royal Society of Medicine* 56:405-10.

Sergent, Ed, and E. T. Sergent. 1947. *Histoire d'un marais algérien*. Algiers: Pasteur Institute.

Smith, P. G., and R. H. Morrow, eds. 1991. *Methods for Field Trials of Interventions against Tropical Diseases*. Oxford: Oxford University Press.

Stanley, N. F., and M. P. Alpers, eds. 1975. *Man-made Lakes and Human Health*. London: Academic Press.

Sydenstricker, E. 1988. Statistics of morbidity. In *The Challenge of Epidemiology*, edited by C. Buck et al., 167-75. Washington, D.C.: Pan American Health Organization.

Townsend, P., and N. Davidson, eds. 1982. *Inequalities in Health: The Black Report*. Harmondsworth: Penguin.

Weil, D. E. C., A. P. Alicbusan, J. F. Wilson, M. R. Reich, and D. J. Bradley. 1991. *The Impact of Development Policies on Health*. Geneva: World Health Organization.

Weisbrod, B. A. 1973. *Disease and Economic Development: The Impact of Parasitic Disease in St. Lucia*. Madison: University of Wisconsin Press.

White, G. F., D. J. Bradley, and A. U. White. 1972. *Drawers of Water*. Chicago: University of Chicago Press.

Whitehead, M. 1987. *The Health Divide: Inequalities in Health in the 1980's*. London: Health Education Council.

World Health Organization Working Group. 1986. Use and interpretation of anthropometric indices of nutritional status. *Bulletin of the World Health Organization* 64:929-41.

Worthington, E. B., ed. 1977. *Arid Land Irrigation in Developing Countries*. Oxford: Pergamon Press.

Part VI
Perspective

The demands that will be placed on agricultural producers and rural society because of population and economic growth and resource and environmental change suggest a number of important shifts in agricultural, environmental, and health research priorities. If these priorities are to be realized, it will be necessary to both strengthen and achieve more effective articulation among national and international agricultural, environmental, and health research systems.

In chapter 13, the research priorities that emerged both from the consultations that preceded the Bellagio conference and from the conference itself are outlined. The research priorities reflect a set of four generic issues that ran through the three consultations and the Bellagio conference: (1) Many of the problems are international in scope. An effective response will involve international collaboration and transnational organization. (2) Much more attention needs to be given to the design of technologies and institutions that will broaden options for choice and action. (3) Capacity to identify and monitor shifts in the sources of agricultural-productivity change, environmental change, and change in health status is exceedingly limited. (4) The institutional infrastructure that will be needed to sustain the required rates of growth in agricultural production as we move through the first decades of the next century is not yet in place.

In chapter 14 David E. Bell, William C. Clark, and Vernon W. Ruttan outline a vision of global agricultural, health, and environmental research systems to meet the needs of the first decades of the 21st century. This vision is informed by a perspective that the family and the community must occupy a central role in efforts to realize society's demands for growth of agricultural production, enhancement of the resource base, and improvement in health. This means that much more effective organizational and institutional linkages must be built between the suppliers and users of knowledge and technology. And it means that bridges must be built between the "island empires" of agricultural, environmental, and health research.

CHAPTER 13

CHALLENGES TO AGRICULTURAL RESEARCH IN THE 21ST CENTURY

Vernon W. Ruttan

In this chapter I summarize the implications from the Bellagio conference and from the three consultations that preceded the Bellagio conference for agricultural, environmental, and health research. In each section the discussion of specific research priorities is preceded by a brief discussion of the changes that have contributed to advancing the several research priorities.

Biological and Technical Constraints on Crop and Animal Production

It is apparent that the gains in agricultural production required over the next quarter century will be achieved with much greater difficulty than in the immediate past (see chapter 2). Difficulty is currently being experienced in raising yield ceilings for the cereal crops that have experienced rapid yield gains in the recent past. The incremental response to increases in fertilizer use has declined. Expansion of irrigated area has become more costly. Maintenance research, the research required to prevent yields from declining, is rising as a share of research effort (Plucknett and Smith, 1986). The institutional capacity to respond to these concerns is limited, even in the countries with the most effective national research and extension systems. Indeed, there has been considerable difficulty in many countries during the 1980s in maintaining the agricultural research capacity that had been established during the 1960s and 1970s (Cummings, 1989).

It is possible that within another decade, advances in basic knowledge will create new opportunities for advancing agricultural technology that will reverse the urgency of some of the above concerns. Institutionalization of private-sector agricultural research capacity in some developing countries is beginning to complement public-sector capacity (Pray, 1987). Advances in molecular biology and genetic engineering are occurring rapidly. But the date when these promising advances will be translated into productive technology seems to be receding.

The following general conclusions are from the first consultation on biological and technical constraints on crop and animal productivity (see Ruttan, 1989).

Advances in conventional technology will remain the primary source of growth in crop and animal production over the next quarter century. Almost all increases in agricultural production over the next several decades must continue to come from further intensification of agricultural production on land that is presently devoted to crop and livestock production. Until well into the second decade of the next century, the necessary gains in crop and animal productivity will be generated by improvements from conventional plant and animal breeding and from more intensive and efficient use of technical inputs, including chemical fertilizers, pest-control chemicals, and more effective animal nutrition.

The productivity gains from conventional sources are likely to come in smaller increments than in the past. If they are to be realized, higher plant populations per unit area, new tillage practices, improved pest and disease control, more precise application of plant nutrients, and advances in soil and water management will be required. Gains from these sources will be crop, animal, and location specific. They will require closer articulation between the suppliers and users of new knowledge and new technology. These sources of yield gains will be extremely knowledge and information intensive. If they are to be realized, research and technology transfer efforts in the areas of information and management technology must become increasingly important sources of growth in crop and animal productivity.

Advances in conventional technology will be inadequate to sustain the demands that will be placed on agriculture as we move into the second decade of the next century and beyond. Advances in crop yields have come about primarily by increasing the plant populations per hectare and the ratio of grain to straw in individual plants. Advances in animal feed efficiency have come largely by decreasing the proportion of feed consumed that is devoted to animal maintenance and increasing the proportion to produce usable animal products. There are severe physiological constraints to continued improvement along these conventional paths. These constraints are most severe in those areas that have already achieved the highest levels of productivity—as in Western Europe, North America, and parts of East Asia. The impact of these constraints can be measured in terms of declining incremental response to energy inputs—in the form of both a reduction in the incremental yield increases from higher levels of fertilizer application and a reduction in the incremental savings in labor inputs from the use of larger and more powerful mechanical equipment. If the incremental returns to agricultural research should also decline, it will impose a higher priority on efficiency in the organization of research and on the allocation of research resources.

A reorientation of the way we organize agricultural research will be necessary in order to realize the opportunities for technical change being opened up by advances in microbiology and biochemistry. Advances in basic science, particularly in molecular biology and biochemistry, have opened and are continuing to open new possibilities for supplementing traditional sources of plant and animal productivity growth. A wide range of possibilities were discussed at the consultation—ranging from the transfer of growth hormones into fish to conversion of lignocellulose into edible plant and animal products. The realization of these possibilities will require a reorganization of agricultural research systems. An increasing share of the new knowledge generated by research will reach producers in the form of proprietary products or services. This means that incentives must be created to draw substantially more private-sector resources into agricultural research. Within the public sector, research organizations will have to increasingly move from a "little science" to a "big science" mode of organization. Examples include the Rockefeller Foundation–sponsored collaborative research program on the biotechnology of rice and the University of Minnesota program on the biotechnology of maize. In the absence of more focused research efforts, it seems likely that the promised gains in agricultural productivity from biotechnology will continue to recede.

Efforts to institutionalize agricultural research capacity in developing countries must be intensified. Crop and animal productivity levels in most developing countries remain well below the levels that are potentially feasible. Access to the conventional sources of productivity growth—from advances in plant breeding, agronomy, and soil and water management—will require the institutionalization of substantial agricultural research capacity for each crop or animal species of economic significance in each agroclimatic region. In a large number of developing countries this capacity is just beginning to be put in place. A number of countries that experienced substantial growth in capacity during the 1960s and 1970s have experienced an erosion of capacity in the 1980s. Even a relatively small country, producing a limited range of commodities under a limited range of agroclimatic conditions, will require a cadre of agricultural scientists in the 250 to 300 range. Countries that do not acquire adequate agricultural research capacity will not be able to meet the demands placed on their farmers as a result of growth in population and income.

There are substantial possibilities for developing sustainable agricultural production systems in a number of fragile resource areas. Research under way in the tropical rainforest areas of Latin America and in the semiarid tropics of Africa and Asia suggest the possibility of developing sustainable agricultural systems with substantially enhanced productivity even in unfavorable environments. It is unlikely—and perhaps undesirable—that all of these areas will become important components of the global food supply system. But enhanced productivity is important to those who reside in these areas—now and in the future. It is important that the research investment in the areas of soil and water management and in farming systems be intensified in these areas.

There is a need for the establishment of substantial basic biological research and training capacity in the tropical developing countries. There are a series of basic biological research agendas important for applied research and technology development for agriculture in the tropics that receive, and are likely to continue to receive, inadequate attention in the temperate-region developed countries. There is also a need for closer articulation between training in applied science and technology and training in basic biology. When such institutes are established they will need to be more closely linked with existing academic centers of research and training than are the series of agricultural research institutes established by the Rockefeller and Ford foundations and the Consultative Group on International Agricultural Research (CGIAR).

Resource and Environmental Constraints on Sustainable Growth

As we look even further into the next century, there is a growing concern about the impact of a series of resource and environmental constraints that may seriously impinge on the capacity to sustain growth in agricultural production. A second consultation on issues of resource and environmental constraints on agricultural production, which included scientists involved in climate change studies, agricultural scientists, and economists, was held in late November 1989.

One set of concerns explored during the consultation focused on the impact of agricultural production practices that will be employed in those areas that have made the most progress in moving toward highly intensive systems of agricultural production. These include loss of soil resources due to erosion, waterlogging, and salinization; groundwater contamination from plant nutrients and pesticides; and growing resistance of insects, weeds, and pathogens to present methods of control. If agriculture is forced to continue to expand into more fragile environments, such problems as soil erosion and desertification can be expected to become more severe. Additional deforestation will intensify problems of soil loss and degradation of water quality and will contribute to the forcing of climate change.

A second set of concerns stems from the impact of industrialization on global climate and other environmental changes (Reilly and Bucklin, 1989; Parry, 1990). There can no longer be much doubt that the accumulation of carbon dioxide (CO_2) and other greenhouse gases—principally methane (CH_4), nitrous oxide (N_2O), and chlorofluorocarbons (CFCs)—has set in motion a process that will result in a rise in global average surface temperatures over the next 30 to 60 years. And there continues to be great uncertainty about the climate changes that can be expected to occur at any particular date or location in the future. It is almost certain, however, that the climate changes will be accompanied by rises in the sea level and that these rises will impinge particularly heavily on island Southeast Asia and the great river deltas of the region. Dryer and more erratic climate regimes can be expected in interior South Asia and North America. As a partial offset some analysts have suggested that higher CO_2 levels may have a positive effect on yield (Rosenberg, 1986).

The bulk of the carbon dioxide emissions come from fossil fuel consumption. Carbon dioxide accounts for roughly half of radiative forcing. Biomass burning, cultivated soils, natural soils, and fertilizers account for close to half of nitrous oxide emissions. Most of the known sources of methane are a product of agricultural activities—principally enteric fermentation in ruminant animals, release of methane from rice production and other cultivated wetlands, and biomass burning. Estimates of nitrous oxide and methane sources have a very fragile empirical base. Some estimates suggest that agriculture and related land use and land-use transformation could account for upwards of 25 percent of radiative forcing (Reilly and Bucklin, 1989). Other estimates, which take into account the different lifetimes and chemical transformations of the several greenhouse gases, attribute a significantly smaller share of climate change forcing to agricultural sources (Nordhaus, 1990).

The alternative policy approaches to the threat of global warming can be characterized as *preventionist* or *adaptionist*. A preventionist or meliorative approach could involve four policy options: (1) reduction in fossil fuel use or capture of CO_2 emissions at the point of fossil fuel combustion; (2) reduction in the intensity of agricultural production; (3) reduction of biomass burning; and (4) expansion of biomass production. Of these, only energy efficiency and conservation are likely to make any significant contribution over the next generation. And the speed with which either will occur will be limited by the pace of capital replacement. Any hope of significant reversal of agricultural intensification, reduction in biomass burning, or increase in biomass absorption is unlikely to be realized within the next several decades. The institutional infrastructure or institutional resources that would be required do not exist and will not be in place rapidly enough. We will not be able to rely on a technological fix to the global warming problem. The fixes, whether driven by preventionist or adaptionist strategies, must be both technological and institutional.

This forces me into adopting, although reluctantly, an *adaptionist* approach in attempting to assess the implications of global climate change for future agricultural research agendas. Thus, in this context, an adaptionist strategy implies moving as rapidly as possible to design and put in place the institutions needed to remove the constraints that intensification of agricultural production is currently imposing on sustainable increases in agricultural production. I am referring, for example, to (1) commodity policies—such as those of the United States, the EEC countries, and Japan—that encourage excessive use of chemical inputs as substitutes for land; and (2) resource policies, such as those that inhibit the rational conservation, allocation, and use of surface water and groundwater. If we are successful in designing the policies and institutions needed to deal with existing resource constraints and management, it will place us in a better position to respond to the more uncertain changes that will emerge as a result of future global climate change. In this section I discuss some of the research implications that emerged from the second consultation (Ruttan, 1992).

A serious effort to develop alternative land-use, farming-systems, and food-systems scenarios for the 21st century should be initiated. A clearer picture of the demands that are likely to be placed on agriculture over the next century and of the ways in which agricultural systems might be able to meet such demands has yet to be produced. World population could rise from the present 5 billion level to the 10-to-20-billion range. The demands that will be placed on agriculture will also depend on the rate of growth of income, particularly in the poor countries, where consumers spend a relatively large share of income growth on subsistence — food, clothing, and housing. The resources and technology needed to increase agricultural production by a multiple of three to six will depend on both the constraints on resource availability that are likely to emerge and the rate of advance in knowledge.

Advances in knowledge can permit the substitution of more abundant for increasingly scarce resources and can reduce the resource constraints on commodity production. Past studies of potential climate-change effects on agriculture have given insufficient attention to adaptive change in nonclimate parameters. But application of advances in biological and chemical technology, which substitute knowledge for land, and advances in mechanical and engineering technology, which substitute knowledge for labor, have in the past been driven by increasingly favorable access to energy resources — because of declining prices of energy. There will be strong incentive, by the early decades of the next century, to improve energy efficiency in agricultural production and utilization. Particular attention should be given to alternative and competing uses of land. Land-use transformation, from forest to agriculture, is presently contributing to radiative forcing through release of carbon dioxide and methane into the atmosphere. Conversion of low-intensity agricultural systems to forest has been proposed as a method of absorbing CO_2. There will also be increasing demands on land use for watershed protection and biomass energy production.

The capacity to monitor the agricultural sources and impacts of environmental change should be strengthened. It is a matter of serious concern that only in the last decade and a half has it been possible to estimate the magnitude and productivity effects of soil loss even in the United States. Even rudimentary data on productivity effects of soil loss are almost completely unavailable in most developing countries. The same point holds, with even greater force, for groundwater pollution, salinization, species loss, and others. It is time to design the elements of a comprehensive, agriculturally related resource monitoring system and to establish priorities for implementation. Data on the effects of environmental change on the health of individuals and communities are even less adequate. The monitoring should include a major focus on the effects of environmental change on human populations.

Lack of firm knowledge about the contribution of agricultural practices to the methane and nitrous oxide sources of greenhouse forcing was mentioned at numerous times during the consultation. Much closer collaboration between production-oriented agricultural scientists, ecologically trained biological scientists, and the physical scientists who have been traditionally concerned with global climate change is essential. This effort should be explicitly linked with the monitoring effects currently being pursued under the auspices of the International Geosphere-Biosphere Programs (IGBP).

The design of technologies and institutions to achieve more efficient management of surface- and groundwater resources will become increasingly important. During the next century, water resources will become an increasingly serious constraint on agricultural production. Agricultural production is a major source of decline in the quality of both ground and surface water. Limited access to clean and uncontaminated water supply is a major source of disease and poor health in many parts of the developing world and in the centrally planned economies. Global climate change can be expected to have a major differential impact on water availability, water demand, erosion, salinization, and flooding. The development and introduction of technologies and management systems that enhance water-use efficiency represents a high priority because of both short- and intermediate-run constraints on water availability and the longer-run possibility of seasonal and geographical shifts in water availability. The identification, breeding, and introduction of water-efficient crops for dryland and saline environments is potentially an important aspect of achieving greater water-use efficiency.

Research on environmentally compatible farming systems should be intensified. In agriculture, as in the energy field, there are a number of technical and institutional innovations that could have both economic and environmental benefits. Among the technical possibilities is the design of new "third"- or "fourth"-generation chemical, biorational, and biological pest-management technologies. Another is the design of land-use technologies and institutions that will contribute to reduction of erosion, salinization, and groundwater pollution. In both developed and developing countries, producers' decisions on land management, farming systems, and use of technical inputs (for example, fertilizers and pesticides) are influenced by government interventions such as price supports and subsidies, programs to promote or limit production, and tax incentives and penalties. It is increasingly important that research on the design of interventions take into account the environmental consequences of landowners' and producers' decisions induced by the interventions.

Alternative food systems must be developed. A food-system perspective should become an organizing principle for improvements in the performance of existing systems and for the design of new systems. The agricultural science community should be prepared, by the second quarter of the next century, to contribute to the design of alternative food systems. Many of these alternatives will include the use of plants other than the grain crops that now account for a major share of world feed and food production. Some of these alternatives will involve radical changes in food sources. Rogoff and Rawlins have described one such system based on lignocellulose—both for animal feed and for human consumption (Rogoff and Rawlins, 1987).

A major research program on incentive-compatible institutional design should be initiated. The first research priority is to initiate a large-scale program of research on the design of institutions capable of implementing incentive-compatible resource-management policies and programs. By incentive-compatible institutions I mean institutions capable of achieving compatibility between individual, organizational, and social objectives in resource management. A major source of the global warming and environmental pollution problem is the direct result of the operation of institutions that induce behavior by individuals and of public agencies that are not compatible with societal development—some might say survival—goals. In the absence of more efficient incentive-compatible institutional design, the transaction costs involved in ad hoc approaches are likely to be enormous.

Health Constraints on Agricultural Development

The third consultation, held in June 1990, focused on health constraints on agricultural development. One might very well ask why this topic was included in a series of consultations on agricultural research. Since the mid-1960s a number of commonly used health indicators, such as life expectancy and infant mortality, substantially improved for almost all developing countries. Concerns about nutritional deficiency as a source of poor health has receded in a large number of developing countries in the last several decades (BOSTID and IOM, 1987; Commission on Health Research for Development, 1990).

Yet there are a number of other indicators that suggest that health constraints could become increasingly important by the early decades of the next century. Daily calorie intake per capita has been declining for as much as two decades in a number of African countries. While dramatic progress has been made in the control and reduction of losses due to infectious disease and in the control of diarrheal disease, little progress has been made in the control of several important parasitic diseases. The sustainability of advances in malaria and tuberculosis control are causing serious concern. The emergence of AIDS, combined with the other health threats, could emerge as a major threat to economic viability in both developed and developing countries.

There is also a second set of health concerns arising out of the environmental consequences of the intensification of agricultural and industrial production, concerns that were discussed in the second consultation. As the environmental impacts of agricultural and industrial intensification become clearer, it appears that they are already imposing significant health burdens in some countries, particularly in parts of the former Soviet Union and Eastern Europe, and they may become more burdensome in the future.

If one visualizes many of these health threats emerging simultaneously in several countries, it is not too difficult to construct a scenario in which there are large numbers of sick people in many villages around the world. The numbers could become large enough to be a serious constraint on food production capacity. It was this set of concerns that guided the dialogue in the third consultation.

Evidence on the question raised at the beginning of the consultation—does health represent a serious constraint on agricultural development?—is at best ambiguous. Scattered data from countries such as India, Indonesia, and the Ivory Coast indicate loss of days worked due to sickness in the 5 to 15 percent range. In the former Soviet Union and Poland substantial numbers of days of work are lost due to respiratory disease associated with atmospheric pollution. There have also been major "plagues" in the past that resulted in mortality levels sufficient to seriously impinge on food supply. The AIDS plague is unique in that it is killing people who would be at their most productive age. The result will be a rise in the dependency ratio—the ratio of the old and young relative to workers in the more productive age groups.

Specific Issues

Let me turn to some of the more specific research implications that emerged from the third consultation (Ruttan, 1990).

The capacity to design systems of health delivery that are capable of reducing the incidence of illness continues to elude health-policy and planning agencies in both developed and developing countries. The systems that are in place in most countries can be more accurately described as sickness recovery systems than as health systems. They are health care rather than health maintenance systems. A major deficiency is the lack of a system for providing families and individuals with the knowledge needed to achieve better health with less reliance on the health care system. The point was made several times during the consultation that many countries have been able to design reasonably effective agricultural-extension or technology-transfer systems to provide farm people with knowledge about resources and technology needed to achieve higher levels of productivity. But we have yet to design an effective system to provide families and individuals with the knowledge in human biology, nutrition, and health practices that will enable them to lead more healthy lives.

The residuals produced as a by-product of industrial and agricultural production have become an increasingly important source of illness in a number of countries and regions. The most serious impacts are occurring in the formerly centrally planned economies of Eastern Europe, the former Soviet Union, and China. Levels of atmospheric, water, and soil pollution have resulted in higher mortality rates and reductions in life expectancy. The effects are evident in the form of congenital malformation, pulmonary malfunction, and excessive heavy metals in soils and in crops grown on contaminated soils. Many of the health effects of agricultural and industrial intensification are due to inadequate investment in the technology needed to control or manage contaminants. Rapid industrial growth in poor countries, in which investment resources are severely limited, will continue to be accompanied by underinvestment in the technology needed to limit the release of contaminants. The situation that exists in Eastern Europe presents a vision of the future for many newly industrializing countries unless better technology can be made available and more effective management of environmental spillover effects can be implemented.

Lack of location-specific or site-specific research capacity represents a major constraint on the capacity of health systems in most developing countries. It is no longer possible to maintain the position that health-related research results can simply be transferred from developed-country research laboratories or pharmaceutical companies to practice in developing countries. Local capacity is needed for the identification and analysis of the sources of health problems. It is also needed for the analysis, design, and testing of health delivery systems. The international donor community has been much slower in supporting the development of health research systems than have agricultural research systems in the tropics. For example, there is now in place a network of more than a dozen international agricultural research centers (IARCs), sponsored by the Consultative Group on International Agricultural Research, that play an important role in backstopping national agricultural research efforts.

The only comparable internationally supported center in the field of health is the International Centre for Diarrhoeal Disease Research in Bangladesh. Furthermore, the capacity to conduct essential research on tropical infectious and parasite diseases—research that was supported by the former colonial countries, the United Kingdom, France, the Netherlands, and Belgium—has been allowed to atrophy.

High birthrates are both a consequence and a cause of poor health. The demographic transition—from high to low birthrates—has in the past usually followed a rise in child survival rates. This suggests that improvements in health, particularly of mothers and children, is a prerequisite for decline in population growth rates. But high population growth rates, particularly in areas of high population density, are often associated with dietary deficiencies that contribute to poor health and high infant mortality rates.

The issue of how to achieve high levels of health and low birthrates at low cost in poor societies remains an unresolved issue. Several very low income countries have achieved relatively high levels of health—as measured by low infant mortality rates and high life expectancy rates—but often at a high cost relative to per capita income (see chapter 7). Other societies that have achieved relatively high incomes continue to exhibit relatively high infant mortality rates and only moderately high life expectancy levels.

More effective bridges must be built, both in research and in practice, between the agricultural and health communities. At present these two "tribes," along with veterinary medicine and public health, occupy separate and often mutually hostile "island empires." But solutions to the problem of sustainable growth in agricultural production and improvement in the health of rural people and of the consumers of agricultural commodities require that each of these communities establish bridgeheads in the other's territory. Multipurpose water resource development projects have contributed to the spread of onchocerciasis. Successful efforts to control the black fly have reopened productive lands to cultivation. The introduction of improved cultivars and fertilization practices has helped make the productivity growth sustainable. But examples of effective collaboration either in research or in project development are difficult to come by.

Some Generic Issues

I would like to list a set of four generic issues that ran through all three consultations.

The first is that many of the problems that we have discussed are international in scope. This means that many of the institutions that will be needed to enable societies to respond to the constraints on sustainable increases in agricultural production must involve international collaboration and transnational organization. We can no longer get by with slogans such as "Think globally and act locally." We will have to institutionalize the capacity to respond to scientific, technical, resource, environmental, and health constraints. In the area of health, for example, it seems clear that almost every source of illness or poor health that exists somewhere—whether the source is an infectious organism or environmental change—will exist everywhere else. This statement may be an exaggeration, but it is only a slight exaggeration.

The second is that much more attention needs to be given to the design of both technologies and institutions that will broaden options for choice and action. We noted, in our discussion, that the highest incidence of AIDS is likely to occur, at least during the next several decades, in those parts of the world where the technologies and institutions needed to sustain food production are exceedingly weak. Wider technical options will be needed in both food production and utilization.

The third is that capacity to identify and monitor the sources of agricultural-productivity change, environmental change, and change in health status is exceedingly limited. We know very little about either the levels or the trajectories. We talk about soil erosion, but we don't have the monitoring capacity to know the extent to which it is weakening our capacity to produce. We are fighting a defensive battle against the health effects of the contamination of our food supply rather than anticipating the sources. One of the puzzling aspects of the data available so far is that the health effects of increased use of fertilizer are less than expected in spite of high levels of nitrate in ground and surface water. Neither the developed nor the developing countries have in place adequate surveillance systems for disease.

The fourth is that the institutional infrastructure that will be needed to sustain the required rates of growth in agricultural production as we move through the first decades of the next century is not yet in place. We are going to have to build institutional infrastructures that facilitate more effective collaboration among engineers, agronomists, and health scientists in order to deal with issues of production, environmental change, and the health of food producers and consumers. The social science disciplines and related professions (law, management, social service) have not demonstrated great capacity in the area of institutional design. Plant breeders have been much more effective. They don't just analyze the sources of yield differences, they utilize the agronomic and genetic knowledge that is obtained from their analyses to design improved cultivars—plants and animals that are responsive to management and resistant to the assaults of nature. In the social sciences, once we complete our analysis we feel that our job has been finished. We tend to stop at the level of analysis. We only rarely bring the knowledge we have acquired to bear on institutional design.

Notes

Earlier drafts of this chapter have been published in *Journal of Asian Economics* 1 (Fall 1990): 189-204; *Canadian Journal of Agricultural Economics* 39 (1991): 567-80; *Outlook on Agriculture* 20 (1991): 225-34; *Choices* 7 (3rd Quarter, 1992): 32-37; *Technology and Economics*, ed. Robert M. White (Washington, D.C.: National Academy Press, 1991), pp. 85-105; *Agricultural Research Policy: International Quantitative Perspectives*, ed. Philip G. Pardey, Johannes Roseboom, and Jock R. Anderson (Cambridge: Cambridge University Press, 1991), pp. 399-411; *Southeast Asian Agriculture and Japan*, ed. Natsuki Kanazawa (Tokyo: Nihon University Regional Research Institute of Agriculture in the Pacific Basin, 1991), pp. 81-98; and *The Economics and Management of Water and Drainage in Agriculture*, ed. Ariel Dinar and David Zilberman (Boston: Kluwer Academic, 1991), pp. 903-12.

References

Board on Science and Technology for International Development (BOSTID) and Institute of Medicine (IOM). 1987. *The U.S. Capacity to Address Tropical Infectious Disease Problems*. Washington, D.C.: National Academy Press.

Commission on Health Research for Development. 1990. *Health Research: Essential Link to Equity in Development*. London: Oxford University Press.

Cummings, Ralph W. 1989. Modernizing Asia and the Near East: Agricultural research in the 1990s. Washington, D.C.: U.S. Agency for International Development, Bureau for Science and Technology. Mimeo.

Nordhaus, William D. 1990. To slow or not to slow: The economics of the greenhouse effect. New Haven, Conn.: Department of Economics, Yale University.

Parry, Martin. 1990. *Climate Change and World Agriculture*. London: Earthscan.

Plucknett, Donald H., and Nigel J. H. Smith. 1986. Sustaining agricultural yields. *BioScience* 36:40-45.

Pray, Carl E. 1987. Private sector agricultural research in Asia. In *Policy for Agricultural Research*, edited by Vernon W. Ruttan and Carl E. Pray, 411-31. Boulder, Colo.: Westview Press.

Reilly, John, and Rhonda Bucklin. 1989. Climate change and agriculture. In *World Agriculture Situation and Outlook Report*, Agricultural Research Service, WAS-55, pp. 43-46. Washington, D.C.: USDA/ARS.

Rogoff, Martin H., and Stephen L. Rawlins. 1987. Food security: A technological alternative. *BioScience* 37:800-807.

Rosenberg, Norman J. 1986. Climate, technology, climate change, and policy: The long run. In *The Future of the North American Grainery: Politics, Economics, and Resource Constraints in North American Agriculture*, edited by C. Ford Runge. Ames: Iowa State University Press.

———. 1991a. Challenges to agricultural research in the twenty-first century. In *Technology and Economics*, edited by Robert M. White, 85-105. Washington, D.C.: National Academy Press; and in *Agricultural Research Policy into the 21st Century: International Quantitative Perspectives*, edited by Philip G. Pardey, Johannes Roseboom, and Jock R. Anderson, 399-412. Cambridge: Cambridge University Press.

———. 1991b. Constraints on sustainable growth in agricultural production: Into the 21st century. *Canadian Journal of Agricultural Economics* 39:567-80; and *Outlook on Agriculture* 20(4): 225-34.

Ruttan, Vernon W., ed. 1989. *Biological and Technical Constraints on Crop and Animal Productivity: Report on a Dialogue*. St. Paul: University of Minnesota Department of Agricultural and Applied Economics.

———, ed. 1990. *Health Constraints on Agricultural Development*. St. Paul: University of Minnesota Department of Agricultural and Applied Economics.

———, ed. 1992. *Sustainable Agriculture and the Environment: Perspectives on Growth and Constraints*. Boulder, Colo.: Westview Press.

CHAPTER 14

GLOBAL RESEARCH SYSTEMS FOR SUSTAINABLE DEVELOPMENT: AGRICULTURE, HEALTH, AND ENVIRONMENT

David E. Bell, William C. Clark, and Vernon W. Ruttan

It is clear from even a casual reading of the contributions to this volume that the battle to achieve sustainable growth in agricultural production must be fought along a broad multidisciplinary front. Poverty undermines health and degrades the environment. Environmental problems such as soil erosion, waterlogging and salinity, and fertilizer and pesticide residues link the agricultural agenda with issues such as malaria and schistosomiasis control, sanitation, and water and food quality on the health agenda. Environmental changes under way at the global level, such as acid rain, ozone depletion, and climate change, will require changes in food production and health practices at the producer and community levels. Effective bridges must be built between the "island empires" of agricultural, environmental, and health sciences.

A second perspective that emerges from the chapters in this volume and from discussion at the Bellagio conference is the central role of family- and community-level decisions in achieving growth of agricultural production, enhancement of the resource base, and improvements in health. This means that much more effective organizational and institutional linkages must be built between the suppliers of knowledge and technology and the users. It also means that the institutions must be designed to place the users in a stronger role relative to the suppliers. During the discussions at Bellagio a vision of the institutional infrastructure that will be needed to supply knowledge and technology in the areas of agricultural production, resource management, and health began to take shape. In this concluding chapter we draw on the papers and discussion at the Bellagio conference and at the three earlier consultations to outline our vision of the structure of global agricultural, health, and environmental research systems.[1] We are under no illusion that the process of evolving an effective global research system that will be capable of bridging the island empires of agriculture, environment, and health will be easy. In his paper for the Bellagio conference, Douglass C. North emphasized that the design of an institutional framework that will make possible sustainable agricultural development in the 21st century will require a clearer understanding of the way institutions evolve than is available at the present time.

Agricultural Research

Our vision is strongly influenced by the experience of attempts, beginning in the late 1950s, to establish a global agricultural research system (Ruttan, 1986; Baum, 1986). For the architects of the post–World War II set of global institutions, meeting world food needs and the reduction of poverty in rural areas were essential elements in their vision of a world community that could ensure all people freedom from hunger.

In the immediate postwar years much of the burden fell on the United Nations Food and Agriculture Organization (FAO). But John Boyd Orr, the first director general of the FAO, burdened with the memory of the agricultural surpluses of the 1930s, was highly critical of the view that knowledge and technology represented a serious constraint on agricultural production capacity. "No research was needed to find out that half the people in the world lacked sufficient food for health, or that with modern engineering and agricultural science the world food supply could easily be increased to meet human needs" (Boyd Orr, 1966:160). In the first two postwar decades, assistance for agricultural development in the poor countries was conducted largely in a technology transfer and community development mode. By the late 1950s, it was becoming apparent, however, that the gains in production from simple technology transfer had largely played themselves out.

The inadequacy of policies based on the technology transfer or extension model led, in the late 1950s and early 1960s, to a reexamination of the assumption about the availability of a body of agricultural technology that could be readily diffused from high-agricultural-productivity to low-productivity countries or regions. The result was the emergence of a new perspective that agricultural technology, particularly yield-enhancing biological technology, is highly "location specific." Evidence was also accumulated to the effect that only limited productivity gains could be achieved by the reallocation or more efficient use of the resources available to peasant producers in poor countries.

The new vision that emerged as a guide to the sources of growth in agricultural production was the product of both experience with the improvement in agricultural technology and a reinterpretation of the role of peasant producers in the process of agricultural development.

It was apparent, in retrospect, that a number of colonial agricultural research institutes had played an important role in increasing the production of several tropical commodities, particularly export commodities such as rubber, sugar, tea, cotton, and sisal. The Rubber Research Institute of Malaysia and the sugar research institutes in Barbados, Java, and India were important examples. The initial success of the Rockefeller Foundation's agricultural programs, initiated in 1943 with the establishment of the Oficina de Estudias Especiales in cooperation with the Mexican Ministry of Agriculture, was of more immediate relevance. The program focused on food crops important in Mexico, particularly wheat and maize, rather than export commodities.

In the early postwar development literature, peasant producers had been viewed as obstacles to agricultural development. They were viewed as bound by custom and tradition and resistant to change. In an iconoclastic work published in 1964, Theodore W. Schultz advanced a "poor but efficient" view of peasant producers. They were viewed as making effective use of the resources available to them. But they lived in societies in which productivity-enhancing, "high-payoff" inputs were not available to them.

Schultz, drawing on the experience of the Rockefeller Foundation program in Mexico and on case studies by anthropologists and agricultural economists, identified three high-payoff investments needed to enhance the productivity of peasant producers. These were (1) the capacity of the agricultural research system to generate locally relevant knowledge and technology; (2) the capacity of the industrial sector to develop, produce, and market new inputs that embodied the knowledge and technology generated by research; and (4) the schooling of rural people to enable them to make effective use of the new knowledge and technology.

These insights, from experience and analysis, shaped the response to the food crises of the 1960s and 1970s. The immediate response was the transfer of large resources, including food aid, to the food-deficit countries. The longer-term response was the mobilization of resources to develop a system of international agricultural research institutes and to strengthen national agricultural research systems (see chapter 4).

In 1959 the Ford and Rockefeller foundations collaborated in establishing an International Rice Research Institute (IRRI) in the Philippines. This was followed by the spinning off of the international activities of the Rockefeller-supported Mexican maize and wheat programs to form the International Center for the Improvement of Maize and Wheat (CIMMYT) and the establishment of the International Institute of Tropical Agriculture (IITA) in Nigeria and the International Center for Tropical Agriculture (CIAT) in Colombia. It became apparent by the late 1960s that the financial requirements to maintain the research and development programs of the four institutes were stretching the capacity of the two foundations. In 1969 consultations were held among the Ford and Rockefeller foundations, the World Bank, the FAO, the United Nations Development Program (UNDP), and several bilateral donor agencies, leading to the organization of the Consultative Group on International Agricultural Research (CGIAR). The initial membership consisted of the World Bank, the FAO, and the UNDP as sponsors, as well as nine national governments, two regional banks, and three foundations.

The leadership of the consultative group is now centered at the World Bank, which provides a chairperson and a secretariat. Each institute or center is an independent corporate identity governed by its own board of trustees. The CGIAR established a Technical Advisory Committee (TAC), with its secretariat located at FAO headquarters in Rome, to provide technical oversight of the research institutes and to advise the CGIAR on priorities and resource allocation among centers. The TAC has been charged with the responsibility of organizing comprehensive reviews of the programs of the centers, of evaluating new initiatives, and of overseeing coordination among centers in common program areas such as cropping systems research.

By the early 1990s the system had expanded from an initial 4 to 18 centers. The initial centers focused their research mainly on the major food crops grown in developing countries—rice, wheat, maize, potatoes, and cassava. These were joined in the 1970s by centers focusing on livestock production and animal disease, on arid and semiarid areas, on food policy, and on germ plasm resources. In the late 1970s and early 1980s, crop and farming systems research programs were developed to achieve more effective understanding of soil, water, climate, weed, and crop interaction. In the late 1970s several donors to the CGIAR were instrumental in establishing independent research centers to work on soils, irrigation, and agroforestry.

As the new seed-fertilizer technology generated at the CGIAR centers, particularly for rice and wheat, began to come onstream, some donors assumed that the CG centers could bypass the more difficult and often frustrating efforts to strengthen national agricultural research systems. But experience in the 1960s and 1970s confirmed the judgment of those who had participated in the organization of the international centers that strong national research centers were essential if the prototype technology that might be developed at the international centers was to be broadly transferred, adopted, and made available to producers.

The location-specific nature of biological technology meant that the prototype technologies developed at the international centers could become available to producers in the wide range of agroclimate regions and social and economic environments in which the commodities were being produced only if the capacity to modify, adapt, and reinvent the technology was available. It became clear that the challenge of constructing a global agricultural research system capable of sustaining growth in agricultural production required the development of research capacity for each commodity of economic significance in each agroclimactic region. One response by the CGIAR donor community was the establishment of a new center, the International Service for National Agricultural Research (ISNAR), to provide analytical and planning assistance to national agricultural research systems in strengthening their organization and management. Another response, particularly during the 1970s, was substantially expanded support for national agricultural research systems.

During 1990-92 5 new centers were added to the CG system, thus increasing the number of centers from 13 to 18. In 1990 the International Irrigation Management Institute (IIMI), the International Center for Research on Agro-Forestry (ICRAF), and the International Network for the Improvements of Banana and Plantain (INIBAP) were brought into the CG system. In 1992 the International Center for Living Aquatic Research Management (ICLARM) was added to the system. This expansion was not accompanied by an expansion of the resources available to the system. Support to the system in 1990-92 actually declined in real terms, producing a "quiet crisis in the system" (see chapter 4).

The crisis has not only been financial. A number of the CGIAR centers have experienced the difficulties associated with organizational maturity. There is a natural life-cycle sequence in the history of research organizations and research programs (Ruttan, 1982:132). When they are initially organized they tend to attract vigorous and creative individuals. As these individuals interact across disciplines and problem areas, the organization often experiences a period of great productivity. As the research organization matures, however, there is often a tendency for the research program to settle into filling in the gaps in knowledge and technology rather than achieving creative solutions to scientific and technical problems. Since the mid-1980s the managers of several of the CGIAR institutes have been addressing, during a period of budget stringency, the problem of how to revitalize a mature research organization.

Efforts to strengthen national research institutes have also been only partially successful. The 1970s witnessed a remarkable expansion of agricultural research capacity in a number of developing countries. The national research systems in India, Brazil, Malaysia, and several other developing countries began to achieve world-class status in their capacity to make advances in knowledge and technology available to their farmers. A number of other countries, such as the Philippines, Colombia, and Thailand, achieved substantial capacity to conduct research on their major agricultural commodities. During the 1980s the buffeting of a global recession and debt crisis had the effect of weakening the commitment of a number of aid agencies and national governments to strengthening agricultural research. In Africa many national agriculture research systems that have received generous external support even during the 1980s have failed to become productive sources of knowledge and technology (see chapter 4).

The role of technical support for decision making by farmers and the capacity to supply to producers the technical inputs in which the new technology is embodied have been continuing areas of controversy. In general the developing countries have been relatively extension intensive. The ratio of extension workers to agricultural product has been much higher in developing countries than in developed countries (Judd, Boyce, and Evenson, 1987). Weak linkages between research and extension and between extension and farmers have represented a serious constraint on the diffusion of new technology (see chapter 6). During the late 1970s and early 1980s the World Bank devoted very substantial resources to the support of an intensive "training and visit" (T & V) system of delivering information about practices and technology to farmers. The system involved a highly regimented schedule in which the field-level worker was involved one day each week in intensive training about the information that he or she was to convey to farmers (Benor and Harrison, 1977). In retrospect it appears the system erred in placing the extension worker rather than the farmer, or the farm family, at the center of the technology adoption process.

A second constraint on the effectiveness of the transfer of agricultural practices and technology to producers is the weakness of the private sector as a source of both the supply and delivery of knowledge and technology (Evenson, Evenson, and Putnam, 1987; Pray, 1987). The emergence of more liberal economic policies since the early 1980s in a number of developing countries is, however, leading to rather rapid growth of private-sector suppliers of agricultural technology and to increased research by the suppliers.

The global agricultural support system is still incomplete. The deficiencies discussed by Carl Eicher, B. L. Turner and Patricia Benjamin, and Judith Tendler in chapters 4 through 6 continue to deprive farm families of the support that they need to meet even current food-consumption and income needs. Yet the vision of the agricultural support system that will be needed to sustain growth in agricultural production is reasonably clear. During the past several decades implementations of the vision have been less than adequate in some developed countries and in all but a few developing countries. With the ending of the cold war it may now be possible to extend the vision to farm families in many of the formerly centrally planned economies. One important step will be to place farm families and the farm enterprise in those societies at the center of the agricultural production process. Another important step will be to link the agricultural research systems in the formerly centrally planned economies with the emerging global agricultural research system.

Health Research

At the Bellagio conference Godfrey Gunatilleke outlined a vision of the gains in health status that can be achieved by even a poor society that devotes significant resources in support of an effective national health policy. Sri Lanka has achieved health indicators—a life expectancy of around 70 years and infant mortality below 20 per 1,000 live births—comparable to the levels achieved by many societies that are much more affluent (see chapter 8). But a vision of the global health research system needed to sustain national health policy has emerged more slowly than the vision of a global agricultural system. Only within the last decade has the health research community begun to articulate the form that such a system might take.

For most of the last century—since the time of Koch and Pasteur—health research has been thought of principally as laboratory-based biomedical research, seeking "silver bullets" against specific infections or diseases—new vaccines, new drugs, new surgical techniques. This focus, plus the remarkable improvements in health in recent decades, led to the misperception that all the new knowledge and new technology needed to protect families and communities around the world from debilitation and illness could be generated in the universities, research institutes, and pharmaceutical company laboratories of the industrialized countries.

This limited conception was clearly wrong and has been changing rapidly. Three gains in perception are especially important.

The first is the recognition that health technologies, to be useful, must be applied in particular social settings. Achieving health improvements requires not only technology but also policies, organizations, and processes that are adapted to the varied economic, social, cultural, and historical circumstances among and within countries. Even vaccines, the simplest of technologies, cannot be applied in Lagos by the same means they are in Liverpool.

An effective health research system, capable of conducting the essential national health research described by Adetokunbo Lucas in chapter 7, needs epidemiologists, economists, management specialists, and other social and policy analysts in addition to biomedical scientists. Such skills are scarce in industrialized countries. They are grossly deficient in developing countries. But they are essential to identify the precise nature of health problems in different national and local settings, and to design, test, and apply appropriate solutions.

A second gain in perception is the recognition that the principal actors in achieving improvements in health are individuals and families, especially mothers. Preventing illnesses and promoting health depends first and most of all on "maternal technology"—the ability to use basic knowledge about nutrition, cleanliness, home remedies, and when and how to call on health professionals (Mata, 1988).

An effective health research system, therefore, must be organized not simply to serve physicians but to support the flow of health knowledge and technology to families and communities—and to provide for the reverse flow of information from families and communities to researchers about the actual nature of health problems and how they are changing. Such a conception of linking researchers directly to primary actors is customary in agriculture, where research results have long been aimed at farmers as decision makers. But it is a recent conception in health, even in industrialized countries.

A third gain in perception is the recognition that the world's health research efforts are overwhelmingly concentrated in industrialized countries, seeking technologies to address the diseases of the more affluent societies. Only about 5 percent of global health research financing is directed to the major diseases and health problems of the developing countries, where more than 90 percent of the world's burden of preventable deaths occur (Commission on Health Research for Development, 1990). An effective global health research system must address this huge imbalance and provide for a large increase in the resources devoted to the health problems of the developing countries.

Combining these three perceptions with the traditional power of biomedical research, one can begin to perceive, dimly, the shape of a global health research system and how to move toward it.

Such a system—in health just as in agriculture—will need to be based solidly on national research systems, capable of supporting decision makers as they identify and confront health problems. A national health research system requires, first of all, skills to measure the patterns and determinants of disease, disability, and death and skills to monitor changes in health status over time. It requires also skills to design, test, and evaluate means for applying improved health technologies in local environments and for making research results available to those who need to use them, from national policymakers to local families. Every nation needs the capacity to conduct such country-specific research to guide its health activities, and the establishment of such capacity should clearly be given top priority (see chapter 7).

Beyond the capacity for essential country-specific research, health scientists in every country will wish to join, as and when they can, in the international effort to advance the world's frontiers of knowledge concerning the social and biological pathologies of ill health and disability and the new technologies to overcome them. In poor countries, the conditions for world-class science are difficult to establish. Nevertheless, a significant number of developing countries—to name just a few, Thailand, India, Egypt, Mexico, and Brazil—are beginning to have the capacity to make significant contributions to world knowledge in the health field.

Thus, national health research systems need to begin with the capacity to guide national health activities, and to go on, as conditions permit, to participate in global frontier research. In most developing countries, there are only rudimentary health research capabilities at present. It is urgent for developing countries, and for the international health assistance community, to commit themselves to building steadily stronger national health research systems. Such systems will need to start small and to focus initially on the most pressing health problems. But they should be designed with a view to dynamic change over time as financial and personnel resources grow and as health problems change with the demographic and epidemiologic transitions through which the developing countries will pass over the coming decades.

Thinking about how to achieve an effective global health research system thus begins with the development of strong national systems. But national systems must not be thought of as separate, freestanding entities. On the contrary, it is essential that they be linked together by strong international ties, and that they draw from the common, growing pool of worldwide health knowledge, with each country adapting advances in health science to its own specific circumstances.

Moreover, it would be a mistake to think of a global system as centered in the industrialized countries, with all scientific advances pioneered there and rippling outward to the developing world. We have already seen major health improvements developed in the third world, as ambulatory therapy for tuberculosis was pioneered in Madras, and oral rehydration therapy for diarrhea in Dhaka. As the amount and quality of developing-country research steadily rise, a global research system will increasingly be multicentric—one in which the flow of ideas and new knowledge moves in all directions along networks of information and collaboration encompassing scientists from many countries, rich and poor alike.

Thus the guidelines for moving toward a global health research system include (1) the development as rapidly as feasible of strong national systems, especially in developing countries where they are currently very weak, and (2) the rapid evolution of international collaborative mechanisms and arrangements. There is much work here for years to come.

In the discussions at Bellagio, two aspects of this overall vision received special attention and illumination.

The first was the necessity for building direct relationships between the national health research system and action for health at the community and family levels. In chapter 8, Dan Kaseje described the elements of a community-based health system in Kenya that he helped design and implement; it relies directly on the actions of individual families and communities. The model views the mother as the key health provider and builds on the strong motivation to carry out her tasks resulting from concern about the current and future well-being of her children and family. The "Harambee" model recognizes the strengths and resources of the community; seeks to facilitate and enhance these strengths; recognizes that communities have always been responsible for their own health, even without the intervention of health professionals; and recognizes that the mother is the most important and knowledgeable health provider. This mother is not, however, left without resources to carry out her responsibilities. She is reinforced with a strong program of health education, the availability of appropriate technology and materials, and support from nongovernmental organizations and official health programs. The system described by Kaseje does not work perfectly and should not be overly idealized. Kaseje himself expressed considerable skepticism about the possibility of breaking the professional and bureaucratic inertia in order to extend and sustain the program he has described.

It is clear, however, that the resources needed to enable the family to provide effective health services to its members are very similar to those identified three decades ago by Schultz as enabling peasant producers to become effective suppliers of agricultural commodities. The high-payoff health inputs include the following:

> (1) The capacity of the health research community to produce the new knowledge and the materials that are appropriate to the resource and cultural endowments of rural communities.

> (2) The capacity of national, regional, and local institutions to make the knowledge and the materials available to families.

(3) The formal schooling and informal education of families, particularly mothers, to make effective use of the knowledge available to them.

The second issue on which the papers and discussions at Bellagio shed light is the nature of the international apparatus needed for a global health research system.

In the field of agriculture, the CGIAR-sponsored international research centers serve as leaders of applied science for the third world and as accelerators of linkages between frontier science and third-world problems. There is no comparable set of internationally supported health research centers in poor countries of the tropics. Lucas notes in chapter 7 that there are only two international centers of significant size in the field of health — the International Centre for Diarrhoeal Disease Research in Bangladesh and the International Centre for Insect Physiology and Ecology in Kenya (which is concerned with entomology that is relevant to both health and agriculture).

There are strong differences of opinion within the international health community as to whether a system of international health research centers, analogous to the CGIAR centers, would be appropriate or effective:

> On the one hand internationally organized efforts have the advantage of achieving a critical mass of scientists concentrating on and physically located close to high-priority problems. . . . Internationally organized research efforts can focus on specific problems in a multidisciplinary way and demonstrate economies of scale in their operations, making them attractive to external funding. On the other hand, international center salaries are high and their activities, if not carefully targeted, can supersede rather than complement national efforts. (Commission on Health Research for Development, 1990:58)

At the Bellagio conference there was something approaching consensus that present constraints on foreign assistance funds suggest that it would be unrealistic to expect resources to be mobilized in the mid-1990s to support a system of international health research centers in the tropics. It seems more likely that the predominant model of international collaboration in the health field will be international networks linking scientists in national institutions (both in industrialized and developing countries) in goal-oriented research programs aimed at specific health problems. A successful example of such collaboration is the Special Programme for Research and Training in Tropical Diseases (TDR), cosponsored by UNDP, the World Bank, and WHO. Started in 1976, TDR focuses on six specific diseases (including ma-

laria, schistosomiasis, and leprosy) and, in addition to supporting research, invests approximately 25 percent of its annual budget of
$30-35 million in strengthening research capacity in developing coun-
tries.

While international networks of national centers evidently can
work effectively in supporting research on particular diseases, there is
one extremely important function they cannot perform. The field of
health research conspicuously lacks an overview mechanism. In agriculture, the CGIAR (as distinct from the set of centers it sponsors) has
built highly valuable methods for surveying the worldwide agricultural research scene in relation to the needs for research results, reviewing ongoing research activities (both those of the international
centers and of other institutions), and proposing changes in current
research priorities and institutional arrangements, including, where
necessary, the development of new research facilities.

There is no analogous effective, independent organization in the
health field for assessing progress in research, especially on developing-country health problems; for identifying neglected areas; and for
promoting necessary action. The result is clear. At present, of the
three leading infectious-disease causes of death in the world (acute
respiratory infections, diarrheal diseases, and tuberculosis), only diarrhea is addressed by a major, sustained research effort. That is why
the Commission on Health Research for Development came to the
conclusion that "a health analogue of the CGIAR assessment and promotion structure could be of great value and should be established"
(Commission on Health Research for Development, 1990:59). This objective is clearly an urgent one.

Environmental Research

If the global research system for agriculture now faces the challenges
of maturity and the system for health confronts those of adolescence,
then the global environmental research system still requires prenatal
care.

To be sure, research for environmental conservation has a long and
productive history in many parts of the world. Since World War II,
this research has been given impetus and direction by at least three
waves of concern over the implications of natural resource availability
and environmental change for the sustainability of improvements in
human well-being. Early work focused on the adequacy and protection of the material base for agricultural and industrial production. By

the mid-1970s, increasing attention was also being given to the impact of residuals generated by that production on air and water quality and human health. Today, rapidly growing awareness of global change in the earth system has provided yet another dimension to our environmental concerns.

Most environmental research to date has been performed in universities, initially with support from major philanthropic organizations such as the Ford Foundation. Prodded by the United Nations Conference on the Human Environment in Stockholm in 1972, national governments have become increasingly involved as supporters, producers, and users of environmental research. Over the last decade, there has also been an explosion in the number and variety of nongovernmental organizations active on the world's environmental scene, some of them producing research of the highest caliber and relevance (Livernash, 1992). International programs for environmental research have also expanded dramatically since their "modern" birth in the International Geophysical Year of 1957. Nonetheless, most important international institutions for environmental research are barely 20 years old—for example, ICSU's Scientific Committee on Problems of the Environment (SCOPE), UNESCO's Man and the Biosphere Program (MAB), IIASA, and, of course, UNEP (Caldwell, 1990). Today's major research programs on global change—the World Climate Research Program (WCRP), the International Geosphere-Biosphere Program (IGBP), and the Human Dimensions of Global Change Program (HDGC)—are younger still (Jaeger and Ferguson, 1991; Miller and Jacobson, 1992; Perry, 1991).

This impressive and expanding array of activities nonetheless falls far short of the global system of environmental research needed to provide the knowledge base for sustainable development. Still lacking is a coherent institutional structure that can link the world's environmental researchers both upward to the international level of policy negotiations and downward to the community-level consumers, producers, health workers, and extension agents on whose actions sustainable development must ultimately depend. In the wake of the Rio "Earth Summit," however, several initiatives are under discussion that could supply important components of such a system and move it substantially closer to reality.

The most ambitious of these is START—a System for Analysis, Research, and Training proposed in 1991 by the IGBP in collaboration with the WCRP and HDGEC. START is planned as "a global system of regional research networks to stimulate research, modelling, and training activities related to global [environmental] change in both the natural and social sciences" (IGBP, 1992: 5). Its regional focus is based on the realization that global change wears local faces. The origins, the impacts, and the options for managing global environmental change will be different in different parts of the world, and must be understood within their local environmental and social contexts. The initial START planning document divided the world into 13 "scientifically coherent" regions (Eddy et al., 1991). Within each region, the research network is planned to consist of one or more research centers plus an unspecified number of regional research sites (for example, university departments and field stations). The networks aim to provide scientists from all parts of the world the knowledge and infrastructure necessary for them to participate fully in ongoing research concerning global environmental change. If planned funding from the international community is forthcoming, the first of the networks—probably in the tropical Asian monsoon region—could be fully operational by mid-decade.

In addition to the comprehensive plans of START, a number of more focused regional initiatives are also being pursued around the world. Some examples follow:

> In Asia: A Smithsonian-sponsored program, Sustainable Management of Tropical Evergreen Forests, has linked leading centers throughout Asia in a unique network for research, training, and data collection (Ashton, 1991). Although the tropical forests program has been launched largely through the efforts of private foundations and host-country contributions, Japan and the United States—through their recently announced "Global Partnership Plan of Action"—have promised increased governmental support of environment and conservation research in the region (Lepkowski, 1992).

> In the Americas: The Inter-American Institute for Global Change Research (IAIGCR) has been established as a "regional network of research entities . . . [that] seeks to achieve the best possible international coordination of scientific and economic research on the extent, causes, and consequences of global change in the Americas" (IGBP, 1991; Declaration of Montevideo, 1992). Close integration with the START initiative has been emphasized throughout the planning of the IAIGCR.

> In Central and Eastern Europe: A number of environmental re-

search, development, and training institutions have been formed to address the special problems of this region. One notable example with support from a number of Western countries is the Regional Environmental Center in Budapest. Since its inception in 1989, the center has helped "to set up environmental surveys, grassroots and non-governmental organizations, new environmental legislation and remediation campaigns" (*Nature*, 1992). Its major activity has been building a data base on environmental conditions in the region, coupled with a computer network to disseminate these data to smaller offices for use by local researchers.

Globally: Increasing attention is being given to the need for a permanent international research institution that could tackle environmental problems transcending individual regions and that could link national centers for environmental research into a truly global system. This function is currently performed on a largely ad hoc basis—for example, through studies of ICSU's Scientific Committee on Problems of the Environment, or the Intergovernmental Panel on Climate Change. But the time may well be ripe for complementing such ad hoc efforts with a more permanent home or homes. The International Institute for Applied Systems Analysis, with its focus on problems of global change (IIASA, 1991), has been put forward as one leading candidate (Maddox, 1992). The Carnegie Commission on Science, Technology, and Government has proposed the establishment of a Consultative Group for Research and Environment (GREEN), modeled on the Consultative Group on International Agricultural Research, that would combine the functions of resource mobilization, priority assessment, and research monitoring and evaluation in areas related to the environment.

How these and other initiatives will relate to one another or to existing national research centers is not yet clear. Most of the parties involved seem aware of the need for addressing such relations. Early indications are that their potential complementarities could dominate the inevitable competition for people, programs, and funds. The recent formation of a professional secretariat for START in Washington can only improve the prospects for successful integration of emerging international environmental research efforts.

Against this optimistic assessment, however, it must be noted that in the dialogue leading to recent environmental research initiatives there appears to have been little consideration of appropriate linkages with agricultural and health research systems (see chapters 10 to 12). This is a serious omission for two reasons. First, it virtually guarantees that many of the lessons painfully learned in the course of building today's relatively mature network of agricultural and health research systems will be lost on the fledgling environmental effort. Second, it perpetuates the "island empire" problems referred to at the outset of this chapter. We address possible measures for mitigating these shortcomings in turn.

Lessons from the development of current agricultural and health research systems that should be incorporated in new environmental efforts reflect a growing appreciation of the central role of family- and community-level decisions in shaping sustainable development:

1. Means must be designed to assure that research priorities reflect the environmental problems confronting individual families, farmers, and resource users in the field. The small "charmed circle" of puzzles that excite lab scientists or program administrators should not be allowed to dominate the agenda. The World Bank's recent report, *Development and the Environment* (World Bank, 1992) is surely correct in its conclusion that "the current environmental debate has paid too little attention to the problems of clean water, urban air pollution, indoor air pollution, and severe land degradation" that each year kill millions of people, undermine the health of hundreds of millions more, and significantly reduce productivity of people who can least afford it (World Bank, 1992:4; see also Norberg-Bohm et al., 1992).

2. We must resist the temptation to search for universal "silver bullets" that will solve specific environmental problems whenever and wherever they occur. Most causes, impacts, and solutions will be intimately associated with particular social circumstances and landscapes. Effective research systems will therefore require significant, site-specific components, and must avoid focusing activity in a few elite laboratories of the high- income countries. The need for elite laboratories will remain, in part because of needs for special research and data-processing equipment, in part because of the need to bring top scientists from many disciplines together for particular aspects of the necessary research. But specific measures must be implemented to assure that such regional centers do not bleed talent, funds, and equipment from the essential national and local nodes of the research network. A recognition of the need for simultaneous and complementary

strengthening of the local, national, and regional dimensions of the emerging global environmental research system seems well embodied in the plans for START (Eddy et al., 1991). But a practical vision of "essential national environmental research"—how it is to be funded and linked to international efforts—is only beginning to emerge.

3. A "technology transfer" strategy for research and development will be no more successful in dealing with environmental problems than it has been for sustaining improvements in agricultural productivity or human health. This applies not only to conventional north-south transfers, but also to the current spate of enthusiasm for grafting the clean-energy systems of advanced Organization for Economic Cooperation and Development (OECD) nations onto the formerly socialist economies of Eastern Europe. Less obvious, but perhaps even more important, experience in the agriculture and health sectors warns against the wholesale transfer of institutions as a means of enhancing environmental conservation. This is especially the case in the area of common-pool resources, where an uncritical tendency to transfer solutions based on full private-property rights or centralized regulation to small-scale, low-income situations has had disastrous consequences. Appropriate alternatives often exist, more finely attuned to local social and environmental conditions (Ostrom, 1990). In general, the need is not to transfer environmental technologies and institutions from "advanced" to "developing" regions, but rather to promote more widespread sharing of knowledge, know-how, and experience around the world. In particular, in environment as in agriculture and health, the need is to enhance the voice and power of users relative to suppliers of needed research and development.

4. An effective global environmental research system must be much more broadly inclusive than is presently the case. The need to better incorporate knowledge users in the system has been stressed in this chapter. The need for an expansion of the capacity to monitor global change has been emphasized in chapters 10 to 12. The environmental R & D potential of the formerly centrally planned economies must also be tapped, although this will require institutional innovations to end the traditional exclusion of such societies from the "global" research system. Finally, the private sector must be encouraged as both a supplier and a deliverer of the knowledge needed for environmentally sustainable development. Perhaps no single factor has so inhibited the development of effective global research systems for agriculture and health as the failure to promote incentive and reward

structures that can induce constructive private-sector involvement. In the environmental field, there is a vast potential for private-sector engagement in topics as diverse as energy efficiency and biotechnology. But a number of issues involving intellectual property rights, liabilities, and government-industry relations will have to be resolved before the potential can be fully tapped for the benefit of sustainable development (Schmidheiny, 1992).

In summary, an effective global environmental research system will have many of the features of effective agricultural and health research systems. The behavior of consumers of environmental services and of the producers of the residuals—households, farms, and factories—that erode environmental amenities will have to be recognized as central to the process of environmental change (see chapter 5). The resources that will be needed to place households, farms, and factories in a position to respond constructively will depend on (1) the capacity of the environmental research system to provide the knowledge, including the essential national environmental research, needed by household, farm, and factory decision makers; (2) the capacity of national, regional, and community institutions to provide the knowledge, technology, and incentives to those who make decisions about resource use; and (3) the depth of understanding possessed by household, farm, and factory decision makers about the consequences of their own actions and the actions of the economic and political institutions in which they participate.

Bridging the "Island Empires"

We have argued that the "island empires" of the agricultural, health, and environmental sciences can learn from one another as they strive to build global research systems that can support sustainable development. Whether they can, or even should, move beyond passive learning to active cooperation remains to be seen.

There seems little merit in any grand organizational scheme that would attempt to pull the already diverse networks of research in the respective empires under a single roof. And the most dynamic of the existing empires—that dealing with environmental research—simply does not have enough experience in the tough business of actually running a global network to seem credible as a leader of any major bridging movement. What does seem both feasible and desirable, however, is to begin some modest effort at active bridge building.

At a minimum, the principals of the three empires might agree to meet regularly—perhaps in the spirit of the G-7 summits—in order that they and their senior staff members could get to know one another and exchange information on current activities. An exploration of possible collaboration in global monitoring and other data-gathering activities might be a good early agenda item for such meetings. The new U.N. Commission on Sustainable Development, established at the 1992 Earth Summit, would be one logical convener for such meetings. But private foundations and NGOs could do a lot to get the ball rolling.

At a deeper level, it is essential to realize that the global agricultural, health, and environmental research systems outlined in this chapter have important common elements. The global systems outlined here can be effective only as the underlying sciences—particularly the biological and the social sciences—advance. Advances in the biological sciences and the social sciences are necessary to enlarge the world's understanding of the natural and social phenomena in global change. They are also needed in order to expand the capacity to apply advances in knowledge to the natural and human dimensions of development in the poor countries, where most of the world's people live.

The need to enlarge scientific capacity in the poorer countries of the world should not be viewed as a burden on either the developed or developing countries. Rather, it is an opportunity to multiply the intellectual talent necessary to advance knowledge relevant to the achievement of sustainable development. Completion of the development of global research systems in agriculture, health, and environment is a necessary component of a global effort to establish and mobilize the intellectual capacity and energy that will be needed to sustain development.

Notes

The authors are indebted to Carl K. Eicher, C. Bonte-Friedheim, B. L. Turner, and John S. Perry for comments on an earlier draft of this chapter.

1. The dialogues and recommendations from the initial three consultations, held under the auspices of the Twenty-First Century Project, have been reported in three University of Minnesota Department of Agricultural and Applied Economics Staff Papers (Ruttan, 1989; Ruttan, 1990a; Ruttan, 1990b) and are summarized in chapter 13. A revised version of the second consultation report has been published by Westview Press (Ruttan, 1992).

References

Ashton, P. 1991. Sustainable Management of Tropical Evergreen Forests: A program proposal. Cambridge, Mass.: Harvard Institute for International Development, Harvard University. Mimeo.

Baum, Warren. 1986. *Partners against Hunger: The Consultative Group on International Agricultural Research.* Washington, D.C.: World Bank.

Benor, Daniel, and James Q. Harrison. 1977. *Agricultural Extension: The Training and Visit System.* Washington, D.C.: World Bank.

Boyd Orr, John. 1966. *As I Recall.* London: MacGib and Kee.

Caldwell, L. 1990. *International Environmental Policy: Emergence and Dimensions.* 2d ed. Durham, N.C.: Duke University Press.

Carnegie Commission on Science, Technology, and Government. 1992. *International Environmental Research and Assessment: Proposals for Better Organization and Decision Making* (New York).

Commission on Health Research for Development. 1990. *Health Research: Essential Link to Equity in Development.* Oxford: Oxford University Press.

Declaration of Montevideo. 1992. Declaration of Montevideo on an Inter-American Institute for Global Change Research. Montevideo.

Eddy, J. A., T. F. Malone, J. J. McCarthy, and T. Rosswall. 1991. *Global Change System for Analysis, Research and Training (START).* International Geosphere-Biosphere Program, International Council of Scientific Unions, Report no. 15. Boulder, Colo.: University Center for Academic Research, Office of Interdisciplinary Earth Studies.

Evenson, Robert E., Donald D. Evenson, and Jonathan D. Putnam. 1987. Private sector agricultural inventions in developing countries. In *Policy for Agricultural Research*, edited by Vernon W. Ruttan and Carl E. Pray, 469-511. Boulder, Colo.: Westview Press.

International Geosphere-Biosphere Program (IGBP). 1991. The Inter-American Institute for Global Change Research. *Global Change NewsLetter* 8:4-5.

———. 1992. A quick start for START: Guidelines for regional research networks and centers. *Global Change NewsLetter* 9:5-7.

International Institute for Applied Systems Analysis (IIASA). 1991. *Agenda for the Third Decade.* Laxenburg, Austria: IIASA.

Jacobson, Harold K., and Martin F. Price. 1990. *A Framework on the Human Dimensions of Global Environmental Change.* New York: International Social Science Council/United Nations Economic and Social Council Series 3.

Jaeger, J., and H. L. Ferguson, eds. 1991. *Climate Change: Science, Impacts and Policy.* Proceedings of the Second World Climate Conference. Cambridge: Cambridge University Press.

Judd, M. Ann, James K. Boyce, and Robert E. Evenson. 1987. Investment in agricultural research and extension. In *Policy for Agricultural Research*, edited by Vernon W. Ruttan and Carl E. Pray, 2-38. Boulder, Colo.: Westview Press.

Lepkowski, W. 1992. U.S.-Japan global partnership action plan revived. *Chemical and Engineering News* 70(29): 16-18.

Livernash, R. 1992. The growing influence of NGOs in the developing world. *Environment* 34(5): 12-20, 41-43.

Maddox, J. 1992. Dangers of disappointment at Rio. *Nature* 357:265-66.

Mata, Leonardo. 1988. A public health approach to the "food-malnutrition-economic recession" complex. In *Health, Nutrition, and Economic Crises: Approaches to Policy in the Third World*, edited by David E. Bell and Michael R. Reich, 265-75. Dover: Auburn House.

Miller, Roberta B., and Harold K. Jacobson. 1992. Research on the Human Components of Global Change: Next Steps. Human Dimensions of Global Environmental Change Program, International Social Science Council, Discussion Paper 1. Paris: International Social Science Council.

Nature. 1992. West's gift becomes a model. *Nature* 355:672.

Norberg-Bohm, Victoria, William C. Clark, Bhavik Bakshi, JoAnne Berkenkamp, Sherry A. Bishko, Mark D. Koehler, Jennifer A. Marrs, Chris P. Nielsen, and Ambuj Sagar. 1992. *International Comparisons of Environmental Hazards*. John F. Kennedy School of Government, Harvard University, CSIA Discussion Paper 92-09. Cambridge, Mass.: Harvard University.

Ostrom, Elinor. 1990. *Governing the Commons: The Evolution of Institutions for Collective Action*. Cambridge: Cambridge University Press.

Perry, John S. 1991. Global change: From rhetoric to reality. *Reviews of Geophysics*, supplement, April, 39-45.

Pray, Carl E. 1987. Private sector agricultural research in Asia. In *Policy for Agricultural Research*, edited by Vernon W. Ruttan and Carl E. Pray, 411-31. Boulder, Colo.: Westview Press.

Ruttan, Vernon W. 1982. *Agricultural Research Policy*. Minneapolis: University of Minnesota Press.

———. 1986. Toward a global agricultural research system: A personal view. *Research Policy* 15:307-27.

———, ed. 1989. *Biological and Technical Constraints on Crop and Animal Productivity: Report on a Dialogue*. St. Paul: University of Minnesota Department of Agricultural and Applied Economics.

———, ed. 1990a. *Resource and Environmental Constraints on Sustainable Growth on Agricultural Production: Report on a Dialogue*. St. Paul: University of Minnesota Department of Agricultural and Applied Economics.

———, ed. 1990b. *Health Constraints in Agricultural Development*. St. Paul: University of Minnesota Department of Agricultural and Applied Economics.

———, ed. 1992. *Sustainable Agriculture and the Environment: Perspectives on Growth and Constraints*. Boulder, Colo.: Westview Press.

Schmidheiny, S. 1992. *Changing Course: A Global Business Perspective on Development and the Environment*. Cambridge: MIT Press.

Schultz, Theodore W. 1964. *Transforming Traditional Agriculture*. New Haven, Conn.: Yale University Press.

World Bank. 1992. *Development and the Environment: World Development Report 1992*. Oxford: Oxford University Press.

CONTRIBUTORS

David E. Bell is Clarence Gamble Professor of Population Sciences and International Health, Emeritus, at the Harvard School of Public Health. Before joining Harvard in 1981, he was vice-president for international programs at the Ford Foundation (1966-81); administrator, U.S. Agency for International Development (1962-66); and director, U.S. Bureau of the Budget (1961-62). He is an economist with long-standing interests in institutional development, beginning when he was the field leader of a team of advisers (1954-57) helping the Pakistan Planning Board prepare that country's first five-year development plan. During 1987-90 he served as senior consultant to the International Commission on Health Research for Development.

Patricia A. Benjamin is a doctoral candidate in the Graduate School of Geography and a research assistant in the George Perkins Marsh Institute, Clark University. She has been engaged in research on the human dimensions of global change and is currently serving as a Social Science Research Council fellow for doctoral studies in Tanzania.

David Bradley is professor of tropical hygiene at the London School of Hygiene and Tropical Medicine, in the Department of Epidemiology and Population Sciences and the Ross Institute. He is a physician and biologist. He lived for ten years in East Africa, working on schistosomiasis and on domestic water-supply policy in relation to disease, then for several years in Oxford on the genetic determinants of susceptibility to leishmaniasis and other infections. His recent work has been on malaria epidemiology and environmental change. He was one of the authors of *Drawers of Water* (1972) and of *Sanitation and Disease* (1983) and is editor of the *Journal of Tropical Medicine and Hygiene*. He has for many years been closely involved with WHO programs on tropical diseases, diarrheal diseases, and the building of research capacity in developing countries.

William C. Clark is assistant director of the Center for Science and International Affairs in the John F. Kennedy School of Government at Harvard University. Before joining the Kennedy School in 1987, he led a team of scholars from Eastern and Western countries in the Program on Sustainable Development of the Biosphere at the International Institute for Applied Systems Analysis in Austria. His current research focuses on policy issues arising through the interactions of environment, development, and security concerns in international affairs. He has been a member of the U.S. National Academy of Sciences' Committee for Global Change, and he serves on the steering committees for the U.S. Office of Interdisciplinary Earth Studies and the International Institute for Applied Systems Analysis's work on environmentally sound restructuring of national economies. He is coeditor of *Environment*, a monthly magazine of international environmental affairs. In 1983 Clark was awarded a MacArthur Prize Fellowship for his achievements in environmental policy.

Carl K. Eicher is University Distinguished Professor at Michigan State University. His research and teaching over the past three decades have focused on agricultural development in sub-Saharan Africa. He is coeditor of a number of books, including (with John Staatz) *Agricultural Development in the Third World* (1984, 1990). In 1986 he received the Foreign Francqui prize from Belgium and was honored in 1991 with the Michigan State University Distinguished Faculty Award.

Godfrey Gunatilleke is executive vice-chairman of the Marga Institute, Centre for Development Studies, in Sri Lanka. He was consultant to the World Health Organization on intersectoral action for health and to the International Labor Organization on the World Employment Programme, and he has served as adviser on development issues to several United Nations agencies. Currently he is president of the Association of Development Research and Training Institutes for Asia and the Pacific. His research has been focused on the linkages between social, economic, and political factors in development. His publications on health-related issues include *Changing Needs of Children* (1985).

Dan C. O. Kaseje is with the International Federation of Red Cross and Red Crescent societies. From 1989 to 1992 he was director of the Christian Medical Commission in the World Council of Churches, Geneva, Switzerland. He has held key positions in the development of primary health care in rural Kenya. He was at the same time teaching community health at the University of Nairobi in the medical school. He has been extensively involved in research and training in the field of community-based health in many countries in Africa.

J. A. Lee is professor of environmental biology at the University of Manchester, England, and head of the Department of Environmental Biology. His current research interests center on the responses of plants to extreme environments (including polluted environments) and on the effects of global change on seminatural ecosystems. He is chairman of the Natural Environment Research Council's Arctic Ecology Special Topic Programme and a member of its Polar Sciences Committee. He is vice-president of the International Association for Ecology, and from 1984 to 1990 was an editor of the *Journal of Ecology*. He has served on several national committees concerned with the effects of atmospheric pollutants on forests, crops, and seminatural ecosystems.

Adetokunbo O. Lucas is professor of international health at the Harvard School of Public Health. Born in Lagos, Nigeria, he obtained his medical training in Britain. In Nigeria he taught clinical and community medicine in Ibadan from 1965 to 1976. For four years prior to his appointment as professor of international health, he served as chair of the Carnegie Corporation's grant program concerned with strengthening human resources in developing countries. For the ten years preceding his work at Carnegie, he directed the Special Programme for Research and Training in Tropical Diseases based at the World Health Organization in Geneva. He has been awarded the Harvard Medal on the occasion of the University's 350th anniversary and the Mary Kingsley Medal from the Liverpool School of Tropical Medicine.

David Norse, formerly senior policy and planning coordinator for the Agricultural Department of FAO, is now with the Environmental Change Unit, University of Oxford, and the Overseas Development Institute, London. He has worked on agricultural development and environmental problems for over 25 years, first in Malawi and then in

Barbados, followed by senior positions in the British Civil Service in London and the OECD in Paris. He has written or contributed to over 100 scientific and economic papers or books on plant pathology and crop protection, global modeling, and long-term food and agricultural development problems in both industrialized and developing countries. He contributed to the U.N. Conference on Environment and Development Agenda 21 on sustainable agriculture and research needs.

Douglass C. North is Luce Professor of Law and Liberty in the Department of Economics at Washington University. He has been the editor of the *Journal of Economic History* and president of the Economic History Association (1972). In 1987 he was elected to the American Academy of Arts and Sciences. His current research, on the formation of political and economic institutions and the consequences of these institutions on the performance of economics through time, is available in *Institutions, Institutional Change and Economic Performance* (1990).

Kirit S. Parikh has been the director of the Indira Gandhi Institute of Development Research, Bombay, which he founded, since 1987. From 1980 to 1986 he led the Food and Agricultural Program of the International Institute for Applied Systems Analysis (IIASA), Austria. He has been professor of economics and head of the Indian Statistical Institute, New Delhi. He is a member of the Economics Advisory Council of the prime minister of India. He has authored or coauthored books in the areas of planning, water resource management, appropriate technology, energy systems, national and international food policies, trade policies, and general equilibrium modeling. In 1978 he was given the Vikram Sarabhai Award for Outstanding Research in Systems Analysis and Management Sciences.

Martin Parry is professor of environmental management and IBM director of the new Environmental Change Unit at the University of Oxford. Previously he was professor of environmental management at the University of Birmingham and coordinator of the Atmospheric Impacts Research (AIR) Group. He is chairman of the U.K. Climate Change Impacts Review Group and a member of the Scientific Advisory Committee to the World Climate Impact Studies Programme. He was lead author of the assessment by the Intergovernmental Panel on Climate Change (IPCC) of potential impacts on agriculture, and was director of the IIASA-UNEP research project (1983-86) on climate change and agriculture. He has written extensively (including three books) on the potential effects of climate changes.

Stephen L. Rawlins is project leader for an interdisciplinary cropping systems research team with the U.S. Department of Agriculture's Agricultural Research Service (ARS) at Prosser, Washington. He has served in both research and leadership positions, including several years as a member of the ARS National Program Staff in Beltsville, Maryland. There he planned and implemented a number of interdisciplinary national programs, including renewable energy, natural resource assessment, and global-change research. He organized and served as first director of the ARS Systems Research Institute, and brought the discipline of systems engineering into ARS through the organization of a formal training for ARS scientists in this discipline. His research has been in the field of soil and plant physics and the analysis and management of policy-relevant agricultural research systems.

Vernon W. Ruttan is Regents Professor in the Department of Agricultural and Applied Economics and the Department of Economics, and adjunct professor, Hubert H. Humphrey Institute of Public Affairs, University of Minnesota. His research has been on the economics of technical change, agricultural development, and research policy. He has been elected to membership in the National Academy of Sciences. His collaboration with Yujiro Hayami, *Agricultural Development: An International Perspective* (1973, 1985), has become the leading work in its field.

Judith Tendler is a development economist and professor of political economy in the Department of Urban Studies and Planning at the Massachusetts Institute of Technology. She has published two books, *Electric Power in Brazil: Entrepreneurship in the Public Sector* (1968) and *Inside Foreign Aid* (1975). Specializing in Latin America and particularly Brazil, she has also published a number of comparative evaluation studies of programs in the government and nongovernment/nonprofit sectors. She has served as a consultant to the World Bank, the Agency for International Development, and the Inter-American, Ford, Rockefeller, and MacArthur foundations. Her research focuses on public-sector performance in developing countries in the agriculture, infrastructure, and small-industry sectors and on similar issues in the nongovernment/nonprofit sector.

B. L. Turner II is professor of geography and director of the George Perkins Marsh Institute, Clark University. His research emphasizes nature-society relationships and has ranged from agriculture and environment in the ancient Maya lowlands of Mesoamerica to induced intensification and agricultural change in tropical cultivation. He currently heads several research efforts investigating global land-use and land-cover change. He is the editor of the widely acclaimed *The Earth as Transformed by Human Action: Global and Regional Changes in the Biosphere over the Past Three Hundred Years* (1990).

Index

Compiled by Mary Rasmussen

A *t* after a page number indicates a table is on that page. A *b* after a number indicates that it is a bibliographic record.